Masterminding the Deal

Breakthroughs in M&A strategy and analysis

Peter J Clark and
Roger W Mills

LONDON PHILADELPHIA NEW DELHI

Publisher's note

Every possible effort has been made to ensure that the information contained in this book is accurate at the time of going to press, and the publisher and authors cannot accept responsibility for any errors or omissions, however caused. No responsibility for loss or damage occasioned to any person acting, or refraining from action, as a result of the material in this publication can be accepted by the editor, the publisher or either of the authors.

First published in Great Britain and the United States in 2013 by Kogan Page Limited

120 Pentonville Road
London N1 9JN
United Kingdom
www.koganpage.com

1518 Walnut Street, Suite 1100
Philadelphia PA 19102
USA

4737/23 Ansari Road
Daryaganj
New Delhi 110002
India

ISBN 978 0 7494 6952 8
E-ISBN 978 0 7494 6953 5

British Library Cataloguing-in-Publication Data

A CIP record for this book is available from the British Library.

Library of Congress Cataloging-in-Publication Data

Clark, Peter J., 1950-
Masterminding the deal : breakthroughs in M&A strategy and analysis / Peter Clark, Roger Mills.
pages cm
Includes bibliographical references and index.
ISBN 978-0-7494-6952-8 – ISBN 978-0-7494-6953-5 (eISBN) 1. Consolidation and merger of corporations. 2. Corporations–Valuation. I. Mills, R. W. (Roger W.), 1951- II. Title.
HD2746.5.C554 2013
658.1'62–dc23

2013011421

Typeset by Graphicraft Limited, Hong Kong
Printed and bound in India by Replika Press Pvt Ltd

To Lillian and Natalie

CONTENTS

List of figures and tables viii
About the authors xii
Foreword by Bill Weinstein xiii
Preface xvii

Introduction 1

01 The next merger boom is already here 7

1.1 Business-merger waves: patterns, theories on causes, issues 8
1.2 Four post-1980 business-merger waves, four phases 24
1.3 The fourth (and final?) post-1980 wave is already underway 28
1.4 Merger wave issue I: (T)APP-synergy divergence as the wave progresses 33
1.5 Merger wave issue II: whipsaw-merger market entry and exit missteps 35

02 Debunking the six merger fallacies that destroy value 42

2.1 Myth 1: Increased understanding of historical merger failure means that would-be acquiring firms are more inclined to avoid mergers 43
2.2 Myth 2: Significant increases to target company's debt levels do not significantly reduce the probability of the related deal's success 45
2.3 Myth 3: The heroic figure in the acquisition drama is the all-conquering acquirer, while shareholders of the acquired company are victims, with their firms accurately depicted as led by underperforming managers 50
2.4 Myth 4: There is no inherent conflict of interest between dealmakers and other parties compensated on the basis of fees earned upon deal closure, and the interests of acquiring firms' shareholders 53

2.5 Myth 5: Price-to-earnings and similar multiples techniques are the leading merger valuation methodologies 56
2.6 Myth 6: Stories and process: PMI success is primarily a matter of sound process and responsive organization 60

03 Criteria: First, get the merger valuation methodology right 66

3.1 You can't manage what you can't measure *especially* when it comes to M&A 67
3.2 Criteria-setters: preeminence of continuing shareholders of the acquiring firm 70
3.3 Overview: four alternative merger valuation methods 74
3.4 Event studies (ES): exceeding the limits of rational market theory 78
3.5 Total shareholder return (TSR): most appropriate for round turn financial acquirers? 82
3.6 Value gap (VG): do synergies offset the price premium necessary to acquire the target? 91
3.7 Incremental value effect (IVE): two-scenario DCF analysis, adapted to mergers 107
3.8 Reconciling the tier I merger valuation methodologies 111
3.9 Multiples: critical confirmation role in merger valuation 117

04 Merger segmentation comes of age 134

4.1 The case for segmentation by merger type: precedent 135
4.2 Four categories, nine merger types: different deal types mean different M&A success 147
4.3 Applying the nine merger type framework 160
4.4 The path forward in merger segmentation: towards M-Score© 163

05 Mergers *still* fail, but does it matter? 169

5.1 More confirmation that historically, most mergers fail 170
5.2 No effective refutation of MMF 174
5.3 M&A's core contradiction, segmentation and stakeholders' different merger perspectives 180
5.4 Moving forward: expanding upon Hayward's three causes of merger failure 185

06 The merger megaboom's signature IPO: Facebook 191

6.1 The straw that stirs the drink 192
6.2 Social networking and the 2011–19 merger megaboom 197
6.3 Direct and indirect merger market effects of social networking sector acquisitions, 2011+ 202
6.4 Vapor numbers: *when* is the social networking valuation? 207

07 Towards systematic investigation and implementation of post-merger synergies 218

7.1 Synergies: definitions, approaches, issues 219
7.2 Net realizable synergies and merger success: value gap revisited 228
7.3 A key category-based net realizable synergy investigatory framework 235
7.4 Post-merger priorities explored 249
7.5 Other PMI implementation issues: choosing the PMI implementation team 261

08 The seven keys to merger success 273

8.1 Merger success: the seven keys 273
8.2 Some implementation considerations 294

Epilogue 299
Appendix A: Acquisition purchase premium-related issues 300
Appendix B: Debunking the extreme acquisition leverage fallacy 305
Bibliography 314
Further Reading 319
Acronyms and glossary 322
Index 329

LIST OF FIGURES AND TABLES

List of figures

FIGURE 1.1 US merger patterns 1926–2004: percentage of companies taken over, quarterly basis 8

FIGURE 1.2 Meeting minimum expected return: internal vs external investment approaches 12

FIGURE 1.3 A pattern of merger wave expansion and collapse key events: post-1980 merger wave 1: 1982–90 (LBO) 14

FIGURE 1.4 Identifiable merger phase and acquisition purchase premium (APP) percentage ranges 15

FIGURE 1.5 Merger phoenix/economic reset: landmark events in post-1980 merger wave 4 (2011–19 merger megaboom) anticipated 20

FIGURE 1.6 A perfect merger storm: dot com II/merger megaboom 32

FIGURE 3.1 Coley and Reinton (1988): An initial step towards merger segmentation? 90

FIGURE 3.2 Value gap consequences of merger market dynamics 95

FIGURE 3.3 Kaufmann (1988): Patterns of APP 98

FIGURE 3.4 Transaction timing during the merger wave and corresponding APP percentages 99

FIGURE 3.5 Considering *both* VG determining factors, over the business-merger cycle 101

FIGURE 3.6 VG under real world multiple bid circumstances 102

FIGURE 3.7 Gordon Formula I: components of the second stage equation in the two-stage DCF method (DCF2S), issues 112

FIGURE 4.1 Revisiting Coley and Reinton 1988: simple steps towards merger performance improvement 137

FIGURE 4.2 Bid dynamics of bottom-trawler (type 1) negotiations, in value gap terms 152

FIGURE 4.3 Merger segmentation and value management by acquirer: overview 153
FIGURE 4.4 Considering both VG determining factors, over the business-merger cycle 162
FIGURE 5.1 Perspectives on merger returns 177
FIGURE 6.1 Mergers and prices: symbiotic relationship 200
FIGURE 6.2 Facebook 'valuation' reference points as of April 2012 210
FIGURE 6.3 The post-IPO price waterfall, including share purchaser groupings as suggested by Rogers (1963) 211
FIGURE 6.4 Factors influencing Facebook's ongoing valuation 212
FIGURE 7.1 Synergy implications of VG analysis, assuming the Azofra/AMS APP ceiling percentages 230
FIGURE 7.2 Net realizable expense synergies: framework, examples 240
FIGURE 7.3 Net realizable revenue synergies: framework, examples 244
FIGURE 8.1 Pre-bid synergy insight – the two major synergy categories, classified by forecast reliability 287
FIGURE A.1 The rising tide dilemma and TAPP 301
FIGURE B.1 Towards capital structure reflecting present, future CAP lifespan positioning, dynamics 311

List of tables

TABLE 1.1 Signature events of the four post-1980 merger waves 16
TABLE 1.2 Some explanations for merger wave development: four categories 19
TABLE 1.3 Shocks by category: the four post-1980 merger waves 22
TABLE 1.4 Cross-influences between the four post-1980 merger waves 25
TABLE 2.1 Acquirees are not always losers 52
TABLE 3.1 Alternative interpretations of deal success: deal closing vs returns in excess of capital cost 73
TABLE 3.2 Overview: the four alternative tier I merger valuation methodologies 75
TABLE 3.3 Total shareholder return (TSR) basic equation 83
TABLE 3.4 TSR variants 86

TABLE 3.5 VG summarized 93
TABLE 3.6 APP and influences 97
TABLE 3.7 Changing of the merger valuation guard: ES vs IVE 109
TABLE 3.8 Gordon Formula II: components of the second stage equation in the two-stage DCF Method (DCF2S), issues 113
TABLE 3.9 IVE: Constructing the two scenarios 114
TABLE 3.10 Reconciling share price with business fundamentals: Vodafone analysis by Mills Clark's VRQ method, v02.06 125
TABLE 4.1 Towards a merger segmentation framework: some related investigation 139
TABLE 4.2 Nine merger types framework v2 148
TABLE 4.3 Four adjustments to Table 4.2 success profile ranges 161
TABLE 5.1 Nine merger type framework (adapted from Table 4.2) 182
TABLE 5.2 Merger success objectives by stakeholder groups 183
TABLE 5.3 Perspectives on Hayward's three factors 186
TABLE 6.1 Bank M&A adviser fees, 2009 194
TABLE 6.2 Major corporations emerge, in both net eras 198
TABLE 6.3a Direct merger market effects – social networking's boom 202
TABLE 6.3b Indirect merger market effects – social networking's boom 203
TABLE 6.4 Foundations of fake: 'Value' distortions in pre-IPO price indications 209
TABLE 7.1 Which synergy orientation is the acquirer exhibiting? 221
TABLE 7.2 Synergy scope – three alternative approaches 224
TABLE 7.3 Diagnosis of possible post-merger improvements by synergy type 236
TABLE 7.4 Revenue synergy: alternative approaches and issues 245
TABLE 7.5 Ten post-merger pitfalls and fallacies 249
TABLE 7.6a PMI priorities 1–5: From defense first to return to normalcy 250
TABLE 7.6b PMI priorities 6–10: From invest-to-save to M&A post audit 256
TABLE 7.7 Post-merger implementation team composition 262
TABLE 8.1 Overview: Seven keys to M&A success 274
TABLE 8.2 Merger success key 1: Getting the merger valuation criteria right 276

TABLE 8.3 Merger success key 2: Optimal timing in the four phase merger wave 278

TABLE 8.4 Merger success key 3: Exploiting the new merger segmentation 280

TABLE 8.5 Merger success key 4: Consideration of APP indicated maximums 281

TABLE 8.6 Merger success key 5: Synergy integrated with target bid dynamics 283

TABLE 8.7 Merger success key 6: Real synergy elements distinguished from illusions 291

TABLE 8.8 Merger success key 7: Avoiding the desperate acquirer's journey to value destruction 292

TABLE 8.9 Searching for promising targets 295

TABLE B.1 Four scenarios: HLT resulting in extreme overleverage, plus three alternatives 307

ABOUT THE AUTHORS

Peter J Clark has more than two decades of corporate management consulting and advisory experience in the United States, United Kingdom and Continental Europe, spanning all aspects of acquisition- and company-valuation analysis and practical application. He has been involved in more than $4 billion worth of M&A transactions, in roles ranging from acquisition program development to target company identification and analysis, bid pricing and M&A strategy, and postmerger integration. Past clients include both buying and selling principals and also deal intermediaries, primarily investment groups. He is the author of three previous company valuation and merger valuation books and lectures on corporate valuation and merger valuation at a major international university.

Roger W Mills has more than two decades of corporate advisory experience in North and South America, the UK, Continental Europe, the Middle and Far East, and Australia. His expertise spans all aspects of M&A analysis, company performance improvement, and valuation investigation. In addition, he has bought and sold companies and divisions, including those within his own business portfolio, and has advised on divestitures and target company investigation and pursuit. He is the author of numerous books in this field. He lectures on corporate valuation and merger valuation at a major international university and also runs M&A executive masterclasses for acquisition decision makers from global corporations.

You can contact Peter and Roger by emailing **pondbridge@gmail.com**.

FOREWORD

Masterminding the Deal: Breakthroughs in M&A strategy and analysis presents a tough-minded and systematically analytical examination of the criteria, methods and causal factors relating to acquisition success.

That, historically, most mergers fail (based on failure to achieve minimally required returns to acquiring firms' shareholders and/or speculative purchase bids well in excess of the level of realistically achievable synergies) is today accepted as conventional financial wisdom, for good reasons. No recent acquirer is likely to brand his or her own deal a flop, yet *others*' past transactions are accurately viewed as disappointing at least two-thirds of the time. But the future does not necessarily have to be a repeat of merger cycles past. *Masterminding the Deal* helps management of acquiring companies to significantly improve their deal performance results – today and in years yet to come.

Some of the more diagnostic M&A analyses in the past have hinted at some of the elements thought to be critical to improving acquisition performance, such as increasing post-merger synergies, avoiding acquisition chases resulting in overpayment and Winner's Remorse, and rejection of merger evaluative criteria with scant regard to the essential financial interests of the principal stakeholders in merger transactions, that is, the buying firm's ongoing shareholders.

But while such suggestions might help reduce the incidence of the more spectacularly embarrassing (and often, career-damaging) merger missteps – meltdowns of the AOL/TimeWarner or RBS/ABN Amro magnitude – mere stories about merger experiences gone awry or pundits' vague M&A overviews fall short of the need for a complete program for merger success. Stated another way, merely suspecting where some of the potholes are located in the road does not necessarily ensure that it is safe for the driver to zoom ahead at high speed. At best, the combination of merger failure fables and each year's new lot of acquisition brainstorm concepts only suggests some areas to avoid.

Masterminding the Deal's depth of insight represents a point of differentiation from prior M&A works. Rather than merely restating established (and therefore, already well-known and widely applied) observations about, say, the importance of discounted cash flow-based methods in M&A analysis or the central role of synergies, this book proceeds further, presenting practical and actionable frameworks for the acquiring company chief executive and his or her senior team who are adamant about ensuring that their *next* merger is a success. This achievement is illustrated in three major topic areas, as follows:

1. *Pursuit of maximum achievable synergies.* The authors introduce the concept of net realizable synergies (NRSs) in Chapter 7 to identify that specific subset of post-merger improvements available to offset the acquiring firm's acquisition purchase premium (APP) bid amounts. Each of the four distinct synergy categories is examined separately in that chapter in terms of component elements, offsets, timing issues and feasibility. Co-authors Clark and Mills specify which synergy categories are most important and why; identify the unique diagnostic and analytical approaches required for accurate evaluation of each synergy category; and describe which two of the four synergy categories are most useful for shaping bid pricing strategy *before* the deal is finalized.
2. *Merger segmentation.* In M&A analysis to date, investigation of success and failure characteristics has not yet evolved into a useful and useable framework capable of guiding acquirers' specific deal strategies. While one or two characteristics that set apart more successful mergers from the others become apparent from time to time (eg Coley and Reinton, 1988; Goedhart *et al*, 2010), mere identification of a couple of attributes is a far cry from today's requirement of an in-depth framework that codifies merger prospects by success probability. Such a framework should be capable of guiding the buying firm's target selection and, to a lesser extent, deal pricing. Chapter 4 in this book, entitled 'Merger segmentation comes of age' represents a giant step forward in terms of eventual development of such a framework.
3. *Revealing the value-destruction from past M&A analysis shortcomings.* A definitive perspective about the most defendable merger valuation (MV) methodologies has long been needed. Such clarity is required both to minimize MV destruction due to reliance on spurious methods, and also to hone merger performance improvement actions. Clark and Mills respond to this challenge in their third chapter. So long as MV success is imagined as being

> subject to whatever subjective theory this month's M&A dabbler conjures up, the end consequence is no reliable merger methodology at all. By *first* addressing the critical question of *which* M&A stakeholder group has primacy in setting deal success-failure criteria (who determines merger success?) the stage is set to critically assess the few remaining existing and emerging methods suitable for assessing acquiring firm M&A performance in future periods.

This book's immersion in M&A practitioners' key issues of importance, the in-depth examination of potential causal factors of merger success and near-forensic levels of investigation and examples give this work a special punch. Its combination of practical examples and academic gravitas means that this work is for students of any background, in any role in the M&A decision chain, or any level in the corporate hierarchy.

Regardless of whether the individual searching for M&A truth has only recently become involved in acquisition analysis or sees him or herself as a seasoned acquisition pro, this book has much to offer. Its uncompromising, no-punches-pulled style provides strong mental armor-plating against the porous merger generalities of the past. In this respect the book elevates *every* deal participant's M&A game to a higher level and thus is a welcome development for all in the acquisition community. This book is critical for managers who in the past have been subjected to a variety of 'new merger insights' of debatable worth.

Clark and Mills are unsparing in their criticism of several of M&A's more notorious analysis black holes, including but not limited to 'soft' (that is, qualitative and subjective) motivations-oriented criteria for assessing merger performance, and statistical methodologies that are long on data availability but short on acquisition performance logic. The latter includes the merger academicians' favorite methodology: event studies-based statistical analysis of share price movements.

Regarding merger methodologies overall, the authors' stance in this book is analytical but non-prescriptive: while it is clear what their preferred methods are (and why), characteristics of other alternative viable approaches are described in a way that facilitates adaptation based on the acquirer's situation or objectives. For example, Clark and Mills describe how total shareholder returns (TSR) today remains suitable for use by some intermediate-term financial acquirers buying companies for improvement and future re-sale, even though a combination of two DCF-related methods with backup remains the dominant methodology for most other acquirers and circumstances.

The book is not conducted as a polemic; in the spirit of science it invites and not merely dishes out critical evaluation. Throughout the eight chapters readers will find copious references to and evaluations of the works of others from both scholarly and general management sources.

Having qualified, demolished or reconstituted a variety of analyses about why mergers succeed or fail, the mountain peak of the book then emerges. Chapter 8, entitled 'The seven keys to merger success', is drawn from the critical evaluations in previous chapters. The success keys are not merely listed but also described in detail with a view towards contributing directly and immediately to the acquiring operating company's M&A success.

Chapter 1 is dedicated to the portrayal of waves of mergers and their characteristics since the early 1980s. The analysis of contemporary developments occurs in what the authors refer to as the post-1980 merger era, with special reference to a fourth, current major business-merger expansion period beginning in late 2011. The historical context provided is retrospective as well as future-oriented.

In summary, the main objective of this book is to clear away a vast amount of past deficient analysis and to retrieve and reorganize what is of value in evaluating merger success and failure, using tough-minded criteria implanted in current finance. Its deductive design resembles a sifting operation that starts with the examination and testing of multiple alternatives, then permitting only those that are worthy of serious consideration by acquiring company chief executives to progress to the next level, along with recommendations and pragmatic how-to steps.

Readers familiar with many of the landmark works in the field will appreciate the manner in which those works are reported systematically and compared analytically. Readers not familiar with such works will find this book a less fragmented and more empirically grounded entry to M&A prevailing intelligence than could have been found previously from other sources.

Bill Weinstein

Bill Weinstein is Professor Emeritus of International Business, Henley Business School, University of Reading (UK) and Fellow Emeritus in Politics, Public Policy & Management, Balliol College, University of Oxford.

PREFACE

Twenty-plus years is a long time for a sequel, even when the subject is Wall Street and takeovers. No, we're not talking about the time gap between the first and second incarnation of Oliver Stone's *Wall Street* movies (although Gekko *is* quoted in this book, once).

Beyond the Deal (Clark, 1991) a predecessor to this work, was written by co-author Peter Clark in response to the new insights about merger success following the rise and fall of the 1980s leveraged buy out (LBO) bubble. At that time, M&A general management writings appeared to that author to be limited in scope, application and insight: compilations of stylish but unproven merger fad concepts or, far worse, huckster pieces gushing about the performance alchemy of mergers, despite the reality that most mergers fail.

That earlier book began the process of addressing the merger performance paradox. In Chapter 5 of this book, *Masterminding the Deal,* that paradox is expressed succinctly: if most mergers fail, then why do they continue? In the 1980s, the pendulum had swung towards a growing consensus that most acquisitions fail (that momentum has since become an avalanche), so the earlier book focused on identifying differences between successful and non-successful deals, on the importance of advantageous timing during the merger cycle plus a section on post-merger integration imperatives. Those areas of emphasis continue in more developed form in *Masterminding the Deal.* As with the earlier work, research underlying this new edition started years before publication, in late 2010, when hints of a possible future M&A resurgence first began to appear.

There is major emphasis, in *Masterminding the Deal*'s third chapter, on merger valuation – that is, how to determine whether or not deals succeed – going far beyond the single methodological approach emphasized in the first book. Observations about critical differences in M&A prospective target companies and deal types become a full merger segmentation framework in this edition's Chapter 4. Also in this book, synergy expands from post-merger afterthought to critical merger consideration before and after the deal's close.

Also, while the earlier work was a solo effort, this book, *Masterminding the Deal*, reflects the substantial insight and major contribution of Roger W Mills, a merger and valuation thought leader in several spheres of worldwide corporate and merger valuation practice as practitioner, academic, adviser and investment (including acquisitions) reviewer-auditor.

Introduction

Masterminding the Deal anticipates a resurgence of record M&A transaction volume in this decade. In this book, the authors provide the analysis and implementation approaches designed to significantly increase merger success by acquiring firms leading the way in the next great merger boom.

This future expectation – which presumes that both major market disruptions and political shocks can be avoided until around 2019 – is no radical guess of a *Dow 36,000*[1] soothsayer variety. Mounting evidence and past patterns suggest that the latest business-merger wave has already started. The forces underlying the present merger expansion period point to high deal volume, over a sustained period.

Facebook's IPO and that firm's startling acquisition of Instagram in April–May 2012 mark the beginning of the second phase of the boom. But risks of merger missteps persist: in some technology-related sectors (mostly social networking firms, this cycle), the attitude of some overly-enthusiastic acquirers appears to be to shoot first and aim afterwards, with mind-boggling acquisition purchase premiums (APPs) reducing chances for merger success.

Achieving success in the 2011–19 merger megaboom is not just a matter of showing up and finalizing the deal. Today, the fact that most mergers fail (MMF) is so widely accepted that it is met with the grudging acceptance of an unwelcome but necessary statement of reality.

The difference between buying companies mastering the next M&A boom or being victims of it depends on understanding and applying the new critical instruments of merger success as explored throughout this book:

- *Right timing.* Avoiding transactions during high risk periods in the merger cycle, when success probabilities are low, due to the quality of remaining targets, APPs are high both in absolute terms and relative to achievable synergies, and other factors.

- *Right criteria.* Assessing whether or not the deal is successful based on the specific evaluation approaches most consistent with the vital financial interests of criteria-setters: the acquiring firm's ongoing shareholders.
- *Multi-dimensional merger valuation.* Applying the best aspects of the top four merger valuation methods, in combination with multiples-based triangulation analysis.
- *Merger segmentation.* Understanding the differences between deal types exhibiting high probabilities of success (for example, consolidations involving companies in established industries, correctly priced) and bet-the-company *transformational* deals with appealing future prospects suspiciously perceived only by the acquiring company's chief executive and the M&A advisers whispering in his or her ear.
- *Synergy before the deal closing, not just after.* In today's financial media, every major deal with a high APP brings immediate speculation that the acquirer has overpaid. While synergies are important in the post-merger period, they are even more essential *prior* to the close, to help avoid deal failure caused by value-destroying bidding wars.

About this book

Orientation

This book is directed at the critical interests of operating company acquirers or, more specifically, to the interests of the shareholders who ultimately own those firms. In past years, the lack of singular focus on the financial requirements of this group when it comes to merger analysis has contributed to the persistence of some merger criteria and valuation techniques which, we contend, *destroy value*. The range of parties involved in M&A is expansive, spanning financial and operating company acquirers, selling companies and their representatives, other deal intermediaries and a multitude of M&A pundits always searching for a new angle to either talk up or talk down the deal, placing themselves at the epicenter of the merger discussions.[2]

By contrast, the acquiring firm's ongoing shareholders are invisible yet omnipotent, the latter at least when it comes to merger performance being judged. *They* are the ones who are ultimately responsible for the risk capital necessary for the deal to proceed; thus it is *their* selection of criteria for merger valuation – that is, the basis for determining whether the transaction is successful or not – which has primacy over the interests of all other M&A interested groups.

Uses and users of this book

Operating company acquirers

Consistent with the description of this book's primary orientation, senior management of firms that are presently involved in M&A initiatives or that may become so in the future will embrace this book as one of their core M&A planning and implementation resources, guiding their acquisition programs. Merger questions of central importance to the board and the financial community – including what target companies and types of firms to pursue (and which to avoid), when to act, how much to pay, and how to determine whether the deal is successful, are addressed in this book.

Merger intermediaries and deal instigators

Your corporate clients are changing their approaches to M&A planning, analysis, pricing, valuation and synergies. To retain present accounts – and for a chance of amassing a commanding market share in deal volume terms over the remainder of the present 2011–19 merger megaboom – a working knowledge of key concepts and approaches described in this book is essential. The 'buy side' will find much to disagree with in this book, including the notion of synergy-based advance limits on merger bids and the proposition that nearly all deals should be avoided in the second half of the merger wave's concluding phase.

Other merger practitioners and advisers

The days when merger principals would tolerate and sometimes even welcome vapid but hollow acquisition concepts are finished. Except perhaps to the acquiring company CEO equivalent of individual investors who buy shares of social networking company IPOs on the first day, such prose disqualifies its creators, rather than creating new leads. Some of these middlemen will be washed out in the years ahead; amongst those that survive will be the firms and individuals who return to merger valuation's basics, as detailed in this book.

Those investigating company merger performance and effectiveness

Those with a vested interest in acquisition-intensive companies long ago discovered that relying primarily on the CEO's defensive retorts in response to questions such as, 'So will this deal be a success?' is unsatisfactory. To those parties – which range from representatives of investing institutions to investigatory-oriented business media reporters – this book provides an important step towards a more complete understanding of merger performance today. Those specifically involved in target company diagnosis and practical synergy investigation – both before and after the deal is closed – will discover insights, frameworks and techniques of use to them in this edition. This book's content is already extensively used in a university-level mergers and valuation course.

An overview of the chapters of this book

1. The next merger boom is already here

Are you wondering when the next merger boom will start? Stop wondering – it already has. At this writing, the fourth post-1980 merger boom is now beginning its second (of four) phases. This chapter provides an overview of the reasoning underlying our contention that the next great M&A expansion period *has already commenced,* along with guidance on how to ensure that your firm's merger timing is right in the boom years ahead.

2. Debunking the six merger fallacies that destroy value

The time has come to clear away the mistaken and dead-on-arrival M&A beliefs that suppress merger performance and, in some instances, lead to acquisition failure. Included in this chapter are fundamental differences in the core objectives of acquirers and their acquiring company clients, and the demise of those high leverage transactions (HLTs) that destabilize the target.

3. Criteria: First, get the merger valuation methodology right

The phrase 'You can't manage what you can't measure' is heard in the daily operations of the company. And yet, methods of merger valuation (MV) – of determining whether or not the deal is successful – have historically been dominated by some techniques that are at best severely limited and in some instances may lead to value-destructive merger decisions. The approach described at the end of Chapter 3 combines three separate emergent MV methods.

4. Merger segmentation comes of age

Observers have long suspected that deals exhibiting certain characteristics perform better than those without those essential features. Relative size of the merging partners, relatedness, plus a half dozen other factors are combined to create a unified framework capable of guiding future target company assessment. Merger segmentation has arrived (finally), with the potential to improve the acquiring firm's acquisition performance.

5. Mergers *still* fail, but does it matter?

The phrase 'most mergers fail but it doesn't matter' used to be a (mostly unspoken) slogan of the headstrong acquiring company CEO who relied on personal charisma and/or energetic media spin to persuade those who doubted the wisdom of a high risk deal. Today, that same phrase means something else: that by applying the timing, merger segmentation synergy diagnosis and other key frameworks and tools contained in this book, the acquiring firm's chances of deal success may be significantly improved.

6. The merger megaboom's signature IPO: Facebook

The first chapter identifies the role of certain signature events in the early stages of the new business-merger boom which direct the attention of financial markets away from the recent recession and towards better times ahead. In the first dot com wave, that event was Netscape's IPO in 1995. In the present second dot com-related boom, another IPO emerges as key event: Facebook's record-setting public offering in May 2012.

7. Towards systematic investigation and implementation of post-merger synergies

Synergies are not just critical after the close but also before, while insights improve target selection and later, merger pricing. While synergy stories of the 1990s type improve understanding of synergy basics, the time is overdue for practical frameworks to identify the true improvement opportunities available. Chapter 7 describes a systematic approach for pursuing the most important of the four major synergy categories.

8. The seven keys to merger success

Merger success requires an approach equal to the challenge. Isolating one aspect of the deal process could increase the risk in other areas, eg the fading organization that acquires the high quality company at the height of the market and at maximum purchase premium, dooming that deal to failure since achievable synergies will never bridge the APP-synergy value gap.

A complete approach and action plan is called for. Those key steps and analyses are described in this book's concluding chapter, based upon frameworks and methods from the preceding parts of this book.

Notes

1 Glassman, J and Hassett, K (2001) *Dow 36,000: The new strategy for profiting from the coming rise in the stock market*, New York, Crown.

2 For such M&A pundits, the need to stimulate blog traffic encourages a radical stance. Deals initially fawned over as marriages made in heaven are just as quickly condemned as disasters.

The next merger boom is already here

01

M&A cycles 'tend to last five to seven years, and we are two years into it'.

(Evercore Partners' Roger Altman, anticipating on May 6 2011 that transaction volume in the newest merger boom will exceed levels of prior cycles (such as the 2002–8 cycle), with $4.5-plus *trillion* in annualized deals as early as 2013; *Bloomberg*).[1]

CHAPTER CONTENTS

1.1 Business-merger waves: patterns, theories on causes, issues

1.2 Four post-1980 business-merger waves, four phases

1.3 The fourth (and final?) post-1980 wave is already underway

1.4 Merger wave issue I: (T)APP-synergy divergence as the wave progresses

1.5 Merger wave issue II: whipsaw-merger market entry and exit missteps

Most mergers *still* fail,[2] based on today's most defendable financial criteria: returns to the acquiring company's shareholders. But new analysis frameworks and approaches aimed at developing superior understanding of transaction timing within the merger cycle, segmentation of target opportunities, and bid limits based on realizable synergies, emerge to improve the odds of M&A success for the acquirer seeking to excel in the next great merger boom. In this chapter, the next great M&A period is described as 'the 2011–19 merger megaboom'.[3]

1.1 Business-merger waves: patterns, theories on causes, issues

Periods of business expansion have been evident since the first recorded histories of commercial transaction activity. In cyclical manner, boom surges are invariably followed by years of contraction. M&A transaction intensity corresponds approximately to periods of growth in the overall economy, as illustrated in Figure 1.1. Researchers Martynova and Renneboog affirm that 'it is a well-known fact that mergers and acquisitions (M&A) come in waves' (2008: 2148). Past merger bubbles display patterns of alternating growth followed by retrenchment.

FIGURE 1.1 US merger patterns 1926–2004: percentage of companies taken over, quarterly basis

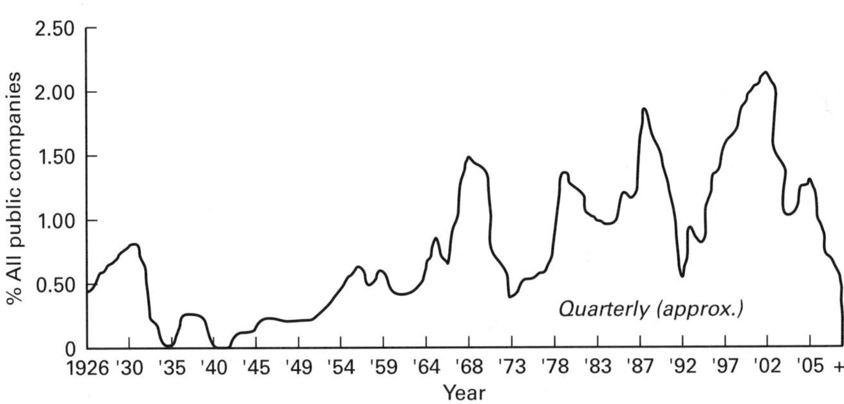

Based on some data cited in Martynova and Renneboog, 2008, Figure 1, 2150, plus other cycle trend sources. Statistics to 1954 are attributed to Nelson (1959), 1955–1962 to *Historical Statistics of the US-Colonial Times to 1970*, 1963–1997 to *Mergerstat Review*. Post-1997 statistics are attributed to *The Value Creators Report*.

During expansion periods, management at the growing company seeks new sources of (external) investment to augment growth from R&D and other internal sources. During the boom, an increase in the publicly traded company's share price occurs, coinciding with improved investor sentiment and surging share prices. This effect ('a rising tide lifts all ships') sometimes encourages a misperception that value has been created in the prospective acquiring company, without effort. When that acquirer later relies on shares as its acquisition currency in deals, a few executives in the company think that appreciation of their firm's share price means that they have more money available to spend on deals.[4]

Such (mis)perceptions represent one part of the behavioral explanation for merger waves, some aspects of which are summarized in Table 1.2. This instinct is to obtain something of worth – such as precious metals or another company – using that firm's inflated acquisition currency. The consequence is Gresham's Law, commonly paraphrased as 'bad money forces out good'.

AOL's disastrous acquisition of TimeWarner in mid-January 2000 is one example as AOL's share 'currency' was highly valued by the target's chief executive, Gerald Levin, rendering that unthinkable deal plausible. The (first) dot com bubble popped two months after that deal was consummated; a few weeks later, TimeWarner's shareholders quickly came to regret both the nonsense deal as well as its basis for payment. Post the acquisition in early 2000, new AOL TimeWarner's share price plunged along with other vapor valuation companies in the tech bubble.

If buoyant future expectations for the acquiring firm and its target mark the arrival of the acquisition gold rush periods, the opposite sentiments precede merger market slumps. Reduced cash flows (CFs) threaten the viability of the newly completed deal secured at a heady premium to the target's pre-announcement share price (acquisition purchase premium, APP). Economic conditions appear to be weakening. Analysts debate whether there are sufficient funds in the newly combined entity to service the deal's debt and also fund new investment required to stay ahead of industry rivals in competitive terms.

For a while, overall merger volume remains robust, despite such concerns. The merger wave is maturing and questions of when/how to get out occur to a few merger market participants who are beginning to lose their nerve. At this point in the cycle, the shattering end to the merger wave is several years in the future. Deal volume is bolstered by some of the mid-cycle failed deals, as new targets are suddenly available for late entrants eager to buy: one company's refuse is another one's treasure, at the right price. Kaplan and Weisbach (1992: 107) 'consider that 34 per cent to 50 per cent of classified divestitures are unsuccessful'. But eventually, the cheap dispositions of quality targets dry up and merger volume recedes back to rock bottom, as M&A financiers exit from the market.

Patterns: historical periods of merger intensity

Figure 1.1 begins with the Roaring Twenties' speculative bubble and ends with a comparable period of exuberance, 2004–5, the peak of the subprime mortgage derivatives bubble. At the height of that business-merger cycle, it sometimes seemed that only Nouriel Roubini anguished over the conversion of near-worthless financial manure (mortgages that borrowers either could not or would not pay off) into tranches of securities then marketed by financial market hucksters as valuable.

Never again? Each new business-merger repeats the old insanity to some extent. (Chapter 6 considers some of the company pricing distortions emerging with the new social networking companies and their shares, focusing primarily on Facebook.)

Despite the Depression's central role in 20th-century US economic planning culture, the 1920s period is conspicuous by its modest dimensions, in terms of M&A transaction volume. Note that in the period immediately preceding the start of the Great Depression, quarterly takeover volume never exceeded 1 per cent of all publicly traded US companies. That level of merger intensity was easily passed by the M&A surge of the late 1960s to early 1970s, and later by each of the three post-1980 merger booms examined elsewhere in this chapter.

Fast forward to the growth stock era of the mid-1960s and the conglomeration mania bubbling up a couple of years later. 'Multi-companies' (aka conglomerates) were touted in the early 1970s as financial value magic. The two parts of the conglomerate fiction were that 1) a holding company with diverse investments in numerous sectors was better positioned than a single core business company to withstand downturns affecting any one industry and, 2) a diverse business unit portfolio could help facilitate value-maximizing cash flow transfers from cows (cash generators) into stars (cash-hungry but high value separate business units or SBUs). In the early 1970s, crunchers at conglomerates such as ITT, LTV and Litton micro-managed business performance *statistics* but not the business. Believing their own press releases that a competent central management team could manage almost anything, fundamentals about the newly-acquired company were relegated to a secondary role, behind the quarter-to-quarter (or even week-to-week) 'hot indicators'.

What this conglomeration business model failed to emphasize was that the market imposes a 10+ per cent discount on such adventurism into unknown businesses, and that then as now, one-dimensional cruncher acquirers frequently lack the operational acumen to achieve anything beyond superficial near-term improvements (synergies) to the target company. Loading up the target company with new debt reduces the level of future investment required to remain competitive; the post-1985 leveraged buyout consequence is often value destruction.[5] It is no coincidence that, to many, General Electric is widely viewed today as the only true US conglomerate.

But then the world changed. In the early 1980s, a different type of merger wave appeared. The combination of enduring low inflation levels, radical changes to several core industries' bases for competition, a relaxed regulatory environment compared to prior eras plus Professor Michael Jensen's concept of the myopic, self-absorbed agent manager and T Boone Pickens's notion of entrenched US corporate underleverage and underperformance, combined to create conditions for merger booms of a type and intensity that the world had not experienced before.

Explaining the persistent urge to merge

Different analytical approaches emerge to help the persistence of acquirers' fervent interest in combining with other firms.

One dimension is active versus passive. In the *active* notion, the buying companies' top management expands through acquisition into new markets and in new directions, thereby directly *causing* M&A activity levels to soar. Or, the opposite occurs: initially reluctant buyers passively rush to make defensive acquisitions in reacting to conditions and circumstances over which they perceive they have no control. The latter group's hope is that protective actions might somehow help insulate their firms from unknown but feared future shocks.

Investment-based rationales as depicted in Figure 1.2 are consistent with this activist conception: 'NPD' in that exhibit stands for new product development. 'PMI' is a commonplace abbreviation-acronym for post-merger integration: improvements made to the acquired target firm (and some related areas in the acquiring company) in the weeks and months after the deal is closed. Company top management, concerned that they might not be able to achieve the financial markets' minimum expected returns through internal investments alone (eg new capital expenditures, internal projects) decide to augment that outlay with additional *external* investment in the form of suitable mergers (Copeland and Dolgoff, 2006).

Andrade and Stafford (2004) also view merger-related external investment as part of effective management's overall tactics for growth: 'A significant portion of merger activity should be explained by factors that motivate

FIGURE 1.2 Meeting minimum expected return: internal vs external investment approaches

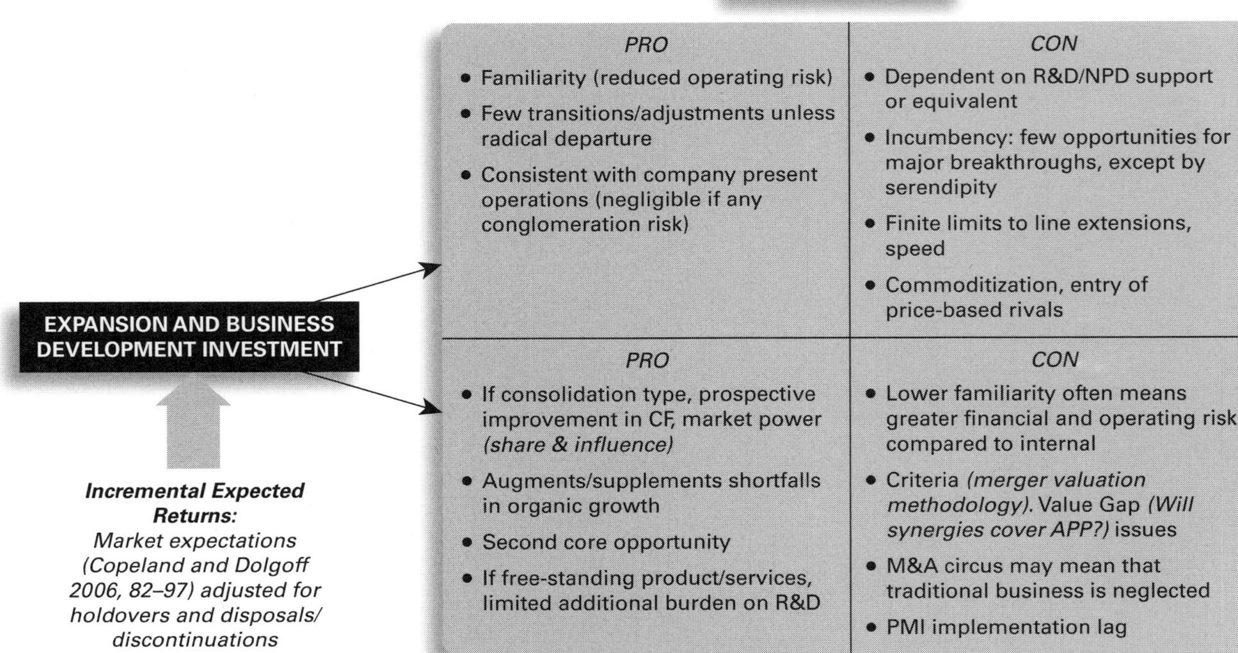

firms to expand and grow... Mergers and internal investments should be related, since they are similar ways of adding to a firm's asset base and productive capacity.' Timing and other characteristics of the investment-propelled merger program are dictated by the size and success of prospective internal investments. Internal investment opportunities are well understood, at least compared to an external target company understood only from limited publicly available intelligence and other information that may become available during a due diligence period.[6] If management can depend on sufficient financial returns from internal investments, then there's no need to pursue the less familiar external M&A opportunities.

But that was before profitability began to decline in major industries, from telecommunications to pharmaceuticals, publishing to travel agencies. With new profitable investment opportunities drying up, attention turns outside the firm. Consolidation-type mergers have increased as a percentage of total acquisition volume in each of the past three merger booms, a trend that is already beginning to manifest itself in the latest 2011–19 merger megaboom.

One key point of differentiation between internal (R&D) and external (M&A) investments is that there is no acquisition purchase premium involved in the former: the factory's cost basis for that new fabrication machine is the direct cost to vendor plus merchant. For a merger however, a buyer has to pay more than the stated purchase price as reflected by current share prices. Otherwise, present shareholders will not give up their ownership rights.

The additional premium increases the riskiness of external investments relative to internal, as more incremental cash flow (CF) must be generated to break even, all other factors and considerations being the same.

The last merger wave crashed. Three years later, and next wave is just around the corner (but this time we'll do it right!)

The four phase pattern of the M&A expansion-retrenchment cycle endures. Figure 1.3, depicting threshold events over the 1982–90 leveraged buyout M&A era, is from Clark (1991). Related Figure 1.4 highlights the four characteristic merger wave phases along with APP percentage ranges typical for each.

The Roman numerals in Figure 1.4 correspond to four identifiable phases characterizing each of the post-1980 merger waves. Since both components of the bid price – the pre-announcement share price of the target company and the APP percentage premium required to secure control of that firm – tend to rise as the merger wave ages, deals closed earlier in the cycle face a

FIGURE 1.3 A pattern of merger wave expansion and collapse key events: post-1980 merger wave 1: 1982–90 (LBO)

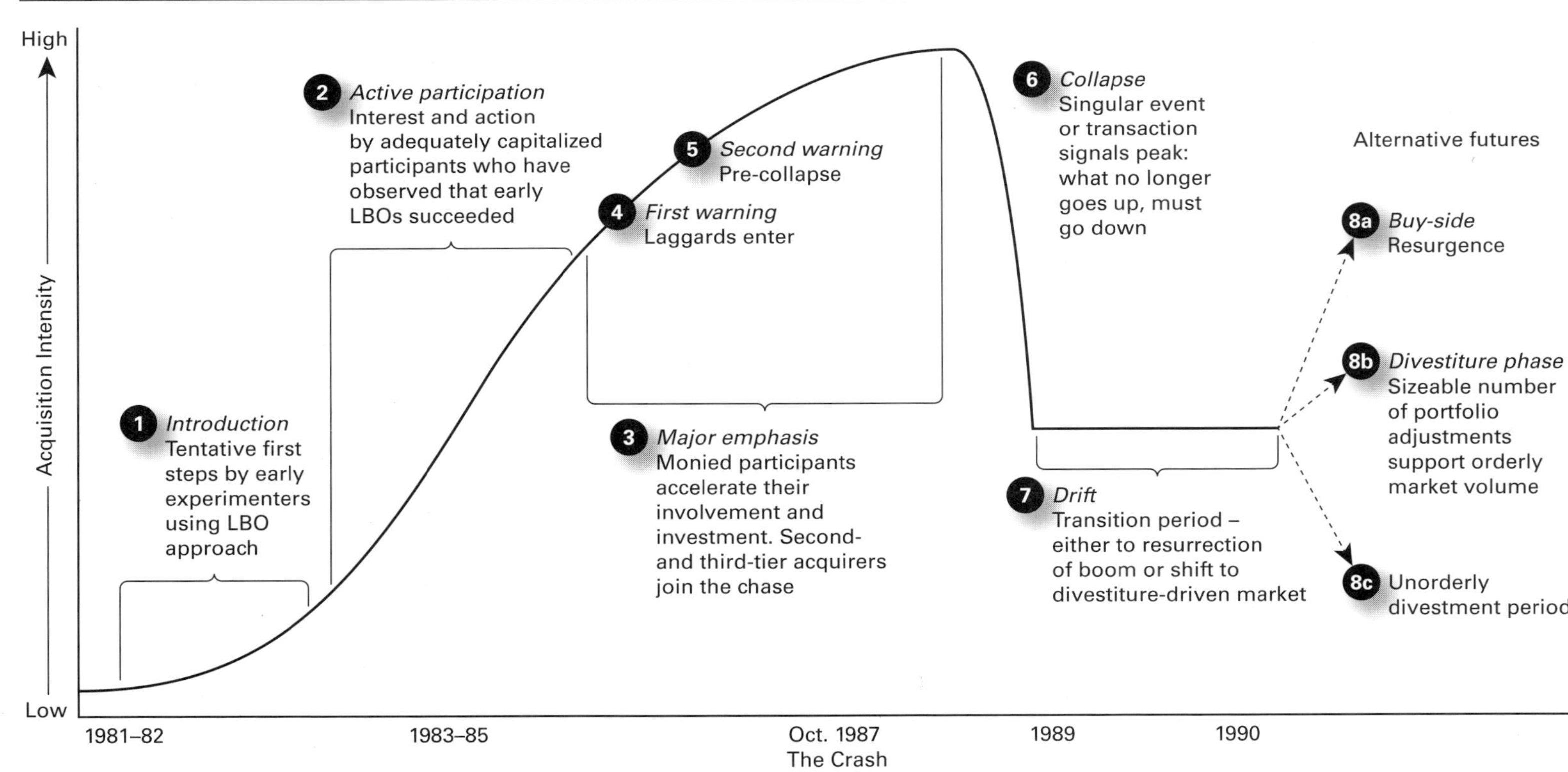

FIGURE 1.4 Identifiable merger phase and acquisition purchase premium (APP) percentage ranges

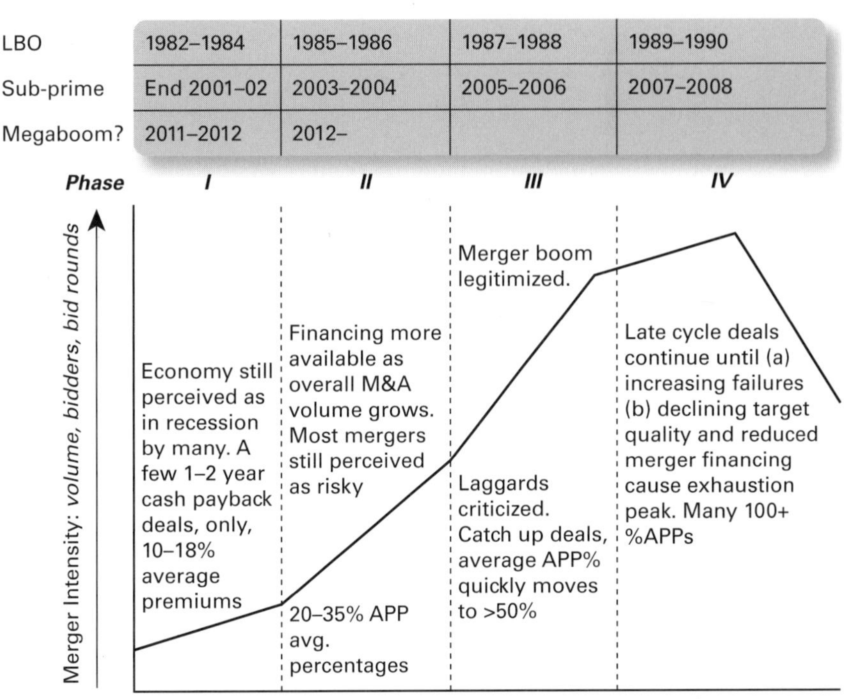

higher chance of success. As Akdogu *et al* (2005) suggest, 'There is ample reason to believe that the... (specific merger's) tendency to create or destroy value may differ depending on... whether it is early or late in the wave.'[7]

Phase I: Green shoots are coming up – or are those weeds?

Finally emerging from a long, painful recession, optimism and cash gradually return. Initially, business mass media insist that the recession never ended, sometimes even when customary gross domestic product (GDP) indicators suggest otherwise. Conjecture about a *double-dip* recession persists, at least for a while.

But then others look at the last three post-1980 merger waves when quarterly GDP either *did* decline temporarily (wave 1, LBO, 1982–90), or came close, (prior to wave 2 dot com I, 1996–2000)[8] and as a result come to view the double-dip scaremongering as irrelevant. Even if it happens, all that occurs is that the start date of a robust new merger wave is delayed for a few quarters, at most.

But the recent past is still troubling, and deals are suspect. With banks obsessed with repairing their own ravaged balance sheets first and their boards wary of the return of the recession, acquisition financing is limited to non-existent during phase I. At this point in the business-merger cycle, cyclical targets are trading at the low end of their seven–eight year price-earnings (P/E) multiple ranges. On an opportunistic basis, a few maverick all-cash buyers decide to act despite the adverse merger market sentiment. Some cheap targets become newly available as their owners lose patience during phase I. Except for occasional bottom-trawler deals of this type, overall merger activity remains almost dormant.[9]

Phase II: Jump-starting the new business-merger expansion period

Something is needed to steer the financial community's attention away from the wreckage of the last, crashed wave. That challenge can be daunting. Some company and country sovereign debt defaults – both actual and slightly disguised – still occur at this point in the cycle, with the potential to fracture already fragile market confidence. But as the second phase progresses, the nature of such threats to the nascent merger wave is perceived as moderating.

The development that forces the market's sights upwards towards the expansion business-merger wave yet to occur? Consider the role of the new merger wave's *signature event,* which occurs either late in phase I or early in phase II; see Table 1.1.

It is *not* important that the signature event is unique. It *is* important that the event is *perceived* by financial markets as fresh and novel. Both the first

TABLE 1.1 Signature events of the four post-1980 merger waves

Period	Wave Name	Signature Event
1982–90	LBO	RJR Nabisco Acquisition
1996–00	Dot com I	Netscape, Worldnet IPOs
2002–08	Subprime	Countrywide Financial Acquisition
2011–19(?)	**Megaboom**	**Facebook, LinkedIn IPOs**

internet boom and social networking had roots in developments occurring one decade earlier. It doesn't matter; by the time that dot com I (1996) and new generation social networking (2010) burst on to the scene, gushing analyst-cheerleaders proclaimed that something new, something not to be missed had occurred.[10]

When the signature event performs its role successfully, the financial community's sights are redirected – away from the dark past, towards a brighter future. Promise begins to push fear away. Concerns about repeating the excesses and errors of bubbles past are brushed aside. As the title of Reinhart and Rogoff's 2009 book proclaims, *This Time is Different.*

APP percentages creep upwards in phase II, not because merger market confidence has completely returned, but because M&A financing is now available for top rank acquirers. Availability of merger financing early in the wave is now viewed by some acquirers as an M&A competitive advantage. Moderate risk-takers reason that they had better pursue their deals quickly, lest they lose that edge as merger financing is extended to more firms as the wave progresses.

Then there are the incendiary transactions that signal that the slow recovery may be exploding into an outright boom. Earlier in the merger wave, APPs in a modest 10–22 percentage range predominate. Then something occurs such as Facebook's acquisition of Instagram in April 2012 at a price that was *double* the previous *week's* market value for that photo sharing services company.[11]

Phase III: So how come you missed out on the market's major upward move?

By the time the merger wave's third phase begins, everyone has arrived at the same realization, seemingly at the same time: *It is now safe to pursue deals again.*

The merger boom is legitimized in different ways, ranging from deal success stories embellished in the financial press to macho proclamations of corporate war chests as merger-expansion-oriented chief executives signal their readiness for M&A battle. Then there are the consultant infomercials restating merger conventional wisdom from the acquisition bubbles past. A few of these advisers acknowledge that *most mergers fail* (see Chapter 5).

That board member who criticized your idea about a major deal at a purchase premium of 22 per cent more than the target's price as of the originally proposed announcement date? Now that same director badgers you about why you aren't pursuing that same target company, but now at a higher APP because of the later point in the merger wave.[12]

Ask any stock picker on Wall Street or in the City of London, or any corporate marketer whose career depends on being viewed by his or her superiors as at the forefront of his or her field. It is far less damaging to make a best-efforts guess and then fail than sit on the sidelines and do nothing while the market roars ahead without you.

Reminiscent of merger bubbles past, M&A targeting and bid pricing discipline begins to give way to the imperative to complete a major deal. Increasing urgency to *get the deal done* is manifested by multiple bidders and multiple bidding cycles.

The chase for the hotly pursued target assumes a life of its own, outshining less dramatic developments such as ensuring prudent limits on APPs based on precedent and careful examination of *realizable* synergies, which often differ from the levels that the bidding team feels is necessary to prevail as the selected pursuer willing to overpay for the acquisition by the most. Concerns that confusing merger *activity* with merger *performance* in this manner ultimately results in merger train wrecks of the RBS Fortis/ABN Amro or AOL/TimeWarner variety, brings a terse, predictable response from the deal's apologists: *This time is different.*

Middle of phase IV: Feeling tentatively for the edge of the cliff

Attempting to snap a panoramic picture from the top of a steep precipice can be a terrifying proposition, whether you suffer from vertigo or not. Inch a bit closer to the edge, and much more of the horizon becomes visible. But how close to the edge of the cliff (to the ending months of the merger wave) do you dare go for fear of falling off the cliff (of experiencing merger failure)?

Such is the high risk nature of aggressive merger activity during the wave's concluding phase, the fourth. Slick perception-bending propaganda featuring spin-phrases such as 'soft landing' or 'managed retreat' might persuade a few to remain active in the merger game until the end. Direct compelling sales propaganda to a few laggards who regret that they have missed the market's big move to date, and there might even be some late participants available to scoop up the share positions that earlier buyers abandon, fearing that the edge of the cliff is near.

Observing years of active merger activity at defendable purchase premiums, the laggard reasons that the timing is finally perfect to proceed. It isn't. Excessive delay means that the major merger opportunities in this wave are in the past, that late movers have been whipsawed.

Phase IV has a well-deserved reputation as the most treacherous of the four merger wave periods. APPs rise to triple-digit percentage levels, rendering the task of first discovering and then securing sufficient synergies to offset those premiums nearly impossible.[13] Deal financing remains available for a while, enabling some of the companies that bought earlier in the wave to bail out of their earlier investment. The purchasers? The late-to-the-boom laggards, eager to make up for lost time. Sheep led to slaughter.

Over the years, various researchers have offered their explanations of merger waves. Four of the five categories of explanations are shown in Table 1.2. The fifth, referred to as merger phoenix/economic reset, is depicted by Figure 1.5 and results from the other four.

TABLE 1.2 Some explanations for merger wave development: four categories

	Description	Subsets	Research
Phenomenon	Reacting to shocks and similar unforeseen developments: threats, opportunities.	Overall Industry-specific Company-specific	Mitchell & Muherin (1996) Gort (1969)[14]
Behavioral	Perception of under-/over-market (share price-based) valuation: either target, or prospective buyer's shares, or both.	Focus on worth of prospective buyer's securities, in both absolute and relative terms.	Ang & Cheng (2006)[15] Dong *et al* (2006)[16]
Operational	Acquisition as alternative investment form required to meet expected returns.	Mergers as contingent investment when internal growth insufficient. Accelerated growth by merger.	Becketti (1986)[17] Copeland & Dolgoff (2006)
M&A stakeholders	Any or all of the three M&A stakeholder groups (acquirers, sellers, major intermediaries) shape merger environment in accordance with their business models.	Buyer's a) merger performance criteria, b) motivations. Divestment patterns and reasons. 'Bleak House' explanation: bankers	Kaplan & Weisbach (1992) Ch. 6 (dealmakers)

FIGURE 1.5 Merger phoenix/economic reset: landmark events in post-1980 merger wave 4 (2011–19 merger megaboom) anticipated

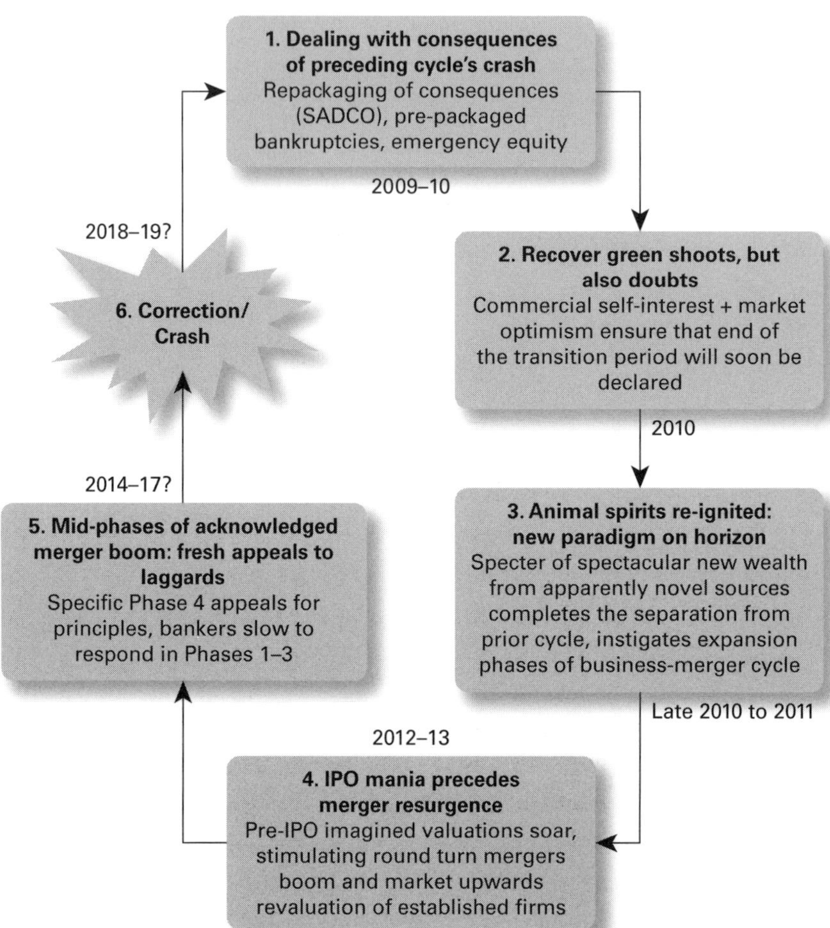

Traditional and non-traditional categories of merger wave explanations

Economic, regulatory and technological shocks drive industry merger waves.

(Harford, 2005)

Shocks, behavior, operations

Phenomenologists prescribe to the notion that merger activity arises from company reactions to perceived shocks, threats and changes. These shocks may affect the economy overall such as credit rationing, deflation, or emergence of the net. They may be industry-specific (radical, sudden deregulation without prior preparation in telecommunications, airline and savings and loan or building association companies), or company-specific. Examples of the latter include the loss of a critical account (Marconi) or slippage of legacy businesses and sectors into commodity status (Dell, Hewlett-Packard). Some different dimensions of shocks with the capability to influence merger activity are shown in Table 1.3.

While such disruptions may help explain why some companies believe that they are motivated to seek out mergers before they are fully prepared, those managers who are willing to have their firm's M&A strategy dictated by external developments are comparable to corks bobbing on a stormy sea. Buffeted back and forth by forces that they scarcely understand (but may think they do) a couple of the first movers succeed, while the others find themselves savaged by the new changed environment.[18]

Following the 1970s partial deregulation of telecommunications and savings and loan associations (S&Ls)[19] in the United States, advisers and consultants eager to plunge their snouts deep into the merger fee trough were at the time quick to point out to management of such firms that they now had new freedom to make purchases that would have been prohibited a few years earlier. Ambitious but without acquisition experience, the results of these naïve acquisitions were often failure: AT&T's multiple forays into computers and S&L adventures in general commercial lending.

No one appears to have advised these M&A marketplace neophytes to stay away, in part because that advice would have reduced deal advisory fees and underwriting income. Just because such acquisitions *could* be made based upon newly relaxed regulations doesn't mean that they *should* have been made, for reasons including two in particular: lack of management knowledge or ability relating to the new business areas; and unfamiliarity with bidding wars dynamics, which can quickly hike prices up to buyer's remorse[20] levels.

By contrast, behaviorists examine merger motivations leading to new merger waves from the perspective of *perceptions* of under- or overvaluation. *Perceptions* is italicized for a reason: even with rational market theory coming under increasing attack from more and more researchers and other observers (eg Fox, 2009), the notion that – except for obvious

TABLE 1.3 Shocks by category: the four post-1980 merger waves

In the phenomenology category, Baker and Kiymaz (2011, 26) support Mitchell and Mulherin's (1996) contention that major merger waves coincide with **industry-level clustering patterns**, and that these clusters are characterized by **'technological, economic and regulatory shocks**

	SHOCK: Technological/ Conceptual	SHOCK: Regulatory	SHOCK: Economic
1 LBO 1982–1990	Eclipse of mainframe computing ROE, CF, HLT	Privatization: Bell System Deregulation: S&L, Airlines	Stagflation broken
2 Dot com I 1996–2000	Internet I DCF Valuation goes mainstream	Beginning of 'regulatory light'	Friendly offers, globalization
3 Subprime/ Derivatives 2002–2008	Li's Coppula Broadband proliferation/ 3G	Repeal of Glass-Steagall TBTF/moral hazard	Accelerating PLCs: Apple Megamerger relaxation
4 Dot com II/ Merger Megaboom 2011–2019	Internet II (SN) Segmented merger valuation	Limited banking reforms: Volcker	QE Commodity bubble

speculative extremes involving either buyers' or sellers' panics – firms can be under- or over-valued strikes many as suspect.

Consider the source: look behind the proclamation of under- or over-valuation and you often see a not particularly subtle attempt at generating some company news and thus share action, regardless of the legitimacy of the contention. Proclaiming that share prices accurately reflect true value – the essence of semi-strong concepts of market efficiency – does nothing to encourage the stock picker's customers to take advantage of market mis-pricing, as pricing mistakes are presumed to not occur.

The group referred to here as operationalists are addressed in Table 1.2 in this chapter. One advantage of the pragmatic mindset that accompanies such a merger perspective is to quash high risk, low reward 'visionary' deals that have worth primarily in the pursuing chief executive's imagination. While it would have been advisable for AOL management to evaluate TimeWarner primarily on the basis of solid synergies between the two companies, that would have resulted in an APP far too modest to result in a transaction. But with merger bid ceilings set by realistically achievable synergies (see Chapters 3, 7 and 8 in this book) and with pricing guided not by ego but by a complete synergy diagnosis including realistic joint business development initiatives, chances for success increase.

Towards a stakeholder perspective on business-merger waves and deal activity

The remaining category in Table 1.2 is probably unfamiliar. In the stake-holder perspective depicted there, merger waves are seen as resulting from the rational economic action of each party. That responsible top management of companies on both the buy and the sell side at least theoretically seek to maximize ongoing returns to their shareholders is assumed. Whether or not a specific merger is consistent with management's shareholder value mantra is another matter.

But we've forgotten a major constituency, even though they are normally not principals on either side of the deal: merger transaction intermediaries in general and investment bankers/deal rainmakers specifically. Forget that they are neither the buyer nor seller: without these middlemen there is no robust continuing M&A marketplace.

With a radically altered business model – the Big Bang – banks are still highly dependent on merger fees. In certain markets where the middlemen actually run the market, the principals might fool themselves into imagining that their interests are paramount and shape the nature and future direction of the market – in this case, the global merger market.

The intermediaries wouldn't have it any other way. Casinos in Las Vegas don't go out of their way to make the percentages in their favor widely known if they can help it, and the estate lawyers in Dickens's book *Bleak House* were careful to position themselves as mere facilitators, with no self-interest in the principals' concerns.

The dealmakers run the show. Comprehend that simple truth, and the overt actions of bankers at key points in the merger wave suddenly begin to make sense. *Dealmakers running the merger show* starts with IPO pricing (as differentiated from value): the new business-merger wave's signature event. In the present expansion period, those events involve social networking firms. Bankers bluff and statistical quasi-logic are necessary to craft the case that Facebook is worth more than $100 billion despite multiple current and potential competitors and the possibility of wide swings in profitability at least until the business model stabilizes.

The merger megaboom is on! Phase II of the 2011–19 merger wave began in mid-April 2012 with Facebook's acquisition of Instagram. Mergers become widely considered safe again, even though as prices increase with prosperity, so do the obstacles to merger success, as the price versus value difference widens.

1.2 Four post-1980 business-merger waves, four phases

Post-1980 era business-merger waves differ from their predecessor in key ways, including low structural inflation, widespread use of debt financing for acquisitions, increased awareness of the agency problem (Professor Michael Jensen) combined with dual concerns about underleverage and underperformance (T Boone Pickens).

To date in this era, there have been three distinct business expansion-merger waves: 1982–90 LBOs, 1996–2000 dot com I/friendlies, and the 2002–08 subprime derivatives/financial securitization bubble. Each of those waves is composed of four phases that are typically not understood by participants except in retrospect, after that wave is finished and a corrective recession looms. The dynamics of each phase are described earlier in this chapter. What may be less apparent is how a feature or failure from an earlier merger wave comes to affect objectives and strategies in future cycles.

Table 1.4 compares characteristics of the four post-1980 merger waves. Time period, duration (in terms of elapsed years, actual or expected), and causes of particularly visible value destruction are identified for each of the four post-1980 cycles. The bold arrows show the adjustments in the *next* business-merger wave, as the financial community acts to correct the *preceding* wave's chronic shortcoming.

TABLE 1.4 Cross-influences between the four post-1980 merger waves

	1. LBO	2. Dot Com I	3. Subprime	4. Dot Com II / Megaboom
Period	1982–1990	1996–2000	2002–2008	2011–?
Duration (elapsed years)	8	4	6	8 (based on 2019 end date)
Value destruction	Late phase hostiles	Large friendlies ('strategic') Profitless dot coms	High reward without accompanying risk	**TBD** – missteps in monetizing social networking subscribers?
Next wave adjustment	High leverage transaction (HLT) exemplars	Friendlies	Rediscovery of substantive (financial) basis of merger valuation	Superficial regulatory modifications Eclipse of profitless net IPO

Post-1980 merger wave 1: leveraged buyouts (LBOs) 1982–90

The merger wave exemplified by Gordon Gekko and dramatic takeovers dominated the business expansion cycle of the 1980s, particularly in the United States. As noted, a combination of supportive regulatory and financial conditions set the stage for a resurrection of the merger marketplace in that decade. High leverage transactions (HLTs) represented a reaction to the value-depressing combination of under-leverage and under-management. For the first half of that bubble at least, financial acquirers might imagine that financial restructuring combined with commonsense reductions in superfluous discretionary spending might cause the merger equivalent of something for nothing: the target company that could be substantially or sometimes completely purchased with its own underutilized balance sheet.

With early 1990s studies criticizing hostile takeovers as contributing to some of the worst abuses of that period including late phase deals with such high APPs that they were effectively in danger of collapse at the time of merger (including RJR Nabisco, MCC (Maxwell Communications Company) and various media properties), the reaction for the next wave was predictable, if naïve. It could be presumed that hostile transactions played a large role in the 1980s merger excess; next time make sure that the deal is perceived by target company management as friendly (read: at such a high bid price that opposition disappears).

Post-1980 merger wave 2: dot com I (plus friendlies), 1996–2000

Some suggest that the next wave began around 1993, which is reasonable if you primarily base that starting point on the basis of the brief recession that followed the LBO bubble. However, we assume the post-1980 wave 2 began in 1996, because of volume considerations and emergence of the commercial net in 1995–6 (Netscape's signature IPO happened in August 1995). On that basis, wave 2 was the briefest of the four post-1980 business-merger expansion periods, at four years.

Note the 180 degree change in order to emphasize friendly transactions as contrasted with noteworthy battles of LBO wave 1, such as for RJR Nabisco. Schwert (2000) expressed what many others were sensing, then and now: that the so-called hostile-friendly difference in deal types was often irrelevant, as every transaction in which the seller was taking responsible actions to maximize *its* shareholders' wealth almost always started with some degree of antagonism. Equally important, the myopic approach to pursuing a transaction that is warmly embraced by selling company shareholders almost guarantees overpayment on such a massive scale that synergies cannot even come close to covering the APP.

Upon receiving a bid for Huffington Press from flailing AOL in early 2011, Arianna Huffington's response was conspicuous because of the *absence* of the standard issue dismissive language that is almost every seller's tactic to try to extract the last dollar from an over-eager suitor. No response? The acquirer has already exceeded the *upper end* of the seller's range (best to nod agreeably before the overpayer wakes up to the mistake). An exception occurs when the seller-target fears that a rebuff might risk scaring away a once-in-a-lifetime deal in terms of its generosity. The price of Huffington's agreeable silence was that AOL grossly overpaid for the company, paying an extremely full price of 10 times sales.[21]

Profitless dot coms presented a separate, significant problem. As examined in Chapter 6, IPOs usually help spur merger activity in the first half of the new wave as smaller firms become absorbed in consolidation-type mergers, while some firms outside of the golden segment seek to buy their way into the new *can't miss* sector via merger. Both developments roared during the first half of wave 2, the first dot com bubble, but then suddenly collapsed as suspicions arose that some of the acquired companies were not worth the cocktail napkins upon which their thrilling but profitless business model ideas were written.

How does wave 2 of the dot com II social networking companies compare to the present 2011–19 merger wave, wave 4? Profitless social networking companies are effectively banished from today's IPO markets while concerns about inexperienced management and sometimes suspect plans for advertising revenues mean a more suspicious eye, less of the naivety that led to first Greenspan's and later, Shiller's alarm about *irrational exuberance* in the late 1990s.

Post-1980 merger wave 3: subprime/securitized financial derivatives, 2002–8

The third of the four post-1980 waves was dominated by the debatable concept of universal banking combined with repeal of the Glass-Steagall Act of 1934. In retrospect however, the key causal feature underlying wave 3 was Li's experimental Copula, suitably referred to in Salmon's insightful 17

March 2009 article in *Wired* entitled, 'Recipe for disaster: the formula that ruined Wall Street.'

For those market players unwilling and/or unable to understand the complex equations underlying the use of multiple tranches (or groups) of subprime mortgages and related derivatives, Li's Copula was incendiary, as it was perceived by the layman as justifying unthinkable loans to normally ineligible borrowers.

It was only a matter of time before the simple truth became apparent to everyone, after the crash. *Extend massive amounts of money to deadbeat borrowers, and bad things occur.* Thus Countrywide Financial, the king of subprime mortgage loans originations appeared to be a profit juggernaut in the mid-2000s – a perception soon revised and then reversed three years later. Barclays ducked a value-destruction bullet by *failing* to 'win' the acquisition bidding war for ABN Amro.

Deals in the concluding phase of the 2002–8 wave were shotgun marriages aimed at saving the world financial markets. JPMorgan Chase absorbed Bear Stearns, Merrill Lynch collapsed into Bank of America while new bulge bracket player Barclays selectively acquired some parts of collapsed Lehman Bros.

1.3 The fourth (and final?) post-1980 wave is already underway[22]

While it is true that the only absolutely reliable method for verifying a merger wave is after the fact, a close second is to monitor the progress of the new emergent wave as it evolves.

Some parallels

Some similarities have been noted already in this chapter. The presumed start year of this latest wave was soon after the United States officially emerged from recession-based GDP. Purchase premium (APP) percentages are rising, with triple-digit deals not limited to fading companies desperate for a turnaround, regardless of the value-destructive overbid amount. Wave 4's signature IPO, Facebook, is reminiscent of wave 2's comparable event, the 1996 Netscape IPO.

Merger volume is increasing in fits and starts, with wave 4's initial phase marked by early acceleration for a few quarters followed by retrenchment. While this early phase volatility is unsettling to dealmakers and others in the financial community and press, initial inconsistency tallies with past patterns of how new merger booms begin. Market direction is only straight up or straight down in the cartoons.

 Alex reprinted with permission from Peattie & Taylor. Website: http://www.alexcartoon.com/. *Alex* appears regularly in the Finance section of *The Telegraph* (Lon.): http://www.telegraph.co.uk/finance/alex/.

Describing wave 4's phase I M&A volume and the present merger wave's future direction, Scott Bok, CEO of bankers Greenhill & Co, on March 5 2012 commented that:

> You had a significant upturn beginning last year, and for the first seven months it looked like everything was in track for a normal cyclical recovery. And then around August we hit an air pocket... as a result of the problems in Europe... (Now) companies are more optimistic and they are looking for opportunities to put their cash, and even their stock, to work in some cases... More than a third of our revenue was not linked to completion of an M&A transaction.[23]

Bok's observations contradict the winter 2011–12 perspective that instability in the sovereign debt of PIIGS (Portugal, Ireland, Italy, Greece and Spain) could derail the new business-merger wave before momentum for post-1980 merger wave 4 can become established. The Greenhill chief executive's 'more than a third' comment indicates that almost 65 per cent of his firm's revenue is *still* dependent on merger activity, despite a staggering recovery in 2010–12. Thus Bok and other bankers have a vital interest in bringing about the embryonic fourth post-1980 business-merger cycle in a way that is to *their* advantage, in *Bleak House* manner if necessary. There are no merger transaction fees until and unless principals can be convinced that the markets are safe again for merger adventures.

Wave 4: led by high tech

> The early extreme excesses of NetPhase I are just part of the stage-setting for what is to come: NetPhase II, when the Dot Coms grow up, when the major new corporations of the 21st century begin to be built, and when the new internet champions soar.
>
> (Clark, 2000)

Bok's comments pertain to the overall M&A market. Focus on the pacesetting tech sector alone – rather than acquisitions overall, from all sources – and a more buoyant indicator of wave 4's possible future emerges. By mid-2011, *The Economist* cited Ernst & Young statistics indicating a resurgence in technology-related acquisition activity, with quarterly deal volume rebounding to around 75–80 per cent and deal financial amount at the height of the preceding 2002–8 business-merger cycle (wave 3).[24]

The fourth major business-merger wave began around March 2011. Not coincidentally, that was about the same time that the *first* $100 billion pre-IPO vapor valuation price guess for Facebook was articulated (it came public in May 2012 at an indicated value for the firm as a whole of $104 billion). A key feature of the merger megaboom will be the introduction of a new type of (mostly) profitable businesses that begin their lives as public companies with the question not being the dot com I concern of *will those companies survive* but instead, *how will those firms handle their explosive success?*

Wildcard: QE

No one at this time knows the full consequences of massive sustained quantitative easing (QE) beginning at the time of the collapse of the *last* wave. Assurances that massive excess liquidity can simply be soaked up as economies recover is contradicted by basic economic theory, which suggests that a large surge in liquid funds must eventually become manifested in a return to inflationary expectations, once *de*flationary fears are put to rest.

While some might argue that a possible trend return towards higher levels of structural inflation increases the attractiveness of *all* assets (including merger target companies), negative effects on merger activity levels are nonetheless suggested by reduced merger financing availability and competing high returns from passive financial investments (particularly as the sense grows that MMF – most mergers fail – evolves from provocative notion to widely accepted fact; see Chapter 5).

Will the fourth post-1980 wave endure until 2019?

A 2019 expected end date for this merger megaboom is broadly consistent with the duration of early post-1980 era patterns. Wave 1, LBO, lasted eight years. But will wave 4 last that long? This, the second dot com bubble, is still highly experimental. Road show bombast notwithstanding, no social networking (SN) company has yet discovered the secret to keeping the product (subscribers) and the customers (advertisers) both happy at the same time, although Twitter comes close. SN subscribers are notoriously fickle: Facebook is the *third* company of its type, not the first.

There's also the earlier dot com era's (wave 2, 1996–2000, four elapsed years) precedent of very brief bubbles: everything happens faster on the internet, including business-merger cycles. Then there's the overall tendency over three decades towards briefer and briefer product-service life cycle duration. From consumer electronics to 3D printers, cosmetics to m-commerce, there is always at least one well-financed competitor in each segment that attempts to mobilize its superior speed-to-market as a basis for competitive advantage.[25]

Evercore Partners' Roger Altman described merger waves as lasting 'five to seven years' in the quotation shown at the beginning of this chapter. Apply those durations to a post-1980 wave 4 starting in 2011, and the consequence is a fourth post-1980 business-merger wave ending between 2016 and 2018. However, Altman also predicted that the present merger cycle began in 2010 ('we are two years into it'), which would suggest an even earlier end to merger megaboom, in 2015–17.

A perfect storm?

> The most recent wave of M&As, as well as previous ones, is fueled by many factors: low interest rates, a bull market, deregulation, global expansion and industry restructuring.
>
> (Andre, 2004)[26]

Destructive strength of the individual tsunami is in direct proportion to the combination of conditions occurring at the wave's earthquake epicenter. The particular combination of conditions and characteristics – strength of the earthquake shock, depth of the epicenter and the ocean in the immediate area of the shock – all influence how powerful the wall of water becomes, and how far the wave travels.

Confronting the notion that merger wave 4 could end *before* 2019 is the unprecedented combination of origin (epicenter) factors that have sustained past merger booms. Typically only two or three of the factors identified in Figure 1.6 are in place. At the time of writing, *all six* appear to be in place for the merger megaboom, suggesting a duration comparable to that of the first post-1980 wave (LBO): eight years.

FIGURE 1.6 A perfect merger storm: dot com II/merger megaboom

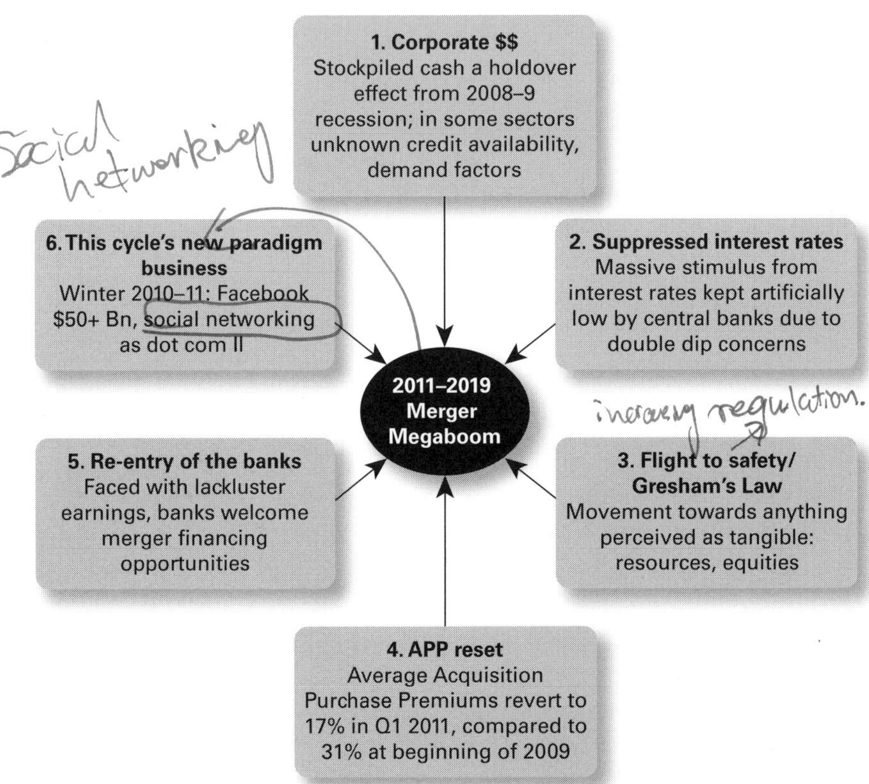

The cash hoard alone (point 1 in Figure 1.6) may be sufficient to ensure that wave 4 lasts to 2019. Company cash hoarding persists, even as the recovery gains momentum: as of May 6 2011, *Bloomberg* estimated that 3,000 of the largest public companies still had approximately $4.8 *trillion* in cash and short-term investments in their coffers.[27]

Private equity firms – often the earliest to act as the new merger wave starts and the last to leave – sat on $940 billion in unspent capital as of October 2011. Much of this 'dry powder' will end up being deployed in buyout transactions as the present wave progresses. As *Bloomberg's*

Chassany reports: 'About 41 per cent of dry powder is held by leveraged-buyout funds, according to UK research firm Preqin. LBO funds raised in 2008 have about $91.5 billion in unspent commitments.'[28]

1.4 Merger wave issue I: (T)APP-synergy divergence as the wave progresses

(See also Appendix A.)

Both overall share price indices and APP amounts and percentages required to close deals normally rise over the course of the business-merger wave. Phase I begins modestly, with APP percentages typically in a 10–15 per cent range. The list of available target companies at that point in the cycle is dominated by emergency divestitures from the last collapsed cycle, and solid but unsexy companies from cyclical industries, then at their nadir.

The merger market heats up, with demand increasing and a broader range of target companies available, as sellers inclined to get out take advantage. By the time the merger wave's final phase (IV) reached its mid-point, carefully considered M&A examinations are replaced by a buyers' panic, as late-to-market acquirers scramble for the remaining few quality targets. Some of the factors contributing to overall share price increases over the course of the business cycle are indirectly referred to in this chapter; researchers concentrating on that topic provide a perspective on causes and implications.[29]

The passage of time leads to business amnesia. Even those who are reluctant at first to plunge back into the merger game, following the painful memories of M&A carnage from the last wave, eventually convince themselves that this time will be different. Or if it isn't different, they'll be nimble enough to get out before the *next* merger bubble pops.

Aspiring acquirers' cash flows (CFs) rise, creating upward pressure on overall share prices, as more cash is available to chase quality targets and merger speculation returns. Merger market momentum is boosted when certain types of transactions – such as companies in cyclical industries and moderately-priced consolidations – are proclaimed to be 'safe'. Share prices of companies in sectors particularly attractive to potential future acquirers (in this wave, that includes cloud computing and some segments within social networking) enjoy an additional bonus to their share prices, with that extra amount target speculation: the possibility of future pursuit by an ardent acquirer, as the cycle gains momentum.

But two problems arise as a consequence of the rise of both share prices overall and increases in merger enthusiasm as the cycle progresses. The first has to do with the accuracy and usefulness of APP indicators in later phases of the wave. As detailed in Part A1 of Appendix A, the APP indicator that appears to accurately reflect the bid price dynamic early in the cycle may be understated by Phase IV, as the denominator in the APP ratio is not an unchanging target company share price. Stated another way, the target's share price tends to move upwards as the business-merger wave advances with the rest of the market ('a rising tide lifts all ships') as investor sentiment improves, distorting the raw APP calculation.[30]

This issue has greater implications. It is not just that total acquisition purchase premium (TAPP, an adjustment to APP taking into account both the successful acquirer's bid amount based on pre-announcement prices and also appreciation of the target's baseline price since the beginning of the cycle) sources in later phases of the bubble. It is also that synergies relating to the proposed business combination do not rise with either APP or TAPP levels.

Comparisons of the APP with apparent realizable synergies frequently appears in some reports as the financial community seeks an early indicator of whether or not the proposed deal with be successful or not (merger evaluative criteria are examined in Chapter 3). No bidder ever *knowingly* admits to overpayment, as that is effectively an admission that the acquiring company's funds have been misspent and implies value destruction from the perspective of acquiring company shareholders. But comparing the amount (or percentage) of the premium paid (APP) against the present value of net realizable synergies (NRS) by ratio, percentage or amount provides one such early indicator. This technique is comparable to the value gap (VG) merger valuation methodology described in the third chapter.

In the expansive phase of the business-merger cycle and often afterwards, APPs tend to increase. In May 2011 at the time of the Altman quote found at the beginning of this chapter, the pre-announcement to final deal price average premium was thought to be approximately 17 per cent. One half year earlier, APP percentages were described as 5–7 points lower, that is, around 10–12 per cent. The beginning of the merger wave in phase I is when realistic estimates of synergies (Ss) and price paid are most likely to coincide. As the merger wave progresses, a disparity arises, as APPs increase but Ss do not.

Rising APPs. Prices paid increase as the merger wave progresses through its four phases because of the increasing level in pre-announcement prices (the 'T' in TAPP – 'the rising tide that raises all ships'), and increasing required APP percentages due to increasing merger speculation and decreasing availability of quality targets.

Static Ss. But for a particular proposed acquirer-target business combination, most synergy elements are not subject to upward revision as the merger wave progresses. Assume that the savings in post-merger synergies expected from combining overlapping IT platforms and departments in a deal originally contemplated between A and B in the middle of phase I is $1 billion. The factors underlying that analyzed amount are unlikely to change over the course of that same merger wave. So the synergy savings estimate pertaining to this part of the Ss calculation when the deal between A and B is finally closed in early phase IV, *remains* about the same: approximately $1 billion.

1.5 Merger wave issue II: whipsaw-merger market entry and exit missteps

A second Wave 4 issue of importance involves whipsaw, referring here to merger market participants' missteps when entering or exiting the merger market. *It's about those claims of expert timing (guaranteed to escape fast-exploding merger bubbles).*

Timing

The financial (as contrasted with trade-, or operating company) acquirer's boasts about its astute market timing is all part of that group's standard advertising pitch, thus unlikely on its own to reduce concern about casino-grade bets involving very high leverage transactions (HLT) in the waning days of the merger cycle, as collapse into recession looms. The reality of such self-proclaimed timing acumen is of course often considerably different to actual performance. Unless these 'experts' possess a crystal ball (they don't) or have operations-honed instincts of when the target's markets are going forward or not (again, nothing there), the timing expertise claims amount to only so much spin.

Terra Firma/EMI, Cinven/Spire Healthcare (UK), Zell/Chicago Tribune – notable late phase merger mistimings – suggest instead that at least in some acquiring firms, the problem instead is that the buyer believes his or her own promotional fluff. Overconfidence leads to mistakes in knowing when the exact time arises in phase IV to *get out*. By the time you understand that signal, it is too late: others are coming to that exact same conclusion at the same point, resulting in a sellers' panic. The stampede for the exits scares away any remaining last-phase buyers who might have been receptive to a deal, and private placements are out of the question, except perhaps at terms that reflect the seller's desperation.

Entry decisions

Markets consider prospects five years *forward,* but some acquirers only look nine months *backwards.* In widely-traded exchanges, stock prices are based on forward perspectives, consistent with the DCF approach of determining specific company worth on the basis of future projected cash flow generation, discounted at the appropriate cost of capital. By contrast, individual investors – a group that includes chief executives of acquiring firms on the basis that acquisitions are external investments – are often influenced by recent developments.

Alarmist stories about double-dip recessions persist into the second phase of the merger wave, spooking some acquirers, or at least delaying their actions. This lag effect means that the popular business press is crowded with disaster stories about the *last* bubble almost until the mid-point of the merger wave that occurs *next.*

At the very least, any tendency to assign greater importance to recent events may contribute to timing errors at both extremes of the merger wave. In phase I, the aspiring acquirer ignores the fact that new expansion periods almost always start within 18 months of the end of a prolonged recession. Cheap prices are missed as that acquirer is haunted by the possibility that the overall economy might technically slip back into recession for another quarter or two, before recovery gains traction. Even in those exceptional instances where there *is* a short-lived dip into recession based on customary GDP criteria (such as in the early 1980s, prior to the start of the LBO business-merger wave) the eight-year duration of the overall robust recovery period is only postponed by a few months.

End-of-cycle timing is usually only understood after the fact. By the time the high timing risk deal is consummated late in phase IV, the acquirer already has its excuses lined up. Negotiations started back in phase III, so this isn't really an end-of-cycle deal. At almost any time during the merger cycle, there are some market Cassandras who always see the worst and proclaim that the end is nigh. By the time that the business-merger cycle slips into its final phase, the acquirer is numb to those warnings: *other deal-makers are still in the game, right?*

'It's unique'

Every deal tends to be described by the acquiring company's chief executive officer as unique. They aren't. Ask a group of acquiring executives the probability of deal success, and responses tend to be consistent with the MMF indications cited in Chapter 5 of this book – that approximately two-thirds of all deals fail, based on prevailing financial return-based criteria.

But that only applies to others' transactions. Ask an executive to assess his or her own past deal performance, and an optimistic spin is predictable. Even if it is true that two-thirds or more of that acquiring company's deals have become merger train wrecks, don't hold your breath waiting for such an admission.

Hubris (as described by Roll, 1986) or deliberate self-distortion are factors. Another consideration is that the acquiring CEO's deals are perceived to be unique and thus customary indications of merger success and failure do not apply. When the transaction is imagined to be unique, timing signals based on prior merger waves are likely to be ignored. The possibility of a serious merger timing misstep – involving entry (acquisition) or exit (divestment) or both – soars.

One of the deterrents to merger learning – as evidenced by an acquirer improving its M&A performance by making adaptations based upon prior experience – is a tendency to treat every merger event as unique.[31] When each new acquisition possibility is treated as a one-off, neither the deal nor its positioning within the prevailing merger wave is likely to be perceived correctly.

Is this proposed transaction occurring during the sluggish initial quarters of the wave, when both target company pre-bid share prices and APPs are modest but financing is scarce, or is one of those lamentable deals occurring a month before the cycle's exhaustion peak – one of those dead-on-arrival mistakes that the pundits will point to in complaining about that wave's excesses? The deal misperceived as unique is adrift, with no signposts pointing away to the future. Timely entrance and exit are left to personal pique or chance.

Spotting the south-pointing compass indicators

> One of Gordon Brown's clunkier traits as chancellor was to seize on a phrase 'an end to boom and bust...'
>
> (*Private Eye*, September 16–29 2011, 'The Credibility Gap', p 8)

An indicator that is so consistently wrong as to be reliable – the compass which points in the exact opposite direction than it should – can be highly valuable to effective merger timing. Correctly diagnosed, the acquirer simply takes the opposite of the indicated action.

Uncovering and correctly diagnosing these south-pointing compasses can be difficult, but few are widely understood. For example, the top executive or senior politician (such as former UK Prime Minister Gordon Brown when he was Chancellor of the Exchequer, above) who at the height of the market bubble proclaims that the boom-bust cycle has been defeated, unknowingly signals to those who know what to watch for that the end of the business-merger wave will begin soon, a year to 18 months from the time of the indicator.

The naïve statement of unrealistic optimism does not *itself* cause any change in business or merger fundamentals. Instead, such indicators serve as a signal that favorable conditions have already passed. Stated another way: when *everyone* acknowledges that the boom is on, the expansion period is probably nearing its end.

Availability of merger financing and changes in unemployment levels during phases I and II are among a group of less visible but no less important indicators. The would-be acquirer who either doesn't know what to look for or how to correctly interpret that indicator misses valuable timing advantage.

Merger wave supply and demand dynamics

Each merger wave represents a closed-ended system, with a finite of quality targets over that period. By itself, a visible reduction in the quality of targets provides one indication that the end of the merger wave is fast approaching. Factor in *higher* bid prices and APP percentages paid for targets of *lower* quality, and an even clearer advance indicator flashes.

For whatever the reason, the aspiring acquirer has to date missed out on top candidate companies in that would-be buyer's target industry or segment. Independent observers comment that more must be paid for less, if that would-be acquirer wants to avoid being shut out. Making decisions on the basis of fear instead of analysis and conviction, that player is a conspicuous victim when the shakeout occurs a few months along. While a handful of desperate acquirers may proceed anyway, figuring that this is the best they can do, more careful acquirers decide to stand aside – in effect, winning in the merger game by staying away (see 8.2 in Chapter 8).

Reluctance to leave money on the table

The merger wave reaches its sixth anniversary, indicating that the end is almost assuredly less than two years in the future, assuming that the maximum duration of post-1980 waves past (number 1, LBO, 1982–90: eight years) as a limit. But some deals are still being done, and money is still available for late entrants to finance a bid. The odds are stacked against such deals, both because of the aforementioned demand-supply imbalances and because the post-bubble recession is now only months away, with the threat of abrupt reductions in CF to try to support a high end-of-bubble bid.

This worst-of-both-worlds situation presents a compelling case for staying out of the market. But contaminating influences may distort what should be a straightforward decision. Aggressive deal arrangers or criticism from major investors for missing opportunities earlier in the wave may cause these timing signals to be ignored.

Notes

1 Saitto, S, 'Altman sees dealmaking surpassing $4 trillion record.' http://bloomberg.com/apps/news?pid=newsarchive&sid=aEAhsRH.WyqM. Accessed May 6 2011.

2 This was also the title of the first chapter to the predecessor of this book, co-author Clark's *Beyond the Deal* (1991: 3): 'Fact: Most mergers don't work.'

3 The 2011–19 business-merger cycle still appears to be on track despite a soft 2012 following some resurgence in merger activity in the preceding year.

4 Share prices also increase for many quality targets, cancelling some or most of that acquirer's presumed purchase advantage. Although a primary area of interest to some merger valuation academicians into the 1990s, the basis of payment (cash versus stock) has become less provocative in recent years as nearly every completed transaction involves a mix of stock and cash – there are few 'pure' deals of either type, and targets usually apply formulas to adjust for different mixes in payment form composition.

5 In part, this helps explain financial acquirers' continuing over-reliance on high leverage transaction (HLT) techniques today, decades after that tactic has lost its effectiveness. Refer to merger fallacy 2.2 in the next chapter.

6 The issue of developing *pre*-close synergy intelligence of the target's business is addressed in Chapter 8.

7 Akdogu, E, Harford, J and Moeller, S (2005) 'Value creation and merger waves.' Phrase in parentheses added by this book's authors. APP percentage is calculated based upon the prevailing bid price amount for shares of target,

divided by share price levels twenty trading days *before* the date that intended acquirer indicates purchase interest. Refer to Appendix A.

8 Post-1980 merger wave 2 (dot com I, 1996–2000, four elapsed years) is interpreted here as briefer that both waves 1 (LBO, 1982–90, eight elapsed years) and 3 (subprime, 2002–8, six years) on the basis that world M&A transaction volume was less than $20 trillion in 1992–4 and still below $23 trillion in 1995. Also, 1996, the presumed initial year for wave 2, coincided with the widespread use of the commercial internet, the major business development of that decade. *The Economist* (Jan 7 1999) 'After the deal', http://www.economist.com/node/181251 Accessed Jan 7 1999. In Spring 2012, the UK appeared to temporarily dip back into recession based on traditional GDP measures, while the US eluded a return to recession measured on that basis.

9 Such acquisitions by 'bottom-trawler' acquirers represent one of the nine types of merger types as shown in the acquisition segmentation framework presented in Chapter 4 (Table 4.2).

10 Anderson *et al* (2011) 'The coming wave of social apponomics', *Strategy+Business*, 62.

11 Facebook's pre-IPO acquisition of Instagram is examined in Chapter 6. Post-IPO, the astronomical purchase premium paid for Instagram is viewed as indicative of FB's concern about financial community criticism of a deficient mobile strategy.

12 From Appendix A: as the merger wave progresses through its four phases, APPs increase as a result of two separate yet related developments. First, later phase deals usually call for increased APPs in percentage terms; second, the pre-bid share price of the target company is likely to be much greater than earlier in the cycle, due to improved market sentiment.

13 See Chapter 3, Part 3.6 for more on this.

14–17 Refer to Further Reading.

18 The phrase 'but may think they do' refers to the questionable third-party guidance that sometimes tricks merger market participants into believing that the keys to success in new target company areas are better understood than they are. The one sure thing about social networking companies is that many of those firms' business models are still works in progress (see Chapter 6).

19 The UK equivalents of S&Ls are building societies: deposit-taking financiers of home mortgage loans and some types of residential income property.

20 See Holt and Sherman (1984) and Bazerman and Samuelson (1983).

21 'In 2010 it made $31 million in revenues, so (it) is being bought for 10 times sales. Even if it manages to double that in 2011, it's still a massive price.' Reece, D (Feb 7 2011) 'AOL shareholders are right to be in a Huff over

$315m website purchase', *Telegraph* (London) http://www.telegraph.co.uk/finance/comment/damianreece/8309579/AOL-shareholders-are-right-to-be-in-a-Huff-over-315m-website-purchase.html. Accessed Feb 8, 2011.

22 As also noted in the Introduction, expectations expressed in this chapter of a business-merger expansion period starting in 2011 and extending until the latter years of this decade presumes that there are no major economic and/or political shocks which significantly alter, delay or misdirect that wave.

23 'View from the top', *Financial Times,* March 5 2012, 18.

24 Excluding private equity (PE) deals, *The Economist* (Aug 27 2011) Figure, 'Another merger surge' in 'Moving up the stack', 57.

25 *The Economist* (Sep 12 2011). 'Shorter cycles?' Buttonwood, http://www.economist.com/blogs/buttonwood/2011/09/global-economy?fsrc=nlwlnewel09-12-11lnew_on_the_economist. Accessed Sep 12 2011; Agarwal, G and Gort, M (2002) 'Firm and product life cycles and firm survival', *Technological Change*, 92: 2,184–90; Clark (2001) *The Value Mandate*, 60–64.

26 http://www.camagazine.com/archives/print-edition/2004/march/regulars/camagazine15502.aspx. Accessed July 25 2011.

27 Saitto, S, 'Altman sees dealmaking recovery surpassing $4 trillion record', *Bloomberg,* http://Bloomberg.com/apps/news?pid=newsarchive&sid=aEAhsRH.WyqM. Accessed May 6 2011. Estimates described therein as based on 'recent company filings'.

28 'Private equity has $937 billion in "dry powder"', *Bloomberg,* http://www.bloomberg.com/news/print/2011-10-17/private-equity-has-937-billion-in-dry-powder-preqin-reports.html. Accessed Oct 17 2011.

29 See Lucas, 1987; Levy, Solomon and Ram, 1996; Tvede, 2006; Zarnowitz, V, 1999. Refer to Further Reading.

30 Expressed here as a ratio (bid amount/target's pre-announcement share price), the rising denominator referred to here is the target's pre-announcement share price. In the illustrative exhibit in Appendix A (Figure A.1), the Phase IV acquisition indicating a nominal APP percentage of 75 is instead revealed to represent an adjusted (or total 'T') APP of over 300 per cent if the original baseline share price of the target is used, instead. Despite this limitation of APP, it is the difference between purchase premium and realizable synergies (APP minus NRS in Chapters 3 and 7) that is most often cited in remarks about a deal being perceived as *overpaid.*

31 Leschinskii and Zollo (2004: 1): 'We find that acquisition experience does not improve post-acquisition experience...'. Experience by the acquiring company's prior management is likely to be ignored and treated as irrelevant, as those prior merger disappointments are attributed to predecessors' incompetence.

02 Debunking the six merger fallacies that destroy value

CHAPTER CONTENTS

2.1 Myth 1: Increased understanding of historical merger failure means that would-be acquiring firms are more inclined to avoid mergers

2.2 Myth 2: Significant increases to target company's debt levels do not significantly reduce the probability of the related deal's success

2.3 Myth 3: The heroic figure in the acquisition drama is the all-conquering acquirer, while shareholders of the acquired company are victims, with their firms accurately depicted as led by underperforming managers

2.4 Myth 4: There is no inherent conflict of interest between dealmakers and other parties compensated on the basis of fees earned upon deal closure, and the interests of acquiring firms' shareholders

2.5 Myth 5: Price-to-earnings and similar multiples techniques are the leading merger valuation methodologies

2.6 Myth 6: Stories and process: PMI success is primarily a matter of sound process and responsive organization

Before considering merger valuation alternative methods – that is, the criteria for evaluating M&A success or failure and thus the first step in improving acquiring company merger performance – it is necessary to understand the six erroneous perceptions that restrain acquisition performance.

2.1 Myth 1

Increased understanding of historical merger failure means that would-be acquiring firms are more inclined to avoid mergers

False

While merger volume dips during intra-cycle merger waves (as shown in Figures 1.1 and 1.3 in Chapter 1), volume quickly rebounds as soon as merger sentiment rebounds, supportive merger financing and/or cash reserves become available, and a signature event such as a blockbuster IPO and/or major, precedent-shattering acquisition occurs. The merger market's sights are set to the future: scare stories about slipping back into recession and remaining there are brought to an abrupt halt.

While the notion that most mergers fail is today widely regarded as fact following numerous studies, MMF is by no means universally accepted. For example, in 'Where M&A pays and where it strays: a survey of the research', Bruner (2004: 68–9) presents the hypothesis that company merger objectives – and by implication, the corresponding M&A success criteria – should reflect the specifics of each acquiring firm and its particular circumstances. Brouthers *et al* (1998: 348) take the idea of customizing merger valuation criteria based on acquiring company characteristics to the next level; those authors argue that the buying firm's imagined key success factors (KSFs) should be taken into account when assessing that firm's merger performance.

Tellingly, the name of Brouthers *et al*'s paper is 'If most mergers fail, why are they so popular?' Explanations for the persistence of high levels of M&A activity despite past disappointing performance fall into two categories: those factors which pertain to principals (acquirers) and those which have to do with transaction intermediaries (deal arrangers, bankers and other advisers).

The reality that, historically, most mergers failed is extensively documented. As further explored in the first part of Chapter 5, the breadth and number of multi-company studies affirming MMF is today so extensive as to end further debate. As one example, Carroll and Mui (2009) describe Bain & Company's large sample research on the topic: 'A Bain study of 250 executives with responsibility for mergers and acquisitions found that 90 per cent accepted historical data that two-thirds or more of takeovers reduce the value of the acquiring company.'[1]

Findings from all three of McKinsey & Co's merger research initiatives are broadly consistent with Bain's findings. More than 20 other major scholarly and general management studies support the McKinsey and Bain findings (see Chapter 5). *And yet, the urge to merge never completely disappears.* You might expect that after the value carnage is finally acknowledged after the bubble crashes, future aspiring acquirers would be reluctant to forge ahead during the *next* merger wave, beginning a few years after the collapse of the old. Not so. As soon as the critical mass for the next merger wave comes together again, it is full speed ahead, as if none of the past merger train wrecks ever happened.

What are possible explanations for this seemingly irrational response? Hopes that booms might occur without the corresponding corrections? Alluring new industries? Bankers minimizing the reality of deal failure lest their merger-related income is threatened? Naïve belief that the lessons about past merger missteps have been learnt and thus will not be repeated (aka *merger learning*)? At different times and in different merger cycles, any of these considerations may provide a part of the explanation.

Our experience suggests that there is another factor that stands in the way of improved future M&A performance by acquirers: the egotistical and mistaken contention that *each and every* merger event is unique. That misguided notion provides acquiring company management (as well as its M&A advisers) with maximum latitude to pursue almost any possible target that catches their attention, at whatever price is necessary to secure control. Avoidance of higher risk target company industries and deal types (such as shown in Table 4.2 in this book's Chapter 4)? No overpayments that threaten deal to success (merger valuation leading criteria; see Chapter 3)?

You don't understand – our deal is unique (thereby justifying tolerance of overpayment and pursuit of this year's doubtful but stylish merger concept from the pop-biz magazines). But deals *are* similar, as confirmed by a repeat of the same primary reasons for merger failure, year after year. Such as – bids far in excess of realistically achievable synergies; pursuing much larger and/or unrelated (and thus, poorly understood) targets; jumping in to the merger market just when the bubble is about to collapse; desperation mergers designed to momentarily distract the financial markets from other shortcomings by acquiring companies; becoming enthralled by targets in the new concept industry, even though business models are still unstable and consistent profitability unknown and letting the bid team run roughshod over those setting maximum bid limits based on analyzed synergies; becoming trapped in multiple-bidder, multiple bid cycle acquisition chases to (acquiring company) value destruction.

2.2 Myth 2

Significant increases to target company's debt levels do not significantly reduce the probability of the related deal's success

False

The high leverage transaction (HLT) technique is part of the persistent fiction that companies might still today be acquired using the targets' underutilized borrowing capacity. This once provocative notion is now 30 years past its prime. For a handful of underleveraged and undermanaged companies in the early 1980s, HLT worked, creating value by improving those target companies' capital structures while improving operating performance by introducing new incentives to eliminate waste. (See also Appendix B.)

But companies quickly adapted, and few if any structurally underleveraged companies have existed since the mid-1980s, at least in developed markets. Piling on extra debt to a company that is already close to its maximum debt level (based on optimal capital structure-based analysis) makes things worse, rather than better.[2]

> Blindly using debt to expand or acquire, therefore, does not guarantee success. Many private equity managers have found out the hard way that purchases inspired by cheap debt can be a disaster.
>
> (Lex, *Financial Times*, March 6 2012)[3]

> We take a buck, we shoot it full of steroids, we call it leverage... leverage debt... It's a bankrupt business model.
>
> (Gordon Gekko, character played by Michael Douglas in the Oliver Stone film *Wall Street*, 1985)

Back to 1982, when HLT techniques worked *(at least until everyone caught on...)*

Increasing the chronically underleveraged company's debt-to-equity (D/E) leverage ratio *may* increase that firm's value, in two different ways: a) reducing the discounting rate at which future expected cash flows (CFs) are discounted, and b) assuming that the means by which D/E is increased is by adding further debt and that the firm has presently unfunded profitable expansion projects on hold, by adding to revenue-driven growth. Also, the hypothesized discipline role of additional principal and interest payments on debt *may* add some extra value as a consequence of reductions of unnecessary expenses and other outlays, presuming that working capital is not already tight.[4]

The word 'may' appears in italics in the first sentence above because of the following proviso: that the acquired company is not already at or above its optimal capital structure (OCS) as manifested by the firm's debt-to-capital ratio (D/C). OCS has numerous interpretations and interpreters; this absence of consensus indirectly has contributed to HLT persisting long after it has ceased being effective.[5]

OCS approaches generally guide the company towards a target range of company leverage relative to financial and operating risk:

- As a typical company's cost of equity (CoE) is around 2 to 2.5 times *greater* than the related after tax cost of long term debt as explained by the capital asset pricing model (CAPM), value is created if all other things are equal if there is more debt and less equity is in the capital mix.
- However, heightened risk of default and bankruptcy must also be taken into account. If these risks and costs soar because of what the financial markets perceive as destabilizing levels of borrowing, then the apparent reduction in weighed average cost of capital (WACC) may instead be cancelled or even exceeded. When the latter occurs, burdensome additional leverage destroys the target's value, rather than increasing it.
- Discounted cash flow-based analysis may assist in providing a perspective on the true value consequences of HLT short-termism. The acquirers apply the standard tools to the acquired target in order to temporarily boost CF and reported earnings: payrolls are capped or in some instances slashed, product prices increased across the

> board, and some promising internal investment opportunities are either starved of funding or cancelled outright. Look forward no further than a few quarters, and some may be tricked into thinking that the company is better off than before these manipulations. But factor in the secondary consequences of these myopic actions (permanent loss of market share, loss of key talent, reduced internal CF generation) and the multiple year DCF diagnosis sometimes results in a different verdict.

During that brief period of the mid-1980s epitomized by *Wall Street*'s Gordon Gekko and Bud Fox, such concerns were overlooked. Back when mobile phones were the size of shoe boxes, such dangers were commonly dismissed and thus precautions ignored. At the hypothetical Teldar Paper stockholders meeting in the movie *Wall Street* – where Gekko/Douglas delivered his immortal 'Greed is good' speech (which today can be cited word-for-word by an alarming number of business students), Gekko pounced on a vulnerable, unsympathetic target: Teldar's profitability had been suppressed for years by gross overstaffing and self-serving agent-managers. Faced with out-of-control costs, Gekko found a receptive audience among shareholders for the fable of the disciplining role of extra debt. The theory is that the requirement to service this extra debt forces cost discipline that may otherwise be missing. The reality is that effective management can accomplish the same thing – but without crippling company investment – by other means.

T Boone Pickens in the early 1980s is described as observing that some managers appear to be more interested in their next lunch appointment than pursuing maximum value for their firms. Tighten cost management and reduce waste, and the Oklahoma oilman reasoned that new cash flows could be generated to service the increases in acquisition-related debt.

Effective value management (VM) – that is, pursuit of maximum continuing value for the benefit of shareholders of the subject company – depends on a clear separation of the objective of *maximizing shareholder value* from the various techniques that might play a role in helping achieve the VM objective. 'Disciplining' debt is one of a dozen arrows in the proficient value manager's quiver. That arrow and others exhibit advantages, disadvantages and secondary consequences. At times, the error of concentrating on the technique (or instrument) instead of the VM purpose results in an illusion of improved company performance, as contrasted with reality.

Why (and how) HLT came undone

The historical time window in which both circumstances central to HLT success (underleveraged companies, undermanaged) was brief, and it closed quickly. The natural opportunities for this simplistic form of financial alchemy disappeared by the late 1980s. But the appeal of something for nothing is compelling, helping to explain how a primitive financing technique obsolete by 1989 continued to be mis- and over-applied many years later.

Provocative financial concepts know no international boundaries, and hyper-leverage techniques began to reappear in emerging countries in the 1990s. In some instances, the result of HLT was disastrous, with the warping of lending practices contributing to Indonesia's 1997 currency crisis just one example.[6]

What happened? Boone Pickens' description of management underperformance was parroted by other pundits; Jensen's agent-manager theory was cited to explain the distorted motivations of me-first corporate managers. Most important, debt levels and D/E ratios both began to rise, eliminating any remaining vestiges of chronic underleverage.

At the onset of 1982, a CEO dragging his feet on the major product with an indicated return well in excess of company WACC would conceivably be praised as being conservative and thus responsible. Three years later, with management consultants preaching the wonders of management by ROE every day in articles and client presentations, that same contemplative manager who delayed would more likely be fired.[7] The emergence of new stock option plans also played a role, increasing managers' stake in the companies that they managed.

The dark side of excessive leverage in deals: the marginal acquisition is sunk

> Firms with below median changes in leverage have positive gains, while those with above median changes in leverage have lower profit rates and market value...
>
> (Trimbath, 2002: 136)[8]

> The acquirer (is) left with a stark new reality: the easy ways to pay back the acquisition debt through the assets, operations or untapped borrowing capacity of the acquired firm had all been exhausted.
>
> (Clark, 1991)

HLTs arguably should have disappeared with the end of the LBO bubble (post-1980 business-merger wave 1) or at least have been strictly limited to very few instances in which the target could both easily assume the additional debt without burden without adversely affecting either forward investment amounts or debt servicing margins of safety, and that firm was chronically underleveraged, as determined both by conservative standards and by the capital structure of other leading firms in that industry. But such action was unthinkable as it would have jeopardized deal volume, and thus threatened the viability of the Two and Twenty fee structure common to many such arrangements today.[9] In a pragmatic post-1980 business world where maximizing short-term paper ROE is not merely tolerated but encouraged, forcing HLT long past its useful life span is understandable, even if the occasional consequence is that the target company's financial structure is trashed.

This is where the vagueness of OCS – there is no single, governing guideline on how to get it right – works to the advantage of those who wished to continue imposing HLT on acquirers even though today the fatally flawed technique usually makes matters *worse*. With no sense of a ceiling on the amount of added debt that the company can endure without collapsing, the conflicted owner-financier wonders, why not raise debt as a percentage of total capital by another 5 per cent... and then another 5... and another?

On paper, the transaction might still appear to the gormless to be slightly plausible, depending on the use deferrals, short-term explosion rates and other tricks of the overleverage trade. In reality, the consequence is similar to that of the burro that finally collapses when its owner adds on one final straw of debt burden on the abused animal's back. *Whoops, the target company is no longer viable. Guess that's a bit too much debt.*

HLT's undeterred zealots bet their companies, and sometimes lose

> A geared business model... made sense in the pre-crisis era, which was marked by steady growth and easy credit. Such a model does not work in a stop-go economy with frequent recessions. Companies have to be very confident that they will not be sabotaged by a sudden dip in revenue, or by a loss of confidence among creditors that makes them unwilling to keep extending funds.
>
> (*The Economist*, June 18 2011: 80)

Having misapplied yesteryear's HLT formula to marginally viable (but not underleveraged) companies that somehow manage to avoid bankruptcy despite the added ballast of unwanted and unnecessary debt, HLT's true believers take the next step to self-destruction. They pursue even weaker targets: marginal companies in decline, but with the siren song appeal of some cash flow generation despite having fallen on more difficult times.

For many of these unfortunate targets, the error of putting the HLT instrument ahead of value management could not have come at a worse time. Facing an imminent crossroads between managed decline leading eventually to exit and resurrection, the imposition of destructive debt had the effect of putting lead shoes on a marathon runner. Some victimized targets might actually finish the race – but no one in the financial community is confused by the financial public relations spin from the debt imposers proclaiming that the target company has been improved.

Zell's acquisition of the *Chicago Tribune* in 2008 endures today as a model of where and how *not* to apply yesteryear's M&A hyperleverage technique. Today, newspapers are the opposite of the cash cow type of target for which HLT was originally intended, but some of the dailies still generate some positive CF at least in the short-term. The sharks sense blood in the water. In 2011, the Project for Excellence in Journalism examined six newspaper holding companies that together controlled 121 separate US newspapers. Their study indicated a mandate for massive investment in digital media merely for those newspapers to survive, since: 'On average, for every new dollar the newspapers were earning in new digital advertising revenue, they were losing $7 in print advertising revenue.'[10]

A worst of all worlds scenario ensued as the late-phase (in merger wave) mistiming of some of these deals effectively eliminated any possibility of refinancing. Result: the *Chicago Tribune*, one of America's great newspapers, was crippled because of the misapplication of a financing technique decades past its prime. Nor was this a unique situation. In the November 27 2008 edition of the *Guardian* (London), Milmo described the fate of the successor firm to North American telecommunications giant Bell Canada: 'The private equity industry's formerly invincible business model suffered another blow yesterday when auditors said the multimillion-dollar acquisition of Canadian telecoms group BCE, one of the world's largest leverage buyouts, could render the business insolvent.'[11]

2.3 Myth 3

The heroic figure in the acquisition drama is the all-conquering acquirer, while shareholders of the acquired company are victims, with their firms accurately depicted as led by underperforming managers

False

While shareholders of the (approximately) one-third of all deals which historically have succeeded (see Chapter 5) may well regard their firms' leaders as heroes, owners of less proficient acquiring firms are more likely to be contemplating shareholder lawsuits because of perceptions of value destruction (Mercier, Vivendi). All targets are not the same (Table 2.1). No one views Arianna Huffington as the vanquished party of AOL's controversial purchase of Huffington Press; as she – the selling *company's chief executive – left that particular M&A poker table with* all *the chips from the table stuffed into her Valentino handbag.*[12]

Media characterizations of M&A acquirers as 'winners' and their targets as 'prey' or 'losers' are simplistic distortions. The massive evidence supporting MMF (most mergers fail) suggests that the seller is more likely to be the winner from the perspective of doing best by its respective set of shareholders.

The newly appointed chief executive eager to make his or her mark in the financial arena pursues an early major acquisition. The visibility of the deal and its role of supporting an image of a dynamic business leader are all-important. Unless the deal immediately implodes, *perceptions* (as contrasted with reality) of deal success or failure matter might be managed through well-timed and well-placed spin (Mathiason, 2010).[13]

Alternatively, the out-of-his/her-depth operating company CEO who epitomizes the Peter Principle (being promoted to one level *beyond* that individual's level of competence) is desperate to divert financial community attention away from his or her performance shortcomings to date. In the same way that medieval monarchs sometimes pursued foreign wars to help silence criticism at home, the corporate ruler welcomes being associated with more successful firms, via the mechanism of acquisition.[14]

Dissecting the good acquirer company management/ incompetent target company management axiom

As with many such maxims, there's sometimes a grain of truth to such broad characterizations; otherwise such stories never would have developed any traction.

In the acquirer-hero column, there's Gerstner's culture-changing leadership and selective acquisitions that saved IBM. At Cisco Systems, Chambers' focused acquisitions have helped to secure that firm's growth and dominance in its sectors. More recently, CEO Jamie Dimon's opportunistic deals

TABLE 2.1 Acquirees are not always losers

Type	Outperformer	Prolonged Underachiever
Examples (acquirer)	Autonomy (H-P) Huffington Press (AOL) 3Par (H-P)	TNT (UBS pursuing*) Boots (UK, KKR)
Other acquisition-relevant factors	Paradox of availability. Optimally managed by seller, unjustifiable APP for most trade acquirers, *all* financial acquirers. Avoid late phase timing. Minimizing acquirer interference, expense overlaps.	Probable support by large institutional investors. Balanced wheat-chaff separation: acquirer group not necessarily preferred option.

* Transaction not concluded at the time of this writing.

catapulted JPMorgan Chase to the top of the bulge bracket, a role at the head of the pack that endures despite becoming yet another bank victimized by unauthorized trading in Spring 2012. At Comcast, AT&T (the former SBC[15]), Wells Fargo and Federal Express, acquiring company top management are praised for deals that *work*.

The victim-acquiree characterization has its own set of past representative examples. NatWest became acquisition fodder for Royal Bank of Scotland (RBS) after the former's value-destroying merger misadventures in the US combined with relatively high back office costs for the industry. Continental European logistics company TNT exhibited anemic profit growth for years, placing the company in the sights of more successful firms in that field seeking to expand.

Shareholders of UK drug store (chemist) chain Boots plc suffered for a decade from then management's unwillingness or inability to slow the pace of chronic market share losses to competing channels; the end result of this under-management was that Boots was targeted for takeover by a group led by KKR; that underperforming target is classified in Table 2.1 as 'prolonged underachiever'.

Not all acquirers are heroic

Exceptions to the axiom that *all acquirers are heroic* are so numerous as to render that characterization futile – and sometimes value destructive, as when deals which should never have happened proceeded anyhow, with loud celebratory spin about 'winning' the deal chase drowning out fundamental concerns about that transaction's viability, in value terms.

'Conquering hero' is hardly a phrase that shareholders of value-diminishing deals are inclined to use when the high profile visionary deals carefully crafted by the company's leader implode. Business reputations of acquirers Jurgen Schrempp (Daimler-Chrysler) and Steve Case (AOL-TimeWarner) were savaged by conspicuously bad deals. The acquisition orgy by Jean-Marie Messier at Vivendi endures as an exemplar of how *not* to manage a transformational, multiple acquisition merger program.

Nor are all target companies managed by directionless underperformers

Fact: selling CEOs at Palm (acquired by H-P), 3Par (H-P again) and Autonomy (H-P's Apotheker again) laughed all the way to the bank after their firms were acquired in record-setting transactions. Skype's two acquisitions (first by eBay and later by Microsoft) demonstrate that sometimes it is better to be on the sell side, assuming that the true objective of the merger program is to benefit shareholders.[16]

Huffington Press management set a price for their company that only a desperate acquirer might consider, and directionless AOL bit. Exactly which of the two principals is the underperformer? Today, Huffington's former shareholders sit back and count their M&A winnings joyfully. Once the short-term distraction of the Huffington Press acquisition period passed, break-up speculation about AOL once again returned.[17]

2.4 Myth 4

There is no inherent conflict of interest between dealmakers and other parties compensated on the basis of fees earned upon deal closure, and the interests of acquiring firms' shareholders

False

Fiercely denied by dealmakers, the reality of an inherent conflict of interest is almost as widely accepted today as fact as MMF (most mergers fail). The business models of deal arrangers and their acquiring company clients are fundamentally different, resulting in unavoidable conflicts of interest.

> Any bank really interested in its clients would shut down most of its M&A department on the grounds that buying other companies almost always works out badly.
>
> (Kellaway, *Financial Times*, January 16 2011)[18]

When the reality that most mergers fail becomes so universally recognized that it becomes fodder for popular business cartoons (see the *Alex* cartoon from Chapter 1) and then lampooned in the only slightly tongue-in-cheek opinion column in the global financial press (Kellaway, above), it is almost impossible for even the most skilled financial public relations spin master to manage perceptions.

Real or imagined, the imagery of bankers ravenously pursuing merger-related fees while value for shareholders of client acquiring firms is relegated to secondary consideration – if considered at all – persists. Today, televised images of Goldman Sachs CEO Lloyd Blankfein awkwardly reacting to questions from Congressmen are singed into the nation's consciousness.

Shock, but no awe

> With little risk and significant dependence on M&A fee income, the rational commercial action on the deal facilitator's part is to pursue maximum number of transactions.
>
> (Mider and Foley, *Bloomberg*)[19]

For the prospective buy-side merger client wondering how vigorously to press for merger fee relief, one consequence of the financial markets' black comedy of recent years is that *no one is in awe of Wall Street or the City any longer.* Any of that Masters of the Universe hype left over from the LBO era is today obliterated – as if the notion of grown men dressed up as furry mammals at Predators Balls in the late 1980s wasn't already hilarious enough.

The only thing more comical is the curious logic that seven-figure bonuses are necessary to retain self-described 'talent' of the caliber of the rascals who came close to destroying the world's economy. If they receive a higher bonus, does that mean *more* value destruction, or *less*? Only now can we begin to comprehend the type of thought processes that spawned dead-on-arrival deals such as Palm (acquired by H-P) or EMI (by Terra Firma). In both instances, the worth of the target was written down from billion to zero or close to it by the acquirer within a few years of the close. Shrewd.

Bleak House *under threat?*

> Quarter after quarter. Nomura's results seem to confirm an immutable law of investment banking: a good deal for bankers, a bad one for investors.
>
> (Lex column, *Financial Times*, April 29 2011)[20]

When principals to the deal no longer view dealmakers and other deal intermediaries with awe, it becomes difficult to sustain the *Bleak House* scenario described in Chapter 1. That scenario: M&A intermediaries effectively *control* the M&A arena, as a combined consequence of principals' past *perceived* dependence on guidance from such sources; and actions and arrangements by middlemen to stimulate maximum M&A deal volume, as their completion fees are based directly on the volume of deals closed.

But emphasize deal volume over more important considerations such as M&A performance from the acquirer's perspective, and the historical pattern of MMF continues into the future. The deal originator gets his or her bonus, while two-thirds of the acquiring companies' chief executives face threats to their careers when the value consequences of deals which should never have happened become apparent.

Does such a return to sanity mean a 67 per cent reduction in annualized deal volume? If acquiring company management (and its advisers) pursue deals first on the basis of whether the transaction can be *closed* and only secondarily on whether that transaction will be a financial success as judged by the acquiring firm's shareholders, then deal numbers are under pressure. You cannot fool all of the people all of the time, and today even overly eager acquirers are aware of the reality of MMF.

But deal volume reductions are not necessary if efforts are directed at the more successful deal types (see merger segmentation, Chapter 4) and if deal pricing discipline results from advance synergy intelligence. Bankers and principals alike require this support, as Christofferson *et al* (2004: 93–4) explain:

> Acquirers must undoubtedly cope with an acute lack of information... Even highly seasoned buyers rarely capture data systematically enough to improve their estimates for the next deal. And external transaction advisers – usually investment banks – are seldom involved in the kind of detailed, bottom-up estimation of synergies that would be needed to develop meaningful synergies before a deal.

2.5 Myth 5

Price-to-earnings and similar multiples techniques are the leading merger valuation methodologies

False

Multiples are at best a second echelon technique, never to be applied on their own, but which may occasionally be used in confirming the findings from more formidable methodologies, such as described in Chapter 3.

> The time-worn and traditional approach to valuation, still used by Wall Street analysts and investment bankers, is a multiples approach... One common example of a multiple is the average of the comparable's market price per share divided by their earnings before interest, taxes, depreciation, and amortization (EBITDA).
>
> (Copeland, in Thomas and Gup, 2009: 69)

> Market multiples are sometimes criticized as overly simplistic and non-rigorous compared to discounted cash flow or other formal modeling exercises.
>
> (Luehrman, 2009: 7)

In its most widely-known form, 'multiple' refers to share price-to-earnings ratios (P/E, numerator), divided by earnings per share (denominator). Copeland refers above to EBITDA-based multiples. Cash flow-based measures of prior performance (particularly free cash flow) are increasingly used in the multiples denominator because of the greater accuracy of CF-based measures (Stern, 1974).

Then there are more suspect forms of multiples, which led by the infamous price-to-revenue (P/R) ratio, which contributed to the rise and crash of scores of profitless dot com companies in 1996–2000[21] (post-1980 merger wave 2), and which today remains at the center of derisory misvaluations of social networking companies. Renren's May 2011 IPO illusory 'valuation' at 72 times revenue is arguably the most notorious example during post-1980 merger wave 4 (see Chapter 6).

Yet multiples are not true valuation methodologies at all, but simply another way of expressing historical financial results. The number-crunchers dutifully following the multiples checklist start with reported sales/earnings/EBITA to date, which are then converted to per share form, and which next are compared to analyzed stock prices. That one of these number-crunchers assigns a growth factor guesstimate to devise a forward 12 months' EPS earnings projection based upon results past performance – typically by applying crude straight-line extrapolation techniques revered by pre-IPO price manipulators but nobody else – does not elevate multiples to the upper echelon of merger valuation (MV) methodologies. Simplicity of calculation is important, but not when the method does little more than provide rear view mirror insight into the target's reported financial performance yesterday.

Relegation to a role below other methodologies, for good reasons

The numerous conceptual and calculation deficiencies that encourage professional business and merger valuation practitioners to relegate multiples to second-tier stature in the corporate and merger valuation universe[22] arise for two different reasons.

The first relates to reliance on accrual accounting earnings information, discredited as the basis for credible company valuation ever since Stern's seminal article was first published in 1974 and by others since then. Multiples are relegated to valuation mediocrity by the unbreakable connection of that technique in its customary forms to accrual accounting-based reported earnings. Expressing EPS in a slightly adapted manner might give some valuation novices an illusion of accurate insight into a firm's cash flow future, but the financial markets are not so easily fooled.[23] The second reason relates to the conceptual and analytical Achilles' heel of multiples, the notorious company-to-company *comparable*. In order to concoct even a slightly plausible argument that the P/E or P/EBITDA of another company has anything at all to do with a different company's worth (company valuation) or combined companies' worth (merger valuation), you first must make a convincing case for similarity of the entities being comparable to each other.

Industry and segment categories are the logical place to start. It makes far more sense to compare drugstore chain Walgreen with competitor CVC than with, say, an industrial company such as General Motors. But even elementary comparisons within the same sector may appear suspect when you realize that the nation's leading research professionals are rapidly abandoning categories by industry – and by implication, the comparables approach that such classification schemes support. In an interview in April 2010, Patrick Dorsey, head of equity research at *Morningstar Reports* – the largest independent equity research organization – described his intention to move Morningstar away from industry and segment categories, largely because companies today have so many unique characteristics that such categories are often useless.[24] And Dorsey comments on only one small aspect of this non-comparable comparables base problem. Two companies that might at first appear to share some superficial similarities are revealed, after a more complete investigation, to exhibit wholly different capital structures and sometimes even different business models and market objectives, all of which lead to significant differences based on the Mauboussin-Johnson (1997) CFROI/WACC competitive advantage period (CAP) measure of company economic viability.

Firms nominally in the same sector may be at different points in their respective economic life spans, adding further difficulties to like-to-like comparisons.[25] From Chapter 1, we learn the problems associated with comparing company data based on different phases in the business-merger cycle, due to the rising tide effect along with an increasing APP component as that bubble matures.

Multiples as a fallback method for when you don't have a clue about the future

> Corporate bidders have access to all publicly available information, but only imperfect information about the target company's future cash flow.
>
> (Varaiya and Ferris, 1987: 64)

The most troubling multiples variant is *price/revenue*: price per share divided by revenue per share. If multiples overall are downgraded as a first-tier merger valuation methodology, then this flawed adaptation also fades into the background, strengthening the argument for primarily reliance on *non*-multiples-based methods.[26]

Like a bad penny, P/R returns in speculative periods or/and in the case of embryonic companies in which either the company's earnings are unknown or cannot be verified and thus multiples based on revenues must be used in early valuation attempts; or to hide fatal shortcomings of a company that will never turn a profit. Why use P/R analysis instead of P/E? There are only two logical explanations, and one of those involves active deceit.

Multiples' popularity, considered in context

When determining the best way to hit a slider, who would you rather talk to: a thousand kiddie league baseball coaches, or Derek Jeter?[27] Exactly.

Multiples depend on the believability of the comparables used, and no two companies are identical.[28] Management invariably attempt to compare their firm with the leader in that industry, and a number is generated. The question persists: 'Does that comparable provide better insight into that firm's economic viability or the proposed deal's success?' Answer: 'Not always.' In the 1996–2000 first dot com bubble, challengers in servers (leader: Cisco Systems) and online auctions (leader: eBay) invoked those companies' multiples to make the case for their own worth. But firms are comparables only in the overly-optimistic eye of the analyst; a beginning company has almost nothing to do with a neophyte in its company except for the same SIC code.

Multiples are extensively used, and not just within the financial community to which Copeland refers. Anyone, from the neophyte business blogger to the corporate executive eager to do a deal but wary of having his or her ambition dependent on spreadsheet calculations by some back office number-cruncher, welcomes the availability of multiples-based methods. But extensive use does not necessarily mean credible calculations. To merger practitioners seeking a fully defendable valuation basis, substance win out over popularity with serious practitioners:

> The (multiples) technique is dismissed by many valuation academicians as little more than an extrapolation of a P/E ratio. Both numerator and denominator in a P/E ratio may be distorted with ease, and the so-called comparable companies that advocates of this technique seek are sometimes non-existent or at least, non-comparable.
>
> (Clark, 2010b: 30)

Necessary, but only after *substantive merger valuation investigation*

Despite its many serious flaws, we *do* use multiples, in numerous company and merger valuation circumstances. The key is to triangulate that technique with fundamental analysis, establishing a vital role for multiples in support of the other primary merger valuation methodologies applied by practitioners today (see parts 8 and 9 in the following chapter).

But from time to time we encounter clients who understandably may be the pacesetters in their own fields but to whom the primary merger valuation techniques (the four primary methods plus multiples are examined in Chapter 3) are black box mysterious. The calculations are at best incompletely understood, leading to distrust. For these managers and others in their companies, multiples play an important role in helping to make merger valuation more understandable. In some instances, this involves translating more credible DCF or value gap methods into their multiples terminology.

The only time when relying primarily on multiples from the start is defendable is when there are absolutely no credible inputs for the three leading methods (excluding ES) – which are examined in Chapter 3. Such situations are rare and risk one of the worst merger valuation mistakes: being satisfied with the quick, slick *but wrong* indication of possible target company worth.

2.6 Myth 6

Stories and process: PMI success is primarily a matter of sound process and responsive organization

Only partially correct

Process and organization are important parts of post-merger integration, but as the PMI side show, not the main event. Meetings and flow charts that are not directed at the most important major synergy-development priorities specific to that merger waste precious time and resources, and thus may be value-destructive. Two critical issues emerge: whether the PMI team knows what the most important synergy opportunities specific to this combination are; *and whether PMI process and organization are directed at those priorities, avoiding all other distractions.*

Re-inventing the PMI wheel

When we encounter yet another general management 'instant' book on M&A, it seems as if post-merger integration (PMI) and post-merger synergies are newly *rediscovered* by that season's group of astonished authors. The inference: that PMI is the neglected stepchild of merger investigation. But such self-serving perspectives are not supported by fact. Since the mid-1980s, PMI has arguably been the *most extensively* investigated aspect of M&A, considering the full range of available insight and research from general management books and articles and also from academic papers in that field.[29]

The new synergy perspective books provide stories of merger missteps, florid process flow diagrams, and much about clashing post-merger cultures. With the exception of Damodaran's seminal (2005) paper, most of the new PMI perspectives tend to be long on generic descriptions and stories of glaring PMI failure but short on the PMI implementation specifics: synergy identification, priorities and achievement.

Opinions abound about the span of opinions and perspectives to be taken into account after the close, differing conceptions of synergies and reporting relationships between the PMI team and the leadership of the acquiring company. While important, such issues are secondary to more substantive questions involving actual synergy *achievement*, as manifested in the following challenge questions:

- How are post-merger synergies segmented, and which opportunities within each of those key divisions are thought to be largest and most achievable?
- Is there an overall model framework for the typical composition of achievable synergies informed by that understanding of PMI segmentation?
- Within each of those major synergy types, what are the considerations in terms of timing, offsetting costs and investment, size of opportunity and implementation feasibility?
- How does the PMI deal with two theoretical synergy sources that are often *mis*diagnosed: management synergies ('m-synergies' in Chapter 7) and some financing-related synergies?

The heart of the synergy diagnostic and implementation problem: some direction from Carroll and Mui

We view Sirower (1997) and the Carroll and Mui's (2009) 'Illusions of synergy' Chapter 1 as among the most useful and insightful of the general synergy analyses to date. The latter affirm a fundamental void in today's PMI analysis:

> A Bain study of 250 executives with responsibility for mergers and acquisitions found that... two-thirds said they routinely failed to achieve all the synergies that had been identified before the takeover[30]... A McKinsey study of 124 mergers found that only 30 per cent generated synergies on the revenue side that were even close to what the acquirer has predicted. Results were better on the cost side. Some 60 per cent of the cases met the forecasts on cost synergies.[31]

Read between the lines of Carroll and Mui's observations, and the diagnosis and implementation deficiencies of most modern PMI investigation become apparent. There is usually no indication about whether the envisioned synergy is recurring in nature or temporary: one-off. Offsets (expenses and other outlays that must be paid to achieve specific synergy opportunities) are rarely calculated.

Revenue synergy ('r-synergies', as defined and described in Chapter 7 of this book) shortfalls cited by Carroll and Mui based upon Christofferson *et al*'s study can and do arise for a variety of reasons, such as overreliance on difficult potential synergy sources like speculative combined company projects, delays or offsets or even the elementary mistake of recording r-synergies on the basis of changes to top-line revenue rather than incremental cash flow effect.

Notes

1. Carroll and Mui refer to Harding and Rovitt's 2004 book: *Mastering the Merger: Four critical decisions that make or break the deal* (Boston, Harvard Business School Press).
2. Emerging markets are sometimes a different matter. With Western concepts of commercial business leverage often unknown, underdeveloped commercial debt and negative connotations related to debt in some societies, the situation of a company with far *less* debt than can be comfortably serviced by internally-generated free cash flow (FCF) still arises from time to time.
3. http://www.ft.com/cms/s/3/ae631f0e-67b2-11e1-b4a1-00144feabdc0.html#axzz1oyrxyx9R. Accessed Mar 6 2012.
4. 'The increased risk of default resulting from recapitalization of the LBOs can force the firm to curb wasteful investment spending and operate more efficiently (Jensen 1986)' in Baker, H K and Kiymaz, H (eds) (2011) *The Art of Capital Restructuring: Creating shareholder value through mergers and acquisitions*. Chapter 23, Bayar, O, 'Going private and leveraged buyouts', Hoboken NJ, Wiley, 427. 'Debt reduces the agency cost of free cash flow by reducing the cash flow available for spending at the discretion of managers.' Jensen, M (1988) 'Takeovers: Their causes and consequences', *Journal of Economic Perspectives*, 2:1, 29. Whether during the HLT halcyon period when this single-dimensional financing technique *worked* or later when *qualified* HLT candidates disappeared, any tinkering with the firm's cash available for debt servicing (CADS) potentially destroys value.
5. In the OCS perspective here, emphasis is on D/E and debt servicing. Other OCS perspectives emphasize different aspects, including: a) the extent to

which the incumbent capital plan does or does not support the company's longer-term financing plan to achieve future growth and to meet or exceed expectations of future performance; and b) the type and order of new capital additions (eg, pecking order method). While judgments about what represents OCS tend to be at least partially subjective and company-industry specific, certain characteristics mark the superior capital structure. Considerations in many firms' OCS include the following: lowest continuing financial cost, adequacy of funding to ensure solvency and to support growth, and extent to which financial charges – primarily interest on debt and principal – are covered by that firm's minimal recurring levels of cash flow from operations (CFFOs).

6 http://en.wikipedia.org/wiki/ 1997_Asian_financial_crisis.

7 A general shift in management measures from asset-based metrics, such as return on assets (ROA) towards return-based metrics and return on equity (ROE) accompanies the brief Pickens-Jensen era. Through leverage, even a mediocre manager might appear to be a top performer, by amplifying modest earnings and CF performance through the exaggerating prism of leverage. For this reason, careful analysts do not abandon ROA, but rather look at both types of measures to develop a more complete understanding of the corporation's true performance and condition.

8 *Mergers and Efficiency: Changes across time*, Boston, Kluwer Academic Publishers.

9 The 'Two' in Two and Twenty refers to the annual management fees, the 20 per cent to profit participation in the acquired company. As piling on debt for a company that doesn't need the extra leverage (but instead needs the CF for investments required to remain competitive, rather than to service debt), applying HLT past its time is arguably more likely to propel the company into bankruptcy (Zell/*Chicago Tribune*, BCE) than prosperity. So the emphasis is on the fee 'Two' part, which is at some firms augmented with an additional 1–2 per cent fee to investors. In both instances, the 2 per cent fee is typically based on the level of assets invested, thus encouraging front-end loads of massive debt. Refer to Table B.1 in Appendix B.

10 Stelter, B (Mar 5 2012) 'A harsh reality for newspapers', *New York Times,* http://mediadecoder.blogs.nytimes.com/2012/03/05/a-harsh-reality-for-newspapers. Accessed Mar 5 2012.

11 'Private equity deal off on fears huge debt will break phone group', *Guardian,* http://www.guardian.co.uk/business/ 2008/nov/27/private-equity-telecoms-bce-canada. Accessed Nov 1 2010.

12 Reece, D (Feb 7 2011) 'AOL shareholders are right to be in a huff over $315m website purchase', *Telegraph* (London). http://www.telegraph.co.uk/finance/

comment/damianreece/8309579/AOL-shareholders-are-right-to-be-in-a-Huff-over-315m-website-purchase.html. Accessed Feb 8 2011.

13 'Hello and good buy: why new CEOs hit the ground running', *InBusiness*, 14–17.

14 The phrase 'Good company/bad price' refers to acquisitions of high quality target companies with minimal synergies, at bid prices reflecting very high APPs. Reasons why such deals are almost always value-destroying for shareholders of the acquiring firm are explained in part 6 of Chapter 3.

15 SBC assumed the better-known 'AT&T' company nameplate when it acquired the remnants of the former telecommunications leader in 2005 following multiple failed acquisitions and mismanagement of the former telecommunications' one-time dominant market position.

16 Sorkin and Lohr (May 9 2011) 'Microsoft in talks to Acquire Skype for $8.5 billion', DealBook, *New York Times*. http://dealbook.nytimes.com/2011/05/09/microsoft-in-talks-to-acquire-skype-for-8-5-billion/?ref=business. Accessed May 10 2011. The sell side M&A counter-strategy is described in the concluding chapter.

17 Ciolli and Nazreth (Aug 17 2011) 'AOL gets last, best hope in private equity', *Bloomberg*, http://www.bloomberg.com/news/2011-08-18/aol-at-57-cents-on-dollar-gets-last-best-hope-in-private-equity-real-m-a.html. Accessed Aug 18 2011.

18 'Finnish lesson on principles for Goldman', http://www.ft.com/cms/s/0/f9c1ffa6-217c-11e0-9e3b-00144feab49a.html#axzz1BDSDYRd2. Accessed Jan 16 2011.

19 'JPMorgan beats Goldman Sachs with T-Mobile Deal', *Bloomberg*, http://bloomberg.com/apps/news?pid=20601087&sid=atBr99scT01s&pos=4#. Accessed March 21 2011.

20 http://www.ft.com/cms/s/3/471d8004-71aa-11e0-9b7a-00144feabdc0.hrml?ftcamp=crm/email/2011429/nbe/LexEurope/product#axzz1KupbFRRI. Accessed April 29 2011.

21 Clark (2000) 26–7, 49 (Fig. 2.3), 78 (Fig. 3.7), 81 (Fig 3.8), 129, 139–42, 144 (Fig. 5.3), 145 'Dot com deathwatch'.

22 Interviews with merger valuation practitioners confirmed this limited role for multiples (primarily forward versions of the EBITDA-type multiples cited by Copeland), presuming that professionals made any use of multiples at all (Clark, 2010b: 131–4, 155–7).

23 Dobbs and Koller (2005) 'Measuring long-term performance', *McKinsey Quarterly*, 16–27; Dobbs, R *et al* (2005) 'Merger valuation: time to jettison EPS', *McKinsey Quarterly*, 83; Varaiya and Ferris (1987: 64–70). Regarding the superiority of cash flow-based measures, the two seminal analyses that frequently arise are Kaplan and Ruback (1995) and Copeland *et al* (1994).

24 Phone conversation with co-author Clark on April 12 2010.

25 Clark (2010b) 190–95, 371–91.

26 The description here is directed at the most controversial applications of P/R. We have also seen the technique used in a prudent manner, such as a pharmaceutical company applying a 4 × P/R multiple to screen out possible targets that are priced too high for a would-be acquirer to contemplate pursuit. Applied in this manner, P/R reduces wasted time and effort.

27 Jeter is captain and star outfielder for the Major League Baseball (MLB) New York Yankees baseball team. A 'slider' is a tortuous pitched ball 7–9 mph slower than a fastball and with shorter but more severe break than a curveball.

28 Alford, A (1992) 'The effect of the set of comparable firms on the accuracy of the price-earnings valuation method', *Journal of Accounting Research*, 30:1, 331–62.

29 Sirower's seminal book (1997) is widely known, along with Chapter 1 in Carroll and Mui (2009) and Damodaran's 2005 paper. Other key PMI works include Variaya and Ferris (1987). Nearly all of Section III of Clark (1991: 265–304) is directed at PMI diagnosis and implementation.

30 Carroll and Mui refer to Harding and Rovitt (2004) *Mastering the Merger: Four critical decisions that make or break the deal*, Boston, Harvard Business School Press.

31 Christofferson *et al* (2004: 92–9).

03 Criteria: First, get the merger valuation methodology right

CHAPTER CONTENTS

3.1 You can't manage what you can't measure *especially* when it comes to M&A

3.2 Criteria-setters: preeminence of continuing shareholders of the acquiring firm

3.3 Overview: four alternative merger valuation methods

3.4 Event studies (ES): exceeding the limits of rational market theory

3.5 Total shareholder return (TSR): most appropriate for round turn financial acquirers?

3.6 Value gap (VG): do synergies offset the price premium necessary to acquire the target?

3.7 Incremental value effect (IVE): two-scenario DCF analysis, adapted to mergers

3.8 Reconciling the tier I merger valuation methodologies

3.9 Multiples: critical confirmation role in merger valuation

Today, the debate about whether qualitative or quantitative criteria should prevail in merger valuation – prevail in terms of the criteria applied to determine whether or not the deal is a success or failure – is a moot point. To the ultimate determiners of *those criteria*, the shareholders of the acquiring company make *their* determination. For the owners of the acquiring firm, there is no debate: quantifiable financial returns have been, are presently, and will continue to be their merger valuation criteria of importance.

But which of the several quantitative-financial merger valuations available is best? Each of today's leading approaches is explored in this chapter, along with multiples.[1] Each approach has strengths and weaknesses. One (event studies, ES) is widely cited by academic M&A researchers but dismissed by merger practitioners. Another (total shareholder returns, TSR) is most suitable for shorter-term owners who make limited changes to the target before attempting to resell the company a few years later. Permanent ownership is out of the question for these financial portfolio round turn buyers.

Partially because of the limitations of ES and TSR and partially because of the growing dominance of discounted cash flow (DCF)-based methods, two other methods emerge as the prevailing merger valuation methods for most acquirers and situations: value gap (acquisition purchase premium minus net realizable synergies) and incremental value effect (DCF company value comparisons, standalone versus combined). Price-to-earnings and other multiples techniques perform an important support role to the VG-IVE combination.

3.1 You can't manage what you can't measure *especially* when it comes to M&A

Managers' subjective merger motivations are sometimes confused with merger valuation criteria. The two are not the same. Merger motivations explain why the deal happened. Leading merger valuation criteria establish the basis for determining whether or not the acquisition was (or if not yet closed, is expected to be) successful or not.

Motivation – such as enhancing the prestige of the acquiring company's management – might be of vital importance to the headstrong buyer, who is hopeful that the transformational deal might earn him or her new visibility in the business community and a reputation as an up-and-coming leader. The mid-market acquirer becomes a possible candidate for the top job at a larger firm, provided the deal is not widely perceived as having been a disaster within six months of the close. Other, less subjective motivations might include expanding the acquiring firm's customer base or enhancing that firm's standing within its industry. For a mature company looking at the end of its economic life, diversifying into new areas may be sought to keep the enterprise alive.

But regardless of the plausibility of the explanation for pursuing the deal, merger motivations are not merger criteria. A momentarily plausible M&A rationale does not mean that the transaction is a success – that is, that the contemplated or already completed transaction is value-creating for the owners of the acquiring company. Developing a defendable basis for determining merger acquisition or failure – in a phrase, *merger valuation* – begins with a clear understanding of the difference between mere enticements for proceeding with the deal and systematic methods for distinguishing the value-*creating* merger from the value-*destroying* acquisition.

The bromide 'you can't measure what you can't manage' has been a mantra of operations-oriented management gurus for years. Sometimes the YCMWYCM theme emerges to justify purchase of yet another set of metrics that promise to navigate the company effortlessly towards top performance. The timing of such sales pitches usually must be separated by a few years, lest the buying company's decision makers remember the mixed consequences of the last set of magic metrics that over-promised and under-delivered.

But that does not mean that YCMWYCM is without merit. When it comes to the company's most important external investment – the large corporate acquisition – phrases such as 'you can't measure what you can't manage' may help prevent acquisitions based on emotions rather than analysis. The niche social networking target company suggests a brighter future for easily impressed would-be acquirers in dead end sectors. Problem is, with no expertise in that field and a high acquisition purchase premium (APP) to secure control of that company, probabilities of a successful merger are miniscule.

Merger excuses and motivations should never be confused with merger valuation criteria

> The gains to acquirers' shareholders are usually zero and often even negative.
>
> (Mueller and Sirower, 2003: 374, citing a range of sources)

Examination of managers' motivations for pursuing deals must be considered in the context of the reality that most mergers fail (MMF; see Chapter 5). Inquisitive researchers' papers about *why* managers chase different deals sometimes help to either spot the next M&A fad, or provide a retrospective explanation for prior M&A evaluation and decision errors. Sirower succinctly expresses today's dominant opinion regarding merger success or failure as follows: 'Acquiring companies destroy shareholder value. That is plain fact' (1997: 16).

MMF is today so widely accepted that the debate has moved forward to two related issues: 1) *why* certain types of value-destructive mergers continued to occur despite broad-based awareness of MMF starting in the late 1980s and growing consistently since that time; and 2) *what* can be done to reduce percentages of failed mergers in future years.

The contribution of the researchers of merger motivation relate primarily to the question of why the urge to merge persists. Since the time of Roll's (1986) analysis of the influence of excessive chief executive pride – hubris – on merger decisions by acquirers, a rich array of works focusing on the question 'Why did they proceed with these deals at all?' has arisen. Some of those exploring these areas include Brouthers *et al* (1998), Bruner (2002, 2004), Epstein (2005), Ghosh (2001, 2002)[2] and Trautwein (1990). Among the explanations identified in these papers are: personal prestige of the acquiring CEO, a desire to expand the buying company's asset size and 'market presence' (generally interpreted as referring to market share and/or negotiating influence with suppliers), or pursuit of a target that suggests a subjectively appealing 'good strategic fit'.[3] Several of these motivations-oriented articles function as forums for authors' opinions about how they believe mergers *should* be evaluated, with limited (or in some instances, no) attention to the paramount financial interests of the acquiring company's shareholders. Epstein (2005) and Bruner (2002, 2004) are especially outspoken in their opinions that reliance on financial merger valuation criteria alone results in an excessively narrow perspective that is both incomplete and potentially misleading.

Insights, provided from the instigators of tomorrow's failed deals

Surveys of acquisition-active executives are of interest when it comes to motivations-based explanations for the continuing urge to merge. As expected, opinions from executives about their *own* M&A success tend to be significantly more positive than the MMF norm, as noted by Mueller and Sirower (2003). In part, this can be explained by the interview approach of researchers. Rather than pressurize executives to explain a controversial past M&A decision considered by many to have been a failure, the tendency is to instead pose general theoretical questions about the attractiveness of growth by merger as an abstract, thereby eliminating chances that such questions are perceived by the interviewee as a criticism of prior (poor) merger performance.[4]

Sample selection also plays a role. The decision makers responsible for yesterday's merger train wrecks have already left (or more accurately, been asked to leave) their company, for good cause. Who is left to survey? Neophyte management dealmakers who have not yet experienced the career-threatening prospect of being held accountable for a controversial deal.

3.2 Criteria-setters: preeminence of continuing shareholders of the acquiring firm

The process of determining *what* the merger valuation criteria and method should be begins with identifying *who* are the most important criteria-selectors. The continuing shareholders of the acquiring firm have primacy when it comes to that determination of merger valuation methods. Their merger expectations are expressed in terms of quantifiable financial returns to them, perceived as resulting from that specific transaction.

The case for acquiring company shareholders as merger valuation criteria-selectors

> Much of the debate (about merger-driven restructuring of the UK retail sector) has related to the benefit, or otherwise, to the customer... about the effect on competition... on employees... (or on) suppliers. Surprisingly one stakeholder group that appear to have been taken for granted in this debate are the owners of the companies involved, and in particular on the shareholders of the acquiring firm.
>
> (Burt and Limmack, 2003: 148)[5]

Opinions about how best to measure merger success are almost as numerous as the number of management writers and academic researchers in the expansive M&A field. Which merger stakeholder groups' opinions are paramount?

In 'Mergers and profitability: a managerial success story?' Ingham *et al* suggest that primacy resides with the originators of the deal, the risk-takers: 'One distinction that can usefully be employed to help disentangle the possible motives of the interested parties is to identify the instigator of the action' (1992: 196).[6]

Burt and Limmack (2003) concur, affirming the primacy of shareholders of the acquiring firm when it comes to setting the rules of the game for measuring M&A performance. After all, it is the owners of the buying business who ultimately are responsible for providing the risk capital that makes the deal possible.[7] The buying company's owners benefit first and most from the value-enhancing acquisition; they are also the first to suffer if the deal is value-destroying after the close.

Those two researcher groups find additional support from others in the M&A performance measurement field, including:

- Tuch and O'Sullivan (2007: 142): 'Shareholders are the ultimate holders of the rights of organizational control.'
- Sudarsanam (2002: 88): 'According to the finance theory perspective, managers' decisions are aimed at enhancing shareholder wealth... This means that the return from investing in the acquirer's stock is at least equal to the cost of capital. If an acquisition fails this... test, the shareholders would have been better off investing their capital in another investment opportunity.'
- Hogarty (1970: 317): '(if) a merger (is) considered to be successful, (it) must increase the present value of the owners' interest in the firm...'.

Re-segmenting the acquiring company's shareholders: implications

The tendency is to treat all shareholders of the acquiring company as a single homogeneous group, presumed guided by similar if not always identical interests. But key differences arise between long-term buy and hold shareholders and financial owners who temporarily buy the target for the explicit purpose of reselling that unit a few years later. Those differences may mean different financial expectations from the merger, necessitating a further segmentation of the acquiring firm's shareholders' set.

Part 2 of Chapter 2 on high leverage transactions (HLTs) identifies the important differences between longer-term company shareholders and transitional owners who may be more inclined to treat the target as a short-term fee and dividend distribution entity. That short-term owner emphasizes the 'Two' (fee) part of the Two and Twenty PE compensation scheme, or similar. The result is maximum growth in financial assets corresponding to increased debt in the target firm, achieved as quickly as possible. By contrast, shareholders who count their ownership periods in firms in terms of decades rather than quarters tend to be oriented more to value gains in the target firm achieved by consistent sound management practices over multiple years, not an imagined instant fix to the balance sheet.

The importance of this distinction becomes increasingly evident as the four major merger valuation methodologies are examined in the pages that follow. While one of those methods, total shareholder return, tends to be highly appealing to shorter-term, round-turn oriented shareholders, TSR's limitations mean reduced appeal to less speculative types of acquiring firm shareholders, who seek target companies that remain as permanent parts of the new combined corporation.

From continuing shareholders' paramount interests to consistently-applied criteria for evaluating acquiring company M&A performance

Hogarty's quote above defines merger success in terms of the present value of future returns to the acquiring company's shareholders. A similar observation is made in Norton (1998) and Sudarsanam (2002: 88) describes shareholders' minimum required returns relative to a comparative standard. The acquiring firm's analyzed weighed average cost of capital (WACC) is identified as the minimum acceptable return rate. According to the finance theory perspective, managers' decisions are aimed at enhancing shareholder wealth. This means that the return from investing in the acquirer's stock is at least equal to the cost of capital.

Merger success is defined – and thus methods for merger valuation established – based not on whether the deal is closed but instead, on the basis of expected or actual financial returns to the continuing shareholders of the buying firm. Bankers and others who refer to closing the transaction as 'winning the deal' have it wrong. When the transaction is value-destroying, then true winning transaction from the acquiring principals' perspective is no deal at all. These alternative interpretations of deal success are shown in Table 3.1.

TABLE 3.1 Alternative interpretations of deal success: deal closing vs returns in excess of capital cost

	Transactional	Financial
How is success measured?	When the deal is closed	Either: (a) positive incremental value effect (IVE) and/or (b) value gap is covered
Success criteria as interpreted by	(a) Transaction initiators/ middlemen unpaid unless deal results (b) Impressionable principals influenced by (a)	Acquiring company's shareholders (continuing ownership)
Advantages	Unambiguous	Aligned with continuing interests of the owners of the acquiring company, the shareholder group who ultimately judges whether merger success or failure has occurred
Disadvantages	Misinterpretation of the interests of M&A middlemen with interests of acquiring company principals	May require 1–2 years to determine, even longer in some circumstances
Issues	May come undone with early collapse of AOL–TWX (2000), HP–Palm (2011) type	Both leading methods require multiple projections and assumptions, reluctance of acquiring firms to monitor later

3.3 Overview: four alternative merger valuation methods

Four quantitative (financial) merger valuation methods of importance are summarized in Table 3.2 and explored below.

Excluded from inclusion in tier I merger valuation methodology

Consistent with the interpreted interests of the acquiring company's continuing owners, qualitative objectives are excluded from Table 3.2.[8] It is not that some of these criteria are not important to some of the company's owners and some other acquiring company's stakeholders: ecological sustainability and corporate governance have both increased in shareholders' ranking of vital interests over the past decade. But qualitative criteria such as Brouthers *et al*'s (1998) nominations to 'enhance managerial prestige' or 'pursuit of market power' prove difficult to identify much less quantify. Perhaps tellingly, these authors are among those who accept that MMF.

Multiples are also excluded from summary Table 3.2 despite Copeland's characterization of price-to-EBITDA as a mainstream method in Chapter 2. As explained in part 2.5 in Chapter 2, multiples indicate past performance results, not forward-facing merger valuation evaluative methodology. The growing practice of company and merger valuation practitioners is to utilize multiples to confirm results from discounted cash flow (DCF)-based methods, the dominant methodology. That important support role for multiples in merger valuation is explored in part 3.9 of this chapter.

There is no such thing as a single infallible merger valuation (MV) methodology

There is no infallible merger methodology. Each of the four methods in Table 3.2 have advantages and disadvantages; partially for that reason the preference choice emerging from the examination in this chapter in part 3.8 is a *combination* of the two DCF-related methods in increasing use today: value gap (VG, 3.6) and incremental value effect (IVE, 3.7):

- *Event studies(ES, 3.4)* are developed from readily available data, and represent the dominant method in academic research of merger performance (Zollo and Meier, 2008: 56). However both short-

TABLE 3.2 Overview: the four alternative tier I merger valuation methodologies

Approach Category	1 Event Studies (ES)	2 Acquirer Total Shareholder Return (TSR)	3 Value Gap (VG)	4 Incremental Value Effect (IVE)
Evaluation basis	Acquirer's pre- vs post-announcement share price trend relative to index and/or industry comparables	Primarily, return based on increase in market capitalization over time period, sometimes compared to WACC	Acquisition purchase premium (APP) minus PV of realizable merger-related synergies	Comparative DCF analysis: target and acquirer standalone future vs combination, with synergies
Source data	Share price (SP)	SP	CF (+ Initial SP (as included in APP))	CF (+ Initial SP (as included in APP))
Limitations in terms of scope, accuracy	Distorted by serial acquisitions (LT version), extraneous post-announcement SP influences (both ST and LT) No control case for acquiring company's future performance WITHOUT acquisition	Divestment bias: round-turn (buy-then-sell) circumstance excludes most successful acquisitions, which are retained by operating company acquirer	Presumes well-developed PMI synergy diagnosis and implementation capability (see Chapter 7) Zero or even negative VG does not always ensure a successful acquisition – other factors may contribute to merger failure.	Possible inaccuracies resulting from multiple causes, including: unrealistic future projection model, components (relationships, amounts, timing), unrealistic synergies, mis-diagnosis or mis-application of imagined 'value drivers'

TABLE 3.2 *continued*

Approach Category	1 Event Studies (ES)	2 Acquirer Total Shareholder Return (TSR)	3 Value Gap (VG)	4 Incremental Value Effect (IVE)
Limitations in terms of scope, accuracy	The notion that acquisition performance may be judged on the basis of a few months/years' post-announcement share price movement defies credibility, stretches SSME to breaking point	Even when evaluated on WACC basis (Coley & Reinton, 1988), may be inaccurate because of timing, other factors hindering comparisons	*(cont.)*	*(cont.)*
Future role as M&A financial measure	Marginal future role. Ease of calculation advantage does not offset logic and contamination disadvantages, absence of explicit APP factor tolerates, if not encourages, M&A overpayment	Primarily limited to financial acquirers, for whom both velocity of RTs *and* returns per transaction important	Increasing visibility and use as a secondary financial measure (to IVE)	Ongoing role: precedent of DCF projection analysis internal investment, synergy assessment

and longer-term event studies are subject to distinct distortions. Studies based on very brief share price analysis periods stretch rational market theory beyond the breaking point. In longer-term ES analysis, isolating the effects of the separate merger transaction is problematic to impossible.

- *Total shareholder return (TSR, 3.5):* supplemented with a cost of capital reference,[9] TSR provides an indication of returns as perceived by that acquiring company's shareholders, although extreme dividend payouts or similar extraordinary distributions to owners from the firm may distort that measure. Comparing one TRS transaction with another can be problematic, as periods of temporary target company ownership differ and involve different phases in the merger wave (Figure 1.4 in this book's first chapter).
- *Value gap (VG, 3.6).* This is arguably the most visible broad measure of merger success in the financial media and some general management publications. Today, it is rare that a major deal is announced and a reporter does *not* express alarm about alleged deal overpayment, based on initial comparison of VG's two components: acquisition purchase premium and net realizable synergies (NRS).
- *Incremental value effect (IVE, 3.7):* Damodaran's (2005) standalone versus combined post-merger company DCF merger valuation approach represents the predecessor to the IVE method as described in part 7 in this chapter. IVE addresses the central question of merger valuation: are shareholders of the acquiring firm better off proceeding with the deal, or are they better off going it alone? As with all projection-based methods, multiple assumptions are required, reducing the appeal of this method to some.

Net financial returns, indications of value creation or destruction

As the word is used here, 'net' means subjecting financial returns to shareholders to a reference rate standard, typically the post-merger combined firm's analyzed weighed average cost of capital (WACC). TSR and IVE develop projected rates of returns to shareholders of the acquiring company, albeit sometimes in different ways.

By itself, a gross indicated return tells little about whether the deal is successful or not. The answer to that question can only be determined *after* the gross return rate is compared to the appropriate WACC. A 12 per cent return rate may indicate either transaction success (if the comparative rate is, say, 9 per cent) or failure (if the reference rate is 14 per cent).

As soon as a major deal comes to be widely perceived as value-destroying, it is only a matter of time before departures at the top of the acquiring company. Smithburg (Quaker Oats/Snapple),[10] Chandler (Unum/Provident),[11] Allen (AT&T/NCR)[12] and Apotheker (H-P/3Par, Palm and Autonomy)[13] all left their firms following M&A debacles.

3.4 Event studies (ES): exceeding the limits of rational market theory

> The efficient capital market hypothesis predicts that any new information, like the announcement of a merger, leads to a quick adjustment of share prices to reflect *unbiasedly* the future changes in profits the new information purports.
>
> (Mueller and Sirower, 2003: 374)

> With respect to the measurement of the performance of M&As, finance and economic scholars have often relied on objective returns such as accounting returns and stock-market based measures...
>
> (Papadakis and Thanos, 2010: 859)[14]

The event studies (ES) category of merger valuation approaches emerges from the observation that when a publicly-traded company expresses purchase interest in a target, that would-be acquirer's share price almost always declines, while the target's share price rises – a mirror opposite to the buyer's shares. Why this effect? Besides the short-term stimulus of the bidder's announcement on market news and thus trading speculation, the concept of market efficiency is at work. In overall terms (that is, including the interests of *both* acquirer and acquiree), mergers tend to improve efficiency (aka, are value-creating) as scale economies and elimination of overlapping costs and other easily achievable synergies (see Chapter 7) are realized. But as Christofferson *et al* observe, these merger efficiencies accrue to the target, in the form of the acquisition purchase premium (APP): 'On average, the buyer pays the seller all of the value generated by a merger, in a premium of from 10 to 35 per cent of the target company's preannouncement market value' (2004: 93).

In a merger deemed to be successful as measured by ES-type methods, the acquirer's share price eventually makes up its early deficit, reflecting the financial community's confidence that the newly combined company will be managed in a way that results in improvements, both in the target and in the combined firm overall. In a word, *synergies*. But if the bid is viewed by the market as so high that synergies cannot possibly offset the purchase premium, and/or if financial markets have little confidence that the acquiring firm's management team will be able to achieve those synergies, there is no rebound. The buying company's initial share price slump at the announcement date continues.[15]

Supporters of this method contend that future changes in the acquiring company's share prices relative to analyzed return requirements indicate whether the deal is (or if applied retrospectively, has been) a success or failure. The ES method is relatively easy to research and to apply, in theory permitting a judgment about whether a specific merger transaction is a success or failure based on limited price data. But concerns arise about both short- and longer-term variants of the method, helping to explain the isolation of such techniques in scholarly studies, with management M&A practitioners and some academic valuation experts of a more practical bent (eg, Bruner, 2002: 94–5), being open to other merger valuation methodological approaches.

Shorter-duration ES

In the case of short-term ES, the notion that a judgment about the success of a specific deal is signaled by a few months price data defies belief and stretches rational market theory up to (and to some, beyond) the point of credibility. The stock market is generally thought of as anticipating future developments five years into the future on a non-residual basis. But the post-merger period is still in effect in many acquisitions one year after the close, and the effectiveness of that PMI period in uncovering synergies is central to the transactions success or failure. One question plaguing shorter-term ES investigation is: how is it possible for an early glance at stock price movements to indicate M&A success when actions critical to success or failure have not yet occurred?

Longer-duration ES

Longer-term ES variants are based on more extensive base data, but the threat of price contamination increases. The acquiring company's share price is not a single-issue referendum on the success or failure of any specific merger deal. As the time from announcement date to analysis date grows longer, it becomes increasingly difficult to isolate the possible influence on the buying firm's share price movement attributable to any one acquisition from the past. Other, additional acquisitions, changes in industry competitive conditions and other factors such as loss of key accounts and talent all affect the company's share price, making it a fool's game to try to isolate any single influence.[16]

Origins: insight into deal success from financial markets' initial reaction to the major merger announcement

Assessing whether or not a merger is successful by looking at the financial markets' initial price response is understandable. The immediate dip in the acquiring company's share price is explained by the fact that while mergers are efficient in overall terms, benefits from the business combination accrue disproportionately to the selling company's shareholders in the form of the acquisition purchase premium (Christofferson *et al*, 2004: 93).

But does the dip in the acquiring company's share price remain, suggesting at least a disappointing merger and possibly a value-destroying one? Sirower's response is consistent with his (and others') belief that MMF: 'Shareholders of acquiring firms routinely lose money... on announcement of acquisitions. They rarely recover their losses' (1997: 3).

Ease of use + unquestioning belief in extreme application of rational market concept

ES approaches dominate the scholarly literature on merger performance, due to the relative ease of calculation, with ample support data compared to the other methods in Table 3.2; and the belief that changes in the acquiring company's share prices from the time that interest in the target is first announced (relative to that firm's analyzed return requirements) provide *all* the necessary information required to determine M&A success or failure. That significant doubts arise regarding the second point – as summarized in this chapter in the pages following and Part 3.7's side-by-side comparison of ES with the competing incremental value effect (IVE) method – does not diminish the attractiveness of this technique to its supporters.

Ease of use sometimes exerts disproportionate influence when it comes to assessing the borderline method. Transition to a superior, different method makes obsolete base data accumulated for the old, flawed method and then there's the issue of which of the alternative methods (or combination) to adopt, instead. The persistent use of the ES method by some does not represent the first time that the shortcomings of a method have been overlooked and the flawed method continues to be defended as appropriate and complete, despite mounting evidence contradicting that contention.[17]

EPS still rules? Today, many years after the publication of Stern's 'Earnings per share don't count' in 1974, some still deceive themselves into thinking that company quarter-to-quarter earnings per share (EPS) results provide the most accurate indication of a firm' performance. *'Likes' as the new clicks?*

Subscriber contact-based metrics for measuring online commercial potential persist, despite indications to date that 2011's *like* buttons on social networking sites are little better at predicting future actual sales consequences than the crude click data of 1998.

Summary of some shortcomings of ES-type methods for merger valuation purposes

This method comes under increasing attack from managerial merger valuation observers, with basic questions plaguing this marginal MV technique, including: 'What good is ample price data when it is almost impossible to separate out a single transaction's results from all of the extraneous noise that can push share price?'

Isolating the price effect of a single transaction becomes a nearly impossible challenge the longer the ES analysis time period. As time passes, other mergers occur, the firm's business model changes and key units are divested. As changes accumulate, questions mount about whether or not the acquiring company's share price alone contains sufficient insight to be useful in assessing the success or failure of mergers.

The acquiring company's share price is at best a detached, indirect indicator of M&A core performance issue – whether the purchase price necessary to secure the deal is warranted based upon realizable M&A synergies. So why has it persisted? Unquestioning belief in the validity of share price as indicator of merger performance dissipates as exceptions to and doubts about rational market theory grow (Fox, 2009). Neither of the two items central to a complete investigation of merger performance – APP nor complete the deal, realizable synergies – is fully visible in the ES method, thus causing that approach to today appear dated and incomplete.[18]

Shorter-term ES studies (six months' analysis periods or briefer) come under particularly pointed attack. The thought that a couple dozen days' share prices occurring can predict whether a deal will be a success or a failure has the unsettling sense of crystal ball predictions. The decisive actions that make or break that merger may not occur until a year after the close. So how is it imaginable that three months' price data contains any intelligence about that future event? The notion that a company's share price reflects intelligence about all of that firm's prospects and potentials from about nine months to around a year and a half (including *all* operations and *all* mergers) is fantastic enough. Stretching the boundaries of share price as a predictive indicator risks reaching a breaking point, credibility-wise.

Tuch and O'Sullivan (2007: 148) summarize some of the key issues pertaining to both shorter- and longer-term variants of ES methods:

> Short-term studies... are at risk from bias, since announcement returns tend to reflect the expectations of investors... Reliability of long-run event studies may also be undermined by thin trading and the overlapping of event periods... Overlapping events are a particularly acute problem in assessing the long-run performance of acquiring firms as, over a period of years, a range of company-specific (including subsequent acquisitions) may influence the price return.

3.5 Total shareholder return (TSR): most appropriate for round turn financial acquirers?

We bought all of Company A's shares in Year 1 at a price of $70 per share each, then sold those same shares three years later for $90/share. Was this round turn buy-and-sell transaction successful? Depends upon whether or not that total annualized return over that ownership period exceeds the greater of the cost of capital or analyzed opportunity cost (return on best available alternative investment).

Our TSR hypothetical describes either a company or individuals purchasing the target's shares, and then assessing success of that transaction several periods or years after the deal's close, following disposition or re-sale of those shares. The TSR method roughly replicates the small investor's round turn – buy and then sell – sequence. Cash returns attributable to the investment are recorded from the time that the target's shares are acquired until the date those shares are sold. The difference in share proceeds plus dividends received are then transformed into an annualized rate of return over the period of possession.[19] For the acquirer of the entire target company, those returns are expressed by the change over time in market capitalization (share price appreciation times the number of shares outstanding) plus total dividends received, as shown in the base TSR ratio in Table 3.3.

The calculation is simple and deal-specific. Similarity to the way that individuals calculate their returns based on the purchase and then sale of a block of shares means that calculation dynamics are transparent and immediately understood by all. But TSR's ease of calculation is offset by some shortcomings:

- *No phantom share sales.* One of these limitations results from the round turn characteristic of transactions normally included in the TSR calculation. In its customary form, TSR only counts those acquisitions that have subsequently been re-sold, brought public

TABLE 3.3 Total shareholder return (TSR) basic equation

Category: Round Turn (RT)	
Method: *Total shareholder return (TSR)*	
(Share price appreciation effect + Cash dividend or equivalents) / Investment time period (*t*)	Replicates individual investor's share purchase return calculation. Merger transaction treated as an extremely large share buy-and-sale round turn.
Positives	**Negatives**
For completed RTs, an easy statistical calculation. Compatible with financial acquirers' business model, in which investment turn velocity is *almost* as important as returns per RT. Thought to reflect financial market (share price) impact of company's performance, strategy, positioning.	Multiple potential distortions including dividend effect, *t:* both duration, buy-sell timing. Comparability. Biased towards (1) divestments and (2) opportunistic short-term turns. Disregards company's ultimate font of value, verifiable short-term operating performance (FCF).

(IPO), or otherwise been disposed.[20] But what happens to successful acquisition that remains a permanent part of the acquiring company? For a financial acquirer whose business model calls for rotating his or her portfolio of companies owned on a continuing basis, this limitation is not likely to be a serious concern. But for the operating company that buys the target and then holds on to it, the TSR ratio fails to provide a clear answer to the question, 'Was that deal a success?'

- *Reference return rates.* On its own, TSR's annualized return rates are only partially indicative of merger performance. Only when that rate is compared to a reference rate of return such as acquirer's cost of capital or analyzed opportunity costs can deal success be determined with greater precision.
- *Comparability of different TSR calculations.* Round-turn transaction dates and duration both tend to be deal-specific, rendering comparisons between different TSR analyses difficult at best.

The base TSR ratio

The acquiring company records returns from two possible sources: changes in the share price of the firm acquired, plus dividends or equivalents received over the ownership period. The inclusion of both dividends received and share price appreciation (change in market capitalization) in the TSR ratio's numerator is justified on the basis that both are inputs that are received by the acquirer of the target company. But both elements comprising the TSR numerator raise some questions from a merger valuation perspective.

Market capitalization (MC) return results are subject to timing. The round turn acquirer that happens to buy early in phase II of the new merger wave and then sells at the beginning of phase IV (see Chapter 1) likely shows a positive MC return result. But assume instead that the acquirer of that same company – identical worth based upon cash flow fundamentals – instead buys at the bubble's peak in mid-phase IV and is forced to unload its position in the recession, 18 months later. *That* acquirer reports a sharp reduction in the MC component in the TSR equation's numerator, even though the underlying worth of the target company as measured by DCF fundamentals is unchanged.

Dividends and equivalent outflows from the acquired firm. Conventional wisdom suggests that an increase in dividends is indicative of improving performance in operating terms. But what if the round turn acquirer is distorting dividend outflows in order to maximize its self-awarded fees? As the HLT fallacy in Chapter 2 attests, extract excessive funds from the acquired company, and the result may be value destruction, regardless of the near-term surge in dividends. In extreme instances, solvency is threatened and the company cannot generate sufficient investment funds to remain competitively viable.

The value damage caused by less extreme forms of dividend manipulation may be more difficult to spot, but that does not mean that the effects are not significant. The product lifecycle of the acquired company is stretched by one year, reducing annual investment requirement on paper at least and appearing to justify increased dividend payouts.

Management of both acquirer and acquiree-target assure the financial community that the change is incremental and does not threaten the company's competitiveness or economic viability (CFROI/WACC in Mauboussin and Johnson, 1997) at all. But is that the truth? First, that new manager at the acquired company was put in that position by the new owners and will never contradict the boss. Viewed solely on the basis of year-to-year investment levels at the target company, the reduction in investment may appear to be slight. What the new managers of the target company do not reveal (assuming that they are aware) is the competitive dynamic.

Assume that rivals a) have already acted to shorten their new product development periods and b) are increasing their competitive advantage by further decreasing the time from product conceptualization to product launch. Increasing speed-to-market in such a manner requires massive investment in new processes and equipment. The target company described above not only failed to keep up, but was falling further behind. The relative changes in fundamentals between the market leaders and the numbers-manipulating target company playing with internal investment numbers to justify increased dividends to the parent will eventually be manifested in differences in share price and market capitalization, once the target becomes an independent, publicly-traded firm again.

Adaptations to TSR

As with ES, ease of calculation sometimes obscures other problems with the technique as a candidate merger valuation (MV) methodology. Table 3.4 considers three different types of possible adjustments and adaptations to TSR designed to improve the usefulness of that approach for MV purposes.

1. Adjustment for extraordinary dividend payout or equivalent

In the TSR base formula's numerator as depicted in Table 3.4, dividends received are combined with increases in market capitalization in determining gross returns. The legitimacy of dividend payouts as an indicator of company worth originates with Lintner's 1956 seminal paper, in which he argues that a close correlation exists between dividend declarations and share prices. In the mid-1950s, dividends often represented a high percentage of firms' earnings available for distribution.[21]

For merger valuation purposes, problems with TSR arise when dividend payouts are bloated to include extraordinary distributions to the new temporary owners. Transitional owners' paramount emphasis on fees and payouts may cause the dividend component in the TSR base ratio to be increased far beyond customary levels for firms in that industry, threatening internal CF generation and competitiveness, and thus value.

TABLE 3.4 TSR variants

Variant	Nature of Adaptation/ Adjustment	Issues
(1) Adjustment for extraordinary (non-recurring) dividend payout or equivalent	Dividend payout factor in TSR numerator limited to historical levels (based on % NOPAT), excess presumed reinvested at historical internal return rates.	To help prevent statistical distortions in gross TSR calculation returns caused by excessive distributions to short-term oriented or transitional owners.
(2) Net TSR: Gross returns compared to higher of analyzed WACC, opportunity cost	More complete indication of whether deal creates or destroys value on TSR basis, after funds' costs included in calculation.	Ensuring that high debt structures correctly reflect increases in operating and financial risk (see Part 2 in Chapter 2, 2.2). Case for *target's* historical WACC when acquirer is transitional owner. Identifying useable opportunity cost rate may be problematic: Analyzed WACC as default.
(3) Point-in-cycle adjustments	Facilitate comparisons (gross TSR, net TSR) with other RT transactions.	Presumed share price at disposition assumptions for one or both of the companies being compared. Diminishes returns advantage from astute intra-wave timing.

NOPAT: net operating profit after tax RT: round turn (purchase followed by sale)

The round turn owners intruding into the day-to-day decisions of the target company management contend that the extra payouts are warranted by reductions in unneeded projects and frivolous expenses. The spin regarding the increased dividends is that these are extra funds, that is, not required in the day-to-day operation of the target business. No longer publicly-traded, there is no one to challenge whether the target could make better use of its so-called excess funds than the parent, such as by advance purchasing of critical raw materials to secure an additional discount, paying down expensive debt, or making internal investments in new growth opportunity areas.

Any single-dimensional orientation to maximizing fees and payouts always brings the threat of excessive cuts to the core of the business. The manager 'encouraged' by its new owners to think first and most about slashing expenses will tend to underestimate the side effects of that myopic policy. Eventually, the suddenly cash-poor company may be unable to compete for top talent or to fully fund projects critical to survival.[22] To deal with this source of distortions and also to discourage short-sighted TSR manipulations that may undermine the value fundamentals of the business, dividends for merger valuation calculation purposes are limited in this variant to historical amounts or trends, with the difference presumed to be reinvested at the target company's historical internal return rates.

2. Net TSR

The base TSR ratio provides an indication of gross returns (numerator) on an annualized basis (denominator) associated with a given transaction. But without a basis for comparison it is impossible to determine that merger's performance indicates a success or failure. Does a 12 per cent annualized TSR return for the merger suggest a viable transaction? Compared to a 10 per cent WACC the answer appears to be 'yes'. But if opportunity cost is 14 per cent, the answer is less certain. TSR often is applied in round turn mergers of short- or intermediate-term duration of six years or briefer. Calculating the appropriate WACC is influenced by the expected term of ownership and type of acquirer.

Operating company long-term buy-and-hold acquirers. Methods for developing a combined post-merger company WACC estimation are detailed in part 3.7 in this chapter on the IVE) merger valuation methodology. The cost of capital calculation requires both a forecast of the post-acquisition capital structure and future estimates of component cost of equity (CofE) and long-term debt (CofD) costs of the combined firm, including effects of changes in company financial and operating risk in later years (Clark, 2010a; Luehrman, 1997: 9).

Transitional owner. If however the acquirer is a temporary, RT business model-oriented portfolio acquirer, then the target firm's capital structure emerges as the correct basis for WACC calculation. There is no permanent combination with the acquirer intended; before being acquired by the takeover firm and after it is sold or disposed, it is the capital structure and cost of the target company that financial markets consider in valuing that firm.

If the transitional owner destabilizes the firm by misapplying high leverage techniques (HLT, part 2 in Chapter 2) calculation of the target's WACC before and after the ownership period is complicated by conflicting influences on capital cost. Normally an increase in debt as a portion of total capital (debt plus equity) means a reduction in company WACC because of the lower after-tax cost of debt compared to equity. But if the target company is already moderately to highly leveraged at the time of original purchase by its transitional owner and the capital structure is trashed with destabilizing debt that threatens the future economic viability of the firm, and WACC likely increases instead, reflecting the effect of soaring operating risk (risk of going out of business) and financial risk (risk of failing to be able service debt) on the equity risk premium component in the Capital Asset Pricing Model (CAPM).

Convention suggests that if opportunity cost (the acquirer's next best return opportunity of comparable risk and duration) is greater than analyzed WACC, then the higher opportunity cost rate is used instead as the performance reference rate for merger evaluation purposes. Large, fast-growing companies tend to have numerous alternative high-return investment opportunities, with the result that determining the best reference OC is sometimes challenging. Luehrman suggests a default assumption if necessary that WACC and OC are identical (2009: 1, 9).[23]

3. Phase-in-business/merger-cycle adjustments

Even if TSR analyses is for adjustments (1) and/or (2) in Table 3.4, it is still difficult to compare returns from one single transaction TSR calculation with another, because of material differences in the period of ownership. Consider the following circumstance: Company A is acquired at the beginning of phase I of the merger wave (Figure 1.4 in Chapter 1) and then sold early in phase III, a couple of years before an exhaustion peak indicates the imminent collapse of that merger wave. During the period of ownership, the share price basis of Company A has risen significantly, although that is not fully apparent until the target company becomes publicly owned once again.

By contrast, a second target company, B, is purchased almost at the time of the wave's collapse in late phase IV. Egos are involved, and the RT acquirer's initial inclination is to try to tough it out and hold onto the target, hoping that the recession period is brief and that shares can be sold to the public at the earliest opportunity. But economic conditions are deteriorating rapidly, and an emergency liquidation is forced during the recession that occurs after phase IV. Further assume that target companies A and B at acquisition are nearly identical in terms of the fundamentals of the business: viability of business model, annual CF generation, cost of capital. The round turn TSR calculation for A is positive; for B, negative. The only difference is timing.

TSR returns from Company A are artificially inflated by booming market conditions. Returns relating to B are suppressed as the market collapses into oblivion. Readjusting one or both calculation periods becomes necessary for any like-to-like comparison.

Early indications that MMF in C & R adapted TSR approach

> Despite the size and boldness of recent mergers and acquisitions, there is now good evidence that most of them have failed.
>
> (Coley and Reinton, 1988: 29)

Coley and Reinton evaluated 116 US and UK merger transactions closed in the 1970s and 1980s. Their investigation was based on a variation of the TSR method, as each transaction's results were compared to that acquirer's analyzed WACC to determine 'success' or 'failure'. On that basis, 23 per cent of Coley and Reinton's sample were successful deals while 61 per cent were not.[24] Sixteen per cent of that sample (the difference between the sum of the two percentages cited above and 100 per cent) could not be classified either way by the two researchers. Assuming these undesignated transactions are split roughly in the same proportions as the other transactions, the adjusted result is a failure percentage of about 68.

The researchers' study represents a watershed analysis in merger performance investigation as the differences in performance results based on relative size of parties and relatedness as exhibited in Figure 3.1. Although Coley and Reinton's investigation only considers the two dimensions even this crude, initial attempt at merger segmentation reveals some important differences in M&A performance. While 86 per cent of large unrelated deals fail, that percentage drops by more than 30 points down to 55 per cent in the case of the small related deal. (Merger segmentation is the focus of Chapter 4.)

FIGURE 3.1 Coley and Reinton (1988): An initial step towards merger segmentation?

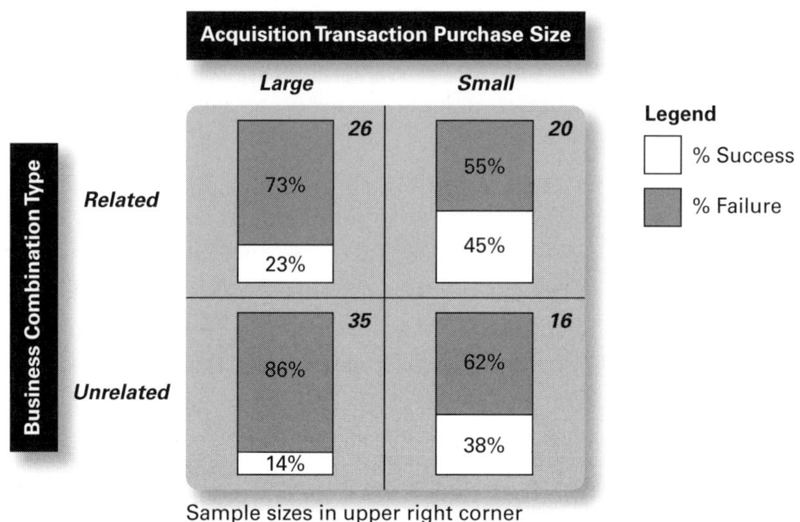

Derived from statistical summary information contained in Coley and Reinton (1988) 30. Similar exhibit in Clark (1991).

Round turns, comparables, and other analytical limitations of the method

TSR-type analyses often involve companies that are acquired and then later sold, usually over an intermediate time period. That characteristic leads to some limitations of the technique and possible distortions of results.

The round turn (buy-sale) characteristic of TSR studies means a bias towards portfolio acquisitions by non-trade financial acquirers. Trade acquirers hope to retain ownership of the target company indefinitely. When Wells Fargo absorbed Wachovia Bank, the objective of the business combination was to establish Wells Fargo as a true US national financial institution, rather than merely achieve a fix-and-then-dump return over a few years. By contrast, private equity firms' emphasis on well-timed entry and exit fits well with those firms' business model, along with their management fee structure, as described in part 2 of Chapter 2 and Appendix A.

If an operating (trade) company divests the acquired target company within a few years, the usual explanation is that the target has underperformed expectations or that acquisition debt is strangling the buyer, or both.

Hewlett-Packard's $2.1 billion acquisition of Palm's surviving operations in 2010 was designed to provide H-P with an established software platform to help in challenging Apple's explosive iPad category. Problem is, with low category gross profit margins of less than 25 per cent, only Apple and perhaps Samsung are able to compete profitably in that segment. Entering a market where it could not succeed, Palm was effectively a total write off for H-P one year later.

In the mid-1990s, Quaker Oats lost 82 per cent of the $1.7 billion paid to acquire drinks company Snapple, within three years.[25] Sirower (1997: 34–5) describes how AT&T's $1 billion bet on re-entering the computer business by acquiring NCR in 1990 ended up with almost half the amount being lost when the company was re-sold in 1994 at a loss of about $450 million. These consequences are consistent with Kaplan and Weisbach's 1992 study, 'The success of acquisitions: evidence from divestitures' in which the authors contend that 'By the end of 1989, acquirers have divested almost 44 per cent of the target companies. We characterize the *ex post* success of the divested acquisitions and consider 34 per cent to 50 per cent of classified divestitures as unsuccessful.'[26]

Best merger valuation methodology for transitional financial acquirers?

The predecessor to this book advocated the use of TSR-type evaluative criteria for all types of acquisitions and acquirers (Clark, 1991: 16–21, 57–8). Since that time, we have updated our perspective. We now suggest that long-term buy-and-hold acquirers including operating companies and institutional investors are better served by the two discounted cash flow (DCF)-influenced methods described in the next two parts of this chapter pertaining to value gap (3.6) and incremental value effect (3.7).

3.6 Value gap (VG): do synergies offset the price premium necessary to acquire the target?

> It is the NPV of the acquisition decision – the expected benefits less the premiums paid – that markets attempt to assess.
>
> (Sirower, 1997: 10)

> A's acquisition of B or B's acquisition of A is in fact good for the buyer's shareholders only if synergism is expected. And the synergism must be at least large enough to justify the premium paid above the seller's current share price.
>
> (Stern, 1974: 39)

Value gap (VG),[27] the third merger valuation methodology in Table 3.2, reflects the commonsense notion that for a merger to be successful, post-merger improvements in the combined company – synergies – must exceed the APP paid by the acquirer to secure control of that target. As the quotation from Stern's 'Earnings per share don't count' (above) attests, this merger methodology approach originates with the earliest days of management's embrace of free cash flow (FCF)-based company value analysis beginning in the mid-1970s.

Following broad-based acceptance of the reality that, historically, most mergers fail and the spectacular collapse of some so-called 'friendly' transactions around the end of the millennium such as Daimler-Benz's acquisition of Chrysler (1998)[28] and AOL's purchase of TimeWarner (2000)[29] financial writers of an investigatory bent became far less inclined to unquestioningly accept management's assurances that 'we have not overpaid'. Today, nearly every major acquisition is accompanied by that analyst or reporter's rough math about APP relative to synergies, either to support the contention that the acquirer has overpaid for the target, or not.

VG is one of two merger valuation methods in Table 3.2 incorporating discounted cash flow (DCF)-based methods, the other being incremental value effect (IVE, 3.7). In VG, projected synergies from the envisioned business combination are discounted back to the present, ideally at the combined firm's projected WACC) rate. In IVE, both standalone and combined company projections apply the two-stage discounted cash flow (DCF2S) approach already well-established in *company* valuation (Mills, 2005: 73).

VG calculation dynamics

Based on the simple VG method, a transaction is considered to be value-destroying (and thus, unsuccessful) when and if the APP exceeds the present value of net realizable synergies,[30] as depicted by 'APP' and 'SYN' in Table 3.5. Issues arise with both components of the VG equation.

APP. As generally calculated, APP is an external market approximate indicator that does not take into account the effect of rising share prices as

TABLE 3.5 VG summarized

Category: Purchase Overbid Coverage	
Method: ***Value gap (VG)*** 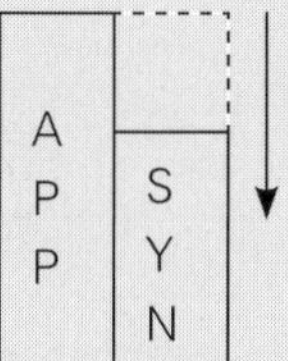 Acquisition purchase premium (APP) calculated on two month pre-announcement basis MINUS PV of ***confirmed and achievable*** synergies of all 4 types (see Chapter 7)	Recognizes that the great majority of acquisitions are value-diminishing at the time of accepted bid, that the real work of achieving merger success starts the day AFTER the close.
Positives	**Negatives**
Debunks the 'good acquisition, even though we overpaid' illusion. Incorporates recognition that 'meeting the prevailing market premium' (APP) may still result in a non-viable deal. New emphasis: As merger cycle ages, escalating APPs become more difficult to offset with synergies. Potential for improved bid pricing/walk decisions: deals from the head, not the ego.	Potential that illusory synergy assumptions not prevented at time of bid. PMI effectiveness difficult to confirm: the *highest* common denominator presumption. In view of CEO of floundering firm: strategic options curtailed as error of the high APP percent deal exposed.

the cycle matures, as noted in Appendix A. Accounting professionals may be inclined to argue that APP should not be used as the basis for this excess payment, but rather the traditional concept of accounting-based acquisition overhead. Continuing use of APP in the VG and similar calculations appears to be due more to inertia than to widely-based acceptance. We expect this side of the VG equation will be refined and revised by merger valuation practitioners in the coming years.

Synergy (S). That there are few perspectives on net realizable synergies (NRS) except for those included in Chapter 7 in this book suggests that the systematic analysis of synergies is still at a primitive stage, illuminating stories of acquirers' past post-merger mistakes notwithstanding.

VG merger market dynamics

While the VG may be expressed as a simple ratio or as a sum (APP/S or alternatively APP-S), that does not mean that this is a passive statistic with little to do with the sometimes tumultuous realities of the merger chase. On the contrary, the difference between the purchase premium and achievable synergies reflects several key forces arising both before and after the transaction is closed.

In Figure 3.2, APP ('acquisition overbid') and S ('realized synergies-plus') are likened to tectonic plates sliding against each other:

- *APP rising: merger success threatened.* If bid-related forces push the APP to higher and higher price levels (four such forces are identified in the figure) while synergies remain unchanged, the chances for a successful deal shrink, because the APP-to-S gap has widened.
- *S shrinking: merger success threatened.* Conversely, if realizable synergies shrivel because of actions or developments such as a competitor poaching key staff, timing delays in the post-merger integration program or adjustments such as reducing previous overly-optimistic estimates of S while APPs remain unchanged, the gap widens and chances of deal success recede further, albeit for a different reason.
- *Both developments occur at the same time: worst case scenario in terms of the deal's success in value terms.* Many of the more spectacular merger train wrecks as described in Sirower (1997) and the initial chapter in Carroll and Mui (2009) involve rapid deterioration on *both* elements in the VG equation. Unum misdiagnosed the basic business model of its target, Provident Insurance, with the result that a high APP bid was paid for a misfit. That situation was made worse when fanciful synergy assumptions for IT platform consolidation and joint sales initiatives dissolved. Terra Firma bought music company EMI for a reported £4.2 billion in 2007. By early 2011, 'the private equity firm wrote down its investment in record label EMI Group Ltd to zero'.[31] A contributing factor was artists' resentment over controls.

FIGURE 3.2 Value gap consequences of merger market dynamics

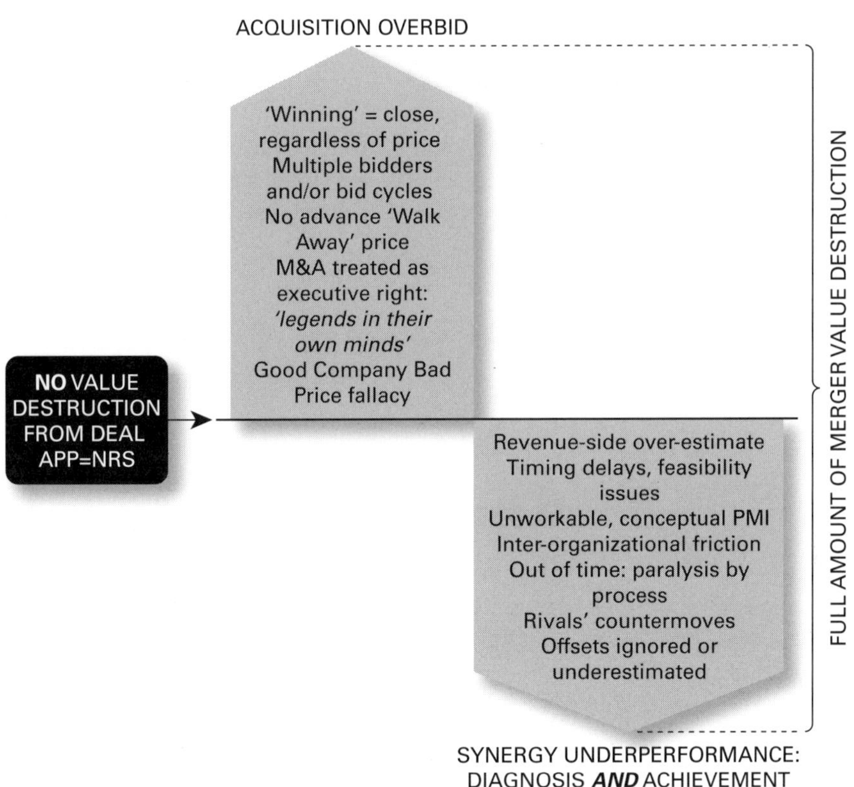

> A threatened talent exodus put EMI management on the defensive at the worst time possible, when competing labels were concentrating on their new strategies in the digital era.

Timing and effectiveness are key to merger success as measured by the VG methodology. VG's imperative is that the acquiring company's management must act quickly and in the right ways to reduce the deliberate overpayment necessary to secure control of the target. Sluggish execution (AT&T's *laissez faire* PMI approach contributed to the loss of nearly half the value of its 1990 acquisition of NCR) or misdirection by the acquirer. Today, Time Warner lifers still wince at the memories of being talked down to by AOL managers proselytizing the era of digital media to them following consummation of the stillborn AOL-TWX deal on January 10 2000.

Are high bid prices (as reflected by high APPs) primarily to blame for the continuing high levels of merger failure?

> For the past two decades, the premiums paid for acquisitions – measured as the additional price paid for an acquired company over its pre-acquisition value – have averaged between 40 and 50 per cent, with many surpassing 100 per cent (eg, IBM's acquisition of Lotus)... The higher the premium is, the greater is the value destruction from the acquisition strategy.
>
> (Sirower, 1997: 14)

The VG methodology is the one approach of the four explored in this chapter which *explicitly* addresses acquiring company overpayment as a major reason for M&A deal failure.

Azofra and Andrade et al *indicated purchase premium percentage ceilings*

Azofra *et al* (2007: 4) suggest an upper APP percentage range for successful transactions of 37 per cent. That maximum APP is almost identical to that from an earlier investigation by Andrade *et al* (2001: 103–20, also Table 3.6): 38 per cent.

Azofra *et al*'s perspective is not single-dimensional. The researchers contend that they were considering both parts of the VG equation – APP and S – in their analysis: 'The purpose of this research is to test whether the price paid for takeovers is related to synergies expected or whether bidders are overpaying for the acquisitions.'

Compare these limits to Porrini's research into APP percentages in transactions from 1990 to 2002: 'Between 1990 and 2002, acquisition premiums averaged 53.2 per cent with 40 per cent of acquirers paying premiums of over 50 per cent and 10 per cent of acquirers were paying premiums over 100 per cent' (2006: 59). Kaufman's 1988 findings, shown in Figure 3.3, are similar to Porrini's, with about 48 per cent of all deals examined involving an APP of 40 per cent or more.

While unrealistic bids may arise at any phase over the merger wave, particularly by a desperate acquirer and/or egocentric acquirer or adviser, Figure 1.4 in Chapter 1 (repeated here as Figure 3.4) shows the approximate correlation between purchase premium ranges and merger boom phase.

TABLE 3.6 APP and influences

	1973–1979	1980–1989	1990–1998	1973–1998
Premium (Median)	**47.2%**	**37.7%**	**34.5%**	**37.9%**
Bids/Deal	1.6	1.6	1.2	1.4
All cash	38.3%	45.3%	27.4%	35.4%
Own industry	29.9%	40.1%	47.8%	42.1%
Hostile bid* at any point	8.4%	14.3%	4.0%	8.3%
N	789	1,427	2,040	4,256

Period covered is from 20 days prior to the first announcement of the merger to the date of that transaction's close.

*The researchers state that 'We define a bid as hostile if the target company publicly rejects it, or if the acquirer describes it as unsolicited and unfriendly' (106).

SOURCE: Based on statistics from Andrade *et al* (2001).

Both Azofra *et al* and Andrade *et al*'s research in effect suggest that no deals should be attempted any later in the merger wave than phase III, thereby placing a premium on the ability to accurately discern the transition points from one merger phase to the next.

Overbids and Apotheker

> H.P. paid an astonishing 80 per cent premium for Autonomy, a business software maker based in Britain. H.P. lost $12 billion in market value within 24 hours of the deal being announced... (For 3Par, H.P. paid) the highest premium ever paid: 242 per cent.
>
> (Andrew Ross Sorkin, *New York Times*, Nov 7 2011)[32]

In the absence of useable synergy insight, the question arises as to whether excessive bids *per se* mean increased incidence of merger failure. If the APP level in percentage terms is, say, two or more times the Azofra/Andrade *et al* 37–8 per cent ceiling, mounting evidence points towards an answer of 'yes' *regardless of synergies achieved.*

FIGURE 3.3 Kaufmann (1988): Patterns of APP

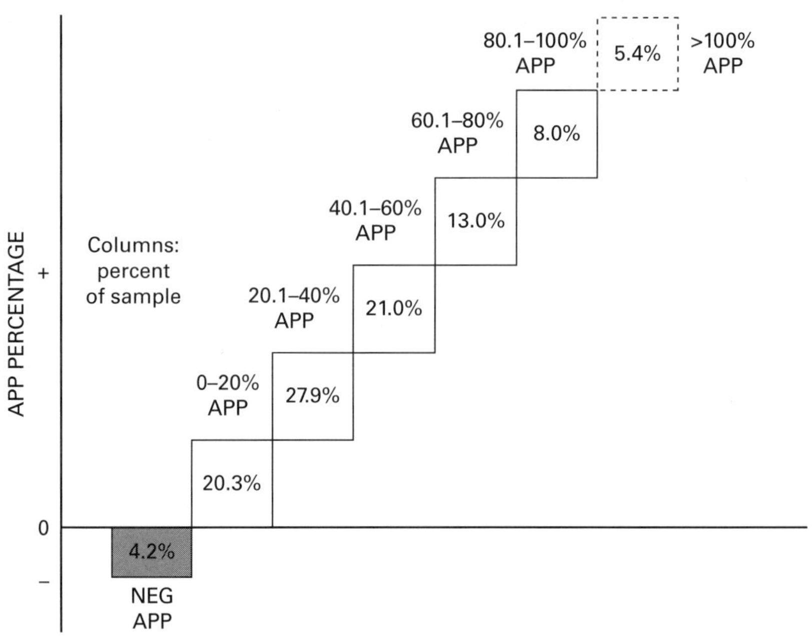

For example, each of three major acquisitions – 3Par, Palm, Autonomy – made by Leo Apotheker during his brief term as chief executive officer of Hewlett-Packard involved APP premiums that were *more than twice* the Azofra/Andrade *et al* 37–8 per cent ceiling in APP percentage terms (refer to the quotation above from Sorkin). On an ES basis, the market's judgment about the Autonomy acquisition was manifested in day one $12 billion plunge in market value. This was despite high regard for the consulting firm as a leader in its field. 3Par – also well regarded in the cloud computing area – quickly became a university of how not to negotiate in an acquisition chase, with a reported APP percentage well in excess of 200.[33]

In the case of the embattled CEO's acquisition of what remained of Palm Inc's software operations, there is no need to guess about whether or not that deal's stratospheric APP predestined an imminent crash. Overbidding for a company that had recently declared that it could no longer compete and thus understandably had few bidders except of the bottom-trawler type (Table 4.2, Chapter 4), Apotheker paid what financial markets refer to diplomatically as a 'very full' price for Palm.

FIGURE 3.4 Transaction timing during the merger wave and corresponding APP percentages

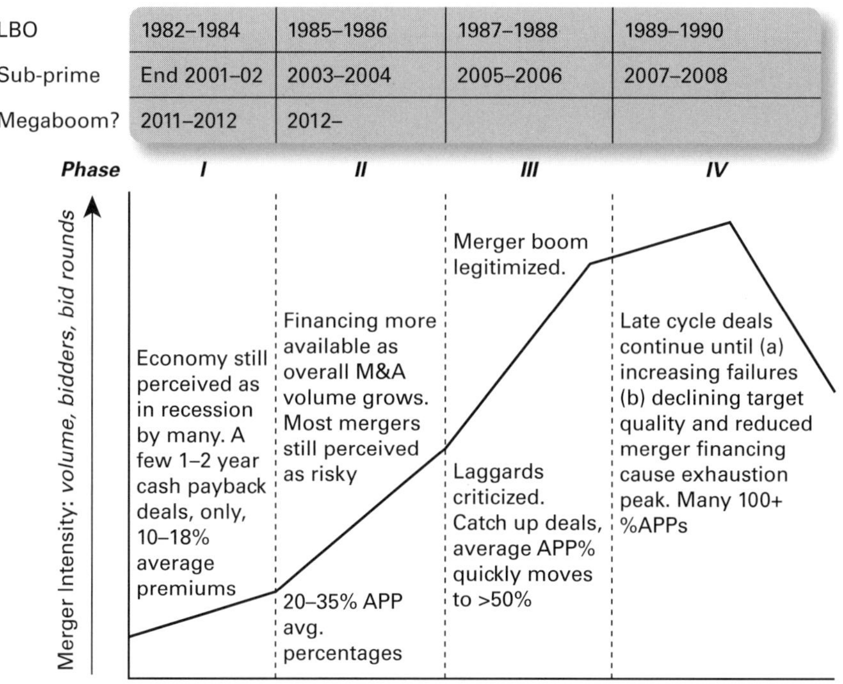

Related exhibit: Figure 1.4, Chapter 1

That 'must have it at any cost' desperation deal was made on the basis that Palm's software capabilities were key to H-P's new adventures in tablet computing, a product category in which gross margins are at 23–4 per cent of sales, effectively ensuring that only Apple and perhaps Samsung are able to make a profit. *Never mind that due diligence shows there are no profits in tablets except perhaps for the initial movers – this is a segment we must not miss!* Could any action by the hard-pressed chief executive of the Palo Alto firm boost value and share price? Yes. When embattled chief executive Apotheker departed H-P in September 2011 after less than a year in the job, H-P's share price surged 7 per cent.[34]

But it's APP *relative to realizable synergies* that matters when it comes to merger success. Overbidding alone does not by itself identify the failed deal. It is the level of pricing *relative to the present value of net realizable synergies (NRSs)* that determines whether the deal is a value-creating success or not based upon the VG methodology.

NRSs versus acquisition premiums over phases of the merger wave

Ever since the publication of Sirower's *The Synergy Trap* in 1997, most acquirers and their handlers chant the mantra that synergies are important to merger success. Seemingly, the stream of pundits claiming special insight into synergy processes and priorities grows with each passing year, and 'synergy' remains a favorite M&A-related topic today. Every year or so, post-merger synergies are identified by yet another new observer as a neglected area of merger analysis, even though since the late 1980s that topic has arguably been the *most* extensively covered aspect of M&A investigation.[35] But conspicuously absent from the synergy perspectives to date have been workable frameworks and segmentation necessary to examine this part of the VG equation adequately.

Synergy is the end result of four different distinct categories of synergies (expense-, revenue-, financial, and management-related synergies) occurring over time and sometimes subject to partial offsetting charges. Synergy isn't just some guess number devised for the financial community as the bidding war causes prices to soar. It results from both operations and execution, from priorities and speed – as there is limited time opportunity in the critical PMI period to pursue many objectives and multiple distractions.

The concept of NRS as introduced here and explored in Chapter 7 also incorporates the dimension of *time*. While the purchase premium is paid at the time of a deal's close, a substantial portion of total synergies such as from IT platform consolidation, require years to fully accomplish, thus requiring discounting those inflows (for merger valuation purposes) back to the present at the combined post-merger companies' analyzed WACC rate. NRSs are compared to APPs in Figure 3.5.

The APP trend line rises in Figure 3.5, as the cycle progresses through its four phases.[36] In part, this is due to merger market fundamentals, as more and more aspiring acquirers chase fewer and fewer quality targets. Market psychology also plays a role. By phase III, a modest boom is transformed into an outright bubble through frantic acquisitions by late entrants fearful of a career-threatening criticism: missing the major upward market move.

Note that NRSs' trend line over the four phases of the merger wave is shown almost flat in Figure 3.5. While target company-originating synergies are sometimes affected by the characteristics of the acquiring firm and/or the capabilities of that particular buyer's post-merger integration terms, neither factor relates to the phase of the merger wave. For any specific merger situation, NRS remains almost unchanged from the beginning of the business-merger cycle to the end of the wave, raising the prospect of a growing – and value destroying – APP-to-NRS VG as the cycle ages.

Individual transaction perspective: two opposing VG views

> In competitive takeover bid situations, the winner tends to be that bidder who most overestimates the true value of the target company... He who bids on a (target) what he thinks it is worth will, in the long run, be taken for a cleaning.
>
> (Capen *et al*, 1971: 643)[37]

Dobbs *et al* (2010: 5) describe the unlikely but theoretically possible merger circumstance in which a negative VG situation arises. In their merger valuation theoretical ideal, synergies (S) from the deal do not merely *match* the

FIGURE 3.5 Considering *both* VG determining factors, over the business-merger cycle

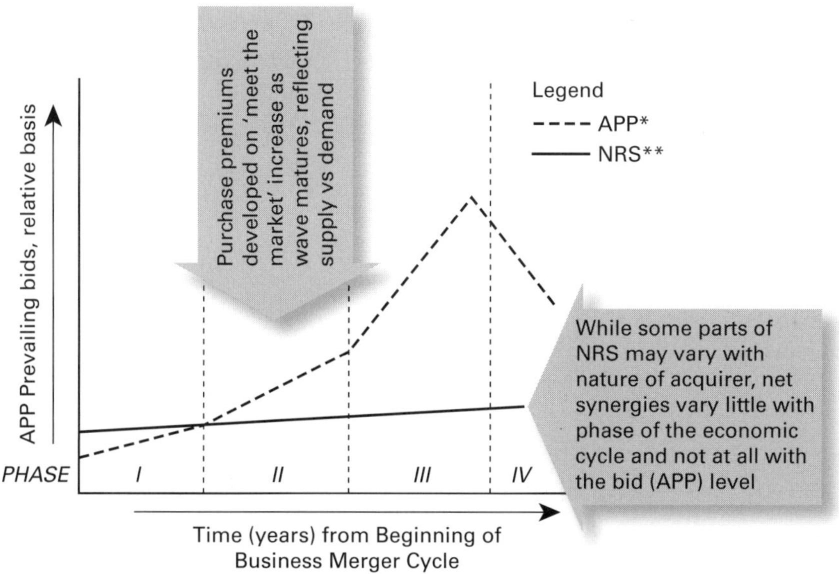

Notes:
* APP refers to Acquisition Purchase Premium: Accepted bid versus pre-announcement indicated share price
** NRS refers to Net Realizable Synergies: PV of synergies from four S categories (Ch. 8) adjusted for timing, feasibility, offsetting charging and/or investments

FIGURE 3.6 VG under real world multiple bid circumstances

elapsed time
3
35%
4
+15%
Acquirer's
reconciling
assumption
VALUE GAP
2
18%
1
20%
Net overall
synergies
E–, R–, F–, M–
0%
0%
ACQUISITION PURCHASE PREMIUM (APP) Pct., accepted bid versus pre-announcement target company share price basis
Analyzed/Assumed **SYNERGIES (S)** resulting from proposed combination with target firm (percentage improvement)

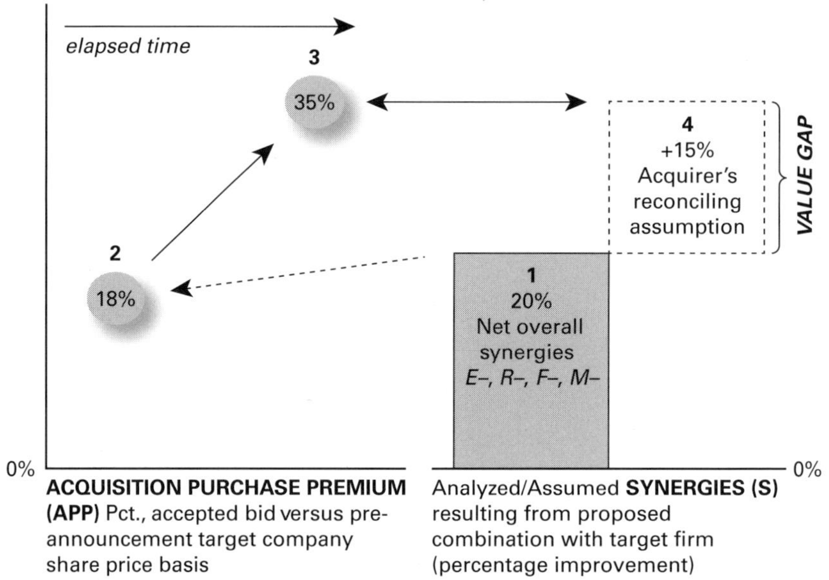

bidder's APP in this merger valuation fantasy, but *exceed* that threshold amount. The merger consultants' Holy Grail of value-creating acquisitions suddenly exists, on paper at least. In theory, that excess synergy *is value available to* the shareholders of the acquiring firm.[38]

But which of the two opposing perspectives – Dobbs *et al*'s theoretical ideal or value gap under real world multiple bid circumstances as depicted in Figure 3.6 is the more likely? For us, the answer is Figure 3.6, showing APP>S, for several reasons:

- *Bid chase to value destruction.* The macho acquiring company CEO doesn't dare being called a wimp for 'losing' the bidding war. Such hubris pushes the buying company and its leader to make excessive, value-destroying bids in order to save face. The relationship between high purchase premiums and the number of bidders and bidding cycles is suggested by the statistics in Table 3.6.
- *Deficient pre-acquisition synergy intelligence.*[39] Higher bids might appear to be warranted based upon indications of higher synergies, but is the analysis credible? Conventional pre-close synergy analysis techniques range from the inadequate (eg across-the-board expense

reduction based on income statement information available in the public domain) to the implausible (eg subjective guesses about management (m-) synergies). The consequence is that there are usually no credible numbers to support a higher bid based on increased analyzed NRSs.

- *Selling company incentive to eliminate any negative* VG. Dobbs *et al* imagine a *negative* VG situation, as synergies are presumed to exceed the purchase premium amount. But do such situations ever arise in the real world consistent with an actual bidding war? Precedent suggests that the answer is 'no'. Selling company management know their company best, and they act quickly to capture any such extra synergies for themselves. The seller insists on a higher minimum bid price, thereby capturing the 'value created for acquirer' for its own shareholders.
- *Consistency with MMF.* Accepted reality today is that historically, two-thirds of all deals fail, based on financial returns to the acquiring firm's shareholders. The VG depiction consistent with MMF is Figure 3.6, in which APP exceeds S.

The sequence as depicted in Figure 3.6 helps explain why so many mergers fail as measured on a VG basis. Bids move further and further away from levels justified by synergies as the orderly pursuit of the target company eventually deteriorates into a buyers' panic rout:

Step 1: Initial synergies analysis, calculations. Acquiring company management develop an initial estimate of realizable synergies based upon analysis of the two largest and most predictable 'S' categories. Expense-related synergies ('e-synergies' in Chapter 7) are augmented by *some* revenue-related synergies ('r-synergies') in developing that preliminary number. In more complete post-merger integration efforts, estimates from those two sources are supplemented by some additional assumed financing synergies ('f-synergies'), primarily tax-related improvement opportunities.

Step 2: Synergies inform initial bids. Whatever the acquiring company's method for estimating realizable synergies, the presumption in Figure 3.6 is that those calculations influence the initial bid and the related APP. The figure depicts an initial target bid that is slightly lower than the level of calculated synergies to date. But the bidding war is on, and higher bids will be needed to close the deal. The acquiring company's CEO asks, 'How much above the target's current share price can we afford to go?' Sirower's (1997) descriptions of the synergy missteps associated with Unum's acquisition of Provident Insurance and his description of the aftermath of the AT&T-NCR deal provide valuable insight into what *not* to do, synergy-wise. Guessing at imagined synergies without factoring in feasibility, time delays and/or offsets (additional costs in order for the synergy improvement to occur) is self-delusional. But impetus to ignore bid discipline as indicated by early synergy analysis does not always originate with the acquirer; sometimes the target itself is to blame. Misled by advisers to expect a king's ransom price, this may stipulate a minimum bid so much greater than realistically achievable synergies that the would-be acquirer's only defendable chess move is to walk away from the deal.

Step 3: Meeting the price challenge of the bidding chase (aka, the Snapple/ABN Amro/3Par effect). But the acquiring company shown in the figure is not the only bidder pursuing the target. In Figure 3.6, the APP percentage thought to be necessary to keep up competing bidders increases from 18 to 35 per cent. Bid dynamics are now dominated by the aspiring acquirer's obsession to keep up with the chase – to not fall behind other bidder(s) who are pushing the price for the target higher and higher with each bid cycle. But NRSs do not keep pace, and an adverse (for bidders) VG situation arises. The only way to prevail as the selected top bidder for the target is to participate in a value-destroying, (failed) transaction. Figure 3.6 shows a single bid adjustment. Multiple bids are a norm for attractive target companies; the statistics in Table 3.6 suggest that there is a close correlation between the number of bids and the level of the APP.[40] By this advanced point in the chase, the CEO of the acquiring firm is on the horns of a dilemma. Even the most non-analytical chief executive realizes that a 'groundbreaking' high bid threatens to cause winner's remorse, when the buyer realizes that he or she has paid too much for the target and that the deal should have never occurred.[41]

Step 4: Rationalizing the value-destructive overbid. The success-threatening excess bid proceeds anyway. The concerned acquirer's only remaining chess move is to mitigate adverse financial community reaction somewhat by attempting to disguise the reality of the excessive bid relative to achievable synergies for that specific deal. Enter the financial public relations spin-masters, who tellingly avoid *any* mention of *any* elements having to do with the Value Gap MV criteria. Instead, 'soft' attributes are emphasized: joint perspectives and similar customers, or the vapid 'marriage made in heaven' proclamation.

Good company bad price (GCBP), some other VG-related fallacies

Fallacy 1: If the target company is excellent quality, it is acceptable to overpay

> In one of the biggest deals last year, Hewlett-Packard agreed to buy Autonomy Corp. for $10.3 billion in a bid to build its software business and scale back on its PC manufacturing.
>
> (Saito, Feb 6 2012)[42]

This might alternatively be referred to as the Huffington Press fallacy, in recognition of AOL chief executive Armstrong's gross overbid in 2011 for the attractive and almost-profitable (at the time of acquisition) complementary company, Huffington Press.[43]

The GCBP situation arises when the chief executive of the acquiring company impulsively 'breaks the bank' and conspicuously overspends to secure ownership of the star-quality target company. The object of this acquirer's affections is either a promising firm such as Huffington, or alternatively, an already established leader in its sector. The acquirer proceeding with these high risk deals is often either a) a desperate company using the acquisition to deflect attention away from its own slumping performance, or b) a late phase acquirer eager to close a deal in the remaining phases of the merger wave, before it's too late.

There is little debate that the acquirer has paid what the financial markets refer to as a 'very full price'. Additional proof of overpayment comes in the content of the acquirer's announcements about VG components, or rather, the *absence* of such disclosure. The buyer already knows full well that APP far exceeds any realistically achievable synergy amounts, and hopes to avoid new concerns about the value-destructive nature of this latest deal from analysts, reporters and biz-TV talking heads.

Fallacy 2: The chief executive who 'loses' the acquisition chase damages his or her reputation and puts his or her firm at risk

> On the day of the announcement that Quaker would acquire Snapple for $1.7 billion in cash, Quaker's stock price fell by almost 10 per cent... Three years

> later,... Quaker sold Snapple to Triarc for only $300 million. Shortly thereafter, Quaker's chairman and CEO, William Smithburg, was pressured by Quaker's stockholders to resign.
>
> (Lehn and Zhao, 2006: 1760, referring to Quaker Oats' ill-fated acquisition of popular drinks producer Snapple, in 1994)

Is this statement justified? Examples from recent years point instead to the opposite of Fallacy statement 2. The heads of Royal Bank of Scotland (RBS), Lloyds Banking Group, Hewlett-Packard, HBOS, Daimler-Benz, AT&T (pre-SBC days), Vivendi, and Quaker Oats (above) all lost their jobs, significantly or entirely because of disastrous acquisitions. The departing CEO is almost always described by spin doctors at the time as 'making a conscious decision to spend more time with his (or her) family'. No one in the financial community is fooled for a nanosecond.

Contrast the fate of those CEOs to the bidders who – whether by acumen, luck or a combination – somehow ducked the value-destructive deal bullet. On the day that he 'lost' ABN Amro to UK competitor RBS, Barclays top manager was initially labeled by the tabloid business press as the loser in that bidding war. But less than one quarter after the close of that stillborn deal, the opposite perspective emerged. By 'losing' ABN Amro, Barclays eventually won. Unfettered by the huge acquisition premiums and debt of the ABN disaster and able to avoid having to fix the Netherlands-based bank when it became apparent that this was another bank that believed in the subprime fiction too much, Barclays' then CEO Robert Diamond was later able to pursue *his* true target: selective parts of defunct Lehman Bros.

Fallacy 3: A quality synergy capability represents wasted money that could better be used to increase the bid

Wrong. Without actionable, accurate intelligence about the true synergies achievable from the proposed business combination, the would-be acquirer is effectively bidding with a blindfold on, guided only by the manic price dynamics of the bidding war. With insufficient synergy intelligence to guide the bidding process, misperception of the meaning of merger 'success' soars. Except to those transactions intermediaries who only get paid if the deal closes and their client is the buyer, success does *not* occur when the document is signed; success only occurs when value is created for the acquiring firm as a consequence of the merger.

Wasted outlay? A robust synergy diagnosis capability supports the acquiring company management by helping them to distinguish value traps from value opportunities. The CEO inclined to value-destructive overbids has a counterweight to the manic environment of the bidding war. Both executives and the board become aware of the absolute bid limits, unique for each proposed merger. Knowing when to proceed and when to walk away? Hardly the place for the acquisition-active company to pinch pennies.

Fallacy 4: So long as the bid is somewhere around the median of bids for that target, criticism of value-destructive overpayment can usually be evaded

The bid tendencies of companies pursuing other companies at around the time provide important insight. In Chapter 4, we explore how and why middle-of-the-range offers tend to result in higher levels of M&A success prospects than bidding blindly. But some problems arise with this fallacious statement.

Bidding groupthink is no substitute for pre-close synergy intelligence: consider bid patterns only, and you miss the other side of the VG. Also, during pricing manias, *all* bidders are inclined to overbid. At such times, *all* bids are value destructive, misleading management of the acquiring company.

3.7 Incremental value effect (IVE): two-scenario DCF analysis, adapted to mergers

> Most companies transacting M&As rely on discounted cash flow (DCF) models to value a target company (Bruner *et al*, 1998).
>
> (Schweiger and Very, 2003: 1)[44]

The IVE method as described here represents an adaptation of Damodaran's (2005) two scenario method. The major adaptation pertains to synergies, as the NYU Business School professor establishes a separate sub-category for synergies that original target company management *could* have achieved but did not; such synergies (described in Chapter 7) *are* included in the IVE methodology.

IVE involves merger valuation decisions made on the basis of comparative analysis of two alternative DCF projections. *Scenario 1* presumes that acquiring and target firms remain separate companies. Separate cash flow projections are developed for each firm, along with separate costs of capital (WACCs) based on each firm's separate capital structure and component costs. As there is no business combination, purchase premium and no synergies are disregarded. *Scenario 2* assumes that the proposed merger progresses. Both NRSs and the APP amount paid by the buyer to gain control of the target are factored into the combined company's projections period. The hybrid DCF discount rate reflects the analyzed post-merger WACC of the two companies together. If the NPV associated with Scenario 2 exceeds the NPV of Scenario 1 to the extent that the excess returns exceed the acquirer's cost of capital, then the deal appears to be value-creating.

Passing of the merger valuation standard: from ES to IVE

At the time of writing, the accrual accounting-based ES method remains the leading merger valuation methodology utilized in merger valuation academia. But DCF-based methods have dominated in *company* valuation by management since the mid-1970s.

Regarding preferred methods for merger valuation, the issue is no longer whether a comparable change will occur, but rather when. Managers and consultants began to move away from dividend-based methods for *company* valuation in the mid-1970s with publication of Stern's 'Earnings per share don't count' article in the *Financial Analysts Journal*. Stern deals with the basics of DCF-based *merger* valuation in one part of that article ('Acquisition analysis', 39–40), thereby suggesting that in its simplest form, the evaluation of M&A success or failure centers on the comparison of the involved companies' worth on a *pre-* and *post-*combination basis.

The IVE method encompasses that type of standalone versus combined DCF diagnosis. If ES is on the defensive except in parts of academia, what is its successor? The side-by side comparison of ES and IVE in Table 3.7 provides an answer.

Merger valuation rationale/basis of value assessment

The salient question is: 'On what basis does the method assess the success or failure of the M&A transaction?' ES-based methodology focuses on (external market) share price movements of the buying firm, over a period of time starting 20-plus days or so before the acquirer's announcement of interest in the firm (see Appendix A) and an analysis ranging from a few months to a few years after the deal's close. IVE looks instead to DCF-based valuation of the two principals (acquirer and acquiree) on a standalone basis and combined, including consideration of both realizable synergies and a purchase premium adjustment in the latter.

TABLE 3.7 Changing of the merger valuation guard: ES vs IVE

	Event Studies (ES)	**Incremental Value Effect (IVE)**
Merger valuation rationale	Changes, trend in acquirer's post-announcement share price suggests market's judgment of deal's success	Merger is value-creating if combined firm exhibits higher analyzed NPV than two firms as standalones, including APP, S, transition costs
Basis of value assessment	External MV (share price)	Internal MV (PV of CF generation)
Effect of individual M&A transaction identifiable?	No	Yes
Analysis period (*t*)	Variable, with indicated result for same transaction sometimes changing with *t*	Preference: corporate value lifespan (CVL) Secondary: perpetuity (DCF2S)
Advantages compared	(1) Data availability (2) Appears to be validated by initial price movement of acquirers' and target's prices (3) Precedent	(1) Consistent with leading company valuation basis (2) Reliance on ultimate source of company worth: internal FCF (3) Correctly developed, incorporates APP, S
Disadvantages compared	(1) Multiple contagions (2) Time: exceeds limits of market predictability (3) Suffers from no specific consideration of APP, S	(1) Three separate forward projections (2) Varying interpretation of: CF drivers, WACC basis, variable amounts

Some limitations associated with ES methods are described earlier in this chapter, including some of the specific foibles of shorter- and longer-term ES versions. As alarming as those limitations are, the more decisive issue is the suitability of *any* limited duration analysis of share prices alone as the basis for making judgments about whether the merger is a success or failure.

Share price looks five years into the future on a non-residual basis. But at the time of acquisition, the target is viewed by its operating company acquirer as a *permanent* addition to the combined enterprise. This is no temporary portfolio addition designed for future IPO or other exit strategy by a financial buyer; for the operating company acquirer this marriage is intended to continue forever.

This mismatch between the short analysis period of the ES approach (even longer-term variants) and the acquirer's long-term ownership intent undermines ES as a dependable merger valuation method. An analogy is attempting to predict how many miles the newly-purchased car will remain on the road based on how long the new model's paint job fades in the first 90 days. The measure is too brief and too unrelated to the fundamentals of that issue to be useful as a consistent M&A success-or-failure indicator.

By contrast, IVE resembles make-versus-buy decisions within companies: two alternative scenarios are developed and compared on a projected basis, with the scenario exhibiting the highest Net Present Value (NPV) result selected. IVE also enjoys the advantage of common sense and easy understanding, compared to ES. ES-oriented merger valuation academicians anguish over a range of alternative calculation and sampling variations: provocative to some merger valuation academicians, the equivalent of rearranging the deckchairs on the Titanic to many others.

The pragmatic, non-statistical acquiring company chief executive seeking a direct answer to the question of whether to proceed with the deal at the stipulated price or not wonders, 'Why can't we simply look at the difference in value based on whether the two companies are combined or remain separate?'

Isolation of individual acquisition transaction

The longer the ES analysis period, the greater the chances that developments unrelated to the specific merger under examination affect the acquirer's share price. But shrinking the ES analysis period brings a separate set of challenges, including the aforementioned mismatch between the metric's evaluation period and the expected continuous future economic lifespan of the new combined company.

In attempting to apply the ES method, it quickly becomes apparent that patterns of share prices might only be considered as providing a hint about the future success or failure of the merger under examination when and if *all three* of the following conditions may be assumed: a) annualized CFs will continue at present levels over the foreseeable future; b) there is only one major acquisition over the analysis period (the business combination in question), and c) other material events or developments do not arise to distort the share price indication.

Analysis period

ES involves analysis periods ranging from a few months to several years after the close, with the implicit presumption that a limited number of trading sessions provide all the information necessary to judge the viability of the deal. By contrast, IVE analysis considers projected data over the full future lifespan of both companies and combined.

Advantages versus disadvantages

ES's primary advantages for merger valuation purposes are two-fold: inertia plus ample availability of base data for use in that methodology; ES's disadvantages start with the analysis period and companies' continuing lifespans. Who cares that calculation data is readily available if the conclusions reached by the method are questionable?[45]

Despite being closely related to the leading *company* valuation methodology, IVE does face some limitations, primarily involving the credibility of multiple future assumptions necessary to develop the standalone versus combined comparative scenarios.

The precedent of making major investment decisions on a DCF basis is well-established. Chances that the large proposed internal investment – a project or a capital expenditure – proceeds without advance in-depth DCF analysis, are miniscule. Comparable rigor should apply to the corporation's major external investments, that is, *mergers*.

3.8 Reconciling the tier I merger valuation methodologies

The big four list of merger valuation methodologies in Table 3.2 shrinks to three when the limitations of ES are fully taken into account. Another of the

FIGURE 3.7 Gordon Formula I: components of the second stage equation in the two-stage DCF method (DCF2S), issues

Initial Period Free Cash Flow (FCF) Running Rate

Variable 1: Estimate of company initial period FCF amount ('rate') as of the beginning of the horizon period

Estimation accuracy issues: amount

Typical calculation basis: Rate at end of 'pre-horizon'. Explicit Projection Period (EPP), other

Projection issues: Sustainable FCF at the end of EPP, sometimes to years, occuring in volatile early launch competitive stages

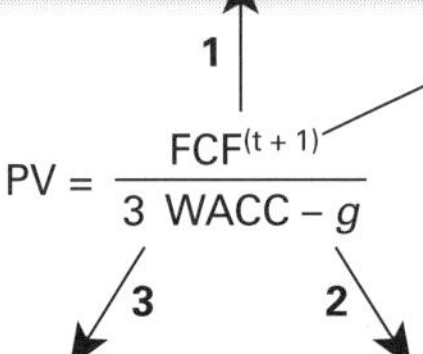

Perpetuity notation. Usually a 4th variable, *time* is transformed into an unchanging assumption, exaggerating any over estimations in variables 1–3

Weighed Average Cost of Capital

Variable 3: Estimate(s) of company's cost of capital over its infinite life span

Estimation accuracy issues: level, variability

Typical calculation methods: CAPM-based analysis (from debt and equity parts), expectations, – based, other

Multiplier effect: Combine an unrealistically low WACC worth Total FCF (Variable 1 × Variable 2), and consequence may be *unreasonable* result derived from what appear to be 3 *reasonable* variables

Projection issues: (a) capital structure (D, E) changes over company life stages, (b) changes in operational and over company life stages, (c) changes in operational and financial risks with maturity, (d) Pickens's high debt model

Subsequent Period FCF Growth Rate

Variable 2: Projection of future FCF growth rate (%) to infinity

Estimation accuracy issues: level, variability

Typical calculation methods: industry, or company change rates, comparable, analysis

Multiplier effect: When combined with an oversized initial FCF (Variable 2), can quickly become an unachievable amount

Projection issues: (a) percentages of small base year amounts, (b) radical steady state (0% growth), (c) curve shape over time

upper tier's four methods, TSR, may be useful for some round turn financial acquirers, so long as comparisons with other TSR transactions are not required.

What remains is the method that is most comparable to today's mainstream method for company valuation, the two-stage DCF approach – IVE plus the

TABLE 3.8 Gordon Formula II: components of the second stage equation in the two-stage DCF Method (DCF2S), issues

Factor	GF Variable	Legacy Approaches	Emergent, Possible Successor
C of C	**WACC**	kWACC (constant), based on CAPM (Fama and French, 2004[46]; Perold, 2004[47])	• vWACC (Clark, 2010a; Luehrman, 1997) • Expectations-based (Copeland & Dolgoff, 2006) • Closed-loop systemic (Madden, 2010[49]) • Options-based (various)
Internal investment (i), related returns	**FCF** (initial FCF, DCF2S Stage 2)	End of EPP (DCF2S Stage 1) annual rate (Cassia and Vismara, 2009[48])	• Future projected FCF deflator • Component analysis: spot (NOPAT, *i*, depr.) • Momentum analysis of FCF during EPP
	g (future FCF rate in Stage 2)	End of EPP (DCF2S Stage 1) annualized rate	• Multiple stages (Mills, 2005; Damodaran, 2002[50]) • Fully variable, *g* component-determined (Clark, 2009)
Analysis period: valuation longevity	**t**	Infinite: $\mathbf{t}^{\infty}$, (t + 1....)	• Multiples of longest major product life cycle (Clark, 2010a) • CAP-based with confirmation (Clark, 2010a) • Category historical precedent (Clark, 2010a)

CAP: competitive advantage period (Mauboussin & Johnson, 1997), CFROI/WACC, CAPM: capital asset pricing model, C of C: cost of capital, kWACC: constant C of C, NOPAT: net operating profit after tax, FCF: free cash flow, t: (time), Valuation analysis period vs WACC: variable C of C over firm's economic life span, WACC: weighed average cost of capital.

TABLE 3.9 IVE: Constructing the two scenarios

	Summary	EPP (Stage 1)	TVPS (Stage 2)	WACC	Confirmation
STANDALONE	Pre-announcement operating and strategic of acquirer and target including incumbent capital, internal investment, management.	Derived directly from two year operating budget. Annualized FCF rate as of end of EPP becomes beginning FCF value for Stage 2	As reflected in current capital structure, component C of D, C of E costs	As reflected in current capital structure, LTD and equity component costs.	Existing share price levels and external market value (MC – MVD = MVE) used to confirm Stage 1 and Stage 2 components in two stage DCF company valuation
COMBINED	Including adjustment for purchase premium less immediate dispositions, terminations, other NRSs guided by four category framework approach (see Chapter 7)		Reflects both purchase premium adjustments and confirmed new, ongoing e-, r- and m- postmerger synergies (see Chapter 7)	Capital structure, financing availability reflect new financing access (f-synergies), combined capital structure	Implied target share price range derived through operations-defined competitive advantage period (ODCAP) analysis

method increasingly cited by the financial investigatory press, referred to in this book as VG:

- The argument that the primary *merger* valuation method should correspond closely to today's prevailing two-stage *company* valuation method – DCF – is supported by the characteristics of the merger transaction itself. The ultimate result of the M&A program is not some theoretical abstract, but a new, combined company. So why not apply an adaptation of the leading company valuation method to merger valuation?
- Viewed in that manner, the question that next demands an answer is, 'How does the value of this new company compare with the two separate entities that preceded the merger?'
- High present visibility and the growing importance of the APP versus NRS issue mandates that VG-type diagnosis is also included in the preference evaluation set.

Illusion: trade-off between current precision and consistency with company valuation methodologies

Understandably, some deal evaluators (principals, intermediaries, others in the financial community) may be inclined to view the ES versus IVE question as a choice between known evidence today and consistency with prevailing company valuation methods, but requiring potentially subjective projections:

The known: to the observer uncomfortable with future projections (dismissed by some as speculative guesses),[51] there's some comfort in relying on readily available price data. There's no ambiguity, no alternative interpretation of today's spot share prices for the acquiring firm; versus *consistency with the leading company valuation methodology.* Mergers involve companies, and based on the fourth method explored in this chapter (part 3.7), IVE, the most complete way to assess the individual transaction's success is to compare the merger partners' value, first as standalones and then combined. An apparent battle beckons between ease of calculation today and completeness of the merger valuation approach.

Rethinking current share prices as value indicators

The presumption that share prices today are indicative of value tomorrow is under attack. As Malkiel (1990: 103–4) explains:

> Stock prices are in a sense anchored to certain 'fundamentals', but that anchor is easily pulled up... For the standards of value... are not fixed and immutable standards that characterize the laws of physics, but rather, the more flexible and fickle relationships that are consistent with a marketplace influenced by mass psychology. Dreams of... getting rich quick may therefore play an important role in determining actual stock prices.

This notion that share prices represent at best an imperfect estimate of a company's true worth contradicts Maubossin and Johnson's (1997: 70) market implied competitive advantage period (MICAP) concept based upon Rappaport's 1986 work.[52] The opposite notion, that internal CFs determine share price rather than the other way around is referred to here as ODCAP – for operations-defined competitive advantage period. Lictenberg (1992: 3) further challenges the notion of share prices as reflecting the firm's value fundamentals:

> The key assumption is that the price of a firm's stock price is equal to the present discounted value of expected future (Cash Flows)... On this view an investor's willingness to pay for (hence the market price for) a security is not generally equal to the expected present value of future (Cash Flows). (Parentheses in original.)

Company valuation is *merger valuation*

With share prices sometimes out of synch with company valuation, the alternative path to determining fundamental worth is to go to the source: DCF. The nominal definition of *merger* valuation differs slightly from the generally accepted definition of *company* valuation. The first focuses on questions of merger success or failure: whether or not the transaction creates value for the acquiring firm's shareholders, taking into account available alternatives and cost of capital. The second involves the worth of the company, typically measured today using versions of the two-stage discounted cash flow (DCF2S) methodology.

While there is no doubt that some alternative definitions for M&A success and thus for merger valuation persist (eg qualitative measures, ES, simple proclamation by the acquiring company CEO regardless of deal specifics, deal completion) the fact that a new company emerges as a result of successful acquisition points to a conclusion that company valuation and merger valuation are close to being one and the same. Such a conclusion positions IVE at the top of the big four merger methodologies list going forward, joining VG.

3.9 Multiples: critical confirmation role in merger valuation

> LinkedIn is valued at 9.65 times estimated revenue... S&P 500 trades for 1.24 times estimated sales... 'It's high-risk and it's tough to justify the valuation,' (says) Shacknofsky, who helps manage about $5 billion for Alpine Mutual Funds.
>
> (Gammeltoft and Vannucci)[53]

Did we say four primary merger valuation methodologies? To many, there is a fifth, described here and in the preceding chapter as 'multiples'. Even we advocates of DCF-based approaches acknowledge that sometimes reliable base data is non-existent. And even today, some acquiring company CEOs insist on looking at prospective targets and bids only in terms of multiples.[54] Copeland (in Thomas and Gup, 2009) affirms that price-to-earnings ratios (P/E) and similar multiples are here to stay in company valuation, at least by middle market business brokers and some on Wall Street. And that means a continuing future role for multiples as a part of future *merger* valuation analyses.

Despite numerous limitations – several of which are described in part 5 of Chapter 2, it is the *attributes* of multiples – particularly ease of calculation plus readily available source information – which ensure longevity of the technique. Or notoriety, as in the case of multiples-based price guesses that sometimes defy credibility (refer to the Shacknofsky quotation above, and Renren's IPO fantasy valuation as described in Chapter 6).

Multiples perform a complementary role to the big four merger valuation methods in Table 3.2. None of the four leading methods is without disadvantages, which is one reason why it is the *combination* of VG and IVE that emerges today as the preferred merger valuation approach for the majority of deals.

Both VG and IVE methods require some projections about future performance in order to generate an answer to the central merger valuation question: 'Is this acquisition value-creating for continuing shareholders of the buying corporation, or not?' VG depends on developing credible estimations of total achievable synergies as a result of the deal. IVE requires three separate future projections of company performance: one projection each for acquirer and target, and a third for the two firms in combination, operating as an integrated entity. By contrast, advocates of multiples contend that simple price-to-earnings (P/E) comparables may be developed from information extracted from publicly available financial sources alone.

Resistance to future projections in the two-part merger valuation method

> Sure, there are some (synergies) for sure. I don't know what they are yet. To say that would be an idiot's game.
>
> (QVC chief executive CEO Barry Diller, commenting on shopping network QVC's proposed 'strategic' acquisition of US television network CBS on July 1 1994)

Based upon his statement (above), Barry Diller's inclination would appear to be to favor merger valuation approaches such as VG entirely because of that method's requirement for an advance estimate of overall NRSs likely to result from the combination.

The importance of synergies to merger success was already well understood and extensively described by the mid-1990s, when QVC contemplated pursuit of CBS.[55] Within a few years, *awareness* of synergies grew to *analysis,* as independent-thinking financial observers began to proclaim overpayment in the case of some major deals when APPs appeared to grossly exceed NRSs). That scrutiny continues today. If acquiring company management fail to respond effectively to suggestions from the *New York Times*' DealBook section or *FT*'s Lex column that the recent bid for the target company represents an overpayment since synergies are insufficient to offset purchase premiums, then the financial community assumes that the concern is justified.

By Diller's apparent reasoning, it is better to avoid speculation about synergies entirely if the numbers would be wild guesses. But the management team quick to make excuses for why it is impossible to develop reliable estimates of synergies reveals itself as bidding blindly if the company then remains in the acquisition chase. But voids in data necessary to estimate synergies plus the potential for wide variability in synergy estimates suggest that an argument may also be made for using multiples-based analysis to support the merger valuation analysis, as multiples-based analysis does not depend on credible estimates of future synergies from the deal:

- Similar to ES, multiples provide an *indirect* rough estimate of the subject company's worth, based primarily on share prices.
- Multiples' numerator, normalized share price, functions as a surrogate for future expected company performance under the principle of semi-strong market efficiency (SSME). The market implied competitive advantage period concept (MICAP, Mauboussin and Johnson, 1997: 70) confirms a correlation between the

company's period of economic viability, future performance in CF terms, and share price.

- While some independent equity researchers such as *Morningstar*'s Patrick Dorsey contend it is sometimes a futile effort to develop categories of companies – the critical aspect of all multiples comparative techniques – some common sense groupings are nonetheless possible based on similar characteristics, such as shared customers and products-services in the same Standard Industrial Classification (SIC) codes.
- In some circumstances, hard information is so limited that there is no practical alternative to primarily relying on multiples. When the People's Republic of China's (PRC) regulatory frameworks were still in their infancy, Chinese joint ventures considering a public offering present a case in point. In many instances, these enterprises are considered to be profitable by their owners and managers, but formal estimations of future and sometimes even past earnings and CFs could not be verified. Without use of P/R or similar multiples-based broad estimation tools, there would effectively be no means of assessing the company's future performance, or determining any merger's future success or failure.
- Even if Dorsey *is* correct in saying that categories of companies tend to be so unstable as to be a waste of time, behavioral finance proponents suggest that what is important instead is whether or not investors *believe* that comparables exist. If analysts and others believe, for example, that major pharmaceutical companies are broadly comparable despite material differences in patterns of revenue and earnings generation,[56] then behaviorists contend that belief in those categories by itself warrants considerations of such groupings.

Precedent: use of multiples as confirmation for other valuation methodologies

Multiples techniques have a long history of use as management sanity checks in merger pre-analysis and as the acquisition chase proceeds and bid levels rise. The supporting role in verifying merger valuation indications from the combined VG-IVE analysis described in this part of the chapter represents a further expansion of multiples' supportive role.

Before pursuit of a potential target even starts, industry rules-of-thumb help prevent wasting time on out-of-range prospects – at least until the seller's indicated price-to-sales ratio comes down to earth, towards something that is more buyer-friendly. As the highly-publicized acquisition chase for Target X enters its third and then fourth bidding round, price-to-free cash flow (P/FCF) histories of prior consummated deals in that industry or segment may help the bidder who is able to put rational judgment ahead of ego to avoid a possible career-ending value-destroying M&A disappointment.

Multiples' merger valuation role – confirming and validating merger value indications as first indicated using VG and IVE methods – emerges because of necessity and opportunity. *Necessity* because, as with the Chinese JV example, the absence of required analysis may otherwise render the valuation task impossible. *Opportunity* because a broadened basis of analysis is well-positioned to gain wide acceptance. Analysts or others may note the limitations of any single technique as described in this chapter: ES, TSR, VG, IVE, and multiples. And yet, it is difficult to argue against a combination of two approaches–one of which (IVE) corresponds closely to corporate valuation's two-stage DCF approach – backed by a separate multiples analysis as confirmation.

Making multiples workable as a confirming merger valuation technique or, if necessary, as a default standalone MV method

Towards the objective of confirming – and thereby, strengthening – the dual methodology VG/IVE approach, the issue is how best to exploit multiples' advantages while limiting disadvantages. Six safeguards emerge to help ensure a constructive support role for multiples in merger valuation analysis. The six constraints or adaptations include: cycle-normalized price, trend comparisons rather than spot, price/FCF as the standard form of ratio for multiples analysis, dynamic sub-categorization including SBU analysis by distinct product or service, performance and solvency adaptation of preliminary analysis, and triangulation from fundamental investigation.

1. Cycle-normalized price

Comparability is the essence of any useable multiples ratio analysis. To ensure that like is compared with like, it is important to verify that the comparison occurs at roughly the same time during the economic cycle, because of the rising tide effect noted in this book's initial chapter and historical changes in multiples indices.

It would not make any sense to compare investment bank Bear Stearns' multiple when the recession struck during the final quarter of 2008 with another bank's multiple at the peak of the cycle. At the end of 2002–8 business-merger bubble, Bear Stearns' bid-asked share price imbalance was so massive that the entire company was momentarily worth less than the real estate value of that firm's Manhattan headquarters alone, on a share bid-asked price basis.

How best to ensure that the two companies being compared are similar not only in terms of type of company, but also in terms of the timing of the comparison? Comparing firms at a similar phase in the cycle and other comparable circumstances is advisable. Such safeguards become mandatory if the multiples investigation spans more than one business cycle. If the point in the cycle is unknown, the default approach is to make the comparison at the approximate mid-point of the cycle, around the end of phase II, as described in Chapter 1.

2. Trend comparisons, rather than spot

Comparing multiples at any single point in time risks distortions in the numerator of the multiples ratio, share price, due to non-recurring and/or extraneous influences.

A single adverse earnings report, one change in senior management ranks, insider stock sales: any of these developments might create a misleading short-term share price distortion without necessarily changing the ultimate source of corporate worth, the future cash flow generation potential and actual performance of the company.

The simplest remedy to this problem also appears to be the most effective: limiting multiples comparisons to analyses over an extended period of time (eg at least 10 consecutive trading sessions) rather than on the basis of a single analysis date alone.

3. Price/free cash flow (P/FCF) as standard multiples ratio

> Groupon was able to show operations at nearly break-even in North America by deep cuts to its marketing and advertising budget, slashing it to $181 million in the third quarter, compared with the $432 million it spent in the first half of the year. But Groupon's growth also slowed considerably during the same period: its revenue rose by only 10 per cent. The previous quarter, revenue had grown 33 per cent and the quarter before that, 72 per cent.
>
> (Andrew Ross Sorkin, October 24 2011)[57]

Post-IPO price collapses of Renren (reported 72 × price-to-sales at IPO date) and volatile online couponing site Groupon (above) place a harsh light on the *least* credible form of all the multiples: price-to-revenue (P/R). The remedy for this credibility problem? Restrict multiples-based investigation to the opposite end of the spectrum, quality and credibility wise: price-to-free cash flow (P/FCF).

The low regard for P/R is richly deserved. Scores of 1996–2000 internet companies that would never become profitable were nonetheless given license to bamboozle public markets by the illusion that a fast pace of revenue growth from a miniscule base today means a new, highly profitable category leader tomorrow.

But P/R's sins go beyond that technique's role in justifying vapor valuation of neophyte companies without the means to *survive,* much less *thrive.* Management and others with an interest in 'guiding' future share price speculation quickly learn how to manipulate the numerator in R/S ratio in particular. Sales statistics can be distorted by numerous techniques, including but not limited to: pipe-filling (premature recognition of future revenues), overly optimistic per cent-completion estimations, blurring of the boundaries between one-time and recurring revenue, and several distortions relating to cash flow from operations (CFFO).[58]

In the early years of the business-merger cycle now underway, one recurring sales multiple distortion of some in the social networking class of 2011–12 is what we refer to here as the 'marketing support shell game'. Early on, as the company is first pursuing a following both in its commercial markets and on Wall Street, massive marketing outlays are made to spur top-line demand. Never mind that unsustainable expenses ensure negative earnings and CFs; the firm's market handlers insist that there is not sufficient information for P/E or even more credible multiple forms (P/CF, P/FCF) and that the historically suspect P/R must suffice. It is only later, after a speculative price has been set based on P/R multiples comparisons, that the company begins to move towards more substantive multiples – that is, those with the potential to reveal how short-term marketing overspending caused a short-term blip in revenues. Reluctantly at first, the transition is made to P/E, with corresponding return of marketing outlays back to sustainable levels.

A partial remedy for the problems associated with multiples with suspect amounts in the denominator of that ratio is reliance only on the form of multiple with the highest credibility, P/FCF or share price divided by free cash flow (or, if period investment information is unavailable, CF). In response to those who may suggest that restricting multiples analysis to such a high standard is overly restrictive as the components of FCF cannot always be discerned, the opposing argument is that for either company valuation or merger valuation purposes, perhaps a candidate disqualifies itself from consideration on a quality basis if future FCF per share cannot be credibly estimated.

4. Sub-categorization by separate business unit (SBU) distinct product-service

The easiest form of multiples comparison is between one entire publicly-traded company and another whole firm. Information on trailing P/Es is widely available, and the analyst can judge the various approaches to and arguments for devising a forward multiple based upon that data and choose the most suitable. Problem is, such simplistic one-to-one comparisons are only valid when both of the companies being compared are 'pure plays' – that is, true single core business entities and those cores are in the same segment or sub-segment (sliver).

In even highly focused companies, two or three different types of separate business unit (SBU) classifications are common. For example, eBay participates in both online auctions and online payment service segments, each SBU with its own distinct business model and value drivers. Apple is in computers, consumer electronics and online content merchandising; while Hewlett-Packard participates in four different segments based on SIC classification.[59]

For the majority of companies, a combination approach reflecting the separate businesses of the corporation is necessary. One example of such an analysis is Brochet and Weber's (2012) analysis of LinkedIn, which is based upon four separate business segments: e-commerce and subscription, software as a service, online search and advertising and online recruitment.

Comparisons based on a minimum sample size of four-plus business unit components are always preferable to a single reference point. When a single business unit is the comparable, it may be unclear whether that example company represents excellent, poor or average performance for that segment.

5. Performance and solvency adaptation of preliminary analysis

Once the results developed from business unit-level analysis are developed, the next issue is to adjust for variations from mean performance in terms of (in order of importance and thus adjustment weight): operating performance, safety and CF consistency. Safety incorporates both liquidity (working capital) and debt servicing (cash available for debt servicing, CADS). Consistency may be approximated by reference to unlevered beta variances if alternative bases for analysis are unavailable.

6. Triangulation from share price indications to estimations of fundamental worth

The Achilles' heel in all the multiples-based analyses (company- and merger-related alike) is internal/external valuation discrepancy. The remedy calls for reconciling cash flow-based performance with external (share price-based) estimations of worth, with internal CF prevailing. As this perspective and approach represents the opposite of the Mauboussin-Johnson 1997 MICAP method, we sometimes refer to this adjustment technique as triangulation or, alternatively, operations defined competitive advantage period, or ODCAP.

While the SSME theory holds that share price-based influenced market value of equity (MVE)[60] equals value based on the combination of the present and future operations-based worth of that enterprise, Fox (2009) reminds us that departures from rational markets are today becoming so frequent that a case can be made for new approaches.

The consequences of failing to make such adjustments are a matter of historical record. The first dot com bubble in 1996–2000 saw multiples-based techniques used to justify outsized IPOs for merely average companies, until those owners discovered *after* investing their money that the business and operational concepts for the 'can't miss' internet concept company had never been thoroughly developed, and that companies were worth far less than their early price hype suggested.

Massive mortgage originations during the third post-1980 wave (2002–8) raised the paper valuations of companies that seemed to have discovered a new source of value; more somber assessments – along with much lower share prices – followed in 2007 and later as the operational CF realities of the broken subprime business model began to become apparent. While rational market theory and SSME presume that external value (reflected in share prices) and internal value (operations-based) are identical, the latter prevails.

A speculative share price can and sometimes is devised for a valueless shell of a company based on hype, misapplications of multiples techniques and similar short-term duplicities. However, if the company generates consistent cash flows net of investment such that return exceeds that company's

TABLE 3.10 Reconciling share price with business fundamentals: Vodafone analysis by Mills Clark's VRQ method, v02.06

Forward VRQ-VOQ Model, Vodafone February 26 2006								
Vodafone Group Plc					**Analyzed price (Feb 2006): 122.5p**			
TVP	FY ends: 31.3							
£M	Feb-06	TVP1	TVP2	TVP3	TVP4	TVP5	TVP6	TVP7
		FY07	FY08	FY09	FY10	FY11	FY12	FY13
MARKET CAPa	70757		12264	16156.58	9696.8	2531.2	3368.3	5419.5
P/CF proj SG		6.3	6					
FCF SG - Note e		7067	7848	6820.28666	5927.154705	5150.980398	4476.447871	3890.246904
TOT ASSTS SG		98807	85868	74623.3913	64851.28952	56358.86657	48978.54559	42564.69433
CF / TA		0.071523273	0.0913960	0.091396096	0.091396096	0.091396096	0.091396096	0.091396096
Tot assts chg			0.8690477	0.86904774	0.86904774	0.86904774	0.86904774	0.86904774

TABLE 3.10 *continued*

WACC @ 10.5%		0.105	0.105	0.105	0.105	0.105	0.105	0.105
Combined CF		0.895	0.801025	0.716917375	0.641641051	0.57426874	0.513970523	0.460003618
DCF		6324.965	6286.4442	4889.582009	3803.105772	2958.047025	2300.762252	1789.527649
CUM		28352.43391						
	Assets	Pct appr	Infl	Addit	Adj Sum	Factor	RV	
RV	42,565	0.25	0.02	12223.36358	54,788	0.460003618	25202.70485	
	Bus Val b	Mkt Sec c	MV Debt d	Strat Val b				
SV analysis	53555.13875	3,769	15,193	42,131	Sum of disc value FCFs, RV			
AMC	74083.18376			74,083	MV adj for assumed £122.5/sh. Price			
Shortfall				31,952				
VRQ%	**43.13%**			0.4313				

NOTES: Reflects version of Gordon and Shapiro (1956), with residual assumed value in distant future years in place of perpetuity assumption. (a) Per Yahoo! finance February 26, 2006, based on closing price of 117p on February 24; (b) Business value per Mills (1998), 36: market capitalization (MC) minus market value of debt (MVD); (c) Cash or equivalent £3.79bn per end of prior fiscal year; (d) Sum of BV of LT debt (£13.19bn) plus current portion LTD (£2.003bn) as of end of prior FY; (e) SocGen projections for Vodafone of December 14, 2005 for TV period Years 1, 2, derived thereafter.

capital cost, share price (external) will always eventually reflect that internal engine of value.

'Triangulation' refers here to the process of testing and verifying the share price indications that emerge from multiples-based company share price indications to ensure consistency with value, as reflected by share price generation. The two are not always the same, and not just in periods of market mania, when clearly discernible buyers' or sellers' panics are occurring. In the 2006 Mills-Clark value risk quotient (VRQ) 2006 illustration of Vodafone, forward projections of CFs were based on conservative forecasts and the company's prevailing investment and expense-control patterns. At that time, and on the basis of management of the firm on comparable basis, the resulting analysis suggested that the share price appeared vulnerable by about 43 per cent, reflecting the disparity at that time between defensible CF internal generation and share price.[61]

In articulating their MICAP concept, Mauboussin and Johnson (1997) suggest that the market value of the company as reflected in the company's share price perfectly relates to the *combination* of that firm's two internal value elements, the subject company's remaining period of economic viability based on the competitive advantage period (CAP) criteria,[62] *and* cash flow performance over that period.

Mauboussin and Johnson's emphasis in their seminal paper is on the duration aspect of that internal value equivalence: the CAP economic lifespan. In that approach, company future cash flows and investment requirements are set, based on prevailing analyst forecasts. Next, the number of future periods is 'solved', by determining the number of future periods of CF generation necessary to reconcile internal worth with external value. But it is the solution *not* pursued by Mauboussin and Johnson that suggests a triangulation opportunity to help verify multiples-based secondary valuation results: solving for the missing CFs, while treating the CAP as fixed.

Despite the valuation calculation convenience of presuming that companies exist in perpetuity in Gordon and Shapiro's (1956) equation, today commonly referred to as the continuous value formula, no one including those authors actually believe that companies continue indefinitely.[63] Instead, credible ranges of real-world company economic lifespans may be accurately estimated based on patterns of historical company longevity from dozens of studies, combined with CFROI/WACC patterns and the time lag between the time that the 1.0 threshold is broached and company collapse (Clark, 2010b: 66–93, 192–3).

Assuming that a credible upper end range for expected longevity can be determined (the maximum end of the range is generally utilized), the focus of the MICAP solution can instead turn to the issue of the other component, the company's free cash flows. Developing forward estimates of investment critical to remain competitive, plus cash flows, and based on recent performance adjusted for significant changes in operational effectiveness and strategy, provides an operations-defined basis for value results. To the extent that the calculation differs from market value of equity (market capitalization minus market value of debt) such as in the preliminary value risk quotient (VRQ) analysis as approximated in Table 3.10, this may suggest adjustments to multiples-based support analysis methods.

Notes

1 See also Chapter 2 on the use of multiples-based techniques in merger valuations.

2 Refer to Further Reading.

3 The *strategic deal* explanation can be among the most value-destructive of excuses for mergers that never should have happened. The 'strategic' adjective implies dynamism, with the unspoken implication of courage to take a prudent chance. What this self-deluding acquirer fails to admit is that he or she is out there and dabbling in areas that are scarcely understood. In 1999, advisers to wannabe acquirer Unum Insurance convinced management that purchase of another disability-related insurance firm, Provident, would be a prudent *strategic* deal. But each firm operated in different and unrelated parts of that insurance segment, resulting in *negative* synergies after that deal's close (from Carroll and Mui 2009: 17–20).

4 If growth by merger is considered in a theoretical sense only, with no criticism of past failed mergers in the conversation, the chances of a positive response are enhanced. Executives tend to keep their options open, especially if there are no failure consequences.

5 'The operating performance of companies involved in the UK retailing sector, 1977–1992', in Cooper and Gregory (2003) *Advances in Mergers and Acquisitions Vol 2. Lose the acquisition game.* Amsterdam, JAI Elsevier Science. Phrases in parentheses added by book's authors.

6 *Journal of Management Studies,* 29: 2, Mar.

7 The owners of the business do not themselves provide the risk capital. But make no mistake: the acquiring company's shareholders bear the risk of the deal.

8 Interpretation by independent party is necessary as shareholders are diffuse and primarily express their opinions by either selling or retaining share

ownership. Stirring scenes in movies such as *Wall Street* and *Other People's Money* when shareholders arise en masse to assert their essential interest in returns are rare, even in today's era of increased shareholder activism.

9 TSR remains a popular method for use by non-trade acquirers who intend to own the target company for only a short- to intermediate-term duration. The WACC applied in many of these deals is the financial acquirer's own cost of capital; that cost of capital approach differs from the WACC calculation used for the incremental value effect (IVE) method, as described elsewhere in this chapter.

10 Lehn and Zhao (2006) 'CEO turnover after acquisitions: are bad bidders fired?' *Journal of Finance,* 61:4, 1760; Carroll and Mui (2009: 27–8).

11 Carroll and Mui (2009: 18).

12 Sirower (1997: 34–5).

13 Wang, X (Sept 23 2011). 'Leo Apotheker's 11-month rise and fall as CEO of Hewlett-Packard: Timeline', *Bloomberg.* http://www.bloomberg.com/news/2011-09-23/leo-apotheker-s-11-month-rise-and-fall-as-ceo-of-hewlett-packard-timeline.html. Accessed Sept 23 2011.

14 'Measuring the performance of acquisitions: an empirical investigation using multiple criteria', *British Journal of Management*, 21. Authors refer to prior research by Zollo and Singh (Zollo, M and Singh, H (2004) 'Deliberate learning in corporate acquisitions: post-acquisition strategies and integration capability in US bank mergers', *Strategic Management Journal*, 25 (13), pp 1233–56).

15 It is often presumed that the answer to the question 'What is the target company worth?' is identical for all potential acquirers. But synergy program scope and PMI ability differs widely among different bidders, and one firm's achievable synergy is not always the same as its rivals. Thus by necessity, the full answer to the question above is: 'it all depends on who the acquirer is'.

16 There is no such thing as a control case for what the acquiring company's share price might have been, without the deal but with all of the other post-announcement events that potentially swing share price.

17 A somewhat similar situation exists today with the continuous value formula ('Gordon Formula', Gordon and Shapiro, 1956). The assumption of an infinite analysis time span (t) for terminal value (TV) estimation provides calculation simplicity but sometimes at the cost of wildly inaccurate TV estimates when combined with untenable FCF growth (g) assumptions, as noted in Clark, 2010b; Copeland *et al*, 1990: 208; Fruhan, 1998: 2–3; Mauboussin, 2007 (refer to Further Reading), 11; Mills, 1998: 83–9 and 2005: 73.

18 By contrast, both of those two critical elements to M&A success *are* visible in the competing value gap (VG) and incremental value effect (IVE) merger valuation methodologies.

19 TSR is alternatively known as 'total returns to shareholders' or TRS. Differences between the small block share purchaser and the corporate acquirer of the entire target company are two-fold: 1) the total company acquirer controls operations of the company while the buyer of a minority shares in the target does not; and 2) the corporate acquirer almost always pays a control premium above full market share price of the firm prior to announcement (acquisition purchase premium, APP).

20 While in theory TSR might be calculated to also reflect companies that remain in the acquirer's portfolio based on dividend returns plus change in market capitalization calculated on a phantom sale basis (requiring estimation of sale proceeds from a hypothetical sale), we have yet to encounter such a variation except among a few venture capital firms. Such a phantom sale variant is not included in the list of possible TSR variants in Table 3.4.

21 'Distribution of incomes of corporations among dividends, retained earnings, and taxes', *American Economic Review*, May, 97–113. The emphasis on dividends as a surrogate for company earnings performance raises a logical question: 'Instead of a surrogate, why not determine company worth on the basis on the ultimate source of that value: the firm's projected CFS discounted by analyzed WACC rate?'

22 The top professionals and value-creators in that industry, 'corporate key contributors' as described in Chapter 7, avoid the troubled company like the plague unless perhaps they have a short-term lucrative project. Arbitrary caps on staffing and investment ensure that the new combined firm is viewed as an unattractive place to work by top talent.

23 'Business valuation and the cost of capital', Case 9-210-037, Boston, Harvard Business School Publishing. Determining the correct opportunity cost reference rate for MV purposes when there are several possibilities involves consideration of factors beyond face rate. Timing and risk are also considerations. Even when the best possible reference opportunity cost is determined, two key differences persist: a) the amount of that comparative investment opportunity is almost always a small fraction of the M&A investment alternative, and b) the merger investment almost always involves a purchase premium (APP), while there are normally no such premiums in the case of opportunity costs.

24 In a predecessor study, also based upon McKinsey & Co research, Magnet (Nov 12 1984) compared TSR-type merger returns to commercial bank certificate of deposit rates in determining deal success or failure. Results were comparable to Coley and Reinton's: 'Over two-thirds of the corporate diversification programs it examined never earned as much as the acquirer would have by investing the money in, say, certificates of deposit issued by a bank.' 'Acquiring without smothering', *Fortune*, 22–8.

25 Lehn and Zhao (2006) 'CEO turnover after acquisitions: are bad bidders fired?' *Journal of Finance*, 61:4, 1760.

26 *Journal of Finance*, 47:1, 107.

27 The method is referred to here as 'value gap' because of growing use of that term by merger practitioners, principals and others to describe the circumstance of an apparent disparity between the amount paid over the target's pre-announcement share price (see Appendix A) and present value (PV) of realizable post-merger synergies. However, the phrase is not universally applied to such analyses.

28 As described in numerous forms, including Alrey, D *et al* (2003) 'DaimlerChrysler post-merger news', Case 903M49, London, Ontario, Richard Ivey School of Business, The University of Western Ontario.

29 Clark, P (Jan 15 2000) 'AOL TWX', *Motley Fool.*

30 Sum of realistically realizable synergies of all four categories (Chapter 7: expense-, revenue-, financial- and management-synergies), including consideration of timing and offsets, discounted at the post-merger combined firm's projected WACC.

31 Chassany, A-S (Jan 7 2011) 'Guy Hands reaped $19 million dividend from Terra Firma in 2010', *Bloomberg*, http://noir.bloomberg.com/apps/news?pid=20601087&sid=arl2VlNf62cw&pos=4#. Accessed Jan 7 2011.

32 'Behind the woes at H.P., Wall St banks lurk', DealBook, http://dealbook.nytimes.com/2011/11/07/as-h-p-shops-its-bankers-do-very-nicely/?nl=business&emc=dlbka23. Accessed Nov 8 2011. Words in parentheses added by this book's authors based upon interpretation of the article's context.

33 Par and Autonomy are both also cited as examples of the 'Good company bad price' (GCBP) value-destroying acquisition in this chapter.

34 Menn, J (Sep 22 2011) 'HP rises over talk about Apotheker successor', *Financial Times*, http://www.ft.com/cms/s/2/4e268022-e472-11e0-92a3-00144feabdc0.html?ftcamp=rss&ftcamp=crm/email/2011922/nbe/GlobalBusiness/product#axzz1YJBzycDZ. Accessed Sep 22 2011.

35 For example, MI (merger integration) cores 1–4 are examined in pages 130–264 of Clark (1991).

36 *Total* acquisition purchase premium (TAPP, Appendix A) increases at an even more dramatic rate, as the TAPP percentage is based on beginning-of-cycle company price levels.

37 'Competitive bidding in high-risk situations', *Journal of Petroleum Technology*, 23:6, 641–53. The word in parentheses, 'target' is added by this book's authors, replacing 'parcel'. Capen's work endures as a frequently cited illustration of 'winner's remorse' – the mis-purchase situation that arises when high bidder 'wins' the deal by overpaying and later regrets that error, which destroys value for his or her (the acquiring company's) shareholders.

38 The key phrase here is 'is available to' shareholders of the acquiring firm, hence the italics. Our experience is that any such 'excess' synergies are a) often claimed by the acquiring company management as their bonus and that b) the synergy-to-APP differential decreases significantly or disappears years later when actual synergies are calculated, two years or so after the beginning of the post-merger period.

39 The issue of pre-close sources of reliable synergy intelligence is addressed in Chapter 8 in conjunction with Figure 8.1.

40 Regarding the negative synergy effect from incompatible distribution systems at Quaker Oats (acquirer) and Snapple (acquiree) refer to Martinson, O (2002) 'Shopping for bargain-priced companies? Avoid asset impairment traps', *Journal of Corporate Accounting and Finance*, 13:3, Mar–Apr, 63–70.

41 ABN Amro (pursuers: RBS/Fortis, Barclays) and 3Par (pursuers: Hewlett-Packard, Dell) are among the more conspicuous acquisition chases to value destruction since the mid-2000s. Even assuming that 3Par is successful in its field, H-P's gross overbid arguably mortgages future worth from that acquisition.

42 'Most takeovers since 2007 seen spurred by data torrent: Tech,' Bloomberg.com. http://www.bloomberg.com/news/2012-02-06/most-takeovers-since- 2007-seen-spurred-by-data-torrent-tech.html. Accessed Feb 17 2012.

43 Reece, D (Feb 7 2011) 'AOL shareholders are right to be in a huff over $315m website purchase', *Telegraph* (London). http://www.telegraph.co.uk/finance/comment/damianreece/8309579/AOL-shareholders-are-right-to-be-in-a-Huff-over-315m-website-purchase.html. Accessed Feb 8 2011.

44 Parentheses in the original. 'Creating value through merger and acquisition integration', in Cooper and Gregory, *Advances in Mergers and Acquisitions Vol. 2: Lose the acquisition game*, Amsterdam, JAI Elsevier Science. 'Bruner *et al*, 1998' refers to 'Best practices in estimating the cost of capital: survey and synthesis', *Financial Practice and Education*, Spring–Summer, 13–28.

45 The ultimate way to test the usefulness of ES methods as indicators of merger valuation success is to compare the results from that approach with other decisive indicators of merger success or failure. Divestitures at a loss (Terra Firma/EMI, AT&T/NCR), significant APP-S value gaps (H-P/Autonomy, AOL/Huffington Press) and/or write-downs (Terra Firma/EMI, H-P/Palm OS) are all possible bases.

46–50 Refer to Further Reading.

51 In 2001, Penman dismisses forward company CF projections as 'voodoo accounting'. Penman, S (2001) 'On comparing cash flow and accrual accounting methods for use in equity valuation: a response to Lundholm and O'Keefe', *Contemporary Accounting Research*, 18:4, 681–92, Winter.

52 Refer to Further Reading.

53 'LinkedIn puts slip to record low as Facebook IPO lures back bulls: options', http://www.bloomberg.com/news/2012-02-15/linkedin-puts-slip-to-record-low-as-facebook-ipo-lures-back-bulls-options.html. Accessed Feb 15 2012.

54 Such situations may necessitate an approach described by co-author Mills as 'fundamental multiples': developing the analysis on a two-stage DCF model basis (Mills, 2005), with subsequent translation into the corresponding multiples.

55 For example, in Clark 1991: 155–74 and 189–202.

56 Clark and Neill (2004) 'New value challenges in the global pharmaceuticals industry', *The Economist* Sixth Annual Global Pharmaceuticals Conference, Shanghai, 8.

57 'Groupon's latest value raises doubt', DealBook, *New York Times*, http://dealbook.nytimes.com/2011/10/24/groupons-latest-value-raises-doubt/. Accessed Oct 25 2011.

58 Some examples of such CFFO distortions include: reporting the proceeds of a loan as operating revenue; mislabeling net interest income as operating income by a non-financial company; and treating proceeds from sale of investments or other assets as ordinary revenue.

59 The March 19 2012 announcement that H-P plans to combine its printer and computer units does not alter the company's diversity based on (SIC) code.

60 Market capitalization (share price times shares outstanding) minus market value of debt (MVD).

61 As of March 20 2012, share price on comparable basis was 170.8p, compared to 122.5 in Table 3.10 as of early February 2006, reflecting change in management as well as significant improvements in both expense controls and new investment philosophy.

62 The end point of CAP is defined by Mauboussin and Johnson as when cash flow return on investment (CFROI) equals analyzed WACC. The CAP persists for as long as the analyzed company's CFROI rate exceeds its WACC rate.

63 The perpetuity assumption is viewed by the continuous value formula's creators as a calculation short-cut: 'It is mathematically convenient to assume that the dividend is paid and discounted at annual rates' (1956: 105).

04 Merger segmentation comes of age

Differences between types of acquisitions may, however, be an important factor in determining which deals are likely to work...

(Pautler, 2003: 13)[1]

Intensified analysis of the causes and consequences of acquisition failure has produced knowledge about what can be done to make acquisitions succeed. This knowledge has been translated into new tools and techniques which may be applied to increase the chances of success...

(Clark, 1991: 7)

CHAPTER CONTENTS

4.1 The case for segmentation by merger type: precedent

4.2 Four categories, nine merger types: different deal types mean different M&A success

4.3 Applying the nine merger type framework

4.4 The path forward in merger segmentation: towards M-Score[2]

No viable marketing strategy calls for pursuing *all* possible opportunities simultaneously, as such scatter-shooting represents a sure path to commercial ruin. So how come it has taken more than half a century for M&A target diagnosis to catch up with Wendell Smith (1956), the pioneer of modern segmentation analysis?

4.1 The case for segmentation by merger type: precedent

Peeling the onion: looking beyond the overall finding that most mergers fail (MMF)

> Segmentation tends to produce depth of market position in the segments that are effectively defined and penetrated.
>
> (Smith, 1956: 5)

Most mergers fail. That recurring headline in articles and research papers is widely-accepted today and substantially supported.[3] To most, MMF is reality, not merely conventional wisdom[4] although a dwindling number of doubters still disagree. But how instructive is the perceived reality of MMF?

The great majority of restaurants fail (Parsa *et al*, 2005) but that doesn't discourage entrepreneurs from dreaming up ideas for new bistros each season. Similarly, the urge to merge is irrepressible, continuing despite acquirers' past merger performance history, for reasons including those described in this book in Chapters 1 and 5. You might as well try to command the ocean's tide to stop as try to suppress gold rush-like enthusiasm for the next new merger wave, arising every 10 years or so.

So what explains the persistence of failed deal behavior despite wide acceptance of MMF? Some excuses are explored in the next chapter, including poor learning from past deal failures (Tuch and O'Sullivan, 2007: 165) and acquiring company chief executive hubris (Morck *et al*, 1990; Roll, 1986). Failure to anticipate cultural differences contributed to post-merger meltdowns at DaimlerChrysler, AOL TimeWarner and PennCentral. But a more fundamental explanation for merger misery is the past absence of effective segmentation frameworks for evaluating, qualifying, and classifying candidate merger opportunities. Without such frameworks, acquisition-oriented operating companies are potential victims for every instant M&A fad imagined by merger pundits and brokers.

A relentless urge to merge arises from within the aspiring acquirer's organization. A gaggle of minions scramble to uncover something, anything that might impress their merger-hungry boss. The would-be acquiring firm's house investment banker brushes the dust off a few companies known to be on the block for years and then presents that company to *their* customer, hoping that the obvious first due diligence question is missed regarding such overlooked firms: 'Why have so many other prospective acquirers passed on these firms before now?'[5]

Without a merger segmentation capability to serve as a sextant for its acquisition program, the acquirer's M&A program is adrift, directionless. The CEO of the operating firm pursuing external growth through acquisition imagines that he or she is in control, and the adviser-banker steering the process towards a completed deal takes care not to pierce this self-delusion. But make no mistake: the acquiring company that is steered by other firms with base objectives and business models that differ from theirs (see Chapter 1) sets itself up for M&A mediocrity and sometimes, failure.

For the operating company acquirer, a basic question arises and demands an answer: 'What is the alternative to a process which too often results in the company being sold damaged goods or paying far too much for the "strategic" acquisition that turns out to be little more than a temporary fad, valueless after a few years?' The starting point to developing an answer lies in the aspiring acquiring company's development of its own merger segmentation framework. Some characteristics of that resource are described in the rest of this chapter.

A merger segmentation re-perspective on Coley and Reinton's (1988) primary findings

Could segmentation be effectively applied to M&A? Yes, that progression has already begun.

Figure 4.1 revisits the four quadrant detail from Coley and Reinton's research into 116 merger transactions, as introduced in Chapter 3. While they indicate that only 32 to 39 per cent of all deals that they studied succeed in *overall* terms[6] that level of deal success is lower than in subsets in the sample as defined by: high levels of relatedness, referring to a target company which is in an industry or segment either very similar or identical to the acquirer's; and smaller size, interpreted here occurring when annualized revenues of the target firm are less than sales of the acquiring company. In Figure 4.1, that improvement in M&A success performance is depicted in terms of the transition from quadrant A (14 per cent of deals successful) to quadrant C (45 per cent success level).

FIGURE 4.1 Revisiting Coley and Reinton 1988: simple steps towards merger performance improvement

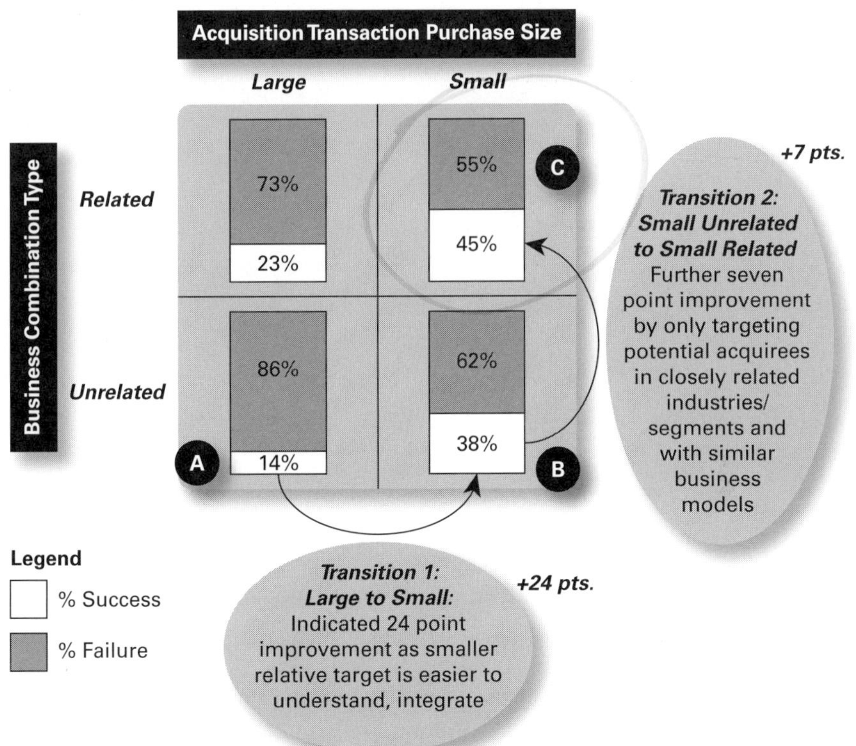

Related Figure: 3.1. Derived from statistics in Coley and Reinton, 1988, 29–30.

A to B: 24 point improvement

Quadrant A represents the starting point of this sequence. Acquired target companies in quadrant A are all a) larger than the acquiring firm on an annualized revenue basis, and b) operate in business segments that are unrelated to those of the ultimate buyer. As a consequence, Coley and Reinton analyzed M&A success at only 14 per cent for this subset of their overall sample.[7]

But alter just one targeting-relevant variable – relative revenue size of target company to the acquiring firm – and acquisition performance improves significantly. If the acquiring firm's selection strategies are modified to include only those targets that are smaller than the acquirer, then the merger success rate improves by 24 percentage points (B). There are several explanations for such a dramatic improvement, including:

- A smaller target is generally less complex and therefore faster and easier for the acquiring company to integrate.
- Management at the acquiring company are less likely to be distracted by the diverse operations of a large, unwieldy acquiree and are thus more likely to concentrate on synergy improvements in their own core business areas, which are well-understood.
- Where functions, departments and projects overlap, there is almost no debating about which of the two companies' (acquirer or target) operations survive. Unless the (smaller) target company's solution is demonstrably superior to that in the acquiring firm, the default option is always to stick to the acquiring company's incumbent practice.

B to C: further 7 point increase in merger success probability

Other changes move the success percentage higher still. In the transition from B to C, the difference is relatedness, as defined above. Pursue only targets that are in the same or nearly same industry based on Standard Industrial Classification (SIC) code classification or similar, and the M&A success rate rises still higher. A primary reason is that such an acquirer tends to be more knowledgeable about the true keys to value development success for that target firm as well as the pitfalls and dangers of competing in that industry or segment; arguably, *that* buyer is less likely to either overpay for the deal and/or miss imminent danger signs. As Flanagan and O'Shaughnessy (2003: 573) declare:

> Core-relatedness and multiple bidders on premiums paid in 285 tender offers for US-based manufacturing firms... The presence of multiple bidders is found to have a greater impact on... premiums when the eventual acquirer is not core-related to the target.

A company primarily involved in online auctions (eg eBay) achieves merger success when the target is in a closely-related field, such as online payments (eg PayPal). *New York Times*' perspective on eBay's other major acquisition of the 2000s, for Voice Over Internet Protocol (VoIP) carrier Skype, is pointedly different: 'eBay has had a mixed record in acquisitions – while PayPal has been a success the company sold Skype in 2009 after it failed to gain much traction with eBay users.'[8]

TABLE 4.1 Towards a merger segmentation framework: some related investigation

Dimension	Research	Merger Success-related Considerations
Relatedness	Harding & Rovit (2004)[9] Bouwman *et al* (2003) Limmack (2003)[10] Fan & Lang (2000)[11] Lang & Stultz (1994)[12] Kaplan & Weisbach (1992) Coley & Reinton (1988)	• Level of understanding of value drivers in target • Naïve expansionism • Superfluous supervisory • Speed-to-market, loss of CKCs[a]
Relative size	Rehm *et al* (2012)[13] Hayward (2002) Azofra *et al* (2007) Loughran & Vigh (1997)[14] Kumar (1997)[15] AMJ[b] (1992) Coley & Reinton (1988) Palepu (1986) and Montgomery[16] Singh[17] (1975)	• Early focus on primary PMI opportunities • Resolution of conflicts • Facilitation of disposals • Other PMI implementation issues
Horizontal vs vertical (see Relatedness)	Tichy (2001) Pautler (2001)[18] Ingham *et al* (1992)	• Scale economies vs market adventurism • Intra-industry differences underestimated • Preferred supplier may be superior to captive • Value development of secondary business • Misdirection of investment priorities • Possible regulatory threat
Location: Domestic vs int'l.	DAG[c] (2009) Houston & Ryngaert (1994)[19]	• Grass-is-greener misanalysis • Oblivious to differences: business practice, culture • Logistics, costs, supervisory • Confusing participation with sustainable mkt. share

TABLE 4.1 *continued*

Dimension	Research	Merger Success-related Considerations
APP1: Over-payment (see Timing in cycle)	DAG (2009) Azofra *et al* (2007) AMS[d] (2001, 2002) Gondhaeler *et al* (2002)[20] Holt & Sherman (1984)[e] Bazerman & Samuelson (1983)[e]	• Absolute APP ceilings relating to merger success • Relationship of APP to synergies (S) • Bid cycles, bid participants • Chronic overbids and the desperate acquirer
APP2: 'Hostility'-related	AMS[d] (2001, 2002) Schwert (2000) Franks & Mayer (1996)[21] Hirshleifer & Titman (1990)[22]	• Role of target's countermeasures in boosting APP • As signal of expectations about necessary APP
Timing in cycle (phase; also see APP1)	Rhodes-Kropf & Viswanathan (2004)[23] Clark (1991)	Early phase: Low APP vs low financing Factors causing higher APP ranges in Phases III, IV Collapse of industry fundamentals: Mid Phase IV+ Late Phase IV: Withdrawal of M&A financing

NOTES: [a]:Corporate key contributors (see Chapter 7); [b]: Agrawal, Jaffee and Mandelker; [c]: Diaz, Azofra and Gutierrez; [d]: Andrade, Mitchell and Stafford; [e]: Relating to Winner's Remorse.

M&A segmentation antecedents

Table 4.1 identifies seven dimensions of merger research into target company differences, including the two – relatedness and size – addressed by Coley and Reinton.

Dimension: relatedness[24]

> There is also the possibility that diversifying into businesses that the acquiring firm has little expertise in can result in less efficient operations after the merger

> (reverse synergy). Lang and Stulz (1994) present evidence that firms that are in multiple businesses trade at a discount of between 5 and 10 per cent on individual firm values and attribute this to a diversification discount.
>
> (Damodaran, 2005: 22)[25]

> Studies focusing on the type of acquisition find that... diversification tends to destroy value, whereas focus conserves it.
>
> (Bouwman *et al*, 2003: 9–10)

The unrelated business tends to be at best incompletely understood by management at the acquiring company. A consequence is merger value destruction as an eager but under-informed buyer operates blindly. Azofra *et al* (2007: 5) group business type diversification with geographic diversification (another dimension in Table 4.1) as related threats to merger success: 'M&As leading to diversification, be it geographically or by activity, tend to have worse results than those that lead to concentration.'

Divestments of recent deals arise as yet another confirming indicator that MMF, since most acquirers are unwilling to absorb a merger mistake: the disappointing acquisition uses up company funds that almost assuredly could be put to more productive use. More important, *that* merger mistake was committed by management past; the new CEO finds it useful to extend the honeymoon period for his or her own regime by dumping his or her predecessor's mistake, providing license to pursue his or her own, hopefully more successful, business combinations.

Kaplan and Weisbach (1992: 107) indicate that a third to half of all divestments result from former business combinations judged by the acquirer as unsuccessful. According to Kaplan and Weisbach, lack of relatedness between merger partners materially increases the incidence of subsequent disposals or spin-offs:

> Divestitures are almost four times more likely when targets are not in businesses highly related to those of the acquirer (ie, the four most important lines of business of the acquirer and target do not have at least one three-digit SIC industry code in common). (p 109)

The buying firm likely claims that it has already anticipated this problem at least in part, by ensuring that top management from the acquired firm are under contract as continuing contributors – or at least advisers – to the post-merger combined firm. It is true that retention of acquired management does emerge as an important consideration in post-merger success, particularly when relatedness is minimal. But to consider such a single-dimensional tactic as a solution for the problem of unrelatedness is an overstatement.

Acquired execs from the target company have become rich from the deal, and are unlikely to be available for longer than a couple of years. That 'solution' adds expenses in the form of duplicate management at the most expensive upper rungs of the corporation, total compensation wise. Speed-to-market is likely impaired compared to independent rivals, thanks to a denser bureaucracy and slower decision processes.

If the acquiring company imposes suffocating controls ('that's not the way we do things here') the victim is likely to be market innovation: an important part of what made the target attractive in the first place. Some value-creation star talent (referred to as 'corporate key contributors' in Chapter 7) leave to join the competition as soon as the non-compete provisions in their contracts permit.

Cyriac *et al*'s (2012) analysis correlates the degree of diversification in the company's basic business with returns. Utilizing TRS (TSR, merger valuation methodology from Chapter 3) method, the authors note an especially damaging characteristic of extreme diversification as shown in Table 4.1: ceilings on achievable positives combined with possible significant chance of loss.

The more focused the company, the more moderate those extremes. The authors' TRS profile for what they refer to as 'moderately diversified companies' is almost identical to that for 'focused companies'. While limiting the firm to one SIC code likely stifles growth by providing insufficient scope for profit and value growth, a two-core company business structure still tends to be valued by the financial community as *focused.*

Another important aspect of the relatedness dimension not considered by either Coley and Reinton or others is whether the business model of acquirer and acquiree – how we make money – conflict.[26] This aspect of the relatedness dimension is considerably more elusive than mere differences in the business classification as defined by SIC code. Acquiring and acquiree (target) companies may share the same SIC code and yet be entirely different enterprises on a *business* model basis, reducing the prospects of merger success.

Airlines

On paper, it may make sense for the airline holding company to include both a high volume discount fare airline division (to compete better with the industry leader, Southwest) in its company portfolio along with traditional operators. But as British Airways[27] and some other traditional carriers have painfully learned, bolting on an airline with a completely different operating philosophy and cost structure often fails.

Consumer versus business banking

Tired of the extreme cyclicality of consumer banking, Citicorp actively sought acquisitions in corporate banking for years, before being acquired itself by Travelers. A successful consumer bank does not necessarily mean a successful investment bank, as Citigroup's difficulties during wave 3 (the subprime-derivatives bubble) attest.

Further examples

Other business model mis-combination examples include mergers stock brokerage and consumer retailing (Henry, 2002)[28] and insurance: Carroll and Mui (2009: 17) describe Unum Insurance's $5 billion acquisition of Provident Insurance in 1999 as another example of the importance of the business model considerations. Both firms were major providers of disability insurance, a surface similarity that encouraged some analysts to initially praise the combination. But those early observers did not look adequately at the critical *differences* in the two firms' business models: Unum sells only to corporations, whereas Provident sells only to individuals. That key difference impacts everything from sales approach and type of salesperson required, to underwriting approaches and claims procedures. What was different in the acquirer's and acquiree's business models? In a word, everything. Buying firm Unum was already aware of the threat of these business model differences to deal success from its own experience, as the acquiring firm in the Unum-Provident deal had previously tried to enter the individual part of the business but then quickly withdrew when that experiment failed.

Dimension: relative size of intended merger partners

The notion of relative revenue size differences between acquirer and target as a key consideration in merger segmentation originates from tactics for dealing with hostile acquisitions. As Trimbath (2002: 45) observes:

> Several authors have reported size as a significant determinant of the probability of takeover. Singh (1975) suggested that, in theory, above a certain minimum industry adjusted size-class, all-firms can reduce the probability of acquisition... provided that they achieve a significant increase in their relative size. This idea was carried forward by Palepu (1986).[29]

Particularly when and if the target and unwanted pursuer and target are both in the same or similar industry or segment (relatedness, above), the possibility of regulatory opposition increases on the basis of perceived market control or unfair trade conditions.

Azofra *et al* (2007: 5) are among those who turn this negative (from acquirers' perspective) into a positive by describing the advantages of pursuing target companies that are much smaller: 'Those operations in which the size of the acquiring company is much greater than the acquired company's also show greater returns.' When the acquiring firm is much larger than its prey, the envisioned result is improved focus on what the buying firm hopes to achieve from the merger. The target of manageable size and complexity is evaluated on a future expense and revenue basis by its buyer. Opportunities arise for the most promising improvements (synergies) to be carefully assessed, ideally resulting in a synergy-informed target bidding approach.

In the opposite situation, when little acquires big such as AOL/TimeWarner (2000) or Conseco/Green Tree (1986), it is clear to all but the buying company's CEO that the acquirer has taken on more than it can handle. Six months after the transaction's closing ceremony, and the acquirer still has an inadequate understanding of the critical operating and strategic nuances of its trophy acquisition's business.

As the name specifies, in an equal-to-equal combination, both principals are approximately the same size. But such marriages of equals sometimes turn out worse than even little-acquiring-big combinations. The acquirer's intention is that referring to 'equals' reduces anxieties among staff in the newly-acquired firm. But that effect is more than offset by chaos in the post-merger integration program. With no firm seemingly designated as dominant, turf-protection battles arise almost everywhere that operations of the acquiring company and the target overlap. PMI progress slows to a snail's pace, and time runs out for securing some of the most important synergy improvements. Eventually there must be an embarrassing reversal on the 'marriage of equals' misstatement for PMI to succeed. This painful lesson was learnt at AT&T following its 1990 acquisition of NCR, and at Daimler-Benz following its 1988 purchase of Chrysler.

Dimension: horizontal merger versus vertical merger

A horizontal merger refers to two companies in the same part of the business while a vertical merger seeks to achieve vertical integration with the acquirer having all – or at least more – control of the commercial sequence from origination to delivery, such as Disney acquiring content developer Pixar.

Tichy (2001: 347) reflects the dominant consensus about the relative attractiveness of the two different types when he says that, 'Horizontal mergers fare best, especially if they are focus-increasing.' Ingram *et al* (1992) examine reasons underlying the sense that horizontal business combinations are more successful than vertical combinations. Horizontals are: 'agreeable due to the belief that economies of scale and increased market power were unambiguously linked to superior performance'. By contrast, vertical acquisitions are depicted by the authors in far less positive terms, as a means of avoiding 'market failure' (p 197).

An offsetting consideration in horizontal mergers is noted by Betton *et al* (2008: 123) – the possible specter of increased regulatory scrutiny based on some interpretations of market shares and market influence: 'A horizontal merger causes a measurable increase in industry concentration (equal to twice the product of the market shares of the bidder and target when using the Herfindahl measure of concentration).' A vertical merger often exhibits the same disadvantages as a merger of two unrelated firms: just because the farmer knows how to grow grain (raw material source) does not mean that he has any expertise in consumer cereal production and marketing (merchandising).

Dimension: geography

Azofra *et al*'s (2007: 5) observation about geographic diversification ('M&As leading to diversification, be it geographically or by activity, tend to have worse results than those that lead to concentration') is indicative of investigation of this merger dimension, as represented in Table 4.1. Diaz, a co-author of the Azofra *et al* paper, offers his own perspective in a separate paper two years later, referring to Houston and Ryngaert's 1994 study: 'Domestic M&As offer a greater potential for obtaining synergies derived, for example, from the elimination of redundant costs by geographical overlapping.'

A tendency to view a foreign market as appealing because some of the disadvantages of the more familiar home market appear to be missing may result in incomplete investigation of the overseas target. This is the greener grass error:[30] misdiagnosing foreign opportunities, not as a result of rigorous analysis of the target and its future prospect, but because the foreign market is different from more familiar domestic areas of operation.

NatWest's 1995 acquisition of niche Manhattan investment bank Gleacher & Company was one of several merger missteps that contributed to NatWest's loss of its independence. Royal Bank of Scotland (RBS) acquired NatWest in 1999.[31] Seeking to diversify into M&A advisory and gazing longingly across the pond at what management considered to be a less-regulated market with greater opportunities than the UK banking marketplace, NatWest (now part of RBS) was well positioned to succumb to the siren song of bankers about the well-shopped small bank, long known to be on the trading block.

NatWest management either failed to ask why trade acquirers in the US had deliberately rebuffed suggestions about Gleacher as an acquisition candidate for years, or didn't care. A visible foreign acquisition in a new field always makes for adoring coverage in the financial press for a few days – or at least until that high-ego deal unwinds.

Idiosyncratic Gleacher was a challenging enough acquisition for a PMI implementation-oriented, tough-minded buyer, which NatWest was not. The triple shocks of discovering that a) Gleacher had already become a marginal player in the movement towards megabanks, b) limitations of the US investment banking environment were at least as oppressive as British regulations and perhaps more so because of more active and effective regulators, and c) that NatWest's experience was irrelevant to effective management of Gleacher, led to rapid retreat – and to neglect of NatWest's base business and operations in the UK. With both RBS and Barclays eager to escape the limitations of the UK marketplace, the *loser* in the bidding war for Netherlands-headquartered ABN Amro – in terms of prevailing as the acquirer – Barclays was the *winner* on the basis of value.[32]

Dimension: overpayment by acquirer

The relationship between overpayment and merger success is examined in part 6 of Chapter 3 on the value gap methodology. Two separate studies suggest that many mergers fail when the acquisition purchase premium (APP) exceeds 37–38 per cent. That M&A failure rates increase when bid pricing has scant connection to synergy diagnosis for that specific deal is commented upon by several researchers.

Dimension: phase timing in the merger wave

The pattern of merger waves is addressed in Clark (1991: 25–8, 50–54) and also in this book in several parts of the first chapter. Two of the three alternative outcomes for the 1982–90 LBO boom as reflected in Figure 1.3 in this current book anticipated collapsing conditions.

Rhodes-Kropf and Viswananthan (2004) perceived late phase deals as increasing the prospect of merger value destruction as eager acquirers overestimate synergies in late periods in order to meet the heightened APP requirement of sellers as the bubble approaches its climax.[33]

4.2 Four categories, nine merger types: different deal types mean different M&A success

> The market is skeptical about M&A, but it is more receptive to some kinds of deals than to others.
>
> (Bieshaar *et al*, 2001: 65)

The dimensions of merger differentiation as explored in Table 4.1 are taken to the next level in this part. Nine distinct different types of business combinations are identified by key characteristics and success probability profile; see Table 4.2.

Four categories spanning nine separate merger types

Four general categories characterize the acquiring firm's purchase objectives, and thus provide a general classification structure for merger segmentation.

Category 1: Opportunistic

(Related merger number, type in Table 4.2, 1 Bottom trawler.) The word 'opportunistic' refers here to the timing of the transaction. Unless the acquirer is a liquidator, this category involves pursuit of companies in segments that are already well known to the buyer. The acquirer acts quickly to exploit temporary negotiating advantage, such as when cash-strapped owners of the target company are eager to sell a SBU whole rather than liquidate that business.

Category 2: Operational

(Related merger types: Bolt-ons (2a), Line extension equivalents (2b).) The acquirer targets acquisitions specifically related to its core business/es. There is no experimentation with unfamiliar industries; the most adventuresome initiative in this type are acquisitions of businesses related to but not identical to the buyer's existing new product and services. The basis of differentiation typically involves geography (sales territories), target customers and/or channels. In some instances, the acquirer's primary consideration is whether to acquire the desired new business (buy) or alternatively, develop that capability within the present organization (make).

TABLE 4.2 Nine merger types framework v2

Success Pct.	Cat.	Type	Description	Example	Success Threats (Excl. Pricing, Phase)
87–92	1	Bottom-trawlers	Dying competitor signals exit, advantage to fast, cash bidders	Marconi, Palm	Obsolescence, incompatible technologies
80–85	2A	Bolt-ons	Fills void in acquirer's existing product/service offer, quickly	P&G/Pantene	Hidden integration difficulties cancel timing advantage
65–70	2B	Line extension equivalents	Next generation/different variant of existing product/service	Volkswagen/ Škoda	Actual synergies limited to scale, insufficient to cover APP
55–60*	3A	Consolidation – mature	Same industry contraction: scale, overhead synergies	Pharma, telecoms	Overestimation of market share gain importance
40–45	2C	Multiple core-related complementary	Logical complements to present offer: products/channels/areas Two or more related elements	Disney/ ABC P&G/Gillette Coty/Avon	Mistaken judgment of development potential (r-synergies)

37–42	3B	Consolidation – emerging	Same industry contraction: Picking winners	ABC Capital Cities/Dumont	Overstated premiums (APP) based on target's prior performance
30–35	2D	Single core-related complementary	Similar to 2C but one or less related elements	Daimler Chrysler	Exaggerated benefits attributed to target in 'marriage made in heaven'
20–25	4A	Lynchpin strategic	Major change in emphasis in acquiring company's business mix and forward strategy	IBM/PwC Consulting	Dependent on extraordinary acquiring company
15–20	4B	Speculative strategic	Radical, high-risk experimentation with company's business mix and model.	AOL/TW Vivendi (Mercier)	CEO's imagined vision inconsistent with market realities

Categories:
1 Opportunistic
2 Operational
3 Transitional
4 Transformational

*Excluding last standing participant

Category 3: Transitional

(Related merger types: Consolidation mature (3a), consolidation emerging (3b).) The industry is consolidating, and the acquirer wants to be at the forefront of that process rather than last man standing. The most common form of consolidation involves companies and industries that are already well-established. Profit and revenue growth rates and cash flow return on investment (CFROI) have all flattened and the remaining primary source of efficiency gains is from rationalization of expenses and functions. Companies in immature industries are also sometimes subject to consolidation forces, but for different reasons: combining R&D efforts and investment budgets in order to ensure survival, sharing of technology or dwindling working capital.

Category 4: Transformational

(Related merger types: Lynchpin strategic (4a), speculative strategic (4b).) 'The roster of companies that have favored transformational deals includes Vivendi Universal, AOL TimeWarner... Enron, Williams and others' (Harding and Rovit, 2004: 53).[34]

The chief executive officer of the acquiring company is motivated to steer the company in a dramatic new direction, and mergers are the chosen mechanism. In many instances, the thought process of the acquiring company's chief executive is that: a) the buying firm faces an uncertain economic future and operating in the present manner and structure is no longer an option; and b) diversification into a new, major (but unfamiliar) industry represents an opportunity to revitalize the company.

Towards a segmentation-oriented acquisition success framework: the nine merger types

The two merger segmentation dimensions considered in Figure 4.1 plus the points of merger differentiation in Table 4.1 go part of the way towards a formal merger segmentation framework: a guideline on what types of deals to consider, which to stay away from and why (as based on estimated model merger success percentages).

Table 4.2 reflects observations and research regarding deals exhibiting certain characteristics. For example, Goedhart *et al* (2010: 3–4) describe how consolidation-type acquisitions typically exhibit higher success rates than most other types of business combinations. Two different types of consolidations are depicted in Table 4.2: 3a (mature) and 3b (emerging).

Factor in other considerations and insights from sources including those identified in Table 4.1, and the analyzed result is the present version of a merger segmentation action framework. The illustrative success ranges shown in the exhibit presume middle-of-merger-wave timing and median purchase premiums for that phase, industry and type of merger. Adjustments to those assumptions are addressed in part 4.3.

Since the purpose of *all* merger-related activity is to maximize value for shareholders of the acquiring company, the ranking scheme in Table 4.2 is the analyzed, estimated probability of success by merger type. The rank order starts with the most assured type of deal (bottom trawler at 87–92 per cent success probability) at the top of the list. Highly speculative so-called 'transformational deals' that promise to change everything (but with 20 per cent or less estimated success probability) are shown at the bottom of the list in Table 4.2.

1. Bottom trawlers (87–92 per cent deal success probability range, estimated)

> Our basic formula was to look for companies (often troubled ones) with growth potential, offer to pay more for them than they were worth, and then fix them.
>
> (Geneen, 1997: 32)

'Trawlers' refers to the mindset of bargain-seeking acquirers; 'bottom' to the status of their prospective targets. The bottom trawler acquirer searches the depths of the available companies lists, actively seeking companies in distress that have recently declared 'We can no longer compete' (Circuit City and Palm in the 2000s), or comparable. The reasoning: a company that is available at a minimal price and APP faces minimal risk of failure because little is at risk. Even if the deal fails completely, proceeds from liquidation are a higher percentage of the purchase price paid than for the other eight types of acquisitions.

Figure 4.2 compares the APP dynamics of customary acquisitions with those of the bottom-trawler acquisition, comparing purchase premiums with synergies as described in the VG description in part 6 of Chapter 3. Since VG is calculated as APPs paid minus net realizable synergies (NRSs), a conventional acquisition expectedly results in a value-destroying (for shareholders of the acquiring company) VG (140 – 120 = 20 in the figure) consistent with the reality of most mergers failing in the past.

However, in the bottom trawler type of transaction, the number of bidders and bid cycles are minimal, thus suppressing the purchase premium. Facing threats to its economic viability, the bottom trawler target's extreme

FIGURE 4.2 Bid dynamics of bottom-trawler (type 1) negotiations, in value gap terms

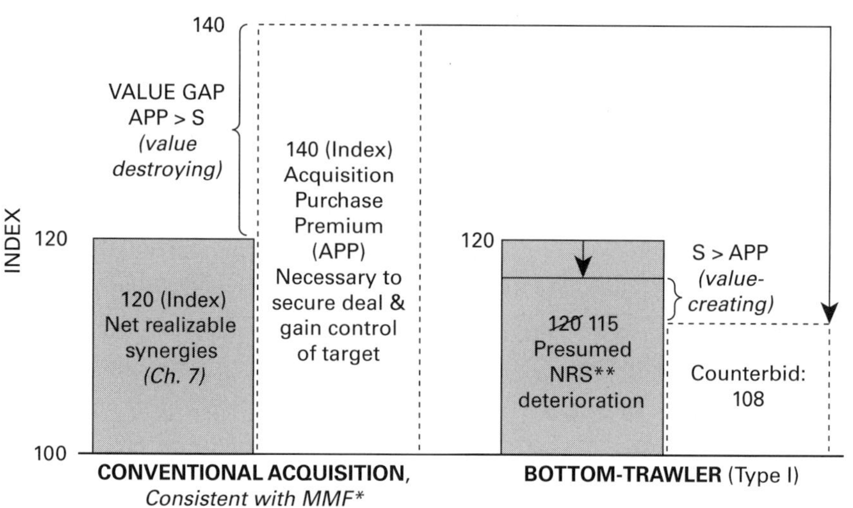

Notes:
100 Index corresponds to pre-announcement share price of target (Appendix A)
* MMF refers to Most Mergers Fail
** NRS refers to Net Realizable Synergies (Chapters 3 and 7)

requirement for immediate funds limits preferred bids to all-cash offers, reducing the number of bidders further. If the company has formally declared that it can no longer compete (UK Woolworths), the APP may slip to zero or even less.

Projected synergies for the bottom trawler target decline with any delays to the sale date. There is already a freeze on all new financing and hiring to preserve cash, while other assets and standalone operations are sold off just to raise survival cash for the parts of the company that remain. Those e- (expense) synergies, which vary in accordance with unit volume levels, decline further (Figure 4.3), as company growth stagnates. The target company is imploding, and r- (revenue) synergies are non-existent. With these reductions in both synergy types and the APP, the opportunity may emerge for a reduced VG lower bid for the bottom trawler company, as depicted in the figure.

One such bottom trawler collapse was Marconi, which failed because of its reliance on a single account, British Telecommunications. When BT awarded a major contract to a Marconi rival, the remnant of what was once a part of the Hanson conglomerate dissolved. The surviving pieces were absorbed by Ericsson at bargain levels in 2005.[35]

FIGURE 4.3 Merger segmentation and value management by acquirer: overview

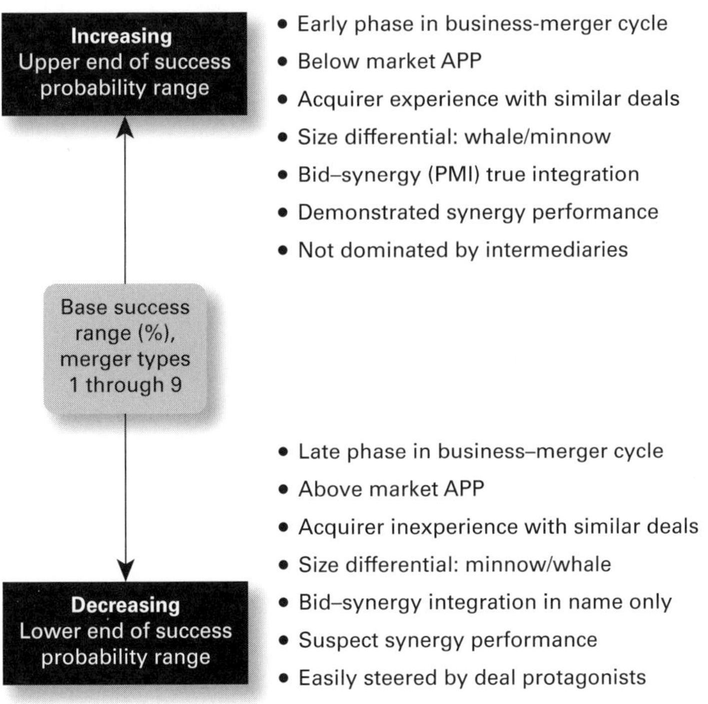

But if the acquirer overbids, the low APP appeal of the bottom trawler deal to the bargain-hunting acquirer is lost. Five years late to market with its Pre™ brand smartphone, Palm management declared 'We cannot compete' shortly afterwards. Hewlett-Packard outbid another suitor and paid $2.1 billion in January 2011 for a business that was effectively written off one year later.

2a. Bolt-ons (80–85 per cent success profile)

As the name implies, 'bolt-ons' imply a target business that fits seamlessly into the acquirer's existing product-service range. A publisher adds a new title in a fast-growing but presently uncovered related segment. A catalogue company that specializes in plus-size dresses for women acquires a company that concentrates on clothing designed for plus-size male counterparts.

Bolt-ons are assigned a success expectation that is only slightly less than that of bottom trawlers. Acquisition of Tropicana® by PepsiCo or Procter

& Gamble's purchase of Pantene are examples. In both instances, the acquiring company was already deeply familiar with both the category and the product, having been involved in somewhat similar products in the past.

Risks associated with bolt-ons are minimal and manageable. Some legacy customers of the target might fear the acquired brand will lose its quality and/or exclusivity. But that risk can be mitigated by careful formulation marketing and channel management and generally does not represent a major obstacle to deal success.

While the original 'with pulp' Tropicana orange juice used to command just one product-width in the grocer's chilled juices section, today's spin-offs – *without* pulp, combined *with* other juices, and so on – multiply PepsiCo's selling space in that high velocity, higher profit part of grocery stores. A related advantage is that Tropicana's expanded footprint also indirectly reduces the space available for competing products.

Pantene, the prestige hair products company acquired by P&G, has been transformed from an exclusive, almost non-advertised (except in print) salon-grade producer, to something slightly more down-market, supported by new advertising and different pricing. Post-acquisition, the abandonment of some snob appeal was more than compensated for on the acquirer's bottom line.

Most, but not all bolt-on type mergers involve identifiable products, although expense- and channel-type varieties arise sometimes. Those high-end US and UK grocery stores that already feature a super-premium range in a part of their conventional stores that then go on to acquire convenience store chains to feature the same lines, represent one example of channel-type bolt-on. Block sales of patents and patent rights (eg AOL, 2012) represent a different form of exception example, involving intangible assets.

2b. Line extension equivalents (65–70 per cent success profile)

Similar to but slightly below the bolt-on deals in terms of success probability profile are product-service line extension equivalents. The illustrative example listed in Table 4.2 is Volkswagen's acquisition of Eastern European automaker Škoda. By acquiring that marque, the parent lowered production costs in two ways: a) through access to new labor markets, and b) by increasing scale economies for VW's existing product platforms. Marketing-wise, the move broadened VW's appeal into lower-price segments without repositioning the parent marque.

The *direction* (up or down market) of the line item extension equivalent is sometimes a factor in that merger's success or failure. When an upmarket nameplate diversifies with a downmarket target, both acquirer and acquiree face potential damage to their respective commercial franchises. The down-market company moving upwards faces the possibility of losing its traditional accounts, as low-end market rivals ignite the flames of customers' fears that extra overhead means the end of the value-for-money positioning (cheap, compared to almost everyone else). When the upmarket brand is perceived as moving downmarket by merger, that sense of exclusivity can rarely if ever be recaptured.

3a. Consolidation mature (55–60 per cent success profile)

The prospective acquiring company's industry is mature: stable and mid-life in terms of corporate economic lifespan (Mauboussin-Johnson's CAP). The sector's rate of profit growth has flattened, with speculation that the rate of increase will soon begin to decrease. Unit (volume) growth has also recently plateaued, although revenue growth may temporarily still be increasing because of aggressive pricing. New pockets of excess capacity arise every year because of new, low-cost entrants and too many legacy competitors. From personal computers to pharmaceuticals, steel fabrication to logistics, the unwritten role is either buy or be acquired.[36]

In this contraction form of consolidation merger, there is mutual understanding by primary participants in the industry that the future value strategy for survivors has changed from offensive (revenue-propelled) to defensive, or expense-based, primarily in the form of scale efficiencies and rationalization of overlapping costs, the two most reliable expense synergies, as described in Chapter 7. The fastest way to bring costs closer in line with capacity is also the oldest technique: plant shutdowns. Akdogu *et al* (2009: 9) observe that: 'Maksimovic *et al* (2008) show that, for mergers in manufacturing industries, the acquirer on average closes or sells about half of the target firm's plants.'[37]

The asterisk in Table 4.2 next to this merger segmentation type arises because of what is referred to in this chapter as the 'last man standing' situation. For both acquirer and acquiree, the consolidation march continues until the sector becomes so concentrated that eventually there are only one or two independent companies (that is, not members of the one or two consolidation groups) still remaining.

In segments from stock brokerage to reinsurance, grocery chains to department stores, a consolidation pattern emerges. Avoiding a deal during the industry's initial consolidation period may be advantageous to both acquirer and target: the careful buyer is able to learn from the mistakes of less patient acquirers, and sometimes pick up some attractive niche businesses that must be divested as a result of that first series of deals. For the target, higher prices (APPs) are the reward for patience, as the remaining acquirers sense that their window of opportunity is closing, and are motivated to act.

But both sets of advantages disappear if parties wait too long and are left as last (men) standing. For the acquirer, the situation in which there are only one or two independents left cancels out any negotiating advantage: the buyer needs to complete the deal as badly as the seller, and capable management at the target company know that. An even worse predicament faces the target which is orphaned – that is, is the last independent but its capacity, customers or patents are not needed. Savvy acquirers wait for this type of company to slip into the bottom trawler type, at a salvage price and with a very high acquisition success probability profile.

2c. Multiple core related complementary (40–45 per cent success profile)

While the business media tends to concentrate on the product similarities between acquirer and target, this combination involves a greater integration challenge than the line extension equivalents (60–65 per cent) in type 2b. The greater depth and complexity of the acquisition type leads to a lower success profile.

The acquiring company likely struggled with that portion of its strategy in the past: Procter & Gamble/Gillette is an example of a combination of this type that appears to be prospering; AT&T's multiple acquisitions aimed at accelerating entry into the computer business in the late 1980s and early 1990s indicate the opposite. P&G's interest in men's toiletries was manifested years before the Gillette deal in the form of the acquisition of Shulton, which failed to advance the acquirer's goals in that segment when the primary salvageable nameplate turned out to be the venerable Old Spice™ brand. Acquisition of Gillette provided P&G with an instantly recognizable name and also a platform for future product growth in that field.

AT&T's multiple attempts at establishing a new core competency in computers first concentrated on internal developments and then Olivetti and NCR, the former National Cash Register. Eager to make up for lost time after the disappointing commercial relationship with Olivetti, AT&T overpaid for UK's NCR in 1990. That second acquisition also ended in ruin, based upon VG methodology: AT&T lost about half of its $1 billion purchase price over four years, before divesting the company in 1994. The combination of high APP and minimal synergies (in part because of AT&T's *laissez faire* post-merger approach in the first years after the close) assured deal failure as measured on a VG (APP-NRS) basis.

3b. Consolidation-emerging (37–42 per cent success profile)

> A merger implementing a new technological innovation may, as the news of the innovation spreads, induce follow-on takeovers among industry rivals for these to remain competitive.
>
> (Eckbo, 2010: 123)

The second of the two consolidation merger types (the first being 3a, consolidation mature) faces a noticeably lower success profile, in part because neither principal to the deal is yet fully established. At first, the two rivals in the same fast-growing segment insist that they will go it alone. At some point it becomes apparent that there are more companies than customers and that actions must be taken to ensure that the firm is one of the survivors. The unthinkable becomes thinkable: combining with your rival with the objective of emerging as the one giant in a sector presently populated only with midgets.

As with the first dot com bubble more than a decade earlier (Clark, 2000: 201–7) commercial and financial markets are both seeking to distinguish market leader from chronic laggard as the new sector evolves and emerges. Almost any entrant can make an initial splash; but as the financial support critical to future growth tends to flow first and most to those firm's perceived as survivors, a defendable market share and customer offer are mandatory, even if it means sacrificing company independence.

Two factors account for the lower success profile compared to type 3a, consolidation mature. The first is reserves: business models of companies in emerging industries are often unstable, with consistent profitability yet to be established. In 2011–12, surprise quarterly losses by several of the new publicly-traded social networking (SN) companies indicate that challenges with subscriber churn, advertising approaches, expense management and sometimes, regulation persist. Despite being proclaimed as the next great thing, margins for error are limited.

A second factor is management. Only a few years from their start-up dates, emerging companies are more likely to be run by entrepreneurs who are great at starting companies, but not so great at building them into major, consistently profitable corporations. The question is not *whether* the transition to professional management will occur at these emerging firms, but rather, *how soon*. Until changes at the top occur, chances for a successful consolidation are reduced – at least relative to consolidations involving longer established firms.

2d. Single core related complementary (30–35 per cent success profile)

This merger type is comprised of deals that are similar to the other type in the transitional category (2c, multiple core related complementary) except that the target business has only a tenuous connection to the acquirer's base business, and thus limited synergy opportunities. Combinations such as eBay/PayPal fall into the 30–35 per cent success envelope; DaimlerChrysler and H-P/Autonomy are indicative of the mirror 65–70 per cent failure probability.

4a. Lynchpin strategic (20–25 per cent success profile)

What's a company to do when its primary business is rapidly disappearing? Assuming that neither selling out nor liquidation are best for shareholders in value creation terms, the company's priority is to capture a supplemental core business quickly in an attempt to elude implosion.[38]

Lynchpin strategic's 20–25 per cent success profile is only slightly more optimistic than outright speculative acquisition bets as represented by 4b, speculative strategic (15–20 per cent). Both of these two M&A types comprising the transformational category involve major changes in the acquiring firm's future direction:

- The business of the prospective target is largely or completely unknown, effectively relegating the buyer to a role comparable to that of the detached financial takeover company acquirer. Little or no new expertise is brought to bear on either day-to-day or strategic management of the target company. The notion that new incentives might encourage holdover management in the target firm to increase firm value persists among such acquirers; but a change in company ownership is not necessarily required for such improved performance.[39]
- Eager to avoid implosion, negotiating leverage is lost and the seller knows it. Especially if the target is well-managed already, the adverse value gap between purchase premium paid and achievable synergies means a deal with minimal chances of success.[40]
- Success chances are reduced by the additional layers of managers in the acquired firm who must be educated continually about the

> company that they are nominally managing. At the very least, bringing the acquiring company's management 'up to speed' reduces performance in the acquired firm (one example: AOL's acquisition of TimeWarner). In chronic situations, top talent departs from the acquired firm, frustrated at inconsistent management by administrators perceived as outsiders.

That the tactic sometimes works – such as in IBM's dramatic turnaround under then-CEO Louis Gerstner in the 1990s – argues against combining this merger type with the lower probability 4b type in Table 4.2, despite the Gerstner-IBM example probably being an exceptional instance. The head-strong manager reads Gerstner's book *Who Says Elephants Can't Dance?* and presumes he or she can make lightning strike twice. Certainly neither his or her minions nor the bankers salivating for deal closure fees are about to contradict that self-image.

4b. Speculative strategic (15–20 per cent success profile)

> Alcohol and aircraft don't mix. But San Miguel, the Filipino conglomerate best known for its beer, ignored that on Wednesday, announc(ing) that it would take a 49 per cent stake in the country's flagship carrier Philippine Airlines as it diversifies further from its core businesses. San Miguel's move away from food and beverages looks sensible.[41]

When we first observed this description, by Lex in the *FT*, of beer company San Miguel's bizarre diversification into air travel as 'sensible', we couldn't help but wonder how much of the acquiring firm's principal product was consumed by those reporters. Apparently Lex has a sense of humor. Financial markets quickly sensed value destruction in the strange combination: 'Since rumors of the deal leaked in January, shares of San Miguel have fallen by 4 per cent. Those of PAL Holdings, which owns the carrier, have gained 8 per cent.'[42]

Speculative strategic deals secure a well-deserved bottom rung in the merger type list with minimal profile success (15–20 per cent). Driven by desperation and/or enticed by the siren song of a dramatic, visionary ego-acquisition, these stillborn M&A deals are easily spotted: consider the merger success dimensions identified in Table 4.1, and such transactions are almost always on the adverse side of each variable, sometimes all of them.

In the last 30 years, similar transactions prompting a collective financial market response of 'Is this a joke?' have included the NatWest/Gleacher deal, Coca Cola's purchase of film producer Columbia Pictures, AOL/TimeWarner, eBay/Skype, and nearly every deal attempted by former Vivendi Universal chief executive officer Jean-Marie Messier.[43]

4.3 Applying the nine merger type framework

The success profile percentage ranges shown in Table 4.2 are intended to be indicative of representative mergers of each of the nine types, meaning a) smaller than the acquirer as measured on a revenue basis, b) secured at an APP percentage level in the median range of past comparable deals of that type.

Some other influences on merger type success

No deal is exactly like another, and a range of influences may either improve, or alternatively, decrease the chances for merger success. Several of these possible factors are shown in Figure 4.3.

Adjustments to Table 4.2 profile success percentages

Considerations such as timing, relative size, relative Acquisition Purchase Premium and geography all potentially modify the model success probabilities by type as identified in Table 4.2. Several preliminary adjustments are identified in Table 4.3, along with the possible effect on profile success probability ranges.

Timing: phase of the merger wave: APP percentages: level, trend, in relation to synergies

The model success percentages shown in Table 4.2 presume a transaction that is closed around mid-point in the merger wave, approximately at the end of phase II and the beginning of phase III (of four).

Deal success indirectly coincides with the timing of the transaction over the merger cycle, with higher success in earlier merger wave phases because of lower relative APP ranges in percentage terms, and a more advantageous relationship between synergies and acquisition premiums. Figure 3.5 in the preceding chapter is shown here as Figure 4.4; they graphically depict reasons why deals consummated in the early phases of the business-merger cycle tend to exhibit greater success than deals closed late in the wave.

TABLE 4.3 Four adjustments to Table 4.2 success profile ranges

Weight (out of 100) Modification Factor	Adjustment to Phase II Success Percentage by Acquisition Type
25 Phase of cycle	Phase 1: +10%, Phase 3: –10%, Phase IV: –25%
40 APP% median based on analysis of precedent: industry *and* phase	Below reported 110%: no effect; 110–125%: 10% reduction; 125 plus% of average 150%: 20% reduction; >150-plus% of average: 30% reduction.
20 Relative size	Target is 90-plus% of acquirer (annualized revenue basis): no effect Target 90–130% of acquirer: –10% Target >130%: –20%
10 Domestic vs international	Domestic: no effect; same continent: –5%, Other international: –10%

Percentages are adjustments to the model success percentages shown in Table 4.2, for example, a 10% downward adjustment in a Type 2A Line Extension Equivalents success probability of 80% indicates a reduction to 72%. Weights sum to 95 rather than 100 because of other factors including but not limited to: culture, first-time CEO of major corporation within first three years in office, rapid obsolescence of company technology.

If early phase transactions tend to be lower risk but sometimes challenging to finance, transactions occurring much later in the wave but prior to that bubble's exhaustion peak[44] (for our purposes here, mid phase III to mid phase IV) show the opposite characteristics: straightforward to finance but with treacherously high APPs and TAPPs (see Appendix A), which threaten the viability of all deals closed then.

As noted in the preceding chapter, merger success based on the VG criteria is not just a matter of high APP but also high APPs relative to NRSs. Late in the merger cycle, the combination of high APPs and flat NRSs (Figure 4.4) means a widening VG, indicating a possible failed acquisition. That exhibit is illustrative and shows relative APP-to-NRS percentages. The exact VG is determined on an individual company basis, thus affirming the importance of in-depth knowledge of available synergies. That said, Chapter 7 in this book suggests that achievement of NRSs of more than 30–38 per cent (on a basis comparable to APP percentages) is unusual.

FIGURE 4.4 Considering both VG determining factors, over the business-merger cycle

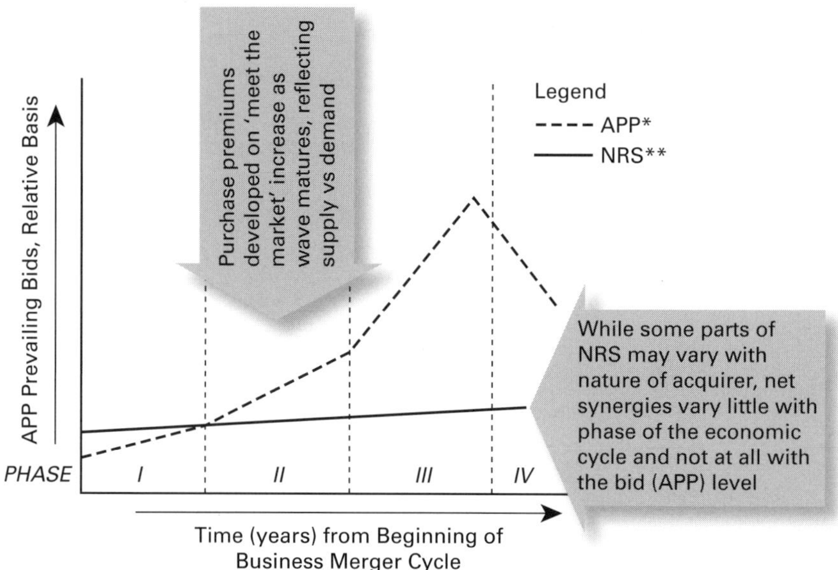

Notes:
* APP refers to Acquisition Purchase Premium: accepted bid vs pre-announcement indicated share price
** NRS refers to Net Realizable Synergies: PV of synergies from four S categories (Ch. 8) adjusted for timing, feasibility, offsetting charging and/or investments

A *Financial Times*' piece in December 2011 entitled 'Quarter of US buyouts in bubble years remain at risk' focuses on the performance of mergers consummated during the hectic final two years of the 2002–08 subprime business-merger cycle. The overview of Moody's report on the performance of 40 large, late phase acquisitions at the end of the post-1980 wave 3 concludes that: 'Many of the large, bubble-era LBOs... have had weak revenue growth and high default rates... since their LBO closings... It may be difficult for private equity investors in lower-rated LBOs to realize returns on their initial investment.'[45]

Domestic versus international

Diaz *et al*'s (2009: 15) perspective on the potential negative effects of geographic diversification on merger success is noted in conjunction with Table 4.1. The issue-behind-the-issue is control. When the target's headquarters and principal operations are located near to those of the acquirer's HQ, candidate synergies can be more easily diagnosed and monitored compared to when operations are separated by thousands of miles. A target based in a different continent than the acquirer also presents possible extra obstacles in the form of communications, logistics, and sometimes, currency transfer. Thus it is no surprise when the new acquiree's headquarters and main operations centers are 'brought home' to the acquirer's headquarters location: examples are SBC/AT&T, BMC/Harris, BT/Dialcom, and General Dynamics/multiple targets.

Distant headquarters locations may be contribute to other potential success-reducing factors, including conflicting business models, control/ownership structures and cultures. Regarding the latter, a private Middle Eastern bank's decision to pursue a merger with another institution based in a different country faced new integration challenges, including but not limited to: transaction (different languages), new regulatory environment, and differing working styles and work ethics.

4.4 The path forward in merger segmentation: towards M-Score©

Even with emergence of frameworks such as v2 of the nine merger types guidelines (shown as Table 4.2 in this chapter) as modified for additional transaction success-influences (see Table 4.3), merger-related segmentation aimed at specifying the probability of any deal's success or failure at this writing is still behind similar diagnostic approaches in other disciplines:[46]

- *Venture capital.* In the past, venture capital success algorithms have provided angels as well as larger latter-stage investors with some means for improving their aim when contemplating which new hardware- or software-related innovations to sponsor, and which to disregard. No such guidance mechanism is universal. Attempts have been made in 2010–12 to apply scoring algorithms to guess at the business success of social networking emerging companies. Many of those SN firms are still struggling to establish viable business models (as explored in Chapter 6), and thus many of these measures exhibit mixed success.
- *Advertising effectiveness(now, web-enabled!)* In the marketing segmentation domain, some reliable frameworks already exist for evaluation of the likely outcome of new product launches supported

by traditional advertising media: print, radio, TV, billboards. In social networking, the measurement gold rush is on, including the great and the merely aggressive as seemingly everyone claims to possess *the* definitive metric for absolutely, positively translating the sideways glance of some distracted Facebook surfer into actual incremental sales.[47]

- *Borrowers' capability to service debt.* With many corporations still experiencing debt hangovers in the aftermath of the subprime-derivatives 2002–08 bubble (post-1980 business-merger wave 3 as described in Chapter 1), financiers must make painful decisions about which clients to a) rollover, which b) to keep on life support (meaning sufficient financing to defer rather than to prevent the inevitable) and which c) to pull the plug on. A systematic scoring mechanism for assessing each borrower's likely future prospects and debt servicing capability is not necessary merely to prevent making refinancing decisions blindly but, in some instances, to insulate that finance provider from possible legal claims by disgruntled shareholders of firms subjected to endgame financing scenarios b) and c).

Regarding the last, Altman's widely-cited Z-Score credit methodology and approach today serves as an aspirational standard for indicators that do not merely provide a postmortem of the reasons *why* that particular borrower collapsed, but also some advance warning indications. For those who know what to look for, and when, an opportunity emerges to manage risk exposure, while there is still sufficient time to avoid or at least to minimize loss. Altman's multi-dimensional, multiple-weighted variable approach to assessing borrowers' risk suggests some of the broad future direction for substantive merger segmentation investigation in the future, including Pondbridge's M-Score.[48]

Distinguishing *decisive* merger success-failure variables (eg as presently hypothesized, triple digit APP percentages and M&A transaction timing from middle of phase IV onwards), from factors presently viewed by us of being of lesser importance, merger success-wise (eg combined firm's relative asset sizes, life stage of industry) is one of the keys to building frameworks essential to the acquiring company CEO.

Merger segmentation has started. Related practical research and framework testing progress forward.

Notes

1 Refers to Bower, J (2001) 'Not all M&As are alike – and that matters', *Harvard Business Review,* Mar 21, 93–101.

2 M-Score© is the name of Pondbridge Limited's proprietary multidimensional merger segmentation and valuation diagnostic approach and related tools, frameworks and analyses, not to be confused with Kelly and Cox's (1936) M-Score.

3 Magnet (1984); see in this book parts 2.1, 1.5 (including discussion of Coley and Reinton, 1988), 3.1, 3.5, 3.6.

4 Bruner (2004: 63).

5 US-based examples include: Long Island Trust, Green Tree, Digital Equipment Corp. (DEC) and Household Finance Corp. (HFC).

6 Researchers Coley and Reinton indicate a 61 per cent failure rate (39 per cent success) for those transactions among the 116 mergers studied designated as either success or failure. Allocate the 16 per cent of total sample which is not designated on a proportional basis, and the adjusted failure percentage increases to 68 per cent (32 per cent success).

7 Sample sizes for all four quadrants are shown in Figure 3.1 in Chapter 3 in this book, also Coley and Reinton, 1988: 30. Sample sizes for each of the three quadrants examined here are significantly smaller than the total sample (n=116) and no consideration is given here for possible distortions caused by an unrepresentative or insufficient sample in each of the quadrants: (A) n=35 merger transactions, unrelated/small (B) n=16, related/small (C) n=20. Also, the transactions comprising each of the four quadrants in Coley and Reinton's analysis are unique and separate to that quadrant only. The two-step (A to B, B to C) sequence described here is illustrative only; we would expect acquiring company management to immediately pursue the *combination* of characteristics that are most consistent with merger performance success.

8 'eBay' (Mar 29 2011) http://topics.nytimes.com/top/news/business/companies/ebay_inc/index.html?scp=3&sq=GSI&st=cse. Accessed Apr 3 2012.

9–23 Refer to Further Reading.

24 The view of diversification as a source of acquisition value destruction is not shared by all. In his footnote 22 on pages 12–13, Sirower (1997) describes the perspective of Harvard Business School's Richard Rumelt in the 1970s: 'Professor Richard Rumelt... found that firms with a pattern of related diversification had consistently higher accounting profitability than firms that had little relation to each other.'

25 Damodaran refers to Lang and Stulz's 1994 paper, 'Tobin's Q, corporate diversification and firm performance', *Journal of Political Economy*, 1248–80.

26 The phrase 'business model' is at times misinterpreted in the business media as referring to an economically viable business strategy and approach, which is different. The expansive IPO road show banker attempting to hype his assigned company may be aware of this misperception but probably does little to correct it, lest the underwriting team and sellers are forced to settle on a lower day one launch price because of disappointing demand.

27 Brothers, C (Nov 12 2008) 'British Airways expands low-cost unit', *New York Times*, http://www.nytimes.com/ 2008/11/12/business/worldbusiness/12skies.html?_r=1&scp=11&sq=go/ per cent20british per cent20airways&st=cse. Accessed Apr 3 2012.

28 'Department store chain Dillard Inc.'s May 1988 acquisition of Mercantile Stores Co. for $2.9 billion in cash seemed a logical expansion... But the two retailers had dramatically different marketing strategies', 'Mergers: Why most big deals don't pay off', *BusinessWeek*, Oct 14 2002.

29 Trimbath, S (2002) *Mergers and Efficiency: Changes across time*, Milken Institute, Boston, Kluwer Academic Publishers; Palepu, K (1986) 'Predicting takeover targets: a methodological and empirical analysis', *Journal of Accounting and Economics*, 8:1 Mar, 3–35; Singh, A (1975) 'Take-overs, economic natural selection, and the theory of the firm: evidence from the postwar United Kingdom experience', *The Economic Journal*, 85, 497–515.

30 Referring to the misperception that any other opportunity are not subject to the limitations of present markets and thus are more promising: 'The grass is always greener on the other side.'

31 Truell, P (Oct 18 1995) 'NatWest to buy Gleacher in $135 million stock deal', *New York Times*, http://www.nytimes.com/1995/10/18/business/natwest-to-buy-gleacher-in-135-million-stock-deal.html. Accessed Apr 6 2012.

32 Werdinger, J (Oct 6 2007) 'Barclays withdraws bid to take over ABN Amro', *New York Times*, www.nytimes.com/ 2007/10/06/business/worldbusiness/06bank.html?_r=1&scp=3&sq=ABN Amro&st=Search. Accessed Oct 11 2011.

33 'Merger valuation and merger waves', *Journal of Finance*, 59:6, Dec, 2685–718.

34 *Mastering the Merger: Four critical decisions that make or break the deal*, Boston, Harvard Business School Press. All four of the companies specified by the authors are widely viewed as being involved in disastrous merger misadventures.

35 'Ericsson agrees to acquire Marconi', *New York Times*, Oct 12 2009, http://www.nytimes.com/ 2005/10/25/technology/25iht-marconi.html?scp=2&sq=Marconi per cent20Ericsson&st=cse. Accessed Sep 12 2011.

36 Gorton *et al* (2005) 'Eat or be eaten: a theory of merger waves', Federal Reserve Bank of Chicago, Apr.

37 'Value creation and merger waves' (Akdogu, E *et al* (2009) 'Gaining a competitive edge through acquisitions: evidence from the telecommunications industry', *Journal of Corporate Finance*, 15:1, 99–112, February); the authors refer to Maksimovic *et al* (2008) 'Post-merger restructuring and the boundaries of the firm', Working Paper, University of Maryland.

38 Rarely (approaching almost never) will the chief executive of the company in terminal decline seriously consider the possibility of liquidating the company, even if that is the value-maximizing course of action. If 'losing' the acquisition chase represents a black mark in the testosterone environment of M&A, voluntarily shutting down the corporation is the kiss of death, as that CEO risks being branded as the individual who *lost the company.* Misinterpretation of Mauboussin and Johnson's 1997 competitive advantage period (CFROI/WACC) concept may also play a role, as management or advisers sometimes mistakenly believe that attempting to extend the company's economic lifespan increases survival chances. When the dying company makes a desperation acquisition in an unfamiliar industry or segment, that action may instead provide the final shock that kills off the acquiring company-in-decline.

39 The notion of superior performance by holdover target company managers responding to new post-merger compensation schemes including an ownership stake is a long-enduring part of management buyout and financial acquirer lore. But some problems arise with presuming that a merger is necessary for improved performance, as comparable incentives could have (and should have) been extended to corporate key contributors before any change in company ownership.

40 The good company bad price (GBPC) fallacy is examined in part 6 of Chapter 3.

41 'San Miguel, jetting off', *Financial Times,* Lex column, Apr 4 2012

42 http://www.ft.com/cms/s/3/24947cae-7e65-11e1-b009-00144feab49a.html#axzz1rF9tW9iK. Accessed Apr 6, 2012. Lex offers a less complimentary assessment of San Miguel's actions later in the same article: 'San Miguel as a food and drink company; now, after diversifying into oil and power, it looks more like a highly leveraged conglomerate. (And investors must never pay a premium for diversification).'

43 Johnson and Orange (2003) *The Man Who Tried to Buy the World: Jean-Marie Messier and Vivendi Universal*, London, Viking.

44 'Exhaustion peak' refers to an indicative date in the merger wave when prices exhibit a final surge with limited volume and no market confirmation. The word 'exhaustion' relates to the chart pattern: an isolated price spike. In post-1980 wave 2, the first dot com business-merger cycle, the exhaustion peak occurred in mid-March 2000, the IPO time of the appropriately named www.lastminute.com (Clark, 2000: 68, 76–8).

45 Dec 6 2011, 'Leveraged buyouts: lackluster performance for bubble era LBOs', *Report Overview*, Moody's, Accessed Jan 18 2012, http://moodys.alacra.com/research/moodys-global-credit-research--PBC_137440. Phrase in parenthesis provided by this book's authors based on context of article. Also, Thomas *et al* (Dec 7 2011) 'Boomtime buy-outs face further distress', *Financial Times*. http://www.ft.com/cms/s/0/15dcf200-202c-11e1-8462-00144feabdc0.html?ftcamp=crm/email/2011126/nbe/InTodaysFT/product#axzz1fpZuWtG0. Accessed Dec 7 2011.

46 No success diagnostic approach can be wholly statistical, and there is *no* inference that M&A success is simply the consequence of crunching various past or projected numbers. The interpersonal relationship between acquiring company CEO and his or her counterpart is critical in early pre- and post-merger months, as are considerations such as the clarity and effectiveness of the combined firm's joint strategic and marketing plan going forward (IVE, Chapter 3). But such acknowledgement does *not* mean that quantifiable approaches aimed at predicting merger success may reasonably be disregarded, either. The self-styled deal arranger/business broker who rejects substantive quantitative measures on the basis of 'I know a good deal when I see it but don't know exactly why' is steered by gut sense plus fee avarice. That anachronism is out of step with the realities of merger performance evaluation today and represents a threat to the career of any acquiring company chief executive who is lured in by the pitch.

47 For example, comScore (Jun 2012) 'The power of like^2', http://www.comscore.com/Press_Events/Presentations_Whitepapers/ 2012/The_Power_of_Like_2-How_Social_Marketing_Works. Accessed Jun 14 2012.

48 Altman, E (2002) *Bankruptcy, Credit Risk and High Yield Junk Bonds*, Oxford, Blackwell; (Jul 2000) 'Predicting financial distress of companies: revisiting the Z-Score and Zeta® Models', NYU Stern School of Business, 1–54; (Sep 1968) 'Financial ratios, discriminant analysis and the prediction of corporate bankruptcy', *Journal of Finance*, 23:4, 589–609.

05

Mergers *still* fail, but does it matter?

> *Study after study of past merger waves has shown that two of every three deals have not worked; the only winners are the shareholders of the acquired firm, who sell their company for more than it is really worth.*
>
> (*The Economist*, 1999)[1]

> *Attempting to restrict mergers because of bad outcomes would be like arguing against the institution of marriage because of what happens at the divorce court.*
>
> (Trimbath, 2002)[2]

CHAPTER CONTENTS

5.1 More confirmation that historically, most mergers fail

5.2 No effective refutation of MMF

5.3 M&A's core contradiction, segmentation and stakeholders' different merger perspectives

5.4 Moving forward: expanding upon Hayward's three causes of merger failure

Additional corroboration to the proposition that most mergers fail is provided in this chapter's initial part (5.1). Today, MMF is largely unchallenged; two groups' opposing contentions are examined in 5.2. Part 5.3 explains M&A's basic contradiction: that merger activity continues (and, in 2012–19, is expected to surge) despite past patterns of deal failure and disappointment. That inconsistency is addressed in the context of: a) different perspectives on merger success by different stakeholders in the M&A process; and b) performance improvements from effective merger segmentation. Part 5.4 considers Hayward's three perspectives on causes of merger failure, including examples and consideration of implications.

5.1 More confirmation that historically, most mergers fail

Extensive evidence supporting today's consensus that historically, most mergers fail, is presented in the preceding chapters. MMF is confirmed by numerous additional citations and references in this chapter.

MMF: The evidence to this point

The indications that approximately two-thirds of all mergers fail as presented in this book's preceding four chapters are persuasive, bordering on conclusive. Besides *The Economist*'s observations at the beginning of this chapter, reference has been made to Bain & Co's survey results as noted in Carroll and Mui (2009) (see Chapter 2; and primary studies in this field cited by Mueller and Sirower (2003) in Chapter 3). References have also been made to the three McKinsey & Co multi-company merger performance research studies, along with three related articles by: Magnet (1984),[3] Coley and Reinton (1988) and Bieshaar *et al* (2001).

MMF: further substantiation

Following are 20 additional points of reference supporting the contention that MMF, amassed over the past two decades, listed chronologically (most recent first).

2012

Skepticism about the ability of big-scale M&A to create shareholder value has grown after a string of megadeals that proved value-destroying – experience backed by many studies.

(Sakoui, Feb 29 2012, 'Harder to slot together', *Financial Times,* 15)

2010

50 domestic acquisitions involving Greek firms. Overall results from the three studies indicate failure rates from 50 per cent to 60 per cent.

(Papadakis and Thanos, 'Measuring the performance of acquisitions: an empirical investigation using multiple criteria', *British Journal of Management*, 21, 859)

2009

Several reviews have shown that, on average, firms create little or no value by making acquisitions.

(Hitt *et al*, 'Mergers and acquisitions: overcoming pitfalls, building synergy and creating value', *Business Horizons*, 523)

The vast body of academic research demonstrates that most mergers add no value or reduce shareholder value for the acquiring firm.

(Bogan and Just, 'What drives merger decision making behavior? Don't seek, don't find, and don't change your mind', *Journal of Economic Behavior & Organization*, 1)

Studies... (on) gains from mergers and acquisitions... focusing on accounting figures tend to find a significant drop in performance.

(Betzer *et al,* May 2009, 'Disentangling the link between stock and accounting performance in acquisitions', *Cardiff Business School Working Paper Series*, 2)

2007

Over the past 20 years, a myriad of business and academic studies have looked at mergers and acquisitions... So far, most studies have yielded little definitive evidence that these deals create value... Companies with 10 or more recent acquisitions were the worst performers one and two years after the announcement.

(Paul, 'Getting a good deal: M&A best practice', *Horizons*, Watson Wyatt, 65)

Most M&As are considered to be unsuccessful.

(Steger and Kummer, 'Why merger and acquisition (M&A) waves reoccur – the vicious cycle from pressure to failure', Paper IMD 207–11, Lausanne, Switzerland, IMD International, 2)

2006

The purpose of this paper is to re-examine the long-term post-merger performance of acquiring firms in the UK and to explore whether M&A creates or destroys value. The results have confirmed... (that) only 35.48 per cent acquirers perform positive abnormal returns, showing obvious wealth loss after M&A.

(Luo, 'Re-examine the long term post-merger performance of acquirers: UK evidence', Nottingham England, Nottingham University Business School, 3)

2004

Most acquiring firms fail to realize positive gains... Acquiring firms are not winners.

(Yook, 'The measurement of post-acquisition performance using EVA™,'[4] *Quarterly Journal of Business and Economics,* Summer 67)

2003

Acquiring company shareholders lost 12 cents at the announcement of acquisitions for every dollar spent on acquisitions for a total loss of $240 billion from 1988 through 2001, whereas they lost $7 billion in all of the 1980s, or 1.6 cents per dollar spent. The losses of bidders exceeded the gains of targets from 1988 through 2001 by $134 billion... The large losses are consistent with the existence of negative synergies from the acquisitions.

(Moeller, Schlingemann and Stulz, 'Wealth destruction on a massive scale? A study of acquiring-firm returns in the recent merger wave', Cox School of Business, Southern Methodist University, 1; published 2005 in the *Journal of Finance,* 60:2, 757)

Studies using methodologies based on the analysis of security returns have generally concluded that... shareholders of acquiring companies experience wealth losses.

(Burt and Limmack, 'The operating performance of companies involved in the UK retailing sector, 1977–1992', 147, in Cooper, C and Gregory, A, *Advances in Mergers and Acquisitions Vol 2. Lose the acquisition game,* Amsterdam, JAI Elsevier Science)

Evidence that M&As destroy wealth can also be found in the event study literature, if one examines the returns to the acquirers over a sustained period after the M&As occur.

(Mueller, 'The finance literature on mergers: a critical survey', 178, Ch 9 in Waterson, M (ed), *Competition, Monopoly and Corporate Governance: Essays in Honor of Keith Cowling,* Northampton MA, Edward Elgar)

2002

Fully 61 per cent of buyers destroyed their own shareholders' wealth.

(Henry, Oct 14, 'Mergers: why most big deals don't pay off', *BusinessWeek*, 2)

M&A deals are more likely to destroy value than to create it... Numerous studies have shown that M&A destroys value for the acquiring company at least half of the time...

(Frick, K and Torres, A, 'Learning from high-tech deals', *McKinsey Quarterly*, 1, 113)

1999

83 per cent of mergers were unsuccessful in producing any business benefit as regards shareholder value.

(KPMG, 'Unlocking shareholder value: the keys to success', *Mergers & Acquisitions, A global research report*, 2)

1998

The overwhelming empirical evidence suggests, at least from an acquiring firm's perspective, that mergers are, at best, break even situations and, at worst, failures.

(Brouthers *et al*, 1998, 347)

Most of the research indicates that between 60 per cent and 80 per cent of mergers are financial failures. In some studies, failure is defined as underperforming in the stock market, while other studies define it as not delivering promised 'synergies' through cost reductions or profit increases.

(Norton, Apr 20, 'Merger mayhem: why the latest corporate unions carry great risk', *Barrons*)[5]

Research indicates that up to 60 per cent of mergers fail to create shareholder value within 10 years.

(Chapman, 'Purchasing's big moment – after a merger', *McKinsey Quarterly*, 1, 56)

1997

Acquisitions that represent a major component of corporate strategy... are likely to fail; approximately 66 per cent of the acquisitions in this sample destroy value.

(Sirower, 1997, 123)

1992

> Some consensus has evolved that takeovers are not, on average, successful for the acquiring firm when judged by the standard profitability or share price criteria... The question is then why managers appear to be pursuing a strategy which seems to be at variance with shareholder wealth maximization.
>
> (Ingham *et al*, 'Mergers and profitability: a managerial success story?', *Journal of Management Studies*, 29:2, Mar, 195)

The volume and diversity research supporting MMF expands with each passing year. Perhaps as a consequence, the number of merger practitioners and others opposing the notion of historical merger failure has dwindled to almost no one today.

Two other indicators point to today's near unanimity of acceptance of MMF. Brouthers *et al* (1998, cited above), a leader of the opposition merger valuation group who prefer qualitative merger valuation criteria, nonetheless affirms MMF's main point: mergers are 'at best break even and, at worst, failures'. Consultants, seeking to differentiate themselves, find themselves hard pressed to develop credible counter-arguments to the MMF notion. When the topic is merger performance, then the requisite MMF caveat (two-thirds of all mergers fail) is a necessary insert in the beginning of the article, if other points are to be considered seriously.

5.2 No effective refutation of MMF

Also, MMF is supported by the absence of effective opposition. To our knowledge, neither the Magnet (1984) nor Coley and Reinton (1988) studies – two of the 1980s foundation investigations in support of MMF – have ever been discredited.

Existing opposition to MMF is primarily from two sources, both of which are considered in the pages that follow. The first is composed of proponents of qualitative, mostly motivations-defined, criteria for assessing merger success or failure. Depending on the researcher, suggestion arises to either supplement hard financial returns-based merger valuation criteria (Chapter 3) with soft, subjective measures or alternatively, to replace the established quantitative merger valuation criteria outright with more qualitative measures and methods.

The second opposing group emerges from among those academicians examining post-merger company operating performance. Within that category is one sub-group whose members contend that instead of damaging the acquiring company, acquisitions help to *improve* operating performance. Healey *et al* (1992) is examined here as representative of that sub-group.

Qualitative merger evaluation proponents: measuring merger success on financial returns alone is too narrow

Epstein (2005), one of the more expansive 'qualitative school' researchers based on the range of management motivations which he cites, acknowledges MMF as follows: 'some studies have even indicated that... 7 out of 10 mergers do not live up to their promises'. His response to the dozens of *quantitative* studies pointing to merger failure from the mid-1980s until the mid-2000s is dismissive: 'the causes of failure have often been shallow and the measures of success weak' (37).

On this issue of analytical robustness, Epstein risks finding himself hoisted on his own petard. Following the research of Henry (2002) and Mueller and Sirower (2003) in particular, explanations of merger performance other than MMF are today on the defensive. At the very least, contrarians attempting to present an alternative basis for merger success management are obliged to first explain the mountain of evidence and analysis in support of the contention that historically, most mergers fail:

- Epstein offers no comment at all about the thousands of crashed deals consistent with MMF. That group includes: Vivendi (Universal), Hewlett-Packard (Palm), Conseco (Green Tree), Unum (Provident), Quaker Oats (Snapple) and Bank of America (Countrywide Financial).
- There are no attempts by the author to explain away disappointing returns from many mergers beyond his 'shallow' and 'weak' broad characterizations.
- Instead, Epstein *does* present a conceptual alternative to MMF: his own personal set of hypothesized M&A success imperatives, such as ensuring 'strategic vision.' His sample set? Deep knowledge of *one* merger transaction, the possibly non-representative acquisition of Chase Manhattan Bank by JP Morgan in 2000.[6]

Epstein (2005: 38) offers the opinion that: 'A more complete discussion would acknowledge that mergers... have often failed because of problems with the strategic vision of the merger, the appropriateness of the deal partner, or the deal structure.' Of his three *keys to merger* success, only the second – appropriateness of the deal partner – is consistent with M&A prevailing quantitative methodologies as examined in Chapter 3 of this book. To the extent that Epstein's reference to the 'appropriateness of merger partner' refers to factors affecting merger success such as relatedness, size, culture and location (see Table 4.1, Chapter 4), his views may reasonably be seen as consistent with some of merger segmentation's key variables.

However, as to that researcher's other two presumed 'drivers': a) Epstein's 'strategic vision' notion is vague, subjective and could encourage hubris-driven acquiring company chief executives into pursuing value-diminishing 'transformational' deals as shown in Table 4.2 (substantially replicated in this chapter as Table 5.1); b) 'deal structure' – cash versus stock – was a prominent research subject in M&A scholarly investigations in the 1980s and early 1990s but has since declined in importance. A half dozen conversion approaches arise for seller's to evaluate mix deals as the merger chase approaches completion.

Bruner's 'All M&A is local' notion of merger performance measurement (2004: 68–9) is as problematic as Brouthers *et al*'s (1998: 348) similar suggestion to assess merger performance on the basis of the acquiring company's key success factors (KSFs). In both instances the disturbing prospect of corporate misuse arises, with a spendthrift acquiring company attempting to avoid the consequences of its pursuit of high risk, value destructive deals, knowing that it might always excuse away its mistake by referring to an easily changed qualitative criterion of the moment. This is the ultimate merger performance escape clause. For what merger performance discipline does compliance with KSFs hold when those lists of imprecise parameters can be and are tweaked with alarming frequency?

Some others items on these motivations criteria lists may from time to time attract the attention of a party to the deal, blurring assessment and thereby threatening M&A performance as measured on a 'hard' financial basis *only*. Expanded opportunities for corporate staff, 'strategic fit' (a term notoriously prone to favorable subjective interpretation) and a more prominent profile in financial markets might all receive nods from the impressionable acquirer as acceptable deal evaluative criteria. Financial markets remain unconvinced that the new non-traditional criteria are workable or suitable.

Healey et al

Is MMF contradicted by evidence of post-close improvements in target company fundamental operating performance? A thorough investigation of challenges to MMF is incomplete without including the contention by a small

FIGURE 5.1 Perspectives on merger returns

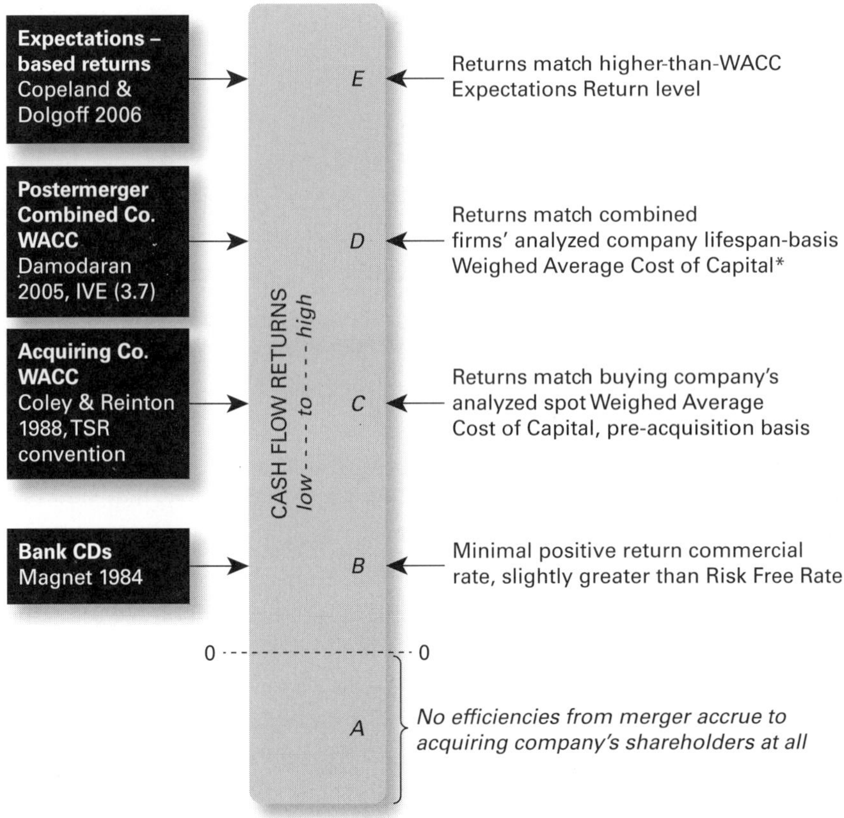

Note
* Depicted here as greater than Acquirer's WACC
Returns rate calculation: APP adjusted or not?

number of researchers including Healey *et al* (1992), who contend that operating performance *improves* as a result of mergers, at least in their study.

An exacting look at Healey *et al* diminishes this challenge, and discredits that study and its sub-group. Aspects examined in the pages that follow include: a) chronic limitations of Healey *et al*'s sample set; b) the absence of any consideration of Acquisition Purchase Premium (APP); and c) the lack of reference to comparable rates of returns (see Figure 5.1).

To the advocates of this notion, post-merger operating performance analysis fills the analytical gap left unaddressed by event studies-type methods, such as those described in Chapter 3 of this book. Healey *et al* contend that:

> Stock price studies of takeovers... indicate that bidders generally breakeven... These increases in equity values are typically attributed to some unmeasured sources of real economic gains... *but researchers have had little success in relating the equity value gains to improvements in subsequent corporate performance.* (Italics added.)

Accordingly, Healey *et al* advocate a separate investigation of post-merger company operating performance, different from the ES approach. Their suggested criteria are 'post-merger accounting data to test directly for changes in operating performance that results from mergers' (p 136).

Despite conspicuous efforts by Healey *et al* to differentiate their approach from ES, the two methods are similar, with the primary difference being that while ES focuses on post-announcement changes in share prices, Healey *et al* examine post-close changes in the post-close combined corporation's future cash flows (CFs).[7]

In commenting on Healey *et al*'s methodology, Martynova *et al* (2006) identify three sets of studies comprising the post-merger operating performance category. The first is composed of studies that assert that companies' performance improve after the close of their deals. Martynova *et al* assign the following research efforts to this sub-group: Healey *et al*, 1992; Heron and Lie, 2002[8]; Rahman and Limmack, 2004[9]. The second and third subgroups are composed of studies which either do not indicate any significant improvement in post-merger operating performance (Group 2) or alternatively, which indicate deteriorating post-merger operating performance (Group 3).[10]

Betzer *et al* (2009: 2–3) dismiss Healey *et al*'s first, improving performance sub-group as a non-representative anomaly. The authors specifically criticize Healey *et al*'s sample as insufficient in terms of both sample size and analysis time period, leading to distorted conclusions: 'Apart from Healey, Palepu and Ruback (1992) who cover a very short period (1979–84) and have a sample of only 50 mergers, studies using accounting measures... find that mergers generate statistically significant losses or at least do not result in significant improvements in performance.' Betzer *et al* note that they have observed this type of distortion in some other research with similar time period-constrained samples.

Do Betzer *et al*'s criticisms of Healey *et al*'s analysis have merit? The sample size does appear to be small. As a comparison, Coley and Reinton's 1988 research involved more than twice as many completed acquisitions: 116. But a numerically small sample does not necessarily disqualify the study's findings, assuming that other characteristics of the sample do not introduce additional bias based on industry selection, type of acquirer or other salient variable. But *that* is where Healey *et al* fall short. All 50 transactions in that study occurred during the brief halcyon 1979–84 period starting during the pre-Reagan recession, until the first two years of LBO merger wave that followed (Chapter 1, Figures 1.3 and 1.4).

If there was ever an era when an acquirer might succeed at almost any deal, 1979 to 1984 was arguably it. The business-merger cycle was then at a low ebb, with easy improvements available in terms of both productivity gains and margins. Share prices and purchase premiums were both minimal over that period. Even if the acquirer's purchase logic were flawed, liquidation value was not significantly less than the amount paid. Volcker's successful efforts at squeezing inflation out of the economy established a foundation for all four of the post-1980 expansion periods.

Superior operating performance? Determined on what basis?

Factor in purchase premiums, and the positive post-merger cash flows indicated by Healey *et al* decline to negligible levels. The fact that purchase premiums were excluded from those researchers' analysis represents a material omission, as APP is an integral part of the target company's total purchase price.

A capable CFO wouldn't attempt to calculate the return on a (internal investment) capital expenditure project without first being assured that *all* costs related to that investment were either known or accurately estimated, including all costs required to acquire that asset. In a similar manner, an external (merger) investment analysis that excludes the full cost of that asset (including the purchase premium) is incomplete and unrealistic.[11] Even if there *is* positive indicated CF generated after inclusion of all cost and investments, that does not necessarily indicate a viable merger. The reference rate is all-important: a 4 per cent rate of return suggests a successful transaction if the reference rate is 2 per cent, but a failure if that comparative rate is 6 per cent.

A range of different reference return rates is illustrated in Figure 5.1. At each different rate level, the proponent for that threshold declares that return performance below that level is deficient – and in the case of M&A, that the acquisition is a failure:

- Magnet (1984) declared that any deal generating less than the return from bank CDs (2–3 per cent at the time) was a failure, as represented in Figure 5.1 as point B.

- Four years later, Coley and Reinton suggested that deals which failed to exceed the acquiring firm's weighed average cost of capital (point C in Figure 5.1) were value-diminishing and thus unsuccessful.
- The incremental value effect approach (point D) adapts the WACC rate threshold to include the projected capital costs and structure of both principals to the deal (acquirer + target) in the combined scenario.
- Alternative investment opportunities (OC, opportunity cost) or return expectations of the financial community may indicate a higher evaluative rate requirement (point E) still.

5.3 M&A's core contradiction, segmentation and stakeholders' different merger perspectives

> There is a paradox in bank mergers. On average, bank mergers do not create value, but they continue to occur.
>
> (DeLong, 2003: 5)[12]

> Any bank really interested in its clients would shut down most of its M&A department on the grounds that buying other companies almost always works out badly.
>
> (Kellaway, *Financial Times*, Jan 16 2011)[13]

Logic suggests that if acquisition failure comes to be widely-accepted (MMF), then mergers are perceived to be a fool's game *and most deals cease*. If prospects for merger value destruction are high (83 per cent according to the 1999 KPMG investigation cited earlier in this chapter), then the expectation is that all M&A initiatives are shut down. Existing funds and new financing both are re-directed to internal investment opportunities instead.

Applying the merger segmentation solution

But that isn't ever going to happen. The urge to merge is a permanent part of firms' value growth strategies. Chapter 1 describes the inevitability of new merger cycles every 10 years or so. The ideal storm convergence of conditions points in 2010–11 suggest that the pre-conditions for robust M&A volume for the balance of the 2011–19 merger megaboom are in place.

But how does acquiring company top management proceed with acquisitions without the ever-present (and high) risk of value destruction? The answer begins with a differentiated M&A strategy emphasizing the types of deals that are most successful while avoiding the others: 'merger segmentation' from Chapter 4. While some highest risk merger types (4a and 4b, transformational lynchpin strategic and speculative strategic) are roughly consistent with the KPMG study's dire indications, the other seven merger types all beat the 83 per cent failure/17 per cent success rate. Look again at Table 4.2 in the preceding chapter on merger segmentation and the nine model merger types, substantially replicated here as Table 5.1.

- The highest four types of mergers in terms of analyzed success probability profile – bottom-trawlers (1), bolt-ons (2a) and line extension equivalents (2b) and consolidation-mature – all exhibit model ranges above 50 per cent;
- 2c, multiple core related complimentary, the indicated success profile is about even money, at a 40–45 per cent range;
- even for the remaining two merger types (3b, consolidation-emerging and 2d, single core-related complementary), opportunistic timing within the merger wave combined with pricing care may improve the chances of prospective candidate targets in those categories enough to justify serious purchase consideration.

Different M&A stakeholders, different interpretations of what merger success means

Then there are those who will point out, correctly, that MMF only coincides with the financial interests of a limited range of stakeholders in the M&A process. Prior to addressing alternative methodologies, Chapter 3 identified the continuing shareholders of the acquiring company as the criteria-setters for merger valuation: those who ultimately determine what constitutes merger success and failure, since they are the ones who ultimately put up the risk capital. But there are other stakeholders in the M&A process, and even though growing consensus is that the financial interests of acquiring companies' shareholders prevail over other merger stakeholders' interests, those other groups assert their perspectives, as summarized in Table 5.2.

Several of those stakeholders advocate their own particular perspectives on what constitutes merger success:

- The dealmaker and some like-minded M&A writers and researchers confuse transaction completion with deal success. The day the deal is signed only represents the point when those compensated on a fee basis are positioned for a payday, nothing more.

TABLE 5.1 Nine merger type framework (adapted from Table 4.2)

Success %	Cat.	Acquisition Type	Description	Examples
87–92	1	Bottom-trawlers	Dying competitor signals exit, advantage to fast, cash bidders	Marconi
80–85	2A	Bolt-ons	Fills void in acquirer's existing product/service offer, quickly	P&G/ Pantene
65–70	2B	Line extension equivalents	Next generation/different variant of existing product-service	Volkswagen/ Škoda
55–60	3A	Consolidation – mature	Same industry contraction: scale, overhead synergies	Pharma, telecoms
40–45	2C	Multiple core-related complementary	Logical complements to present offer: products/ channels/areas, two or more related elements	Disney/ABC P&G/Gilette
37–42	3B	Consolidation – emerging	Same industry contraction: Picking winners	ABC Capital Cities/ Dumont
30–35	2D	Single core-related complementary	Similar to 2C but one or less related elements	Daimler Chrysler
20–25	4A	Lynchpin strategic	Supports major change in emphasis in acquirer's strategy	IBM/PwC Consulting
15–20	4B	Speculative strategic	Radical, high-risk change in overall business model	AOL/TWX Vivendi (Mercier)

Related: Table 4.2, Chapter 4.

TABLE 5.2 Merger success objectives by stakeholder groups

Stakeholder	M&A Economic Interest	Target Objective	Exclusions *(Table 4.2, Chapter 4, Table 5.1)*	Issues
(1a) Continuing SHs, Acquirer	Pursuit of maximum shareholder value on a continuing basis	Avoidance of low success probability deals except where assured synergies exceed APP by 2+ times	Lowest four success probability types: 3B, 2D, both Transformational types (4A, 4B)	Limited to Azofra-AMS APP ceilings, merger wave timing without access to requisite Net Realizable Synergy insight
(1b) Interim SHs, Acquirer	Maximize short to intermediate term return, TSR basis, positioning for profitable round turn re-sale	Established Cash Cow (3A) with upside message for re-sale	Highest three success probability types (1, 2A, 2B) because of size, additional investment requirement, both Transformational types (4A, 4B)	Managing the 2 and 20: Guarding against excessive outflows that cripple valuation of unit on re-sale
(2) Management, Acquirer	(a) Maximize personal benefits (b) Some alignment with 1a, depending on share conditions, amounts	Acquisition consistent with PR value leadership posturing	Highest three success probability types (1, 2A, 2B) because too incremental. If acquirer value is flat to down, active pursuit of Transformational (4A, 4B)	Time in office, options, growth options, level of break-up/buy-out demand

TABLE 5.2 *continued*

Stakeholder	M&A Economic Interest	Target Objective	Exclusions *(Table 4.2, Chapter 4, Table 5.1)*	Issues
(3) Transaction Middlemen	Maximize ongoing M&A transaction dollar volume and thus fees	Higher transaction size opportunities	Highest three success probability types (1, 2A, 2B) due to size, limited bidding attractiveness	Dealing with incompatible business models when the old merger inducements no longer work
(4) Sellers	Maximize APP (thereby maximizing returns to *its* shareholders)	*Target acquirer:* Disregards *all* of the APP value-creating bid rules	1 and 2A: limited negotiating leverage	Determining optimal bidders, bid rounds before proceeding; severity of Rounds 1–2 rebuffs
(5) MMF Deniers	Counter-positioning, to better avoid limitations of returns-centric M&A	N/A	N/A	Reconciling with (a) shareholder primacy, (b) MMF

- Deniers of quantitative financial measures promote their own particular set of preferred *qualitative* criteria, sometimes embellishing the descriptions as (value drivers, etc).
- The initiating principal, the aspiring acquiring company's CEO, may tend to view himself or herself as not subject to the financial rules of merger success or failure cited by others. Emboldened by phrases such as 'strategic imperatives', mergers are treated as executive privilege, sometimes regardless of value consequences for the buying firm and its owners.

Acquiring company CEO longevity plays for time, with newly appointed chief executives particularly eager to make their mark through a bold strategic move. Turnarounds and new internal investment are too slow. Average CEO longevity in office is today around four years, and thus external investment – mergers – receive priority consideration (Mathinson, 2010).[14]

5.4 Moving forward: expanding upon Hayward's three causes of merger failure

None of the alternative stakeholders' perspectives from Table 5.2 have any effect on the primacy of the acquiring company's continuing shareholders as the criteria-selectors for merger valuation (part 2 in Chapter 3). Accordingly, today's dominant consensus that MMF remains unchallenged, although not unopposed.

Focus now moves on to what to do about MMF. A good place to start is the causes of merger failure: just as the answer to Coley and Reinton's finding that around the failure of two-thirds of the deals they examined lies in segmentation on two dimensions, thus the answer to dealing with MMF begins with consideration of the root causes. Hayward presents an uncomplicated prescription for merger failure. In Table 5.3 we expand upon his explanations for M&A disappointment, adding some illustrative examples and implications.

Select the wrong target

No matter how well-conceived all the other parts of the merger process, aiming at the wrong target assures a value-destroying acquisition. Errors in targeting raise the prospect of *negative* synergies: when 2 + 2 = 3. Acquirer

TABLE 5.3 Perspectives on Hayward's three factors

'Acquisitions are complex events that fail for numerous reasons... select the wrong target, pay too much for it, and poorly integrate it.' Hayward (2002: 21)

Misstep	Illustrative Examples	Implications
Select the wrong target	• Conseco/Green Tree • Quaker Oats/Snapple • Coca-Cola/Columbia Pictures	Excuses for the errant acquisitions make little sense to the financial markets, except those portions taking a perspective as incomplete as the acquiring company's chief executive. In extreme instances, disastrous targeting threatens not only merger success, but also the viability or independence of the acquirer (Conseco, Quaker Oats).
Pay too much for it	• H-P/3Par • RBS Fortis/ABN Amro • AOL/Huffington Press	Synergy-informed pricing dynamics characteristic of the most successful mergers are set aside, displaced by (a) chase mania, (b) the Good Company Bad Price fallacy (see Chapter 3), and/or (c) desperation. *Perhaps viable mergers at a defendable price, but that would necessitate Winning by Walking Away (see Chapter 8).*
Poorly integrate it	• AT&T/NCR • Terra Firma/EMI • Unum/Provident	Both hands-off (AT&T/NCR) and oppressive hands-on (Terra Firma/EMI, Daimler Chrysler) ensure that major synergy opportunities are squandered. *As with target selection (see Chapter 3), the absence of a framework and approach sufficient for the challenge means reliance on lesser tactics (see Chapter 7)*

and acquiree businesses struggle to make the best of a transaction that never should have happened.

In the *acquiring* firm, there is pressure from the chief executive to communicate to the financial community that the deal is a success, regardless of the VG-IVE merger valuation diagnosis. If the deal is already suspected to be value-destroying (such as because of a triple-digit APP), formal merger valuation is probably not even attempted. No matter; analysts and the business press are already making their own VG-like estimations. In the *acquired* target firm, adverse selection prevails. Top talent are reluctant to take a step backwards in their professional careers by becoming minions to an overlord firm that doesn't understand its business. Leaving for the competition, once unthinkable, suddenly becomes plausible.

Conseco's acquisition of Green Tree was a merger diagnosis outright miss: a combination of fundamentally different financial businesses, with incompatible customer sets that didn't overlap at all: 'In the year after the Green Tree bid, Conseco shares lost 47 per cent of their value... (while) shares of insurers in the Standard & Poor's 500 stock index rose 8 per cent in the same time.' Dragged down by the dead weight of its ill-advised acquisition, the December 18 2002 headline surprised no one: 'Conseco Makes Chapter 11 Filing.'[15]

In the mid-1990s, Snapple's iconic distribution approach was incompatible with the distribution approaches of major suppliers including acquirer Quaker Oats, an error pointing to seriously inadequate pre-bid due diligence. In the worst instances, the mistargeted acquisition provides an unintended signal to the financial community that acquiring company management either cannot or will not confront a basic problem plaguing that firm for years, and instead is attempting to distract the financial markets from its true problems with adventures of M&A conquest.

Throughout the first decade of the new millennium, AOL management failed to find answers to its most important problem of a deteriorating core business. While that firm's 2011 overpayment for content provider Huffington Press was perceived by many in the financial community as indirectly supporting the content side of the business, problems relating to AOL's deteriorating core remained unaddressed, both before and after that deal.

Pay too much for it

> Studies have correlated variables with acquisition performance have found a statistically significant negative correlation between premium and performance.
>
> (Porrini, 2006: 91)[16]

Conseco's mistake in pursuing Green Tree (above) was made worse by an overpayment more than two times the Azofra *et al* APP ceiling guideline (as described in Chapter 3). *BusinessWeek*'s Henry described the terms of that merger as '$7.1 billion and a huge 86 per cent premium' (Oct 14 2002).

H-P's acquisition of cloud computing company 3Par is described in Chapter 3 as representing the greatest APP ever paid, at 242 per cent.[17] Overpayment to that degree effectively ensures that the transaction will be judged value destroying on a VG (APP-NRS) basis, since achievable returns can never come close to the purchase premium amount.

Multiple cycle bidding wars (such as for 3Par, ABN Amro) almost always result in winners remorse. CEOs of both of the 'winning' companies for those two targets found themselves dismissed soon after those stillborn deals were completed, as the financial community cut through the post-merger hype and came to realize the true nature of those value-destroying (for the acquiring company's shareholders) deals.

Poorly integrate it

Chapter 7 deals with the integration issues between buyer and target. The three examples cited in Table 5.3 were post-merger integration (PMI) failures for three different reasons. AT&T initially imposed almost no PMI guidance at all in the first two years following the 1990 acquisition of NCR, and then abruptly changed to a more activist role after it was too late.

Terra Firma management reasonably imagined that CFs at its new acquiree in the music business, EMI, could generate more cash flow with improved cost controls. But the phrases 'cost controls' and 'rock 'n' roll artist' are rarely included in the same sentence, for good reason. That acquirer faced a crisis as key performing talent fiercely resisted the new owner's ideas about the best ways to run a business in the entertainment field. The consequence of trying to force cost discipline on an uncooperative acquiree? On January 7 2011, *Bloomberg* reported that acquirer Terra Firma 'wrote down its investment in record label EMI Group Ltd to zero.'[18]

Among Unum's PMI mistakes in its acquisition of Provident was a recurring IT synergies mistake: automatic presumption of massive savings from the forced reduction in the number of IT platforms in the two firms. Some savings existed, but the process of reducing the platforms would be slower than anticipated, and involved some unforeseen investment in order to pursue those eventual efficiencies. Poor synergy intelligence means that the acquiring company is bidding blindly, as there is no reliable sense of realizable synergies upon which to build a bid that is consistent with a value-creating acquisition. Or no bid at all if that means a required bid level that ensures an adverse VG metric (APP-S).

The phrase 'cross-marketing' was heard frequently in the weeks following the deal. For reasons described in part 5 in Chapter 7 in this book, this sub-category of revenue-related synergy almost always disappoints. Those Conseco customers who were in high enough tax brackets to be interested in the parent's tax-sheltered annuities hardly fit the profile of mobile home buyers seeking finance. And as *New York Times*' Leslie Eaton observed, 'Green Tree's customers, the mobile home buyers, do not seem likely to be big buyers of annuities.'

Notes

1 'After the deal', http://www.economist.com/node/181251. Accessed June 19 2011.

2 *Mergers and Efficiency.* Notes from the Editors, xix.

3 'A pioneering study by the consulting firm (McKinsey) shows that over two-thirds of the corporate diversification programs it examined never earned as much as the acquirer would have by investing the money in, say, certificates of deposit issued by a bank', from Myron Magnet in his Nov 12 1984 *Fortune* article 'Acquiring without smothering', pp 22–8.

4 EVA™ is a proprietary copyrighted trademark of Stern Stewart & Company.

5 http://online.barrons.com/article/SB892852735409795000.html. Accessed May 14 2011.

6 Our examination of pre- and post-merger performance in multiple industries suggests markedly different patterns for financial companies than for other industries. If a sample set is to be limited to one deal, a case can be made for a reference transaction in sectors other than financial.

7 Healey *et al*'s components differ somewhat from the generally accepted definition for CF: net operating profit after taxes (NOPAT) plus non-cash items (depreciation and amortization) plus some deferrals. Healey *et al*'s 'cash flow' is composed of: 'sales, minus cost of goods sold and selling and administrative expenses, plus depreciation and goodwill expenses... deflated by market value of assets... excludes the effect of... taxes' (p 139).

8–9 Refer to Further Reading.

10 Others reveal a significant decline in post-acquisition operating performance (Kruse *et al*, 2002; Yeh and Hoshino, 2001; Clark and Ofek, 1994). Furthermore, there are a number of studies that demonstrate insignificant changes in the post-merger operating performance (Ghosh, 2001; Moeller and Schlingemann, 2004; Sharma and Ho, 2002)', M Martynova, S Oosting and L Renneboog (2006) *The Long-Term Operating Performance of European Mergers and Acquisitions,* ECGI Finance Working Paper No 137.

11 Acquisition Purchase Premiums (APPs) are normally required to gain ownership control in the case of all merger types (Table 4.2, Chapter 4) except some type 1 (bottom trawler) transactions. If no premium is paid, there is no completed acquisition, since existing shareholders expect to receive compensation in excess of the present market value of their shares. Analysis of returns, and by implication, merger success, without factoring in APP is thus moot.

12 'Does long-term performance of mergers match market expectations? Evidence from the US banking industry', *Financial Management*, Summer.

13 'Finnish lesson on principles for Goldman.' http://www.ft.com/cms/s/0/f9c1ffa6-217c-11e0-9e3b-00144feab49a.html#axzz1BDSDYRd2. Accessed Jan 16 2011.

14 'Hello and good buy', *InBusiness*, 14.

15 *New York Times*, http://www.nytimes.com/2002/12/18/business/conseco-makes-chapter-11-filing.html?src=pm. Accessed Apr 8 2012.

16 'Are investment bankers good for acquisition premiums?', *Journal of Business Research*, 59.

17 A Sorkin (Nov 7 2011) 'Behind the woes at H.P., Wall St. banks lurk', DealBook, http://dealbook.nytimes.com/2011/11/07/as-h-p-shops-its-bankers-do-very-nicely/?nl=business&emc=dlbka23. Accessed Nov 7 2011.

18 'Guy Hands reaped $19 million dividend from Terra Firma in 2010', http://noir.bloomberg.com/apps/news?pid=20601087&sid=arl2VlNf62cw&pos=4#. Accessed Jan 7 2011.

The merger megaboom's signature IPO: Facebook

06

The boom in Web IPOs (those initials increasingly seem to connote insanely popular offerings) has served to pump some life into the market's euphoria.

(Alan Abelson, May 21 2011, 'Facebook for philanderers', *Barrons*)[1]

CHAPTER CONTENTS

6.1 The straw that stirs the drink

6.2 Social networking and the 2011–19 merger megaboom

6.3 Direct and indirect merger market effects of social networking sector acquisitions, 2011+

6.4 Vapor numbers: *when* is the social networking valuation?

Bankers perform a pivotal role in confronting M&A's core contradiction as described in the preceding chapter: the mystery that merger activity persists year-to-year, even though most deals fail. Those same instigators also cause each new merger wave's signature event, as described in

Chapter 1. Whether it is Netscape's IPO in August 1995 preceding the *first* dot com bubble (aka post-1980 merger wave 2, 1996–2000), or Facebook's long-anticipated emergence as a public company in May 2012, Wall Street's active stewardship of the business-merger expansion period ahead is everywhere.

Today's social networking (SN) boom means the emergence of a second top tier group of internet segment leaders, including Facebook, LinkedIn and Twitter. Arrival of the second dot com boom is already stimulating sector and overall merger activity. The gold rush atmosphere surrounding SN IPOs inspires increases in both merger activity and share prices, as firms hurry to utilize their new acquisition currency before the inevitable post-IPO waterfall plunge (see Figures 6.2, 6.3 and 6.5 in this chapter).

That abrupt plunge in share prices in tech deals in particular after IPO Day One reflects a transition from pre-launch hype-pricing towards valuation on a far more substantive basis: DCF analysis, based on the fundamentals of the existing business and future CF performance prospects of that firm.

6.1 The straw that stirs the drink

In the May 1977 issue of *Sport*, reporter Robert Ward quoted New York Yankee slugger (and later, Hall of Fame inductee) Reggie Jackson as boasting 'The team, it all flows from me. I'm the straw that stirs the drink' (per Wikipedia). Jackson wanted everyone to know that *he* was the team's lead instigator, the one who makes the critical difference, whether winning the World Series with three homers in Game 7, or as the center of clubhouse disorder. That chaos inspired the 1970s' nickname for that championship team: *The Bronx Zoo*.[2]

So it is with banker-dealmakers today. With their own business models dependent on revenues from merger *activity* rather than merger *success* (Table 1.4, Chapter 1 and Table 6.1 here – and see the *Alex* cartoon below), bankers are today's 'straw that stir the drink' when it comes to generating business and merger expansion enthusiasm.

Chapter 1 contains several explanations for merger waves, including industry-specific and overall economic shocks, insufficient rates of return from internal investments, and behavioral reasons – the last referring to buyers' and sellers' perceptions of company under- or over-valuation. To

that list we added the concept of *merger marketplace actor* in that chapter. That phrase refers to a notion that deal intermediaries and arrangers with a vital financial self-interest in ensuring continuing levels of M&A transactions actively seek to shape the market upon which they rely for their livelihood.[3]

The notion of bankers making mergers happen isn't just about oversized egos and type A Masters of the Universe personalities. The actor/straw that stirs the drink notion is also supported by *actions*. The internet's roots preceded the 1996–2000 bubble, and SN companies pre-dated the respective business-merger expansion period. *Someone* helped transform those initial developments into major business-merger expansion opportunities later. In the early phases of new merger waves such as now, bankers sensed that under the conditions favoring new M&A activity (Figure 1.7 in Chapter 1), mergers could help pull stock markets out of their recession malaise.

TABLE 6.1 Bank M&A adviser fees, 2009

	Institution	Target & Acquirer Financial Adviser Fees ($Mn)	Number of Deals
1	Goldman Sachs	511.6	324
2	JP Morgan	419.3	320
3	B of A Merrill Lynch	395.7	208
4	Citi	387.1	222
5	Morgan Stanley	349.0	320
6	Barclays Capital	274.7	95
7	Deutsche Bank AG	108.4	221
8	Lazard	108.3	228
9	UBS	43.1	267
10	Credit Suisse	30.1	267

SOURCES: Include some from Fruhan, W (April 21 2010), Exhibit 4: 2009 Fees to Top 10 Financial Advisers in Merger and Acquisition Transactions 'The role of private equity firms in merger and acquisition transactions', 7, CASE 9-206-101, Boston, Harvard Business School Publishing, as well as publicly available ranking information.

Banker self-interest and the M&A core contradiction

Sustaining merger volume starts with convincing the acquiring company's chief executive that his or her firm has a reasonable chance of winning the M&A contest.[4] Confronting such hopes is the reality that most mergers fail.

Prior to 1988, MMF (as measured on objective, quantifiable financial criteria important to the acquiring company's shareholders) might have been sidestepped with an observation that merger performance to date was inconclusive. No longer. It is now necessary for any deal's advocates to demonstrate that their proposed transaction can succeed based on financial returns realizable by the acquiring firm's shareholders – at the envisioned price necessary to secure control, timing and with realistic net synergies factored in – before full financing can be made available from deal financing sources. This makes bankers' job of resurrecting confidence in the merger game much more challenging today than during the three prior post-1980 merger waves. As with merger booms past, there is no selling job necessary for the compulsive CEO acquirer – the one who immediately lurches to the conclusion that a merger is the best option for his or her company, without first considering other major investment alternatives, some of which may offer superior returns on a percentage rate of return and risk basis.[5]

Macho merger language from past merger waves evokes the thrill of the acquisition to this type of acquirer. Such appeals to the emotion of the victorious chase may be sufficient on their own to spur this merger enthusiast to action. By concentrating on the self-described 'unique' characteristics of the target company (along with the imagined 'unique' situation that the acquiring firm finds itself in, this merger enthusiast may be inclined to disregard financial-based merger valuation criteria altogether, arguing that the situation is special and thus conventional performance requirements do not apply.[6] Just ensure that this would-be acquirer is insulated from those who point out the correlation between the numbers of bidders + bid cycles to unsupportable APPs, such as shown in Table 3.6 in Chapter 3.

Other, more careful CEOs of would-be acquiring companies tend to be more wary of making a merger commitment. These executives are *not* motivated by dreams of acquisition conquest. They have observed the merger initiatives of other companies' chief executives, and seen that time in office is halved for chief executives that come to be viewed by the financial community as merger value-destroyers. Since the average chief executive's time in office is already brief (four years), why risk abandoning two years in the top job? Today's chief executive is aware not only of MMF but also that the bankers' recommendations about star targets to consider are sometimes: a) bank client companies desperately seeking to be bought out; or b) well-shopped companies previously turned down by others, for good reason.

Because of the importance of bid price (APP) to realizable synergies to merger performance, the savvy quickly comes to understand that doing everything possible to suppress unrealistic price expectations on the seller's side is key to quick close and early M&A fee income. The chief executive who becomes caught in the upward price spiral of a bidding war is today mocked, not praised for perseverance in pursuing the objective, regardless of obstacles. That banker must hope that the acquirer comes to understand somehow some of the *substantive* ways to improve merger success one deal at a time – such as by starting with the right merger diagnostics and timing (Chapter 3), along with success-oriented target company assessment (Chapter 4), including synergies (Chapter 7).

The new bulge bracket bankers running the biggest casino in the world

Bellagio? MGM Grand? Chump change compared to the casino odds of launching an IPO (but with some comparable built-in advantages to the 'house'). A brand new merger wave means that hundreds of billions of dollars are 'bet' on the new combined company's unknown future performance. M&A is the best and biggest casino in the world, with odds that are better than the best in Vegas or Monte Carlo, even under assumptions that MMF.

Who are the operators of this global M&A casino? The half dozen or so major international banks led by JPMorgan Chase and Goldman Sachs, which did not merely survive the subprime meltdown, but which emerged from that stormy period with sufficient capital and reputation intact to support a return to the offensive during the 2011–19 merger megaboom.[7]

Problem is, every merger wave is preceded by a recession. Until and unless the recession mentality can be shaken off and investors' sights are once again directed optimistically towards a promising future, there is no enduring recovery at all, no new merger wave. Each of the three recessions in the post-1980 era has been successively proclaimed at the time as 'the worst since the Great Depression'. Sustaining that negativity are those writers and pundits who failed to predict the danger signs in the last bursting bubble soon enough to make a difference, and now seem be attempting to make up for lost time by stoking demand for books featuring doom 'n' gloom future scenarios.

Intellectually and sometimes emotionally committed to a negative perspective about the years ahead, which is as deeply entrenched as the mindless optimism seen at the peak of the bubble, these Cassandras[8] see doom around every corner. Even when green shoots of recovery are clearly visible, the crash book authors perceive a dark lining in every silver cloud. For the operators of the great merger casino in 2011–12 (as with their counterparts in 1995 and 2002) the challenge is how to counteract the recession momentum and the deal-killing sentiment that results.

How best to turn the negative sentiment around? The starting point is acknowledgement of fundamental improvement in economic prospects, even as some bad economic indicators prevail. The mix of good and bad news (increases in demand despite financial frailty left over from the last recession) is normal in phases I and II of the new business-merger cycle (by the time that all indicators point 'up', the wave is approaching a peak and a collapse is coming, soon). What is needed from the bankers to help spur increased merger volume is a sentiment-changing major event that communicates to the world that financial markets have now moved forward from the last recession. Something like the signature IPO of post 1980 wave 2, Netscape, or something like the signature IPOs of the 2011–19 merger megaboom: LinkedIn (2011) and especially, Facebook (May 2012).[9] Something to help make sustained bull markets appear possible; something that makes at least some mergers appear to be safe for acquirers, once again.

6.2 Social networking and the 2011–19 merger megaboom

> The early extreme excess of netPhase I is just part of the stage-setting for what is to come: netPhase II, when the dot coms grow up, when the major new corporations of the 21st century begin to be built, and when the new internet champions soar.
>
> (Clark, 2000: xvi)

The new optimism results in not only the carnival atmosphere of IPOs but also getting back to the business of creating tomorrow's major corporations. Even with all the 99 percenters (companies that lost that percentage of their share price when the 1996–2000 bubble burst) in the first dot com wave, that period resulted in the creation of several major corporations.

And dot com II is positioned to accomplish just as much, and possibly more. Profitless wonders of the 1996–2000 era are mostly a thing of the past. While some observe multiple Groupons' reporting and profitability issues in 2011–2012 with alarm, an alternative perspective is that markets have learnt to be wary in the decade-plus since the first net bubble.[10] Concepts written on the back of a cocktail napkin added to the ranks of the 99 percenters in 1996–2000. Such unprofitable companies face extreme difficulty finding banker support in the present IPO era.

In the dot com II column in Table 6.2, the phrase 'Coupon Co' is used instead of any single company's name, both because of Groupon's possible issues and a challenge from within that segment from LivingSocial. 'GameCo' reflects our anticipation of emerging company-type consolidation in that segment, resulting in one or possibly two multiple-product majors. The corresponding merger type in Table 4.2 (Chapter 4) is 3b, consolidation-emerging.

TABLE 6.2 Major corporations emerge, in both net eras

Dot Com I (1996–2000) Post-1980 wave 2	Dot Com II (SN, 2011–) Post-1980 wave 4
Amazon	Facebook
Google	Twitter
Yahoo!	LinkedIn
eBay	'GameCo'
	'CouponCo'

Mergers and share prices

1. Facebook's acquisition of Instagram marks the beginning of the merger megaboom's phase II?

> The $1 billion deal for Instagram reveals quite a bit about the shifting technology industry. Facebook's acquisition of Instagram looks like something of a turning point, as even the Web giant Facebook tries to get a better grasp on a market that requires a rethinking of old rules.
>
> ('A turning point for mobile', *New York Times*)[11]

> History shows that they fail most of the time, but when they win, it's very valuable. There's always the blended question of opportunity and threat.
>
> (LinkedIn founder Reid Hoffman, characterizing Facebook's acquisition of Instagram as an attempt to stave off the competition, even if the price is high.)

Nothing like doubling the price in a week to jolt the merger marketplace.

Facebook purchased Instagram for a cool (cue Dr Evil) 1 *billion* dollars on April 9 2012. Venture capital firms acquired minority positions in Instagram one week earlier, on a basis reported as reflecting a value for that firm of half that amount: $500 million.[12]

Some of the thinking underlying the shock acquisition emerged by mid-April 2012. Instagram was already known as a best-in-class online photo-sharing service, an increasingly important part of interaction on SN websites. Those supporting the move praised Facebook for anticipating the sector's next major evolutionary change, towards the mobile internet. Detractors bemoaned the fact that Facebook apparently could not develop an Instagram-like service internally – at least not fast enough and at competitive cost.[13] The Instagram deal is not just company-transformational, but also *sector*-transformational. After the drama of April 9 2012, you can bet that every present or potential Facebook competitor and affiliate had its key people staying up all night, trying to figure out what this massive vote for the mobile net meant to their firms.

Facebook's watershed acquisition marks the return of the speculative merger, and thus the beginning of phase II of the 2011–19 merger megaboom (Figure 1.2 in Chapter 1). Facebook-Instagram represents the first major acquisition in the present M&A wave (excluding desperation deals by troubled AOL and Hewlett-Packard)[14] in which price and APP considerations were ignored.

One may argue that a lynchpin strategic (type 4a), deal tends to have a higher probability of success than the 20–25 per cent range identified in Table 4.2 in Chapter 4 when the acquirer is a) acting first, and b) effectively changing the industry to its own advantage, as Facebook has. But the market overall tends to ignores such nuances. Imitation is the sincerest form of flattery, and one of the best-known companies in the world has just thrown out the M&A rulebook, starting the new M&A gold rush.

2. Interrelatedness

Rising share prices spur increased merger activity. Conversely, rising merger transaction volume supports overall share prices, as suggested by Figure 6.1.

Baker and Kiymaz (2011) note Melicher *et al's* 1983 paper and related research; they reveal a significant correlation between increases in stock prices and increased levels of merger activity.[15] Those relationships are graphically depicted in Figure 6.1; key dynamics shown in that figure are examined in the pages following.

At the time of the announcement of a major deal involving public companies and a material (that is, greater than 15 per cent) APP, the well-established pattern of the target's price going up while the acquirer's goes down occurs. This reordering reflects both 1) the uneven distribution of any efficiency gains from the merger with target companies' shareholders benefitting to the disadvantage of shareholders of the purchasing firm, combined with 2) the financial community's instant judgment about the likelihood that the acquirer can cover the purchase premium through synergies.

At the beginning of the first phase (of four) of the newly spawned merger wave, both share price indices and merger volume are at record low levels. Both have been devastated by the recession, which just ended recently and is rumored to be re-occurring until the beginning of phase II.[16] Gradually, a few bargain-hunting, bottom trawling acquirers start the merger wave rolling. Those early movers are characterized in the financial media as bold;

FIGURE 6.1 Mergers and prices: symbiotic relationship

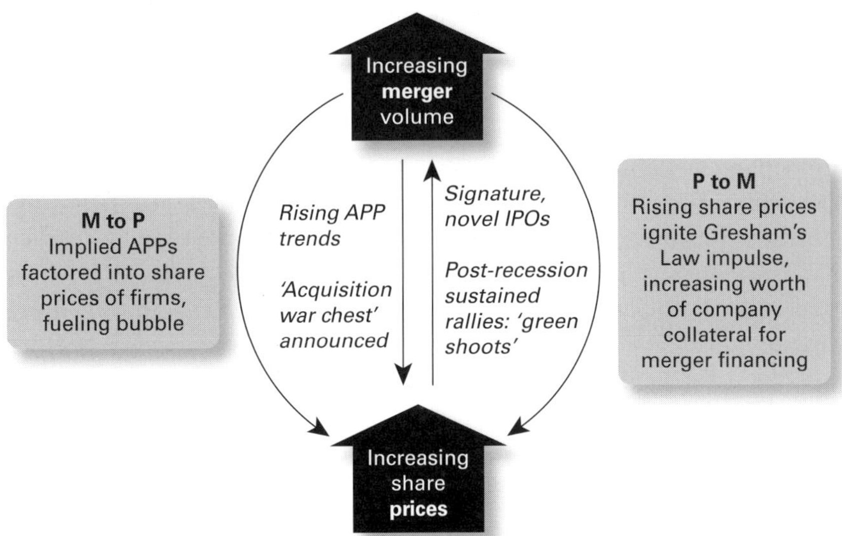

Interpreted/based on Shleifer and Vishny (2003), Golbe and White (1988), Melicher, Ledolter and D-Antonio (1983)[17]

the reality is that special courage is not required, as this represents the lowest risk point during the new merger wave in which to close a deal. Only when the acquisitions begin to move into the slightly more risky categories as shown in the nine merger types table (Table 4.2 in Chapter 4) is the new merger wave established for good.

Time heals all wounds, including the M&A demand-dampening memory of the last wave's collapse and the recession that followed. With the weight of that ballast lessening with each passing day in the new merger wave period, share prices begin to creep higher. Some category 2 (operational, from Table 4.2) and even a couple of category 3 (transitional) deals are consummated.

P to M (in Figure 6.1): Rising overall share price levels, stimulating merger activity

Gresham's Law (see Chapter 1) dictates that bad money forces out good in markets. As applied to countries issuing hyper-inflated currencies in the 1920s and 1980s, this meant that the new payment basis was perceived by recipients as less valuable. Substitution follows: the intrinsically more valuable security tends to be withdrawn and hoarded, even before formal regulations for a switch.

The would-be acquirer's share price soars as the business-merger cycle progresses (Figures 1.3 and 1.4 in the first chapter). The company is essentially the same in terms of the ultimate determinant of worth, internal discounted cash flows (DCF), but the share price has gone up, suggesting a similar circumstance, particularly if shares are being used as all or part of the acquisition currency.

Facebook's acquisition of Instagram called for partial payment in Facebook shares. In Feb 2012, the upper end of the guesstimated pre-IPO valuation for Facebook overall was $103 billion. Thirteen months earlier, that guesstimate for Facebook on a comparable basis indicated a guess at worth of $50 billion (Figure 6.4, January 2011). As share prices increase, so does pressure to acquire today to avoid being excluded tomorrow. Concern arises in the aspiring acquirer organizations that its target may become too expensive in future periods if they continue to delay. Share price rises thus become self-fulfilling prophecies: by acting early, market indices receive upward impetus.

M to P: Increasing merger activity, contributing to company share price increases

Rumors of a growing acquisition war chest at AcquirerCo arise. Not only does that firm's chief executive *not* act to suppress such reports, but he or she also makes media proclamations about interest in future 'strategic' acquisitions. Presuming that this chest-thumping acquirer is large, share prices of companies rumored to be possible targets rise in anticipation. Thus, from mid-phase II of the merger wave onwards (Chapter 1), day-to-day share prices of many publicly-traded companies tend to show a 10-plus per cent acquisition *anticipation* premium.[18]

Our experience is that the excuse for this action is a combination of chief executive hubris and the thought that it is helpful to 'get the word' out, so that suitable candidates might make themselves known to the firm's M&A search team. But ego has its price, and this mistake costs the would-be acquiring firm millions. Negotiating leverage is impaired since the acquiring company CEO has already signaled that he or she is too eager. Share prices of companies in target industries and segments have risen as a direct consequence of the regrettable war chest announcement. Candidate companies first to make themselves known as possible targets sometimes exhibit adverse selection: as AcquirerCo has signaled that it is a somewhat careless buyer, management at those companies which to date have eluded takeover interest may figure that they may have found the ideal buyer.

TABLE 6.3a Direct merger market effects – social networking's boom

	Acquisition Rationale	Description	Examples
DIRECT	**A1** Tier 1 SN: expansion-defensive	Sector leaders utilize the inflated 'currency' of their (vapor) valuations to secure future areas for growth, pre-empt present and potential competition	Perlroth, April 10, 2012 Complementary acquisitions of segment leaders: Types 2A, 2B*
	A2 Tier 2 SN: catch-up, emerging consolidation acquisitions	Internet speed exaggerates Net's tendency to big-little duopolies. If company cannot be leader, rush to Type 3B (Consolidation-Emerging)*	Shakeout in: online couponing services (Groupon versus Living Social), online games (Rovio), SN data diagnostics
	A3 Acquisitions: bricks-to-SN, other clicks-to-SN	Merchandisers avoid being marginalized as channels evolve Established firms broaden their product offering: approaching multiple core	Nordstrom: HauteLook Walgreen: Drugstore.com Wal-Mart: Kosmix Google: YouTube

* Table 4.2, Nine Merger Types Framework v2, Chapter 4.

6.3 Direct and indirect merger market effects of social networking sector acquisitions, 2011+

Facebook's 2012 IPO is positioned to stimulate merger activity for the three remaining phases of the 2011–19 merger megaboom.[19]

Five acquisition rationales are shown in Tables 6.3a and 6.3b, organized into two categories: direct and indirect. Direct (A1, A2, A3), refers to past or

TABLE 6.3b Indirect merger market effects – social networking's boom

	Acquisition Rationale	Description	Examples
INDIRECT	**B1** New value paradigm/ major market move indications	Belief in a sector which defies the customary valuation rules *partially* rekindled: specter of instant wealth by mere sector participation distorts M&A strategies. (Related: fear of missing decade's major development.)	Chand, *Economist* 04.14. 2012. Risk of acquisitions ignored or once again presumed to not apply
	B2 Anticipated APP effect: aspiring acquirers act to beat 'buyers' panic'	Halo effect on Tier 1 leaders permits price-value discontinuities to continue for years; any prospective target or consolidation participant has share price increased by implied purchase premium factor	Perlroth, April 10, 2012 In other sectors, companies follow Monster.com precedent

possible future acquisition activity that results directly from the actions of social networking companies. Indirect (B1, B2) refers to possible secondary effects on the merger market overall.

Direct (a)

a1: Tier 1 SN: Expansion-defensive acquisitions

Facebook has set the precedent of using its shares as acquisition currency, even before its own IPO. The other two companies in the dot com II Big Five, LinkedIn and Twitter, face a keep-up-or-risk-falling-behind dilemma.

As an emerging sector with product and service boundaries overlapping and continually changing, today's partner is tomorrow's competitor. The following 'hit list' appeared in *The New York Times* the day after the Facebook-Instagram announcement, as betting companies are already anticipating Mark Zuckerberg's next possible series of opportunistic targets:

> PaddyPower.com said current odds favored an acquisition of Foursquare, the location check-in service... Evernote, an application that collects and saves notes, is a close second, followed by Dropbox, which has a payout rate of 5-to-1. Spotify, the streaming music service that recently partnered with Facebook, is priced at 7-to-1. The odds that Facebook will buy Tumblr, the blogging site, are 25-to-1.
>
> (N Perloff)[20]

With the precedent for this type of core-strengthening acquisition having been set by Facebook, can the other tier I companies in SN/dot com II sector afford to stand aside? We suspect not.

One of the dot com II Big Five, Twitter, is already using its pre-IPO equity to make incremental acquisitions to refine its market offer. On January 19 2012, Twitter acquired Canadian startup Summify to facilitate management of the massive amounts of information continually entering activity streams and social media subscriber account in-boxes.[21]

a2: Tier 2 SN: Catch-up, emerging consolidation acquisitions

The precedent of dot com I suggests that internet sectors are oriented towards duopolies and sometimes monopolies; fickle changes occur at a click, causing a stampede effect towards preferred products and companies and with the same lightning-fast pace when it comes to dissatisfaction. As shown in Table 6.1, Tier 1's online couponing ultimate champion is not known as of Spring 2012, with both Groupon and LivingSocial still in contention. Look to some supplementary acquisition by each in an attempt to outflank the other, although the persistence of some negative sentiment about the viability of online couponing's base business model will probably mean that acquisitions are of minimal size.[22]

A more classic consolidation-emerging merger type 3b situation arises in games central to the SN sites. Somewhat similar to gaming systems (Nintendo, XBox), the developer is initially hopeful of replicating the early success of its first game, but is forced to consider a combination with others in that segment when internal development attempts disappoint. On April 17 2012, *Bloomberg* reported that Zynga, 'the biggest maker of social games paid $180 million last month to acquire OMGPop Inc, after spending a combined $147.2 million for 22 companies in 2010 and 2011.'[23]

a3: Bricks-to-SN, other clicks-to-SN

The memories of Clickmango and similar bricks and clicks combinations from hell are a distant memory, now more than a decade in the past. The neverending belief that *this time is different* – that the mistakes of boom periods past might somehow be avoided – raise a specter of history repeating itself (Reinhart and Rogoff, 2009). For executive management of the industrial company stuck in low single-digit growth, being part of something with seemingly universal appeal may prove irresistible. Ubiquity is no assurance of profitability – just ask internet service providers (ISPs) and e-mail companies – but such considerations are sometimes ignored in the rush to be part of the Next Big Thing. While we're addressing valuation errors from the first dot com bubble years, don't be shocked to hear this again from some companies presently outside of SN: 'We believe that this acquisition in the social networking space will enhance the valuation of the overall group, as social networking is integrated into all aspects of our operation.' Invariably, first net bubble (1996–2000) terrestrial companies dabbling in experimental acquisitions in internet-related areas discovered that not only was their (the acquirer's) market valuation not uplifted by their adventurism in new tech areas, but markets became concerned at the extra costs and lack of focus resulting from such stillborn M&A strategies, penalizing the buyer still further.

In the 'other clicks-to-SN' sub-category, Google is the elephant in the room. With an existing direct competitor to Facebook (Google+), YouTube and a penchant for entering other internet companies' areas of strength, the issue is less whether a series of additional SN acquisitions is possible, but rather, how quickly and where Google will acquire next.

Indirect (b)

b1: Déjà vu all over again:[24] yet another new paradigm

> There comes a time when people who want to do a deal just throw away the financial spreadsheets.
>
> (Investment banker Rajeev Chand of investment bank Rutberg and Co)[25]

Newly privatized telecommunications companies in the 1980s; first generation internet companies and universal banks[26] in the 1990s; social networking today. If the question involves the merger belief that leads acquirers to destroy value faster and more completely than anything else, a prime candidate for the answer is the new paradigm illusion. This black hole enticement is typically expressed along the following lines: 'Put away all those spreadsheets (Chand, above) and prudent rules for merger effectiveness and prosperity. Simply get in on the ground floor, by acquiring as quickly as possible. Wealth is yours for the taking, like gold nuggets on the ground.'

A Madoff-Sanford level Ponzi scheme? Florida swamp land timesharing offers? No, it's the mirage that the market generates itself when unexplainable wealth arises that defies financial explanation. Such as in May 2011, when 'China's Facebook', Renren went public at reported first day IPO price equivalent to 72 *times* sales,[27] or April 2012, when Facebook acquired Instagram for twice the worth as established by knowledgeable insiders a week earlier. One explanation is that the pricing was determined by throwing darts at the financial pages. Another is that the established rules regarding a target company's value – and by implication, the maximum bid, once APP and synergy considerations are included – is that *the old rules no longer apply.*

In the initial internet bubble of 1996–2000, the phrase encouraged mindless pursuit of anything and everything ending with'.com'. 'Do you get it?' was that period's unsubtle implication that those who delay because they want to understand the full valuation implications before charging ahead were thick. The mania eventually recedes, replaced by shattered dreams and expressions of 'How could we believe such nonsense?' But when bubble-thinking emerges (and there are some indications that it is already underway in the present merger wave), the two implications of importance are a) that when and where the new paradigm illusion arises, irrational pricing prevails – so don't chase; and b) for the patient there are opportunities to pick up some companies at a bargain price, but only after a shake-out.

b2: APP built into share prices

The process by which anticipated purchase premiums come to be reflected in potential target companies' day-to-day share prices is explained with regards to Figure 6.1 in this chapter: mergers and prices: symbiotic relationship. Even before the Facebook-Instagram shock, targets were already being identified. The short list of Facebook's (or Google+'s?) next possible targets include those firms identified by Perloff in her report on bookmakers odds (a1).

Sometimes, the targets nominate themselves. Established online job recruitment company Monster.com appears to be trawling for a consolidation-mature (3a, Table 4.2) type of high success probability merger, based on the comments by chief executive Sal Iannuzzi on March 22 2012: 'We're agnostic as to what type of acquirer it is... The real issue is we know we have value, and we know we can go around and look for opportunities to get that.'[28]

6.4 Vapor numbers: *when* is the social networking valuation?

Shares of acquiring social networking companies represent potential acquisition currency, sometimes even before the acquiring firm is publicly traded (Facebook/Instagram, Twitter/Summify[29]). But volatile swings in the post-IPO prices of SN firms such as Groupon and game producer Zynga prompt the question *when*? The share price three weeks after the IPO is sometimes just a small fraction of pre-IPO price guesses mistakenly referred to as 'valuation' by the financial press and the IPOs arrangers before the launch.

When *is the social networking company valuation?*

In part 2 in Chapter 3, *who* emerged as the critical question to determine the identity of the merger valuation criteria-setters: identifying the groups or individuals positioned to determine what represents merger success and, by implication, how merger performance is measured. Unless MV criteria are consistent with the vital interests of those criteria-setters who have primacy, observations about how deal success or failure is to be measured are nothing more than opinions.

In that chapter and part, continuing shareholders of the acquiring company were identified as M&A's criteria-setters, leading to the emergence of quantifiable financial measures (TSR, VG, IVE and multiples in Chapter 3) of acquisition performance. But when it comes to the worth of post-IPO companies in general – and specifically the worth of social networking companies' shares as acquisition currency – the relevant issue is not *who* but *when*.

Hallucinatory 'valuations' are sometimes not worth the cost to transmit such fiction to financial markets through blogs and – sometimes, alarmingly – from otherwise credible financial news media:

- The quotation marks affixed to pre-IPO 'valuation' above are deliberate. Just because some unidentified source, somewhere whispers (a, Table 6.4, Foundations of fake) that some tech company somewhere, somehow, generates oodles of money, doesn't make it so. Unattributed indications are borderline share manipulation and of suspect reliability. Facebook's plans for an earlier IPO launch were postponed when concerns arose that performance estimates developed in January to February 2011 might have become untenable.[30]

- Price 'quotes' (note another deliberate use of quotation marks) by wafer-thin pre-IPO trading services such as SharesPost[31] or SecondMarket should never be confused with public market prices. Dominated by pre-IPO shareholders and with extremely limited quality company information available, such services operate in the murky twilight zone between private company and fully public firm.
- Share touts notoriously highlight only the upper number in a wide bid-asked range reflecting thin trading ('Spring 2012' in Figure 6.2) as fodder for stories about how some Happybang.com[32] just surged in 'value' from $45 billion to $75 billion over two months despite *no* material improvements in the company's projected future internal CF generation.

No company better exemplifies the importance of the *when* issue than the signature IPO of this 2011–19 Merger Megaboom, Facebook. Figure 6.2 shows seven different Facebook theoretical 'valuation' reference points from the mid-2000s up to April 2012, in the weeks immediately before Facebook's IPO. From 2007 forwards, various slivers of Facebook 'private' shares have been sold, followed by instant carnival-like announcements about the dramatic increase in the subject company's underlying worth. Bad math. Just because a zealot fan of a professional sports team might conceivably be willing to pay $1,000 for one share of that team's common stock with 5 million shares outstanding, that doesn't necessarily mean that the business in total is worth $5 billion.

Different buying groups comprising the whole, with different bid prices

Whether the asset being purchased is shares of stock or the latest Apple product, the first wave of fanatical buyers ('innovators' and 'early adopters' in Figure 6.3) are notorious for deliberately overpaying in order to be first to own shares of the prize company. These zealots are not necessarily indicative of the demand of other buyers, who are temperate and perhaps more analytical (and less emotional) in their assessment of the worth of the company.[33]

Suspect multiplier

By extrapolating that non-representative price quote into the future (b, in Table 6.4, the exhibit appropriately entitled 'Foundations of fake'), the unthinking number-cruncher is committing the Metcalfe's Law error, by presuming that each subsequent buyer is willing to support just as high a price as the one before. The very least adjustment is a declining multiplier

TABLE 6.4 Foundations of fake: 'Value' distortions in pre-IPO price indications

P-as-V Aspect	Role: Description	Issues
A 'WHISPER NUMBERS' *Unattributed reference to purported 'knowledgeable source'*	Even vapor price-as-value guesses require *some* implied connection to knowledge about sustaining sales, profitability. Since this pre-IPO source is rarely specified, credibility is derived from the media source, only.	• Borderline investor manipulation • Risk to collaborating media's credibility • R&P 'informed leak' or just R • Sustaining versus spot • Expense-revenue: unanswered question • Advantageous misuse of 'v' word
B ZEALOT SLIVER PRICE, EXTRAPOLATED *Non-representative partial shares' price becomes new fantasy valuation*	To some, *may appear* to satisfy independent evaluator's requirement for actual market prices. Dual presumptions: price *and* extrapolation basis	• Hiding true nature of the dual presumptions • Media: collaborating bad value math
C SECONDARY VALUATION ARGUMENT *Exit-facilitating search for GF*	Transparent attempt to justify 25–35% higher price basis for no reason other than to ensure some pre-IPO bidders price basis.	• Dealing with the last bidder dilemma • Limited to Tier 1 'iconic' Nets, only

in trying to calculate the worth of the whole firm based merely on an initial small percentage sale: networking's Zipf's Law, as adapted to partial purchases of financial securities.[34]

In the case of Facebook, the predicament of fantasy valuations comes to a head with the bid-asked gap in February 2012 ('Spring 2012' in Figure 6.2). While some expansive estimations came up with a pre-IPO valuation as high as $103 billion,[35] Henry Blodget, cheerleader for bloated dot com company share prices from the *first* internet bubble period, 'concluded that $75 billion was an aggressive valuation for the company.'[36]

Early storm clouds point to a decline in SN share price as permanent investors ignore hyped IPO prices and seek to establish their own sense of the firm's worth based on the present fundamentals and future true prospects of that company. The second dot com bubble parallels the first in many regards, with a startling 'waterfall' pattern of post-IPO share price levels indicating the financial market's level of regard for the tech IPO

FIGURE 6.2 Facebook 'valuation' reference points as of April 2012

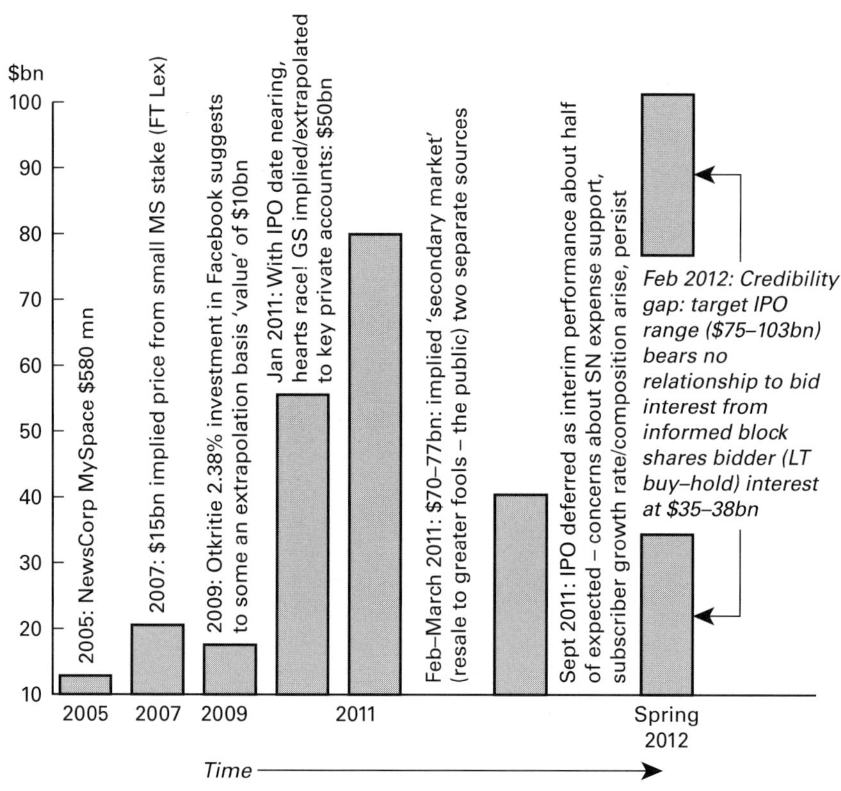

FIGURE 6.3 The post-IPO price waterfall, including share purchaser groupings as suggested by Rogers (1963)

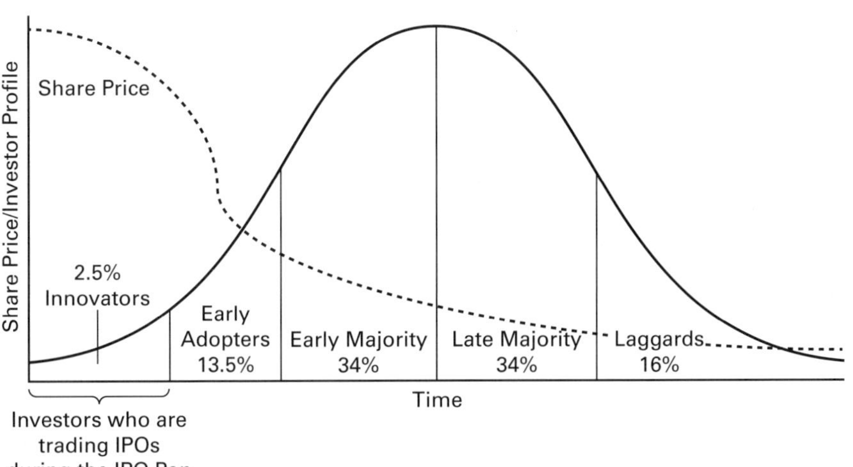

Adapted by B Vojtkova from Rogers, E (1963) *Diffusion of Innovations, 3rd Ed.* New York. Free Press. 247. Reprinted with permission from B Vojtkova.

price-setting process (see Figure 6.3). For those who believe that new SN dot com II shares mean that severe post-IPO drop offs are a thing of the past, think again. The subtitle of the exhibit in Gimein's analysis in *Bloomberg BusinessWeek* of post-IPO price patterns says it all: 'Of the 25 US IPOs with the biggest opening pops in 2010 and 2011, 20 have fallen since.'[37] In an especially disturbing precedent to the Facebook IPO, Renren (referred to some as 'China's Facebook') comes to epitomize post-2010 non-credible IPO pricing, with a share price trend line that resembles a death spiral in the months following *its* IPO.[38]

Detached from the carnival-like IPO atmosphere, movies and growing hype, some hedge funds' expressed level of interest is decidedly more modest, indicating a total company valuation at around $35–8 billion. Contrast that with pre-IPO fantasy valuation maneuvering for Facebook in the weeks immediately before that IPO at $84–103 billion.[39]

Dealing with the Post-IPO 'waterfall'

> Come on: valuing a company at 100 times earnings assumes years of 50 per cent-plus profits growth. Very few companies in history have achieved that. Uncertainty ought to imply caution in pricing a business; at $100bn, there would only be optimism.
>
> (Pratley, *Guardian* (London) Feb 5 2012)[40]

Question: How does one begin to reconcile the massive $35–$103 billion bid-asked valuation gap for Facebook as described above and as depicted in Figure 6.2?

Answer: Don't even try to reconcile those extremes. Wait for the shakeout period to be completed and for the market's sense of true valuation to emerge, instead.

It is not that the issue of the company's worth is seen as unimportant. To the contrary, Facebook's actual (as contrasted with hypothesized) value has a direct bearing on that firm's ability to use shares as acquisition currency, with implications for the sector overall. A valuation at the upper end of the range supercharges prices and adds to merger momentum.

Conversely, valuation nearer to the lower end of that range suggests a bubble which is inflating at a much slower rate than the dot com I (1996–2000) predecessor, with shock deals of the Facebook-Instagram type more likely to be the exception rather than the rule.

FIGURE 6.4 Factors influencing Facebook's ongoing valuation

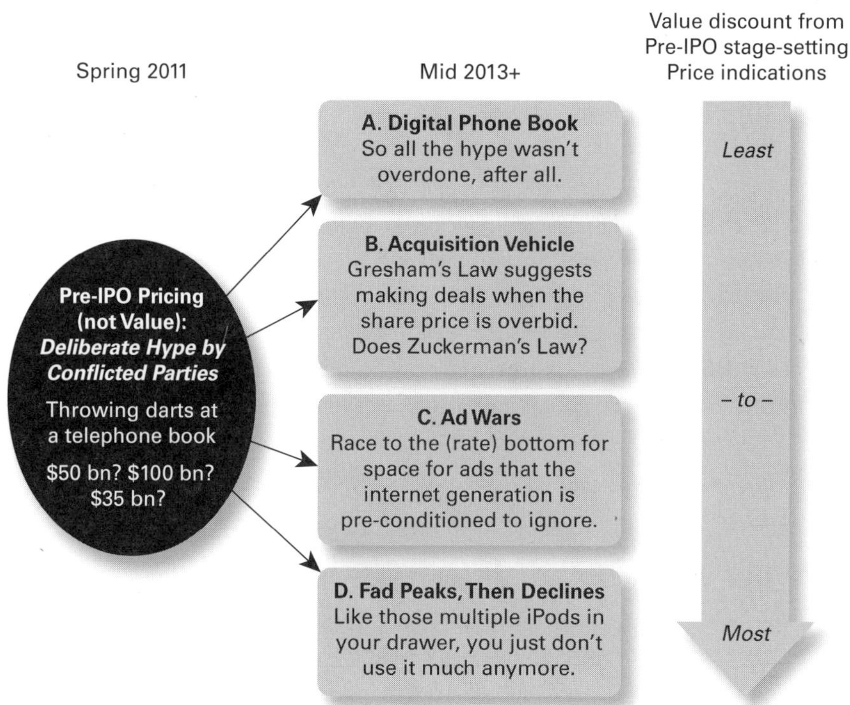

The fact of the matter is that the numbers associated with Facebook's IPO day are irrelevant – except of course to the sellers on that day and the bankers concerned that any headline that does not indicate a $100-plus billion headline on day one (IPO launch day) might be perceived on CNBC or Bloomberg TV as a disappointment, causing the pace of the present boom to slow. Whatever the day one number, it is based upon thin markets and abysmally incomplete information about Facebook's true future prospects and fundamentals. These are quasi-public exchanges dominated by share block maneuverings of earlier investors seeking to cash out, fast. It is only several quarters *after the IPO launch* that sufficient information emerges upon which to evaluate the company based on true value fundamentals. Determining which of the alternative future paths Facebook will follow can only be determined after the IPO hype has died down, when buy-and-hold investors take a careful look at the social networking leader's future on a DCF basis. In April 2012, a few weeks prior to Facebook's controversial IPO, we expressed the expectation that it would take until early 2013 before the hangover from Facebook's IPO fantasy valuation could be overcome. Only after that point in time would the company start to be primarily valued on the basis of reasonably predictable future cash flows, as the true business model of the firm – including strengths and vulnerabilities – begins to be understood in depth by the financial community.

Notes

1 http://online.barrons.com/article/SB50001424052970203869804576327353859494610.html?mod=BOL_hps_mag. Accessed May 21 2011. This chapter was developed shortly before Facebook's controversial IPO in May 2012. Since then, the prospect of post-launch share price deterioration described here has been confirmed, as the financial community apparently shares some of the same mis-valuation and business model concerns described herein.

2 Also the title of the 1979 book by former NY Yankee pitcher Sparky Lyle and sportswriter Peter Golenbock (New York, Outlet).

3 Reference is made in the first two chapters to Dickens' *Bleak House,* in which facilitating lawyers dominate estate litigation, as that process is how that profession makes its money. To those middlemen, the interests of principals are secondary. What matters most to these intermediaries is ongoing exploitation of the market to maximize their fee income. Lip service is paid to the intermediary's intent of supporting principals' interests.

4 'Winning' is defined here solely in terms of the *acquirer's* interpretation of merger success. As described in part 8 in Chapter 3, in terms of the combined

value gap-incremental value effect (VG-IVE) methodology, that definition contains two parts: a), analyzed net realizable synergies (NRS) equal to or at least approaching the final acquisition purchase premium (APP); and b), two stage discounted cash flow-based valuation (DCF2S) for the combined company (including APP and *combined* firms' WACC) that is greater than the sum of the two firms' standalone DCF-based valuations.

5 As noted in Chapter 1, internal investments are usually much smaller than external (mergers), so M&A may be the only alternative in terms of providing significant growth, and on that basis will often prevail despite lower return rate and greater risk relative to internal.

6 'Instead of learning from the past, companies "reinvent the wheel" each time they pursue a merger', Shelton and Dias (2002: 16), cited in Paulter (2003: 24). Refer to Further Reading.

7 Work out the other institutions comprising this new bulge bracket for yourself. Capital requirements mean the practical exclusion of institutions that survived the great recession of 2008–9 only because of government subsidy.

8 *Encarta World Dictionary:* Cassandra (from Greek mythology); daughter of the Trojan king Priam, who was given the gift of prophesy by Apollo. When she cheated him, however, he turned this into a curse by causing her prophecies, though true, to be disbelieved; [as n.] (a Cassandra) a prophet of disaster, especially one who is disregarded.

9 The controversies arising with the execution of Facebook's IPO on the launch day do not detract from the magnitude of that financial event. A company that was little more than a college kid's brainstorm came to be worth more than several of the world's industrial giants. Last time such a description applied? Go back to the *first* dot com era period, 1996–2000 (corresponding to post-1980 business-merger wave 2).

10 Sorkin, A (Oct 24 2011) 'Groupon's latest value raises doubt', DealBook, *New York Times,* http://dealbook.nytimes.com/2011/10/24/groupons-latest-value-raises-doubt/. Accessed Oct 25 2011.

11 Daily Report. http://bits.blogs.nytimes.com/2012/04/11/daily-report-a-turning-point-for-mobile/. Accessed Apr 13 2012. Refers to Wortham, J (Apr 10 2012) 'A billion-dollar turning point for mobile apps', *New York Times.*

12 *The Economist* (Apr 10 2012) 'Instariches', Babbage blog. http://www.economist.com/blogs/babbage/2012/04/facebook-and-photo-sharing refers to Tsotsis, A 'Right before acquisition, Instagram closed $50m at a $500m valuation from Sequoia, Thrive, Greylock and Benchmark', *TechCrunch,* http://techcrunch.com/2012/04/09/right-before-acquisition-instagram-closed-50m-at-a-500m-valuation-from-sequoia-thrive-greylock-and-benchmark/. Accessed Apr 13 2012. *The Economist* (Apr 14 2012) 'Facestagram's photo opportunity' 67: 'Facebook's bid came shortly after Instagram had closed a funding round with a bunch of venture capitalists that valued it at $500m.'

13 In decisions about bolt-ons (merger type 2a in Table 4.2, Chapter 4), make-versus-buy analysis sometimes supplements conventional merger valuation methods, as those are described in Chapter 3.

14 AOL: Huffington Press, H-P: 3Par, Palm, Autonomy (see Chapter 3).

15 Melicher, R W *et al* (1983) 'A time series analysis of aggregate merger activity', *Review of Economics and Statistics*, 65:3, 423–30, cited in Baker, H K and Kiymaz, H, eds (2011: 25).

16 Ending dates of recession periods are usually only diagnosed after the fact. Even if the end of the recession is acknowledged using traditional metrics (two consecutive increases in quarterly GDP), alternative interpretations abound. Also, if speculation of an imminent return of recession conditions gains credibility, the end date issue becomes immaterial as price indices and M&A are both suppressed, reflecting investor and corporate sentiment at that point in time in the business-merger cycle.

17 Refer to Further Reading.

18 Not to be confused with acquisition purchase premium (APP), which applies to actual or prospective bids by prospective acquirers.

19 Repeating the point that at the time that this chapter was written in Spring 2012, Facebook's IPOs had not yet occurred.

20 'Want to place bets on Facebook's next acquisition?' Bits, http://bits.blogs.nytimes.com/2012/04/10/want-to-place-bets-on-facebooks-next-acquisition/?scp=22&sq=%27Twitter%20acquisitions%27&st=cse. Accessed Apr 13 2012. Lower probabilities were assigned to blogging site Tumblr (25-to-1).

21 Ingram, M (Jan 20 2012) 'Twitter acquisition confirms curation is the future', GigaOm, *Bloomberg BusinessWeek*, http://www.businessweek.com/technology/twitter-acquisition-confirms-curation-is-the-future-01202012.html. Accessed Jan 22 2012.

22 For example, Sorkin, A (Oct 24 2011) 'Groupon's latest value raises doubt', DealBook, *New York Times*, http://dealbook.nytimes.com/2011/10/24/groupons-latest-value-raises-doubt/. Accessed Oct 25 2011.

23 MacMillan, D 'Zynga flashes $1.8 billion searching for the new FarmVille: Tech', http://www.bloomberg.com/news/2012-04-17/zynga-flashes-1-8-billion-searching-for-the-new-farmville-tech.html. Accessed Apr 17 2012.

24 One of Yankee great Yogi Berra's more memorable quotations, http://www.yogiberra.com/yogi-isms.html.

25 *The Economist* (Apr 14 2011) 'Facestagram's photo opportunity', 67.

26 Travelers acquired Citibank in April 1998, creating Citigroup.

27 'Investors are forever blowing bubbles and it seems tech ones enjoy it more than most. Following the flotation of Renren, "China's Facebook", last week with a ludicrous valuation of 72 times sales' (May 13 2011), Best of Lex, *Financial Times,* http://www.ft.com/lex/best. Accessed May 13 2011.

28 Frier, S 'Monster CEO says he's open to selling all or part of company', *Bloomberg,* http://www.bloomberg.com/news/2012-03-22/monster-ceo-says-he-s-open-to-selling-all-or-part-of-company-1-.html. Accessed Apr 13 2012.

29 That Twitter used pre-IPO shares as all or part of the payment basis for Summify is suspected but not confirmed. Ingram (Jan 20 2012) suggested that a Summify investor posted a message indicating that the Twitter acquisition was an all-stock transaction. That message was quickly deleted. 'Twitter acquisition confirms that curation is the future', *Gigaom,* http://gigaom.com/2012/01/20/twitter-acquisition-confirms-that-curation-is-the-future. Accessed April 9 2013.

30 'A person familiar with the company said that its revenues were in the range of $2bn a year. However, a report on Reuters last week said the company had made revenues of $1.6bn in the first half of this year, double that of the previous year', Dembosky, A (Sep 14 2011). 'Facebook puts off IPO until late 2012', *Financial Times,* http://www.ft.com/cms/s/2/2b842146-dec3-11e0-a228-00144feabdc0.html#ixzz1Xy1qsEcS. Accessed Sep 14 2011.

31 'SharesPost is an illiquid market with limited supply, so this is a very loose proxy', Shonfeld, E, 'Pre-IPO filing, Facebook trading privately at $84 billion valuation', *TechCrunch,* http://techcrunch.com/2012/01/30/facebook-84-billion-valuation/. Accessed Jan 31 2012.

32 'Happybang.com' was the fictional company valued solely on the basis of staffers' all-night clicks, as shown in the Peattie and Taylor Alex cartoon on page 24 in *Net Value* (2000). Dembosky, A (Feb 6 2012) 'Facebook to be keenly missed by private markets', *Financial Times,* http://www.ft.com/cms/s/0/493319b6-50ee-11e1-8cdb-00144feabdc0.html?ftcamp=rss&ftcamp=crm/email/201227/nbe/GlobalBusiness/product#axzz1lXaSwZAK. Accessed Feb 6 2012.

33 This in part helps to explain the use of emotional appeals such 1996–2000's 'Do you get it?' by bankers presiding over the process. Looking at a purchase on an analytical basis, and several considerations arise that may reduce the price the buyer is willing to pay: future CF generation, worth of comparable companies, stability and profitability of the firm's business model, protection from new entrants and fickle swings in ultimate customers' preferences.

34 Briscoe, Odlyzko and Tilly (Jul 2006) 'Metcalfe's Law is wrong', *IEEE Spectrum,* 37–9.

35 Womack and Spears (Feb 23 2012) 'Facebook insiders push $100 billion value', *Bloomberg*, http://www.bloomberg.com/news/2012-02-23/facebook-insiders-limit-ipo-by-pushing-100-billion-value. Accessed Feb 24 2012.

36 Davidoff, S (Feb 10 2012) 'A $100 billion value for Facebook? That may be possible', DealBook, *New York Times*, http://dealbook.nytimes.com/2012/02/10/a-100-billion-value. Accessed Feb 10 2012. Reference to Blodget's dot com I role: 'Valuation by dot com star guru' Clark (2000: 65).

37 (Nov 4 2011) 'Groupon beware: of 25 hot IPOs, 20 tanked later.' Exhibit title: 'Cold reality for hot IPOs', http://www.businessweek.com/finance/occupy-wall-street/archives/2011/11/groupon_beware_of_20_hot_IPOs_tanked_later.html. Accessed Nov 7 2011.

38 (Feb 16 2012) 'Renren: a friend in need', Lex, *Financial Times*, http://www.ft.com/cms/s/3/bfc785a4-58bd-11e1-b118-00144feabdc0.html#axzz1mcTiIQFi. Accessed Feb 17 2012.

39 Scronfield, E (Jan 31 2011) 'Pre-IPO filing, Facebook trading privately at $84 billion valuation', *TechCrunch*, http://techcrunch.com/2012/01/30/facebook-84-billion/valuation. Accessed Jan 31 2012.

40 'Facebook flotation: three reasons to avoid it', http://www.guardian.co.uk/business/2012/feb/05/facebook-why-not-to-invest. Accessed Jan 5 2013.

07 Towards systematic investigation and implementation of post-merger synergies

The closing ceremony does not necessarily mean the success of the acquisition... For the merger to work, the acquiring investor must achieve additional value in the newly created business combination.

(Clark, 1991:103)

Success will depend more than ever on the merged companies' ability to create added value. And that will depend on what happens after the deal has been done. Yet many deal makers have neglected this side of the business. Once the merger is done, they simply assume that computer programmers, sales managers and engineers will cut costs and boost revenues according to plan, leaving the boss free to bag the next big deal.

(*The Economist*, Jan 7 1999).[1]

CHAPTER CONTENTS

7.1 Synergies: definitions, approaches, issues
7.2 Net realizable synergies and merger success: value gap revisited
7.3 A key category-based net realizable synergy investigatory framework
7.4 Post-merger priorities explored
7.5 Other PMI implementation issues: choosing the PMI implementation team

While 'synergy' is dismissed by some as merger buzzword fluff, the truth is the opposite. Correctly categorized, pursued and implemented, synergies – or rather, net realizable synergies – establish critical guidance necessary for a successful target bidding strategy, while establishing the foundation for efficient and effective operation of the newly combined firm.

7.1 Synergies: definitions, approaches, issues

> The average acquirer materially overestimates the synergies a merger will yield.
> (Christofferson *et al*, 2004: 93, citing challenges in making useable synergy calculations based on limited information)

Post-merger 'synergy': definitions, importance

Perhaps because the word sounds like yet another overly-slick, under-informative, consultant's catch phrase 'merger synergy' has always attracted its share of doubters and detractors. Even into the early years of the new millennium, those who either could not, or would not, embrace the concept of synergy attacked what they imagined the word meant. Decades after the heyday of his conglomerate, ITT, former chief executive officer Harold Geneen dismissed post-merger synergies in the following manner in 1997: 'There's never been a synergy that lasted very long... True synergy is the rarest thing in the world.'[2]

Some other critics of post-merger synergy contend that the notion is too loosely delineated to be taken seriously. Bombast about 'significant synergies' is a standard feature of status proclamations by ardent acquirers as the acquisition chase escalates. Once the deal is closed, the phrase is counted upon to help deflect criticism about overpayment. Not surprisingly, those who swallowed the acquirer's synergy propaganda whole are distressed in later weeks when it becomes apparent that some of those deals have come undone, badly. When the 's' word is *not* heard, it is usually because the acquiring company management fear that the APP-to-NRS value gap (Chapter 3) is so large that a decision is made to try to divert financial community attention elsewhere.

Moving away from the PR bluff treatment of synergies to something more substantive begins with looking at *where* and *how* post-merger synergies arise. Part 3 in this chapter addressed four different primary synergy categories, including some specific initiatives pertaining to each.

Damodaran's modern interpretation for the word 'synergy' corresponds to today's two leading merger valuation methodologies as described in Chapter 3 of this book: value gap (VG) and incremental value effect (IVE):

> Synergy, the increase in value that is generated by combining two entities to create a new and more valuable entity, is the magic ingredient that allows acquirers to pay billions of dollars in premiums in acquisitions... Synergy is the additional value that is generated by combining two firms, creating opportunities that would not have been available to these firms operating independently.
>
> (2005: 3)

Why is it important to investigate synergies? From the perspective of the acquiring company's shareholders and other present or potential owners in the new combined firm, one important reason is to determine whether or not the deal succeeded. With internal investment often too small and/or too slow to significantly propel future company growth, the prospect of increased merger activity emerges. But do investors/owners of the acquiring company trust management of the acquisition-active firm to get it right? To acquire in ways that build company value, instead of destroying it? To assess in a systematic manner whether tangible synergies were and are sufficient to offset management's 50 per cent-plus purchase premium paid for the target? Or instead, whether this deal joins the others in the most mergers fail (MMF) group. Also, to determine whether acquiring company management are merely enlarging the company as a result of their external investments, or also *creating value* in those acquisitions.

TABLE 7.1 Which synergy orientation is the acquirer exhibiting?

Approach	Description	Advantages	Disadvantages
(a) Acquirer-as-victor, expense and time limited	Focus on discretionary budget items over near-term (100 days or less), primarily at target company.	Identified synergies readily quantified. Achievement simple to achieve and confirm.	Myopic in three ways: (1) concentration on acquirees, (2) time threshold, (3) revenue synergies excluded. Indicates that nearly all mergers fail on value gap coverage basis. Process myopic. Offsets and reversals not adequately addressed (applies also to B, C).
(b) Consolidation w/ revenue synergies, extended period	Expansion of (a) to include overlapping aspects of both firms. One year term, inclusion of *some* readily identifiable revenue synergies.	Improves probabilities of not losing top talent from acquiree. Inclusion of more achievable synergies than (a). Includes major technology-market assumed breakthroughs.	Correct diagnosis of CKCs may be problematic. Persistent problem of timing, share and margin calculations in evaluation of revenue synergies. Breakthrough assumptions often speculative (Unum-Provident).
(c) Combined firm, extended scope	Beyond (b): Includes value-performance reforms previously neglected, synergies arising after PMI primary term.	Most complete coverage of potentially achievable synergies, thus most likely to cover value gap (presuming avoidance of gross overpayment).	Synergies beyond one year are dependent on projections. Some managers reluctant to utilize PMI period to address long-enduring value issues.

Synergy analysis issue 1: determining net realizable synergies (NRS)

The concept of NRS is introduced in part 6 of Chapter 3 pertaining to the VG methodology. The NRS-VG connection is revisited in part 2 of this chapter.

Focus on cash flow incremental effect

NRSs are measured on the basis of the discounted cash flow incremental effect associated with the nominated synergy – *not* incremental revenues, or expenditure changes, or increases in subscriber base. When it comes to revenue-related synergies (r-synergies), there remains a somewhat astonishing inclination to record anticipated changes in top-line revenue and sales as synergies. It is only after deducting *all* costs including start-up expenses that the synergy reaches CF.

Offsets: what are the side effects and enabling expenses associated with this synergy?

Next, it is necessary to account adjust for the offsets that invariably accompany these gross prospective synergies. Almost every candidate synergy involves *some* related expense that CF attributes to that synergy-improvement, in some manner. The telecommunications company which following an acquisition originally boasts of tens of millions of dollars 'saved' by dismissing many of its most experienced engineers is shocked to discover that besides the cost of the generous departure arrangements, there are other offsets to its imaginary savings. These side-effects include a) the CF effect represented by loss of some key accounts who become frustrated at the replacements' inability to do the same job, b) extra meetings and concessions, and ultimately c) new, expensive subcontractor contracts to hire back some of the same individuals who were dismissed earlier.

Present value: how long it takes to achieve the synergy (and how long they endure) both count

> Synergies seldom show up instantaneously, but they are more likely to show up over time.
>
> (Damodaran, 2005: 6)

Some synergies may be 'banked' (that is, assumed to be fully achieved) on day one of the post-merger period. Other, sometimes substantial synergies such as IT platform changes, may take three years or longer to completely achieve. To disregard the timing factor is to ignore the time value of money.

For synergy purposes, the relevant discount rate is the same weighed average cost of capital (WACC) in the incremental value effect (IVE) combined scenario as described in part 7 in Chapter 3: reflecting the combined companies' debt and equity portions and financing component costs.

Synergy analysis issue 2: scope

If the scope of synergies available for consideration in the PMI program is overly broad, the post-merger investigation loses focus. Critical deadlines become difficult to set much less achieve, as too much is being examined, all at the same time. Conversely if the synergy scope is too narrow, then NRSs can never match the APP, even assuming bid discipline and moderation. In such instances, a false indicator situation may arise, as even highest probability deals (such as category 1 and 2 transactions from Table 4.2 in Chapter 4) *appear* to be unfeasible based on the APP-NRSs criteria of the VG methodology, even though the purchase is described as a winning deal by acquiring company management.

Synergy scope and determination of merger success or failure (merger valuation)

The scope of the synergy investigation – concerning which areas and budgets of the target company (and corresponding aspects of the buying firm) are included for consideration in the analysis and which are excluded – directly affects the possible total amount of achievable synergies. As a consequence, the synergy scope decision also influences chances of merger success as measured based on the VG method. The smaller the universe of synergies included in the calculation, the less likely it is that analyzed NRSs can match the acquisition premium.

Table 7.2 identifies three different synergy scope alternatives, ranging from least expansive (1) to most (3). Each of the three is then addressed in the pages that follow.

1. Target-immediate

Only the most immediately apparent prospective synergy opportunities are considered in this, the narrowest scope of the three alternatives depicted in Table 7.2.

For a manufacturing, distribution or logistics-shipping firm, scale-based efficiencies emerge as immediate synergy candidates, as consolidation of buyer's and seller's factory and warehouse capacity usually means lower

TABLE 7.2 Synergy scope – three alternative approaches

Narrowest ↓ Broadest	Description	Implications for Synergy Program
	(1) TARGET-IMMEDIATE Primary emphasis on easily identifiable cost reductions in the target company, obviously overlaps	Efforts heavily skewed towards scale and duplication-type expense synergies, bias towards acquirer's resources/ approach *Partial scope, unlikely to cover purchase premium except perhaps in lowest APP percentage (10–20%) range*
	(2) TARGET-EXPANSIVE (1) Expanded to include wider range of prospective opportunities, including improvement opportunities overlooked by prior target management	Consideration of ALL expense-expenditure areas of target Highest promise revenue (r-) and financing (f-) synergies included in scope *More complete investigation than (1), both in terms of areas and potential synergy amounts. Possible coverage of purchase premium up to Azofra-AMS range (~38%)*
	(3) T-E PLUS MISSED OPPORTUNITIES Broadest scope, inclusive of all of (2) plus fundamental improvements in the target's base business which prior management *could* have taken but did not	Target-Expansive is the starting point. Add to that company value-improvement actions with prior target company management could have taken but did not, of all types. (Note: to avoid double-counting, this is to be done only AFTER (2) is completed *Requires skills in Value Management (maximizing company SV on a continuing basis) as a part of the PMI team's capabilities*

costs per unit. Rationalizing sales forces and eliminating overlaps in functional departments emerge among the early improvement opportunities.

In this narrowest scope, contentious and/or difficult to calculate and execute possible synergies are excluded. The result is a short but irreproachable list of nearly assured synergy opportunities. But while the synergy implementation ratio (calculated as the dollar level of NRSs achieved expressed as a percentage of the dollar amount of synergies initially nominated) is high, the amount of synergies may be insufficient to cover all but minimal purchase premia.

2. Target-expansive

The scope in this approach is broader than in (1), with nearly all of the e- (expense-) synergy prospects as described in part 3 in this chapter included. The more predictable forms of revenue synergies (such as product line voids and channel-to-market voids) and financial synergies (eg reductions in overall, continuing financing costs) are also included. With the expanded range and dollar value of synergies under considerations, prospects for offsetting a specific deal's APP are enhanced.

3. T-E plus missed opportunities

The third scope dimension adds to target-expansive (2) with improvement opportunities that the previous managers of the target company missed, regardless of reason. Examples include a) termination of a chronically underperforming research function that has not generated a compound for years that justifies its continuation; b) eradication of performance-killing matrix management practices; or c) an attack on structural overstaffing, through elimination of multiple unnecessary organizational layers.[3]

Some believe that synergies the prior management could have addressed but did not, should be excluded from consideration. Such thinking normally includes the notion that the share price of the target firm has already been adjusted by the market in anticipation of that improvement being implemented, sometime in the future. Problems arise with this arbitrary prohibition, both on a theoretical and on a practical basis. Specific points of importance are:

- The notion that the so-called rational market makes instant share price adjustments for performance improvement opportunities – many of which are oblivious to the managers involved – stretches the concept of semi-strong market efficiency (SSME) beyond the breaking point. An all-seeing, all-knowing force might be plausible in

The Wizard of Oz, but back in the real world is actual achievement, rather than 'could haves'. While Fox concentrates on dramatic macroeconomic malfunctions of rational market theory in his aptly-named 2009 book *The Myth of the Rational Market*, other similar discontinues may arise albeit on a smaller scale as part of target company synergy diagnosis.

- According to Fox, it is not just by chance that financial markets grossly over-valued troubled 'universal banks' rotting from the inside with their undeclared subprime derivatives losses in the mid-2000s. The truth – as known then by canary-in-the-mineshaft economist Roubini and at least suspected by best-selling (*Barbarians at the Gate, Moneyball*) author Lewis – was unknown and/or not accepted by the financial community as a whole in 2005, helping to explain why the rational market provided a wrong share price indication. This is no exception that proves the rule; Fox points to a series of RMT malfunctions, including Long Term Capital Management (LTCM).
- There are reasons to believe that a similar situation arises in the case of post-merger synergies. The share price automatically goes up because the financial market overall believes that those improvements *might have* been addressed by predecessor management, regardless of whether those synergies have *actually* been achieved. Swallow that improbable notion and we've got a bridge in Brooklyn we'd like to talk to you about purchasing.
- Not even the managers directly involved are aware of the available synergies in many instances. Accordingly, it is difficult to imagine how insight reaches the all-seeing, all-knowing rational market. *Because the individuals involved don't know about the synergy, neither does the market.*
- Even more important is what is referred to here as the implementation factor. An automatic share price adjustment for a theoretical achievable synergy implicitly presumes that *any* manager might achieve those improvements. That's (il)logical: it doesn't matter whether the management team is led by Louis Gerstner or a bright chimp. All that's important is that *someone* might achieve those elusive synergies, some day.
- But the rational market appears to act in response to implementation, rather than mere potential. The improvements implemented by

Gerstner in theory could have been achieved by his predecessors at IBM. So how is it then that the so-called rational market indicated in the form of deeply depressed share prices that Big Blue was on its deathbed before Gerstner arrived there? If share prices changed with potential improvements, pre- and post-Gerstner share prices should have been indistinguishable. They weren't, adding fuel to the contention that it is probability of implementation that matters most when synergy scope boundaries are set, rather than mere potential.

- As a practical matter the 'could have' provision potentially excludes improvement opportunities as to render the purpose of NRSs obsolete. Wish to kill off systematic evaluation of post-merger synergies while it is still in its infancy? Then go ahead and proceed to define qualifying synergies so narrowly that the only path forward is 10 steps backwards: back to post-merger synergy's Dark Ages, when public relations proclamations and consultant-speak such as 'strategic intent' prevailed and structured analysis was ignored.
- At this writing, post-merger synergy investigation remains dominated by war stories about PMI programs gone wrong (Sirower, 1997; first chapter in Carroll and Mui, 2009), combined with single function guidelines in which a self-proclaimed subject expert explains how it is that his or her narrow specialty represents the one and only answer to maximum synergies.
- Damodaran's breakthrough 2005 paper, 'The value of synergy' changed the synergy landscape.[4] Synergies were segmented into multiple categories with specific guidelines and methods for pursuing maximum synergy result from each opportunity area; part 3 in this chapter represents an attempt to expand upon some of the Stern School professor's insights.
- If any improvements that pre-acquisition management *could have* pursued are excluded from the synergy scope, there's very little left for the acquiring firm's own post-merger agenda. Even more important, there's almost nothing available to offset the APP.

Other synergy-related issues

Consistent with the importance of synergy implementation to accurate assessment, the specific synergy must be verified as achievable, with feasibility adjustments imposed as necessary.

The duration of the synergy's period is relevant is two ways. One form of synergy estimation error arises when a one-off action – usually a cost-reduction – is misdiagnosed as exerting a continuing beneficial effect on the new combined company. Depending on the level of the WACC discounting rate applied, the present value of that synergy miscalculation may be two to three times, sometimes even more.

That isn't the only duration miscalculation that may arise when it comes to synergy calculation. When continuing value equations derived from the 1956 Gordon-Shapiro Formula are applied to synergies, some expense- or revenue-synergy benefits with a finite duration may mistakenly be calculated as continuing forever.[5] Apologists for this variant of the perpetuity calculation error sometimes point out that the amounts involved are minimal, and thus the effect is negligible. But in the case of synergies, that is not always so. Consider the situation of scale-driven manufacturing improvement of 10 per cent per unit. The correct analysis is to limit the duration to the plant's economic (*not* mechanical) obsolescence point. In fast-changing industries, such a synergy improvement may endure for only two or three years. Imagine the distortion if that short-term effect is erroneously assumed to continue forever and ever!

7.2 Net realizable synergies and merger success: value gap revisited

> Those companies that put priority on pre-deal synergy evaluation were 28 per cent more likely than average to have a successful deal...
>
> (KPMG)[6]

Absent sufficient NRSs to cover the bidder's APP, the deal is deemed to be a failure, both as calculated on the basis of the VG merger valuation methodology from Chapter 3, and also as perceived by the financial community.

Spin-masters' quips deployed at the height of the bidding war suggest that there are ample synergies to justify almost any level of bid that the acquiring company chief executive might be 'encouraged' to make by his handlers. *(Hey, it isn't their money!)* Nuggets are on the ground, there for the picking by anyone. But then the deal closes, and everything changes. The carnival atmosphere evaporates and disappears. Some of the same financial media pundits who celebrated the acquisition at the close openly wonder a few days later in their columns whether or not that deal was value-destroying.

The deal has closed. The real work of making this merger successful has just begun. There is *no* alternative to substantive examination of synergies, in a systematic manner. If the acquiring firm either fails to demonstrate how it can cover the APP minus NRS value gap, or merely rephrases synergy-spin from the chase period, the verdict is the same: the deal has failed, joining the other transactions in the MMF classification.

Examining synergies to determine whether or not that deal should have been consummated, at that price

Synergies' – or more precisely for merger examination purposes, *net realizable* synergies' – central importance to the determination of whether a specific deal is value-creating or not (aka, merger valuation) may be answered with a single phrase from Chapter 3: 'value gap' or VG.

VG merger valuation methodology represents one part of today's two-part preference merger valuation methodology. The other part, which is also detailed in that chapter, is incremental value effect (IVE): a comparison of combined versus standalone company value, calculated on a DCF basis. A part of VG-IVE's emergence as the prevailing merger valuation methodology pair results from the way that NRSs are *explicitly* incorporated into both of those methods. By contrast, the inadequacy of the two other quantifiable merger valuation methods examined in that chapter, event studies and total shareholder return, arise in part because neither ES nor TRS approaches *explicitly* address possible NRSs resulting from the deal.[7]

In the VG method, a successful deal is presumed to exist if the PV of NRSs equals or exceeds the APP paid to gain control of the target firm. Figure 7.1 depicts both APP and NRS elements of that method, in the context of the Azofra/AMS 38 per cent purchase premium ceiling from part 6 in Chapter 3.

While a bid that is higher than the Azofra/AMS 38 per cent APP ceiling might theoretically result in a successful acquisition *if* sufficient additional NRSs are uncovered, several factors argue against such a possibility, including:

- The easiest-to-achieve synergies generally represent a maximum of around 30 per cent APP. A conservative assumption is that in the typical acquisition, up to 20 synergy points may be counted upon from expense reductions and efficiency improvements, with 10 additional points from the combination of three smaller, less predictable synergy

FIGURE 7.1 Synergy implications of VG analysis, assuming the Azofra/AMS APP ceiling percentages

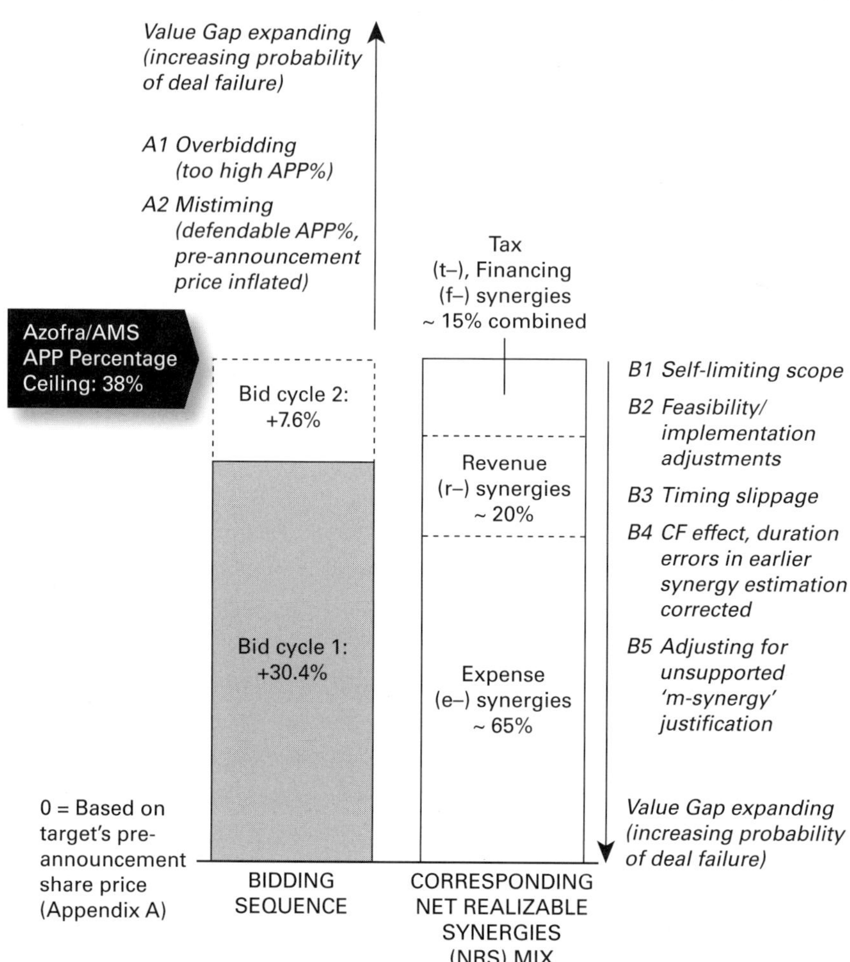

categories: revenue-related, tax-related and other financial synergies (see later in this chapter). That sum is only equal to the first bid threshold (30.4 per cent APP) as illustrated in the exhibit. A full 7.6 points more is required merely to reach the Azofra/AMS ceiling, much less higher bid levels above 38 per cent APP.

- Absence of a credible PMI program capable of uncovering the remaining, required synergies: it isn't that the 30 synergy points represent the total that *can* be achieved. Rather, the 30 points appears to represent the limit of improvements that can readily be presumed as *possible to achieve* without undertaking a systematic PMI approach as described in the balance of this chapter.

- The deal is done, and some members of the board are already complaining about the costs incurred to date. Facing such pressure, requests for necessary supplementary financial support to ensure that the remainder of the synergies can be secured may fall on deaf ears. But except for very low APP percentage deals that tend to occur only in the initial phase of a new merger wave, such a 'synergy-light' approach is insufficient. Starve the M&A implementation effort at this point, and the board arguably fails in its responsibility to ensure that the company's largest investment was worthwhile, in value terms.
- Stretching too far for the low probability guess synergy: self-deprived of a NRS post-merger capability, such as outlined in parts 7.3–7.5 here, desperation sets in. The only apparent remaining ways that the acquirer might appear to narrow the VG on paper is to stretch for unlikely *deus ex machina* synergies, which frequently involve untested and/or experimental concepts. Examples include a radical change in post-merger marketing that a department head imagines will permit cuts of thousands of staff, or the too-good-to-be-true technical fix that promises to slash post-merger data processing costs in half,[8] with no provision for offsets or replacements when that long-odds approach fails. Each of these casino bets is celebrated as genius by sycophants within the acquiring firm. But this is no time for yes-men: the financial markets perceive the emperor's new clothes for what they are (or aren't). Uncorrected, the deal is dismissed as a dud.[9]
- Limited if any upside adjustment in NRS levels occur as the merger wave progresses. The combination of rising pre-announcement share price indices and increasing purchase premiums in percentage terms as the merger wave becomes established and confidence returns means generally higher APPs as the cycle progresses. Problem is, synergies remain mostly unchanged over that period, as graphically depicted in Figure 3.5 in Chapter 3. Except perhaps for some speculative combined marketing ventures (r-synergies; see the next part in this chapter) that could benefit from a rebound in buying as the wave progresses, synergies remain almost unchanged from the time of low-APP bids made at the beginning of the cycle, to don't-miss-out overbids made in the late days of the bubble.

Bidding sequence column

Figure 7.1 sets the Azofra-AMS APP of 38 per cent over pre-announcement market capitalization (MC, target company share price × shares outstanding) as the final, accepted bid amount. In the exhibit, it is presumed that the acquirer reaches that final bid level in two bidding stages: a) an initial bid representing about eight-tenths of the bid maximum (just in case the seller might be enticed by a bargain deal),[10] followed by the remainder in the second bid. Andrade *et al*'s investigation of bid cycles and numbers of bidders described in Chapter 3 of this book strongly suggests that bidding wars involving more than two bid cycles and/or more than one other bidder should be avoided at all costs: emotions and ego quickly drive the APP beyond levels that can readily be justified by synergies.

In Figure 7.1, NRSs are shown as corresponding to a share price that is 38 per cent more than the share price at the announcement date, thereby indicating a successful acquisition based on the VG criteria. Those NRSs are in turn proportioned to the final bid in approximate amounts consistent with Table 7.3 (later in this chapter). Expense (e-) synergies are the most easily achieved, followed in order by revenue (r-) synergies and tax and other financial synergies. How might this deal come undone? Either through deal pricing errors which push the APP out of range (a1 and a2 in the figure), by limitations to available synergies (b1 through b5), or a combination of both.

a1. Overbidding, in terms of APP percentage

In order to ensure that *his* company secures the acquisition object of his desire, the chief executive of the AcquireCo overreaches. In percentage terms, the APP is later criticized as *too rich*. The APP percentage exceeds the Azofra/AMS ceiling of 38 per cent. While it is theoretically possible to achieve a successful acquisition at higher APP percentages, the prospects are remote. Synergy amounts do not increase just because share prices rise. But such bid guidance is disregarded: AcquireCo's chief executive believes that his status as a corporate leader is on the line. Never mind that an increasing number of independent observers are reaching the opinion that at this price level at least, the best strategy is to walk away.

a2. Mistimed APP

In runaway boom periods, pre-announcement share prices of target firms increase by 50 per cent or more, often with little if any enduring improvement in fundamentals of the target company's business. This is the rising tide effect mentioned in Chapter 1. Like a ship raised by a storm's swell, that vessel is elevated not because of its own actions but because of the external (cyclical) forces in the environment.

A 38 per cent premium on a price index of 100 in phase I results in a purchase price of 138. But the same APP in percentage terms (38 per cent) applied later in the business-merger cycle to the same target but now at a pre-announcement share price of 135 results in a bid of 186.3 on an indexed basis (135 × 138 per cent).

But deals concluded late in the merger wave phase do not face an elevated risk of failure merely because the APP is too great to be offset by NRSs. Stratospheric pre-announcement share prices signal the peaking of the bubble. Everyone is saying that things couldn't be better, which means that economic conditions will deteriorate soon, reducing the target's capability to pay off its own acquisition debt.

b1. Self-limiting scope

Other factors generate downward pressure on achievable synergies. Even if the purchase premium remains unchanged from the Azofra/AMS 38 per cent ceiling, the VG increases as the difference between APPs and NRSs expands.

Managers in the synergy development team may have insufficient knowledge of the key target areas and how to extract maximum NRSs from those categories. Alternatively, the potential for synergy development from some less familiar categories may be known, but resources necessary to identify and achieve those amounts are unavailable. For example, the acquiring company may be very popular in proclaiming that there will be no lay-offs in one troubled division within the acquired firm, thereby reducing the scope of predictable savings from the leading synergy category. Or, some tax synergies are suspected, but no one on the team has any expertise in that area, so that opportunity is missed.

b2. Feasibility/implementation adjustments

Some of the early synergy guesses made in the heat of the chase for TargetCo come undone when subjected to tough-minded, exacting scrutiny. The billion-plus in savings counted upon from consolidation of IT platforms from more than 20 to less than five as synergy guess-numbers are brought back to earth when the actual scope of the opportunity and the obstacles are subjected to adequate challenge.

Fearing accusations (true) that at the time of the bidding war, acquiring company management just spewed out whatever fantasy number might temporarily be believed, the defensive CEO at AcquireCo squelches any such serious scrutiny as unnecessary, using phrases such as 'second-guessing'. Doesn't matter – the financial community and especially AcquireCo's core institutional investors are making their own sanity adjustments, and the corrected numbers point to a deal that at best is riskier than first thought and at worst may be stillborn.

b3. Timing slippage

The PMI team has good news and bad news for senior management at AcquireCo. First the bad news: target synergies will take longer to achieve than originally thought. The good news, they proclaim, is that the full amount of the original gross synergies still appear to be on track so there is no need for reducing earlier synergy totals. *Wrong*. As explained in part 7.1, one of the foundation characteristics of NRSs is that the amount represents the *present value* of synergies after offsets. By definition, a timing reduction in NRS, reflects the time value of money in the company-wide WACC calculation developed as soon as the deal was finalized.

b4. CF effect, duration errors in earlier synergy estimation corrected

It is only after the deal chase is over that the high bid submitter discovers some basic errors in the NRS calculation. On second look, it becomes apparent that one-off savings were misdiagnosed as continuing. Some offsets were missed because in the heat of the bidding war those amounts could not easily be calculated and the bidding team was screaming for the new numbers, and necessary adjustment was ignored. But now, corrections must be made.

b5. Deletion of unsupportable 'managerial synergies'

Unable to specify sufficient synergies to match the bid amount, the bid team simply inserted the phrase 'management synergies'. Deliberately vague, this refers to the notion that just by changing management groups, synergies appear.

There are multiple problems with m-synergies. First, every acquirer presumes that it will make things better, even though the reverse is sometimes true. AOL's naïve adventurism at TimeWarner, AT&T's puzzle palace bureaucracy at the time of the NCR acquisition, Terra Firma's attempt to assert its administrative will on EMI – in all three instances, the argument can be made that the acquirer destroyed value, that is, generated reverse synergy. Obviously, this is always fiercely contested, especially in those deals where the transaction is personally associated with the CEO of the acquiring firm.

Second, the fact that 'management synergies' prove to be exceedingly difficult to quantify suggests an Occam's Razor scenario: there aren't any. Correctly and fully calculated management synergies are already represented in the other synergy categories revealed in Table 7.2.

7.3 A key category-based net realizable synergy investigatory framework

> Synergy... is so seldom delivered in acquisitions because it is incorrectly valued, inadequately planned for and much more difficult to create in practice than it is to compute on paper.
>
> (Damodaran, 2005: 2)

The heart of the effective post-merger synergy approach (summarized in Table 7.3) is the four-category PMI diagnostic framework. Expense (e-) synergies differ from revenue (r-) synergies, both in terms of how NRSs are calculated and the nature of candidate improvement opportunities in each. Likewise, tax (t-) and other financial (f-) synergies require distinct approaches and involve issues, offsets, and timing consideration unique to that category. Management synergies – sometimes thought to be the difference between excellent and mediocre management as applied to post-merger synergies – are imagined by their champions as relating to all of the other synergy categories.

Overview: what are the largest and most important synergy targets?

Two overlapping broad classification approaches for examining post-merger synergies exist. The first, operating versus financial(non-operational), is articulated by Damodaran (2005: 3):

> Operating synergies affect the operations of the combined firm and include economies of scale, increasing pricing power and higher growth potential. They generally show up as higher expected cash flows. Financial synergies, on the other hand, are more focused and include tax benefits, diversification, a higher debt capacity and uses for excess cash. They sometimes show up as higher cash flows and sometimes take the form of lower discount rates.[11]

TABLE 7.3 Diagnosis of possible post-merger improvements by synergy type

Class	Operational		Non-Operational		Other
Type	*E* Expense & Expenditures	*R* Revenue	*F* Financial	*T* Tax	*M* Mgmt
Model Percentage	60–70%	15–20%	10–15%		–
Description	Net present value of implied savings, adjusted for offsets	Ongoing CF effect of incremental sales volume directly attributable to merger	Improvements in cap costs, structure	Matching tax exposure w/cover	'Gerstner factor': imagined synergy from 'superior' mgmt. team
Examples	Scale efficiencies Overlapping functional departments Sales force, advertising rationalization Delayering: reorganization	Channel voids PL and geographic voids Lesser Cross-marketing, Integrated service offers, SSS	Lower new funds raising costs Lower WACC	TLCF applied Management of revenue recognition location	
Issues Include:	• Expense-revenue link • Discretionary expenses misdiagnosed as 'free'	• PMI up-pricing • High concept black holes	• Offsetting risks to high leverage	• Regulatory • Duration	• Hubris • Neg. synergy

In a similar perspective, Elgers and Clark (1980) describe some specific origins of synergies within the newly combined firm: 'The incremental value might accrue from expectations of the replacement of incompetent management, scale economies, extension of the product line, improved market control, reduction of business risk, or changes in financial structure.'[12] Elgers and Clark's reference to 'incompetent management' suggests the perspective of advocates of management synergies, as depicted in one of the columns in Table 7.3. 'Scale economies' are among the more readily measurable expense (e-) synergies that may be available when manufacturing, assembly or distribution operations are combined. References to 'extension of product line' and 'market control' point to revenue (r-) synergies. Tax (t-) synergies may reduce business risk and increase post-merger cash inflows, while other forms of financial synergies (f-) are also referenced.

The most important aspect of Table 7.3 is the implied typical distribution of PMI program emphasis on time and resources as suggested by the model percentages. The illustrative model percentages in Table 7.3 presume both an operating company (trade) acquirer, and a target firm that is not already significantly underleveraged at the time it is acquired. In these recurring M&A circumstances, the acquirer attempting to mobilize maximum synergies looks neither to imaginary management synergies nor to financial statement wizardry to make the deal work. The *primary* synergies available to this acquirer in this situation result from the CEO rolling up his (or her) sleeves and getting down to the basics of business improvement: fundamental enhancements to the new combined firm's business model, achieved by simultaneously improving *both* expense- and revenue-related aspects of the enterprise.

For this operating company acquirer, it is the distance separating the bridge (NRS) and the water below (APP) that matters most in answering the question, 'On a Value Gap merger valuation basis, will this particular deal succeed, or not?' But change the nature of the acquirer and the circumstances associated with the transaction, and the model percentages in Table 7.3 also change, with the importance of financial-related synergies sometimes increasing in both absolute terms and relative to the other categories in that exhibit.

Assume that the buyer is a financial acquirer such as a private equity firm, accustomed to looking first to the financing- and tax-related synergy potential of the deal, in a round turn transaction of three to five years expected duration, such as described in Chapter 3. Assume further that the target company's debt-to-capital percentage is still within the upper limit of the band of justifiable leverage.[13] Still within this band (and relying on others to spot the major e- and r-synergy opportunities), this acquirer places a priority on recalibrating debt and equity of the now-private acquiree, in ways that would have been unwieldy at best back when the target was still publicly-traded.

Equity

The company's pre-acquisition single class equity structure is reorganized, including some new interim classes of equity with reduced (or sometimes, no) voting rights and other forms transferable into debt or which can be paid down by alternative provisions, such as PIK (payment-in-kind) arrangements.

Debt

Some of the secured forms of long-term debt requiring period P+I payments are displaced by debenture-grade securities or equivalent, advantageously altering the timing and/or overall cost of debt.

Increased indebtedness remains a primary characteristic of such restructuring, regardless of how eloquently today's financial acquirers describe the extra benefits that they bring to the deal. This means that the threat of the untenable hyper-leverage situation such as Zell-Chicago Tribune (part 2 in Chapter 2) always exists, and may arise when restructuring is misapplied or mis-designed. But even when target company cost of equity (CofE) increases significantly as a consequence of increases in financial and/operating risk, that source of upward pressure on WACC is usually more than offset by lower relative cost of debt resulting from the increase in leverage.

A majority of permanent, ongoing post-merger expense improvements drop to the CF bottom line. Presuming that there are no related delays or offsets, the NRS calculation is the present value of the after-tax worth of those expense synergy savings. Those e-synergies often include but are not limited to scale economies and the elimination of overlapping functional costs.

Revenue synergies are next in importance. Introducing the acquisition partner's product into a known channel, product line, geographic or customer void represents a relatively low risk path to increasing incremental post-merger sales and indirectly, r-synergies.

Consistent with Figure 7.1, our inclination is to suspect that the post-merger investigation is inadequate when either of the following arises: a) the combined percentage of expense- and revenue-synergies is less than 80 per cent of the NRS total, and/or b) e-synergies alone are less than half of the NRS total. The examples of possible synergies that tend to first come to mind – the post-merger plant closing in order to scale back excess capacity, or the new, appealing product available through the acquiring firm's new outlets – obtain that visibility because of recurring instances. When the level of e- and/or r-synergies are seemingly too low on either a financial or percentage basis, the expectation is that the PMI team either has not probed the typical improvement areas in sufficient depth, and/or (they have been led astray, pursuing a provocative but marginal synergy opportunity.

Expense synergies: pursuing and securing what is usually the largest synergy category, first[14]

It is rare that expense synergies do *not* comprise the largest portion of post-merger improvements. Representing more than half of the typical PMI program's NRSs in two sub-categories (Figure 7.2: variable and non-variable), e-synergies are the most likely source of the first quarter quick win that legitimizes PMI investigation while setting the pace for analyses in the other three synergy categories.

E-synergy opportunities minimal in the excellently managed company: implications

While being acquired is not necessarily an indication that significant expense savings or e-synergies are available, the opposite does appear to be true. That is, in a company already managed in a way that maximizes CF-based performance leading to increased value, that firm's leaders have already taken rigorous actions to minimize the negative value ballast effect caused by inefficient operations.

In these 'out of range' companies (except to a desperate over-bidder – refer to the 'good company bad price' fallacy in Chapter 3) production and distribution are already exactingly scaled to unit volume, with excess and inefficient capacity already disposed of. Dynamic operating budget controls (based on Peter Phyrr-type zero base budgeting, but without the documentary complexity) discourage non-essential staffing and budget empire-building.[15]

Borrowing a page from Porter's competitive advantage principles,[16] unless internal support, analysis, research or other overhead functions are *already* either top-most in terms of combined efficiency and effectiveness and/or unique and essential proprietary elements with no other commercial substitute, then company management actively seeks out larger scale and/or more efficient alternatives, thereby minimizing the scope for post-merger e-synergies, if the unexpected acquisition bid arises. But as the description

FIGURE 7.2 Net realizable expense synergies: framework, examples

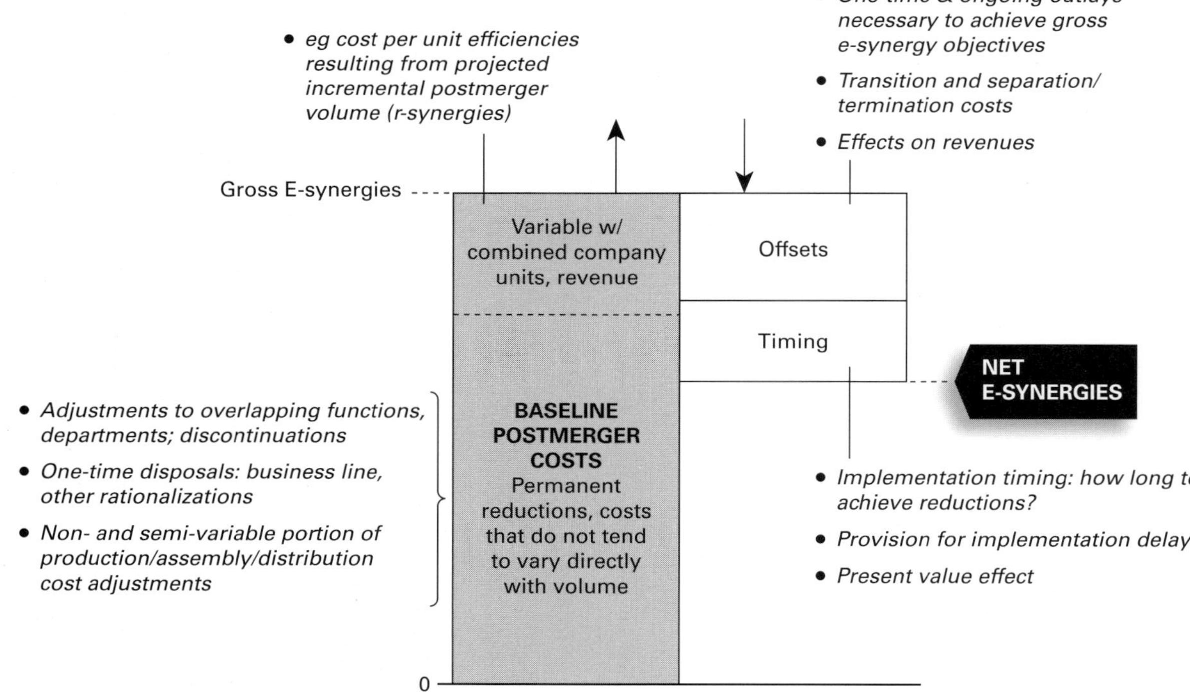

above applies to very few targets, the post-merger e-synergy issue is not whether synergies exist, but which is largest and fastest to achieve. In the post-merger top 10 list of synergy initiatives, it is not unusual for five of the top seven major NRSs to be expense-related.

Non-volume related expense synergies

Figure 7.2 depicts some of the more common e-synergy examples, shown here in NRS format – that is with gross synergies adjusted for necessary expense or investment offsets and timing of anticipated savings, as per the NRS description in the first part in this chapter.

Non-volume related costs are the easiest to calculate e-synergies, as savings amounts are not dependent on separate projections of future company unit volume and capacity utilization. Typical examples of synergy opportunities in this sub-category are function consolidations and eliminations.

Consolidations

A new, combined company functional department (HR, finance, operations, sales administration) comprised of the top performers regardless of original company (acquirer or target) is established. There is no guarantee of continued existence for this post-merger redesigned department: those aspects of the new department which are more effectively provided by externals are reviewed every year, with incremental downsizing as necessary to keep department performance at top levels based on *external* (rather than internal) performance benchmarks.

Eliminations

The acquired retail chain has three different internal groups which all claim to be instrumental in decision making about store layouts. Over the years, an unnecessarily complex matrix of arrangements with advertisers has emerged, with oversized committees today dealing with matters once handled by a single decision maker and small staff. Incremental cutbacks rarely suffice: cut off one head of the Hydra, and another just grows back. If the value contribution of the expansively named unit is difficult to determine, then the rational explanation is that there is no value contribution at all, with corrective action overdue.[17]

Accounting write-offs are disregarded in calculating non-volume related e-synergies for NRS determination purposes. At the target, presume that numerous struggling R&D and other early stage investment initiatives were kept on life support for years because of previous management's sensitivity to EPS effects from write-downs and write-offs. The change in ownership represents the opportunity to re-set the R&D portfolio on a sound footing by terminating marginal projects kept alive even though there is no sizeable future potential for continuing. Probe such life-support expense outlays deeper, and one sometimes discovers pockets of pet projects, superfluous expenditures and non-contributing staff. Eliminate the marginal project and related costs disappear in the fully rigorous post-merger investigation.

Volume-related expense synergies

Scale-related rationalization represents a major expense synergy in product manufacturing, assembly and distribution target businesses. Maksimovic *et al* (2008) state that, for mergers in manufacturing industries, the acquirer on average closes or sells about half of the target firm's plants.

Three essential assumptions affect the credibility of the e-synergy calculation. The first involves the assumed percentage of compatible volume. Except in the case of raw industrial output, almost every volume consolidation involves some additional costs and/or intermediate steps before the two different firms' products can be seamlessly produced using the exact same line or process. The second involves the near-term capacity of existing plant, which can typically be projected with some certainty from operating budgets. The third involves projections of future volume and the duration of assumed efficiency savings.

Of the three, the principal volume-base error is to presume that initial efficiency savings from the combination of ongoing plants or warehouses continues indefinitely, while the reality is that the efficiency benefit is short-lived (sometimes as brief as two years), especially in sectors undergoing rapid technological change. Also, there must be some basis for the presumed efficiency savings other than the team's mathematical calculations alone. In a disciplined PMI program, synergies are not counted until either the improvement amounts have been fully secured, or at least partial or prototype examples support that feasibility presumption.

Revenue synergies: void-fill versus speculative novel concepts

Estimates for the second largest synergy category, r-synergies (revenue) sometimes suffer from a simple but significant calculation error: top-line revenue is miscounted as the synergy amount instead of the much smaller CF effect attributable to those incremental revenues, adjusted for offsets and timing.

The most reliable and predictable r-synergies involve product, channel, customer group or geographic voids, such as when the acquired producer finds an expanded market for its goods and services following acquisition by a larger company with broader market access. By comparison, speculative cross-selling initiatives and new post-merger sales concepts requiring co-operation by both of the merger's principals take longer to implement, and exhibit far lower probabilities of future success.

Duration, offsets and timing adjustments are particularly important considerations for r-synergies:

- *Duration of incremental revenues.* Product and service lifecycles are continually shrinking, rendering r-synergy calculations which assume ongoing CF contribution non-credible. Realistically, catch-up type new revenue initiatives should assume a forward analysis period no longer than a single product-service cycle for NRS calculation purposes. New, breakthrough revenue developments emerging directly as a consequence may merit a slightly longer NRS duration assumption.
- *Offsets.* Unless the full costs related to the void-fill initiative or the new post-merger product are fully accounted for, the r-synergy NRS calculation is overstated.
- *Timing adjustments.* The marketing manager has bad news and good news, informing management that while the new r-synergy launch is going to be deferred for a year, there is no change in the r-synergy initiative – the benefit is simply delayed for one year. But delays in launch and development do reduce the NRS calculation, regardless of misperceptions by marketing staff.

Tax-related synergies: carry-forwards, earnings cover, globalization

Tax synergies are treated by some as a subset of financial synergies. Real life experience along with the requirement for specialist tax expertise to exploit the full synergy potential from this source suggest treatment as a separate category instead.

Tax cover corporate transfer

The primary form of merger-related tax synergies involves making tax cover from one of the two principals available to the other entity. Damodaran

FIGURE 7.3 Net realizable revenue synergies: framework, examples

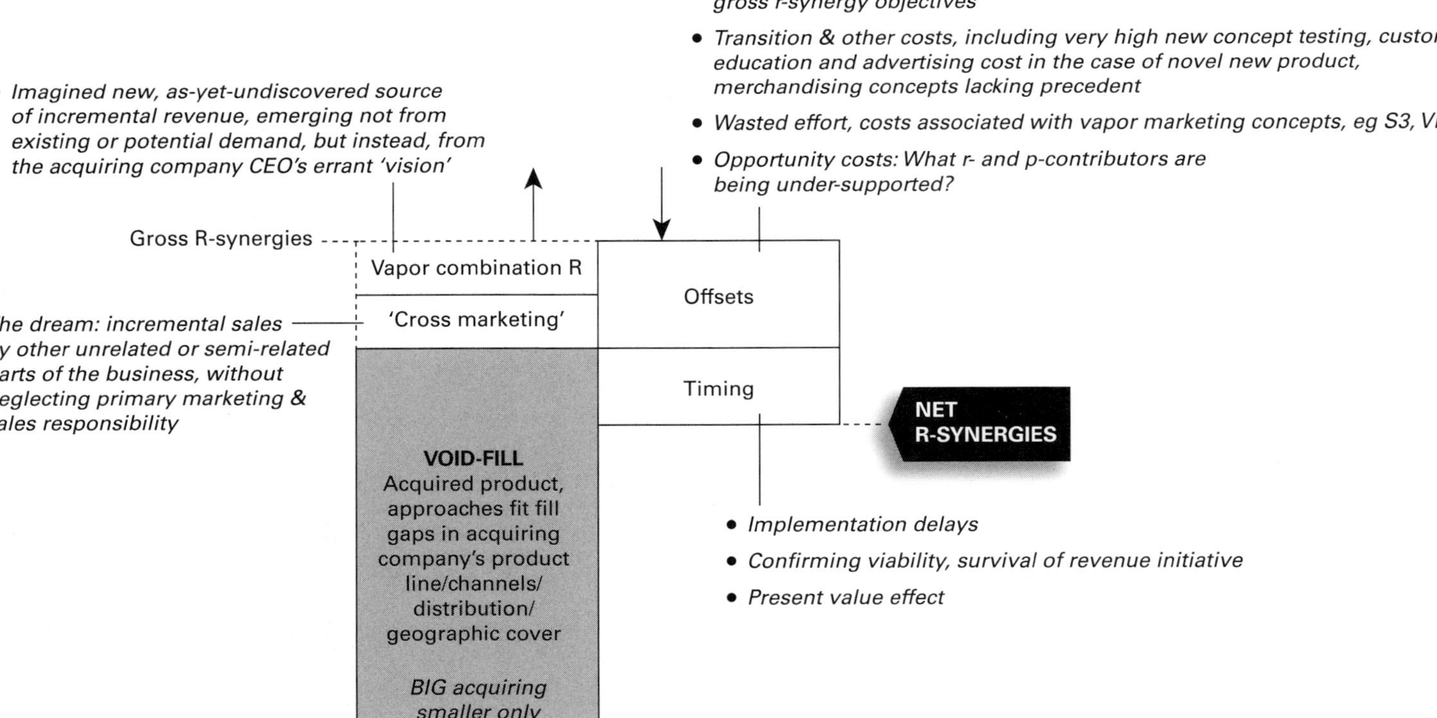

Note:
*Single source of supply, value-for-money

TABLE 7.4 Revenue synergy: alternative approaches and issues

Ease of Implementation	R-Synergy Approach	Description	Issues	*PV of Realizable Synergies*
Easiest	(A) Single source of supply	Acquirer imagines incremental revenues and CFs from convenience factor.	3S typically in eye of provider, but not always valued by accounts. Hidden offsetting costs include costs of inventorying low margin loss leader products.	*Lowest*
-to-	(B) Post-consolidation price increases	Gradual increases in prices reflecting reduced customer range of choice.	Expectations of increased margins not always realized: unforeseen entrants, regulatory opposition, competitors' counter-positioning.	*-to-*
	(C) Missing element	Acquired product/service/brand perceived by acquirer as completing the offer, transforming demand.	Dependent on whether the momentum for ME originates from key accounts or instead, is just a figment of the acquiring company CEO's imagination.	
	(D) Distribution channel void corrected	Pursuing the optimal distribution approach for that product or service.	Licensing and imitation products reduce the incidence of limited availability/channel problem, along with this acquisition justification.	
Most Challenging	(E) Integral to new, evolutionary customer offer	All-new customer offer made possible by the complementary acquisition.	As with ME (C) depends on whether decisive momentum originates from within or outside of the acquiring organization.	*Highest*

explains: 'if one of the firms has tax deductions it cannot use because it is losing money, whereas the other firm has income upon which it pays significant taxes, combining the two firms can result in tax benefits' (2012: 720).

The worth of this form of t-synergy element is calculated as the present value of the tax savings resulting from the combination. Ideally, that estimation reflects the full marginal tax rate – not effective rate – of the profit-generating entity, and can be justified as occurring in one of the newly combined firm's international locations with higher relative corporate tax rates.[18] In the case of a larger company with superior tax expertise either on staff or readily available, the target company benefits from a quality tax-based review of its operations, perhaps for the first time.

Asset revaluation

Asset accounting bases for the acquired firm are typically adjusted upwards at the time of the deal's closing to reflect in part the effect of the APP paid in order for the buyer to gain control. To the extent to which those upward adjustments result in higher balance sheet amounts for depreciable assets such as plant and equipment, an additional form of tax cover for pre-tax income potentially arises in the new combined company: 'This will result in higher tax savings from depreciation in future years' (Damodaran, 2005: 24). Tax rules may vary based on location, which may affect this synergy amount realized.

Other financial synergies: separating the real financial merger benefits from the corporate restructuring mirage

Legitimate financial synergies include access by the acquired company to expanded financing sources at lower overall continuing costs than otherwise possible and, in some instances, lower financing component costs resulting from being a part of a more stable enterprise.

Less convincing f-synergies include contentions that 'corporate restructuring' (at times a euphemism for radically increasing debt as a percentage of total capital) usually increases value. Chronically underleveraged publicly-traded firms are rare today in developed markets. Somewhat similar to the HLT fallacy exposed in Chapter 2, re-leveraging a company's capital structure that is already close to its optimal more likely destroys than creates new worth.[19]

Potential for reduced overall cost of debt (WACD) and overall cost of capital (WACC)

The target has recently been acquired by a larger, better known enterprise, and is now in a position to benefit from its acquirer's superior bank and non-banking financing sources.

Seasonal loans are converted into lower cost, continuing term arrangements, avoiding the target firm's annual scramble for cash to pay off its maturing short-term facility. Able to smooth out its financial requirements and debt scheduling, financial planning improves and emergency borrowing episodes at very high cost become a memory of the pre-merger past. Too small prior to the merger to issue its own low cost commercial paper, the target company now indirectly benefits from the combined firm's facility as it is combining its financing needs with those of its new parent. Consolidated working capital today means no extra financing for liquidity purposes: both the amount and cost of total debt financing declines.

Unused borrowing capacity may or may not result in f-synergies, depending on the particular circumstances. If the acquirer has a large unused open credit facility at a low fixed rate, and has invited the target to make full use of that remaining capacity to finance future growth requirements at a rate significantly lower than the target company could secure on its own in the pre-merger days, then financing synergies arise. The target company's projects thus financed benefit from an increased spread between cost of debt and projected return, resulting in higher profits and value: financing synergies created![20]

But 'underutilized' financing capacity from the other direction – the acquirer responding to what it perceives to be underexploited borrowing capacity in the newly acquired target – doesn't always work as smoothly. First, there is the issue of misdiagnosis of the term 'underutilized', deliberately placed in quote marks here to distinguish a *perception* that the target company might be loaded up with additional debt without value-diminishing side-effects, from what is often a very different reality. This underlying concept of the leveraged buyout worked wonderfully in the case of chronically underleveraged companies in the early 1980s, such as Gibson Greeting Cards, as debt was then minimal and thus debt servicing levels could be doubled without materially affecting the target's debt servicing capability. As Mills observes, this type of legacy capital structure is typically evidenced in markets that are still developing.[21]

Back in today's real world, potential targets have long since moved away from chronic underleverage, for two reasons. First, it is widely recognized by CFOs today that value is destroyed by a capital structure overburdened by expensive equity. Such a practice points to poor financial management, since the WACC is far more expensive than it needs to be. Although buying a company using the firm's own cash hasn't been possible since the mid-1980s – not without trashing the target's capital structure – the dream persists. If predators even *suspect* that a company is underleveraged compared to its ongoing financing needs, it is as if a giant 'Buy Me' sign is placed on the company, in flashing neon lights.

Never mind that the re-leverage game is over because the targets acted years ago to eliminate instances of chronic underleverage. Just redefine sustainable debt levels at 70+ per cent of capital. Overnight, debt-to-capital percentages that would have caused a company to instantly be placed on credit watch two decades ago are proselytized to the financial community as *realistic leverage.*

Sensing that the target has been destabilized in order to apply excessive leverage, storm clouds amass in the financial markets. Concerns arise that the CofE of the re-leveraged company means an untenable overall WACC. HLT target company CofE soars... it is not unthinkable that under conditions of extreme leverage (for example, 90 per cent/10 per cent debt-to-equity structure), the firm's CofE rises from the high teens before the restructuring to greater than 50 per cent, reflecting increases in both operating and financial risk. But WACC doesn't: it increases somewhat, but not as much as the CofE component. If equity represents only a miniscule portion of the restructured firm's overall capital, then the company's overall cost of capital rate is primarily determined by the (much lower) cost of debt.

Defendable reductions to analyzed Beta

All other things being equal, the acquired entity faces the possibility of a reduction in future calculated Beta *if* that newly-combined company results in reduced volatility in terms of future CFs. Such a reduction, in turn, translates into lower WACC and increased company worth, all other things being equal.

The key is the quality of the future projection of the post-merger firm's new Beta. The traditional way of calculating Beta based on five years' or so prior years share price data is almost worthless for purposes of devising future post-merger Beta, because product lifecycles continually shrink and companies' fortunes change accordingly. Dell, H-P, MySpace, Best Buy: last decade's stars struggle today; that pattern continues into the future. Merely adjusting historical Beta by some percentage improvement factor assumption is not credible. Superior approaches call for re-analyzing the internal CF generation dynamics of the new combined firm and the few, key influences (drivers) affecting those future CF amounts and their timing.

7.4 Post-merger priorities explored

TABLE 7.5 Ten post-merger pitfalls and fallacies

The ten PMI pitfalls and fallacies	
1	Process myopia
2	Urgency: the day one value gap reality
3	Failure to allocate PMI budgets, emphasis by model synergy source profile
4	Failure to first stabilize the base
5	'Cutting costs not people'/ringfencing
6	CKC determination not based on true value contributions
7	Big three: IT platforms, operations staff reductions, cross- and new concept marketing
8	Mis- or under-consideration of offsets, timing
9	Attrition and advertising-promotion support errors
10	Double-counting of imaginary management synergy

With limited time available to secure the most important (and most available) NRSs, active knowledge of post-merger priorities and pitfalls becomes paramount. Priorities ensure that the sequence for PMI effectiveness is followed. Tables 7.6a and 7.6b summarize 10 post-merger priorities.

1. Defense first

At its onset, any deal calling for a positive APP is value-destructive, until and unless it is demonstrated that sufficient NRSs can be developed *by this management team* sufficient to offset that necessary overpayment.[22] Fail to develop those synergies and the day one adverse VG situation persists: that transaction slips into the MMF category.

Despite the understandable urgency of the PMI team to amass the maximum possible, as quickly as possible, that is *not* the first priority in the well-planned post-merger program. The initial PMI priority is defensive in

TABLE 7.6a PMI priorities 1–5: From defense first to return to normalcy

	Description	Implications
1 Defense first	This refers to anticipation of competitors' actions aimed at taking advantage of the acquirer's and target's competitive vulnerabilities following the announcement of a deal, with offsetting countermoves.	Unless the base business of the two merger partners is stabilized and secure, an additional value gap-widening threat arises.
2 Post-acquisition reality check for imagined synergies	The initial 'long list' of synergy opportunities devised during the bid (chase) period faces tough-minded challenge, with particular scrutiny of large, experimental conceptual synergies analyzed as too difficult, too time-consuming and/or too expensive to implement.	In the ideal bid team arrangement, independent synergy investigators hold a veto over maximum bid levels. Realistically, no banker-dominated bid team tolerates such a change, as that would mean that many more deals are avoided as too expensive, with a consequence of no fees for deal middlemen. Review of untenable synergy assumptions arising during the chase mania represents a less effective and delayed way to deal with the consequences of bid mania.

TABLE 7.6a *continued*

	Description	Implications
3 Setting the PMI time frame	A brisk pace and consistent progress is required for the postmerger program to remain on track, avoiding pitfalls such as process myopia and target setting without the means or capability to secure the synergies.	The internal PMI team needs dates and deadline to prevent the program from losing pace. But make the mistake of declaring that there will be no further changes after (specified) date, and game players in both companies will attempt to take advantage.
4 Early priority on visible 'quick wins'	Early sizeable synergies communicate to everyone that *this* postmerger program is about action and measurable performance reforms, rather than directionless process and public posturing.	A clearly defined, major synergy is completed (not merely planned) with details provided (1) to convince all that PMI is more than just jargon and (2) to placate 'numbers keepers' with one eye continually on the value gap (APP – NRS) math. Typically an expense- or revenue-synergy large, high probability target.
5 Call for return to normalcy	Following visible quick wins, rest of postmerger program implemented with less company-wide visibility, as rest of the company is encouraged to 'get back to business', *although subject to PMI reforms until the postmerger period is officially over.*	At both executive and operational levels of both firms (acquirer and target), threat arises of company forgetting its operational roots becoming a permanently distracted business combination intrigue.

nature. The business model of the target company – and in some instances, some parts of the business model of the acquiring firm – become vulnerable as soon as the transaction is announced:

- *Key talent.* Opportunistic competitors paint a picture of turmoil and indecision for many months ahead as they attempt to lure away key talent in value contribution terms and entice a half dozen corporate key contributors (CKCs) lacking advance long-term contracts or retention bonuses to change sides, as opponents are weakened.[23]
- *Major accounts* are informed by these same rivals that they will no longer be receiving the same attention as before the deal, since management will be distracted. Besides, it is just a matter of time before price increases to pay for the deal are made public. 'How do you feel about paying for our rival's deal in the form of increased prices?'
- *Principal suppliers.* The propaganda directed at this stakeholder group is that payments will soon slow as cash is redirected to pay for merger financing principal and interest. If concerns exist already about the acquirer's creditworthiness, they are exaggerated by rivals for competitive advantage.

Acquiring company management, guided by the PMI team, must assess which threats to the existing business are most important and develop counter-strategies in advance. Wait until after the deal has closed, and competitors have the advantage: arguments against their whisper campaign appear slow and reactive, thereby adding credibility to rivals' dire predictions.

Ignore defensive actions entirely, and the threat of a different kind of hollow corporation arises: a public shell is purchased, but key parts of what made that target attractive are lost – think of when the Brits in 'Mad Men' attempted to acquire that show's model Madison Avenue advertising firm, Stirling Cooper. By the time of the closing, all that was left was a low-value name, as critical talent and expertise departed.[24] In such instances, the VG widens into a chasm, and the transaction is a sure failure.

2. Post-acquisition reality check for imaginary synergies

Before the deal closed – back when the chase for TargetCo was still in transition from one bid round to the next – management at the pursuing company hoped that financial markets suffered from temporary amnesia, at least as far as pre-close projections about synergies were concerned.

A month ago, a bid of 100 was offered, accompanied by an adamant explanation from the bidder that this represented a full, fair and complete price for the target, 'taking into account all of the realistically achievable synergies'. That initial bid was rejected, and it quickly becomes apparent to the prospective acquirer that a much higher bid of around 140 would be necessary to complete the deal. Unwilling to walk away from the potentially value-destroying transaction, a desperate scramble for extra paper synergies ensued, in order to try to justify a much higher bid. That long odds IT platform reduction notion? Cross-marketing sales thoughts supported by just one marketing analyst's overactive imagination? Go ahead and add everything to the synergy total, irrespective of feasibility. In the heat of the acquisition chase, temporary plausibility might be sufficient to placate the providers of acquisition capital (Just keep your fingers crossed that they don't ask how it is possible that much the lower *maximum* synergies from round 1 have suddenly surged.)

But now the transaction has closed, and the time has come to take the hot air out of the unlikely synergy assumptions underlying the accepted bid. Presuming that the bid sequence up to the time of close was dominated by the pricers – who are inclined to view synergy considerations as unwelcome obstacles to the exercise of their negotiating 'expertise' – time is overdue to determine the true synergy situation.

3. Setting the (internal) PMI timeframe

Post-merger speed is of paramount importance, for several reasons. The NRS calculation is based upon the *present value* of net synergies secured, so a slow start in diagnosing key PMI targets and/or a sluggish pace in implementing major post-merger reforms threaten deal success. Timing delays alone may mean that NRS falls short of APP, dictating a failed deal based on Chapter 3's VG merger valuation methodology.

A PMI period that seems to be never-ending demoralizes employees, suppresses productivity and increases the prospects of an exodus of top talent. Do-nothing post-merger approaches, as exemplified by the period following AT&T's acquisition of NCR in 1990, doom the deal to negligible synergies and thus, failure. *Laissez faire* and PMI do not mix: the acquiring company's top management face likely dismissal on the basis that they didn't do enough to ensure deal success.

And yet, an abbreviated PMI period brings its own, different, set of failure risks. If post-merger priorities are misguided – such as when time and resources are directed towards smaller and/or lower probability synergy possibilities – management runs out of time in the critical first year following the close. If marginal employees with more games-playing skills than business ability come to suspect a finite deadline for the post-merger period, budget shell games and other diversions proliferate, and the mediocre sometimes defy detection in the post-merger period.

Thus a balance must be struck that recognizes the PMI team's need for pace and priority, without issuing an explicit timetable to the organization as a whole. While the PMI team faces specific targets and synergy identification and achievement deadlines, the necessary communication to the target corporation as a whole must be guarded to ensure that synergies – many of which are in the form of people-related costs – are not missed.

4. Achieving 'quick wins' in the first quarter of the PMI program

For all of its visibility in M&A literature and the acquiring company's press releases up to the time of the deal's closing, there will always be some who perceive the word 'synergy' as little more than a corporate euphemism for directionless merger-related process, spun for maximum effect in the financial media.

And then there are those who agree with the importance of offsetting the acquisition overpayment with credible, tangible post-merger improvements, but who are disappointed after the close as few *tangible* synergies emerge, despite the promises. A third interested group is the personnel in the target company, some of whom hope to slow the PMI progress to a crawl, in order to minimize changes to their status quo.

For all three groups and also for deal financiers and the investment community overall, early 'quick wins' are essential to prove that the PMI program is *real:* that it has substance. Typically, opportunities exist in the top two PMI categories (expense- and revenue-synergies) for a quick win. For example: scale efficiencies, facilities rationalization (e-synergy) can be achieved when excess production-assembly capacity of the two firms is rationalized and some performance-enhancing new equipment purchased with some of the proceeds from disposition. Independent verification is provided to attest to the significantly lower costs per unit in the new production order. Another example is when the channel or product line void is filled (r-synergy): a path-to-market channel advantage commanded by either acquirer or target is exploited by the other party. Sales that would not have occurred otherwise are recorded, and incremental CF can readily be determined.

Another example is placing an internal-external spotlight on the synergy target, with the aim of conveying the sense that this is just one example of the synergies being achieved by the PMI team. Given this high visibility, only the most assured forms of synergies are to be considered. The all-new product venture involving talents from both companies might well capture the imagination of the executives; but full costs and implementation issues (including timing) are unknown, raising the unwelcome possibility of a damaging retreat when unknowns arise.

Following substantive proof of progress achieved in the form of the large quick win(s) in the first quarter after the deal close, the balance of the post-merger program continues, but without the same high level of visibility. The point has been made: PMI is important and initial progress has been achieved. All but the most nervous investors and financiers are satisfied and stand aside to await the conclusions of the M&A post audit (see 10, Table 7.6b).

5. Return towards normalcy

The deliberate decrease in the visibility of the PMI program after the quick win(s) stage coincides with a call for a return to normalcy. The work of the PMI team has just begun; however, the new combined company faces a treacherous future if work stops while everyone awaits the remaining three-quarters of the PMI program's expected duration.

Assuming that the quick win occurs no later than the end of the first quarter after the deal's closing, PMI goes underground at this point:

- The quick win provides an unmistakable indication that the process of identifying, analyzing and securing the other major synergy opportunities has just begun. But except for making sure that all inside and outside the organization know that the quick win is only the beginning of the PMI process, post-merger activity fades into the background, deliberately.
- Having secured what is probably the easiest, large synergy (the quick win), the opportunities that remain are more challenging. It should be anticipated that the PMI team will need the next three-quarters just to have any chance of closing the APP-NRS value gap.

TABLE 7.6b PMI priorities 6–10: From invest-to-save to M&A post audit

	Description	Implications
6 The neglected invest-to-save	Ensuring a sufficiently broad PMI scope, taking into account that many of the more important synergy opportunities involve *some* level of offset investment or expense outlay.	Singular focus on expense reductions (major synergy category in most programs) sometimes means unwise elimination of some promising candidate synergy initiatives which require limited offset expenses and/or investment.
7 Missed opportunities	Arbitrary 'no go' areas or the opposite, narrow targets, may result in major missed opportunities.	Sometimes the major synergy opportunity that may mean the difference between merger success and failure is so apparent that it is invisible: de-layering, major dispositions or shut down, budget eliminations rather than incremental budget reductions.
8 Their own medicine	Return to normalcy (5) is signaled by a return to pre-merger levels of market competitiveness and contention.	Relates to Pursuing new accounts (1), key employees of competitors are more than merely guarding against competitors' postmerger tactics. *Rivals* are put on the defensive, dispelling belief in those companies that firm is distracted by its acquisition.
9 Drift to permanent postmerger bureaucracy	Refers to predictable tendency of all internal bureaucracies to seek to extend their lifespans, while expanding their scope.	Except perhaps in the case of the serial acquirer making many small acquisitions (eg, Cisco, Google), mergers are major occasional events for the acquirer, arguing against a permanent internal PMI staff.
10 Independent M&A post audit	Measuring both parts of the value gap equation, independent of interference or selective interpretation by interested parties.	Board level. Without Post-PMI perspective on whether the value gap was successfully covered by achieved synergies, (a) there is no way of confirming that the merger was successful and (b) to adapt future bidding and synergy processes if and when a NRS – APP shortfall arises.

* Net Realizable Synergies

- The carnival atmosphere that has persisted since the original expression of interest must now come to an end. No more combined company assemblies with obtuse post-merger announcements that make things worse in two ways: employees remain concerned about the future after such Town Meetings, and in some instances, a CEO slip about staffing or consolidation might inadvertently jeopardize one of the remaining major synergy opportunities on the PMI team's top 10 list.

Merger fatigue has set in among staff. Instead of spending a third of one's attention on the intrigue of the merger, lower visibility of the PMI program helps get the message across that *this* operating company's main business is making (and/or selling) things, not becoming mired in the palace intrigue accompanying M&A.

Even though a clear message has been given that the PMI process continues, some individuals in the target company in particular will only hear what they want to, and will act both surprised and indignant if the PMI scrutiny comes around to their group. 'I thought that all the post-merger adjustments and layoffs are over.' No such statement has been made, as the PMI senior team completes its work.[25]

6. *Neglected invest-to-save*

As the remaining three-quarters of the PMI program commence, special attention is to be directed at the beginning of this stage to a synergy issue that has been overlooked so far, even by experienced members of the PMI implementation team. These opportunities are described here as neglected 'invest-to-save' (ITS).

The merger is completed and the message is out, across both organizations: search relentlessly for savings everywhere, to help offset the purchase premium which was necessary to gain control of the target. Plans for reductions are everywhere: reduced recruitment, even incidentals such as free coffee. Some promising new product initiatives in place before the deal emerged are put on hold: not the right time.

In such an environment, the notion of having to make some additional investments in order to maximize improvements almost always falls on deaf ears. 'Didn't you get the message about the need for efficiencies everywhere?' And yet, excluding such ITS opportunities from consideration may artificially limit achievable synergy opportunities. Following are two examples, one pertaining to each of the two top synergy categories.

Greenfield as alternative to simple consolidation (e-synergy)

On the surface, the merger appears to involve a straightforward consolidation-mature type of combination: a type 3a transaction as identified in Chapter 4's Table 4.2. With similar end-products and production-assembly processes, next actions appear simple: shut down the less efficient facility and transfer volume to the superior plant. For industries in terminal decline, this is likely the best that can be done. But for sectors which are not yet at commodity stage? Our experience suggests that in some instances an all-new greenfield facility with equipment and processes that enable the firm to regain a past reputation as industry innovator should also be considered.

Applying an IVE two-scenario DCF analysis approach as described in Chapter 3, three possibilities are competitively assessed on a value effect basis. Those three scenarios are no change, simple consolidation, and transfer of all volume to an all-new facility (Greenfield).

Marketing investment to ensure optimum customer retention (r-synergy)

One of the most common marketing-oriented business combinations is also among the most precarious: when two companies in the same field but at different customer-product tiers in that segment are combined: examples are Procter & Gamble/Pantene, Federated Department Stores/Neiman-Marcus and Daimler/Chrysler.

Merger apologists talk of complementary markets and analysis and begin to apply optimistic sales rates per customer to a dramatically expanded customer base. But several months later, customer churn in the new combined company has markedly increased, compared to past levels. High-end brand customers fear loss of exclusivity and perhaps lower quality. Lower-end customers were satisfied with their product's price-to-feature point before the merger; today they fear that prices will soar to pay for the deal and to bring the more downmarket brand closer in line.

7. The missed opportunity

Having built up synergy intelligence from base-level data, sometimes an opportunity for a major synergy or APP offset is overlooked, even though it is staring the PMI team in the face. Praise from the acquiring company's CEO about the target's traditional product may be misinterpreted as ring-fencing that company from aggressive post-merger synergy development.

Johnson & Johnson acquired the clear soap brand Neutrogena in 1994, a prestige product once marketed only via dermatologists and available in luxury hotels. J&J congratulated itself for helping to pay for that deal by gradually introducing Neutrogena into its much wider channel network. But was that value-maximizing PMI? Actions to diversify the nameplate into other cosmetic product areas did not begin until years later. Ambiguity about whether the brand was health- or luxury-oriented didn't help the acquired firm's entry into the personal products mainstream. A more focused effort at developing Neutrogena as a major post-merger luxury brand may have paid off the deal sooner.

Approaches such as de-layering are limited to the most expansive definition of post-merger scope (3, in Table 7.2) and are described in this chapter as APP offsets rather than synergies since savings from such sources are conservatively treated as one-off in nature, rather than continuing.

But with the PMI team probing around the edges of the newly acquired firm at product and expense synergies, sometimes the biggest opportunities to pay down part of the purchase premium is right there: dozens, sometimes scores of sideways-promoted executive journeymen that the combined company can lose without skipping a beat. In fact less is more: efficiency and communications are likely improved as the target company's puzzle palace bureaucracy is culled.[26]

8. (Some of) their own medicine

Competitors persist in circling around key accounts and some key employees despite priority 1, defense first (Table 7.6a). Until and unless the post-acquisition firm signals that it won't stand still for such actions – such as by pursuing some particularly attractive targets of its competitors – the vultures continue. Give the rivals a bit of their own medicine, and signal to customers and competitors alike how the firm continues to compete, even in the post-merger period.

9. Resisting the inclination of some in the PMI team to become part of a permanent post-merger bureaucracy[27]

This priority involves the *avoidance* of a post-PMI inclination. When most of the post-merger objectives on the PMI team's top 10 list have been achieved, the time has come to declare the post-merger period ended. The internal members of the PMI team should begin to prepare to return to their original functional groups.[28]

From time to time, an attempt is made by some members of those PMI teams to transform their temporary roles into permanent positions, in the form of an ongoing PMI bureaucracy within the acquiring firm. But there are almost no circumstances when it makes sense for such permanent costs to be added to the expense structure of the post-merger company.

If and when inclusion of company employees on the PMI team is advisable (see below), the most valuable contributors to the PMI team are insiders from within the target company, because of their direct knowledge of key performance characteristics of the new acquiree. But such insight is limited to a single transaction, with little or no carryover benefit to the acquiring organization in future periods.

Where large companies augment their internal growth through multiple small acquisitions as an integral part of their business model (eg Cisco Systems, Google, some telecommunications firms), an argument can be made for a standing PMI group in the buying firm, but for transaction execution, rather than target company PMI diagnosis. The targets ordinarily pursued as part of such ongoing growth programs tend to be straightforward augmentation-type deals of the category 2 type from Table 4.2 in Chapter 4: 2a, bolt-ons and 2b, line extension equivalents. Given the size and number of such small transactions, the critical skills relate to transaction documentation and closure, rather than in-depth business insight. Bolts-ons and line extensions are often justified on a simple make-versus-buy basis, with simplified integration: the desired part of the target business is retained while the rest of the company is disposed of.

10. Independent acquisition performance post-audit

More than a decade ago, KPMG made the following condemning observation about the state of M&A post-audit examinations:

> Less than half (45 per cent) had carried out a formal post-deal review. This lack of post-deal assessment is concerning. None of the respondent companies were new to the M&A process. Most, in fact, had been involved in several mergers and acquisitions before and, no doubt, carry out more in the future. (1999: 7)

Little has changed since then. The absence of a board-level M&A post audit means that there is no final determination of whether the deal was justified on the basis of the two principal merger valuation methodologies as described in Chapter 3 in this book: VG and IVE. In the absence of an effective examination of merger performance based on the criteria of greatest importance to the owners of the business, the board risks being accused of neglecting its responsibility to the shareholders of the acquiring firm to help ensure that all major investments made by the firm – including M&A investment in other companies – are value-creating.

Sizeable acquisitions require review on a *specific transaction basis*. With merger valuation having only recently emerged from the distortions introduced by subjective, qualitative M&A criteria that are irrelevant to buying companies' shareholders, there is a need for specific transaction investigation based on VG-IVE. Assessments of multiple transaction M&A programs are derived from the correct performance assessment of individual transactions comprising that group.

7.5 Other PMI implementation issues: choosing the PMI implementation team

> External transaction advisors... external transaction banks – are seldom involved in the kind of detailed, bottom-up estimates of synergies that would be needed to develop meaningful benchmarks before the deal.
>
> (Christofferson *et al*, 2004: 94)

The post-merger result can be no better than the collective capabilities of the PMI team. The challenge is daunting: not only to separate out the few *primary* synergy opportunities from all the others, but then to achieve those improvements under intense time pressure and in an environment where many hope that the PMI effort fails miserably. This brass-knuckled post-merger arena is no safe place for 'surplus' employees struggling to secure continuing unemployment in their customary departments and divisions, or for process-myopic advisers who confuse mere meetings and proclamations with PMI progress, or for one-dimensional functional specialists inclined to view PMI challenges through their own narrow cognitive filter.

One fundamental determination is whether the PMI team is primarily composed of internal employees of the firms involved or externals. Some advantages and disadvantages of each are summarized in Table 7.7 and examined below.

TABLE 7.7 Post-merger implementation team composition

	Internal (*Acquirer+Acquiree*)	External
ADVANTAGES	• Facilitate access to critical intelligence; *the numbers behind reported numbers* • Fast track to understanding of critical defensive actions: essential key employees (CKCs), accounts, competitive vulnerabilities • Prior improvements considered but not taken: key to rapid understanding of additional synergy opportunities under broadest scope (TE Plus Missed Opportunities, Table 7.1)	• Objectivity; separate from companies examined • Analytical frameworks, methodologies, tools • Addressing difficult but necessary PMI decisions, such as implementation reductions to NRSs caused by limitations of *acquiring* company management, resolution of acquirer-acquiree synergy conflicts
DISADVANTAGES	• Unfamiliar with key characteristics of effective PMI: NRS notion unknown – likely confuse 'top line' synergy amounts with CF bottom line • Unaccustomed to specific synergy identification and implementation challenges of four main synergy types (e-, r-, f-, t-) • No resistance to synergy misadventures dreamed up by synergy amateurs: the 'Big Win' supposed opportunities which are not • Time urgency missing	• Inadequate awareness of feasibility may result in overreliance on large but theoretical synergies • Sometimes results in limited scope according to specialist area • Dependency: *must* have access to key insiders (not just data), merely to be minimally effective • Possible conflict between need for PMI speed, external's own fee/scope objectives • Illusion of 'free' PMI (integrated with transaction fee)

Internal: superior understanding of the critical characteristics of key synergies

The post-merger synergy team is ideally comprised of members from *both* the acquiring firm and the target. A joint team is preferable despite the potential for intra-team friction, because a team made up exclusively of managers from one company or the other faces limitations.

Acquiring company only

Left to their own devices, staff from the buying company have at best limited insight into where to look and what for in pursuing the top 10 synergy opportunities. PMI analytical traps within the target firm include the negligible improvement candidate (which initially appears to be greater than it really is) and unfamiliar terminology and report formats.

Acquired company only

Conversely, a team dominated by managers from the target almost never reflects the perspective of the group with primacy when it comes to determining whether the deal is a success or failure. Financial return expectations of the buying firm's continuing shareholders are paramount when it comes to merger valuation, but the financial and personal interests of the target's employees differ significantly from those aims. Members of a PMI team dominated by target company employees might attempt to exploit their numerical advantage on the post-merger team by obstructing PMI progress, especially where functions, department and staff of the acquiring firm and the acquired firm overlap.

Advantages of a combined (acquirer + acquiree) staff group as vanguards of the post-merger synergy effort include the following.

Uncovering the numbers beyond the publicly-available performance and solvency numbers. Premerger due diligence-level statistical summaries have already been made available to the acquiring firm. If the target is publicly-traded, other reports and filings are also in the public domain. But what does it all mean? Absent knowledgeable insight into *how* those statistics were compiled and what they do and do not include, the numbers by themselves reveal little.

The phrase 'the numbers behind reported numbers', refers to essential interpretation to transform statistics into useful and useable post-merger insight. For example, special insight about: a) trends of account and supplier concentration; b) keys to those relationships; and c) competitors' price-performance positioning cannot be gleaned from the records alone. Knowledgeable guidance is required to make sense of it all.

Fast understanding of which critical actions are most important in robust defense of the target business in the days immediately following the deal's close. The importance of defensive actions to prevent deterioration in the worth of the acquired firm in the early days immediately following the deal's close has already been discussed. Questions arise about the nature and number of these targets to be defended. Which are most important? Can retention be assured through devices such as stay-put bonuses, or is more required? What are the principal post-merger concerns of key suppliers and customers, and what are they looking for in terms of assurance? Absent insight into these defensive targets, two possible threats emerge.

The first is that the wrong defensive targets are defended, raising costs in the target firm (and *reducing* net synergies) and thus destroying the value and widening the VG. Secondly, without special insight, there is the potential loss of key resources – such as the CKCs who are essential to new product development or to new sales to an emerging category of customers. Their key role is only known when they are gone. By then, it is too late.

Improvements considered but not implemented by prior management represent the key difference between the second (target expansive, TE) and third (TE plus missed opportunities) from Table 7.2. Table 7.2 in this chapter, on synergy program scope interpretations, makes a case for the widest possible working definition for synergies, including some improvements that prior target company management could have implemented but for a variety of reasons did not. Insights to these neglected improvements to the basic business can represent the difference between sufficient NRSs to justify the deal, and falling short. Examples include bloated organizational layers, redundant control structures and sidelined executives retained because of inertia instead of contribution. Some of these overlooked improvements are one-off counter-APPs, while others may be correctly classified as ongoing synergies. One thing for sure: without insider knowledge of past company struggles and deliberations, these additions to scope probably remain invisible.

Some potential disadvantages of the all-internal PMI team include the following.

Insufficient familiarity with core post-merger concepts, principles and approaches, resulting in misguided investigations. Post-merger integration is only today evolving from the level of anecdotal stories and single-dimensional guidelines towards more complete analytical frameworks and methods. Staff dabbling in PMI as a part-time hobby are unaware of the new approaches, some of which are described in this chapter. With no reference point, errors associated with past PMI efforts may be repeated: for example, *laissez faire* inactivity (AT&T/NCR) or over-reliance on unachievable systems efficiencies (Unum/Provident).

When time urgency is missing. Particularly among team members from the acquiring firm, there is not only an absence of the acquirer's urgency to compete the PMI task, but there may also be an active interest in slowing the pace of transition to an unknown future.

The PMI team meets twice a week, and some may confuse activity with achievement. But meetings *per se* mean nothing; the PMI team has accomplished nothing until and unless major, credible post-merger synergies are identified, diagnosed and secured. Anything less represents wasted effort and expense – squandered resources that increase rather than decrease that deal's VG.

Timing affects NRS, which is calculated on the basis of the *present value* of future projected net synergies (gross synergies in CF terms, minus offsetting expenses). The slower the pace of major synergy identification and achievement, the lower the NRS. In both of the leading merger valuation methodologies as examined in Chapter 3, VG and IVE, the timing of synergies (inflows) has a direct bearing on whether the transaction is judged to be successful or not.

External: bringing post-merger tools, diagnosis and urgency to bear

'External' refers here to PMI team members who are not employees of either principal to the transaction. Some advantages include the following.

Objectivity

Assuming that the external team reports to the acquiring company's board and not to that firm's chief executive, the opportunity arises for an independent perspective on the key question: 'Was this deal value-creating for the owners of the acquiring business?'

The acquiring company chief executive's proclamations that 'We have not overpaid' help to deflect uninformed media accusations of value destruction, at least temporarily. But such tactics are not to be confused with in-depth merger valuation and success assessment. Top management at the acquiring company that has just completed a questionable transaction has an interest in limiting the commentary about the attractiveness of the deal to subjects such as 'fit' or 'market presence'. Both such terms are sufficiently vague to permit skilled spin doctors to even make a merger train wreck such as Conseco/Green Tree (see Chapter 5) appear plausible, at least temporarily.

But the board's constituency is neither daytime business TV nor the financial blogs. The board is accountable to the shareholders, who require more exacting determination of merger success that what can be repeated by a terminally cheerful Biz-TV personality as an investigatory sound bite. Because of that board's greater accountability, members need to determine independently whether NRSs exceed the APP. The acquiring company management may hope to avoid an analysis of the two combined companies' worth on a standalone versus combined basis, being concerned about a result that places them in a negative light. For the board, such investigation utilizing Chapter 3's IVE methodology is required. In the absence of an independent, complete point of reference for the critical issues of merger success as determined by the VG method and real versus illusory synergies, the board may face legitimate criticism for neglecting its primary responsibility to protect shareholders' wealth.

Vivendi's Mercier and Bronfman trials are fresh in directors' minds: how can a board without credible independent expertise about what is arguably the third most important factor in merger success (behind only merger targeting and pricing-timing) claim to provide adequate review of the chief executive without its own independent insight into what is traditionally the corporation's largest investment?

Analytical frameworks, diagnostic tools and methods

Company insiders dabbling part-time on PMI are especially susceptible to whatever PMI fad or fashion graces those content-free fluff pieces from various middlemen with their snouts in the M&A fee trough. While there is no assurance that those outside the organization will be any less inclined to pursue the superficial synergy target rather than the substantive, those external advisers with the insights and analytical tools that go well beyond synergy success and failure stories are at least in a position to help. The issue: are tools and capabilities up to the challenge?

Addressing difficult but necessary PMI critical decisions

Just because acquiring company senior management might weave a semi-plausible case for proceeding with their proposed transaction, that doesn't mean that merger success is assured. For good reason: internal analysts fear that pointing out fallacies in their boss's VG math is a fast track to unemployment. But if management overreacts to the post-merger scrutiny of external observers that merely confirms to the financial community that such observations are on track.

Critical assumptions pertaining to synergy amounts, their timing and offsets require tough-minded independent scrutiny. As two-thirds of merger transactions historically involve a purchase price that exceeds NRS, the days of financial markets accepting public relations jargon or statements from easily cowed internal minions that 'we have not overspent' are long gone. In the absence of independent verification that synergies are sufficient to offset the purchase premium paid, the inclination of the financial community in the MMF era is to presume that the deal is value-destroying.

Disadvantages that may arise with external staffing include the following.

Incomplete awareness of feasibility. Detached from the day-to-day business realities of the business and with no creative points for merely re-applying someone else's discovered improvement, externals sometimes exhibit a tendency towards new concepts that prove difficult to implement. Novelty doesn't necessarily ensure that the flash idea is implantable. To the contrary, experimental and expansive, offsetting costs are almost assuredly unknown and only revealed by trial and error.

Limited scope, according to area of specialization. Perhaps one reason for the proliferation of books and articles claiming to rediscover some hidden truth is that post-merger integration sometimes lends itself to domination by self-proclaimed subject experts who imagine that their narrow area of concentration is the *one and only* answer to every major PMI challenge. To a carpenter who is equipped only with a hammer, everything looks like a nail.

But complex post-merger challenges are rarely if ever organized or resolved by narrow functional specialists. The IT manager who looks only at that area, the process specialist who emphasizes schedules with little emphasis on results: the prior absence of action frameworks provides latitude for PMI diagnosis to be distorted as a marketing mechanism. External parties must have access to insider information to be effective. The only initiative that is more of a time waster than a theoretical framework with no connection to reality is the wholly conceptual effort deprived of supportive data.

In the better of two alternative bad circumstances, the PMI effort deteriorates into little more than a series of meetings in which there is an illusion of progress. As ineffective as this outcome is, an even less desirable outcome is if arbitrary savings amounts are allocated by the externals, forcing attention on unfunded discretionary amounts, regardless of whether or not those cuts are appropriate contacts.

Possible conflicts between the requirement for post-merger speed and external fee scope. A fast, well-focused PMI investigation completed within a year is too brief (and with insufficient extra fees) to attract the attention of generalist consultants masquerading as post-merger specialists, where engagements of less than a year and less than seven figures tend to receive secondary attention and second team staffing.

For the banker or other intermediary pretending that adequate PMI support is all included in the transaction fee, budget limitations dictate the short, superfluous PMI effort: the economics of that provider dictate moving on to the next transaction as quickly as possible. The longer the time that the fee-myopic intermediary spends on post-merger administration, the lower the total profit from the deal.

As both internal and external staff members' capabilities as described here are critical to the success of the overall post-merger effort, our experience is that a team combining both types of members, their backgrounds and perspectives represents the most effective way forward.

Notes

1 'After the deal', http://www.economist.com/181251; subtitle: 'Doing deals is easy... Now comes the hard part.' Accessed Jun 19 2011.

2 Geneen, H, *The Synergy Myth and Other Ailments of Business Today*, New York, St Martin's Press, xiii.

3 A secondary beneficial aspect of de-layering, reducing the communications distance between the head of the company and key accounts, may also yield some r- (revenue-) synergies in the form of increased sales because of the more responsive organizational structure.

4 Besides influencing aspects of part 3 in this chapter on specific synergy categories, Damodaran's description of merger valuation based on comparative DCF analyses of the two merger partners as standalones and then combined resembles the IVE merger valuation methodology described in Chapter 3 in this book.

5 'Capital equipment analysis: the required rate of profit', *Management Science*, 3:1, 102–10.

6 KPMG (1999) 'Unlocking shareholder value: the keys to success', *Mergers & Acquisitions, A global research report*, 3

7 The key term here is *explicitly.* One might argue that perceptions of post-merger synergies are indirectly reflected in ES analysis in the form of post-announcement share price levels and movements of the combined firm

post-announcement, but with parties to the transaction often having a poor grasp of achievable – as opposed to touted, during the bid chase – synergies, it is difficult to see how the rational market gains that insight. As for TRS, there is no specific provision for synergies. That change in market capitalization from the time of initial acquisition to the time of round turn sale or disposition can be attributable to several factors, including but not limited to: a) increasing general share price indices over the ownership period, b) increases in market multiples overassigned to CFs over that period, and c) improvements, and as a practical matter it becomes an impossible task to separate out synergies from the other potential influences.

8 Neff, J (Jan 27 2012) 'P&G to cut 1,600 jobs, bank on digital for long-term savings', *AdAge Digital*, http://adage.com/article/digital/p-g-cut-1-600-jobs-bank-digital-long-term-savings/232385/. Accessed Feb 17 2012.

9 The concluding sub-part in 7.1 includes the issue of probability and feasibility adjustments for especially unlikely synergy nominations. Suggesting such adjustments may be career-threatening if made by those within the acquiring company.

10 While the first response of a target's willingness to accept an initial bid may be to congratulate oneself for astute negotiation, early acceptance may instead be indicative of a seller eager to get out, as in Conseco/Green Tree and Compaq/DEC. In the latter acquisition, Digital Equipment (DEC) was hotly pursued by Compaq in the 1990s, even after it became apparent that DEC was not being actively pursued by others. What at first appeared to be a plausible deal has since come to be viewed as a disappointment, helping to propel Compaq into the arms of acquirer H-P a few years later. See also Palepu and Barnett (Sep 14 2004) 'Hewlett-Packard-Compaq: the merger decision', Case 9-104-048, Harvard Business School, Boston, Harvard Business School Publishing, 5.

11 Inclusion of 'diversification' here is controversial. Diversification does not always result in company value improvement and sometimes it contributes to merger value destruction. While it is true that a single-industry corporation may be highly vulnerable to external and internal forces affecting that industry (operating risk) along with possible extra costs and risks associated with the seasonal and term CF patterns specific to that industry – and that diversification may provide some escape from one or both of those risks – offsetting considerations include a) possible loss of corporate focus as management is spread too thin across diverse operations of the firm, and b) additional bureaucracy costs and reduced competitive speed, and c) the well-documented conglomerate discount (such as described by Scherer, F, 1988, 'Corporate takeovers: the efficiency arguments', *Journal of Economic Perspectives*, 2:1, 71).

12 'Merger types and shareholder returns', *Financial Management*, Summer, 66.

13 A significantly underleveraged target that also has underexploited commercial opportunities suggests a rare (today, except in some emerging market company situations) Boone Pickens' early 1980s situation in which the acquirer's post-merger attention is first directed at growing the acquired company to the size it always should have been, using that target's own underutilized borrowing capacity to finance growth. Our interpretation is that the upper end of the band represents the point at which total debt from all sources expressed as a percentage of all debt plus all forms of equity is so great that either a) immediate threat to solvency arises, and/or b) *permanent* damage is threatened to company ongoing competitive or financial viability, as assessed by independent examination by a party with no financial interest in the transaction.

14 'E' synergies are limited here to *expense* savings and efficiencies. In an expanded definition, the category would also include expenditures, with the totals modified to reflect changes in that investment outlay or requirement.

15 Phyrr, P (1973) *Zero-base Budgeting: A practical management tool for evaluating expenses*, New York, Wiley.

16 Porter, M (2004) *Competitive Advantage*, New York, Free Press.

17 Synergy opportunities such as this are at the heart of the case for the widest possible definition of synergy program scope, as addressed in part 7.1. Those inclined to exclude such common sense rationalizations from the synergy scope contend that the market already anticipates these savings and reflects the amounts in the target firm's share price. But as no one has been aware of the duplication in the target firm to date, the implausible notion arises that the rational market responds to a situation that management is not even aware of.

18 A broader geographic scope of operations after the merger expands the opportunities for both advantageous recognition of revenues in lower tax geographies and the opposite, recognition of expenses in higher tax geographies. The primary basis for the geographic designation of revenue or expenses should be other than minimizing tax payment outflows alone. Tax authorities have become increasingly aggressive in their search for geography shifts in expenses and revenue caused by tax considerations alone. One possible partial remedy for the new post-merger combined company is physical relocation of some operations with international tax considerations included as a *secondary* consideration.

19 Here, 'optimal capital structure' refers to a mix of debt and equity components consistent with achievement of maximum value by the new combined corporation.

20 The company-wide WACC represents the correct basis for calculating the difference between project returns and financing costs, not project-specific funding. The spread cited here is for illustration purposes only.

21 Mills, Apr 27 2012 (in conversation with co-author Clark): 'For example, a large power generator in the UK had just undergone a very positive review with the regulator, the upshot suggesting that the company was very well run from an operational perspective. It was with great surprise that the company found itself to be a likely target of a large US company and management found it difficult to understand the economic rationale for the interest. A closer look indicated that the company, which was predominantly equity financed, would be left completely intact from an operational perspective, but that once taken private the expensive equity would be substituted by much cheaper debt.'

22 The phrase 'by this management team' is emphasized because of the management synergy considerations noted in earlier parts in this chapter. There is no universal synergy amount attributable to a specific target. Corresponding synergies in the acquiring firm differ, as do the buying company's past experience and expertise at synergy development.

23 CKCs are designated on the basis of the value effect of those individuals, typically on a simple subtraction basis. A key question arises: 'What happens to value in the new combined company if that specific individual is not part of the new combined company?' If the answer is 'nothing' or minimal, then that individual is expendable, regardless of position or prior role. The CKC diagnosis is necessary to ensure that retention efforts and bonuses are directed to the few, most important targets, and to minimize outside bonuses and retention contracts to those who merely preside over value-development in the firm, rather than perform an instrumental role in creating that corporate worth (see Clark, 2001).

24 'Hollow corporation' refers to a company lacking manufacturing or assembly operations, which causes others to combine the products and services offered to customers. As used here, the phrase refers to the situation that arises when unsecured resources and people are allowed to depart. The acquirer, caught off-guard, likely dismisses the losses as minimal, pointing to the ongoing brand value of the company. Financial and commercial markets know otherwise; as companies become increasingly service-like in nature, the future value of the company walks out the door at the end of the working day.

25 The PMI team leader should expect to have to call upon executive management several times in the last three-quarters if necessary to ensure full cooperation of affected units and individuals. Absolute unanimity of the message that the PMI program continues to be in effect *after* the quick win is mandatory. If the chief executive inadvertently errs by prematurely declaring an end to PMI activity before the full work is completed, the related M&A deal has failed, since synergies are incomplete and the PMI program has lost its legitimacy.

26 In the film *Wall Street*, this type of radical contra-APP was represented by the 100-plus group of vice presidents at fictional target Teldar Paper, when Gordon Gekko played by Michael Douglas proclaimed that an oversized middle- and upper-management bureaucracy represented Teldar Paper's only growth area.

27 This circumstance only applies to internal PMI staff. Part 7.7 considers the advantages and disadvantages of internal and external PMI teams.

28 If the individual's host organization is not inclined to dismiss others to make room for the returning employee, suspicions arise that the PMI team was understaffed. A large acquisition represents the acquiring company's largest external investment; not a suitable destination for 'surplus' staff not in demand elsewhere in the organization.

The seven keys to merger success

08

> *Whether acquisitions create value depends on various factors: how value improvements are measured... the type of deal... the method of payment... the type of target... and the bidder's, the target's or the market's valuation.*
>
> (Bouwman *et al*, 2003: 9)

CHAPTER CONTENTS

8.1 Merger success: the seven keys

8.2 Some implementation considerations

8.1 Merger success: the seven keys

Full merger success is achieved through analyses and actions designed to maximize merger-related value to shareholders of the acquiring company. Hollow processes and vapid merger concepts contribute to the now widely accepted reality that most mergers fail (see Chapter 5). No longer merely a hurried afterthought when the deal is closed, *advance* diagnosis of true synergy opportunities – what is described here and in the preceding chapter as net realizable synergies (NRSs) – become the foundation of a defendable merger plan. Instead of:

> bid as high as necessary to close the deal, and then hope that sufficient synergies might be developed to prevent the transaction from being viewed as a failure,

the new guidance for successful acquirers in the years ahead calls for the following:

> successful deals begin with the development and application of substantive synergy intelligence *well before* the final bid is submitted. M&A success has very little to do with pre-bid maneuverings and topping the other guy's bid. Without *advance* assurance that the deal is justified, even modest merger chases directed at the wrong targets (see Table 4.2) result in massive value destruction and penalties for those responsible.

Most of this chapter addresses the seven keys of merger success, depicted in summary form in Table 8.1.

TABLE 8.1 Overview: Seven keys to M&A success

Key of Success	Description	Chapter(s)
1 Following the right merger success criteria	Central issue of returns over acquisition lifespan to acquiring company's shareholders. Deletion of soft criteria (qualitative/subjective), limited statistical analyses (event studies, TSR), leaves today's two emerging methods, applied in combination: value gap (VG), incremental value effect (IVE).	3
2 Optimal timing within the merger cycle	Late phase (III and IV) deals exaggerate the triple threats to deal success from diminishing supply of quality targets, exaggerated total APPs, collapse in inflows at worst possible time.	1,3,4
3 Exploiting superior understanding of merger segmentation	Historically, most deals fail. Does your acquisition program pursue only the *higher probability* M&A types as identified in the list of 9 M&A types (Table 4.2)?	4

TABLE 8.1 *continued*

Key of Success	Description	Chapter(s)
4 Adhering to absolute & relative limits on acquisition purchase premiums (APPs)	At the very least, premiums either (a) above 38% or (b) greater than the 60th percentile for that phase and industry require extra scrutiny and justification before proceeding with transaction.	3,4,7
5 Bid pricing integrated with in-depth four synergy type PMI investigation	A bid process undisciplined by realizable synergies is vulnerable to value-destructive, success-reducing acquisition over-pricing. The absence of access to complete synergy analysis is no excuse. Primary reliance on the most substantial parts of the two most reliable synergy categories: e- and r-.	3,7
6 Synergy elements: real distinguished from vapor, offsets included	In each of the four synergy categories (e- ,r-, f-, m-) careful separation of the real from the illusory, with (a) acquirer-imagined visions and (b) improvements based on vague or non-existent breakthroughs especially perilous to acquiring company, in value terms.	7
7 Avoidance of transactions by 'wounded quail' acquirers, overreaching egos	Mergers accelerate the decline of firms approaching irreversible decline, rather than saving them. Ego-acquisitions traditionally top the Worst Deals lists.	4–5

M&A success key 1: Following the right merger success criteria

What is the most defendable way (or ways) to determine whether or not the specific merger is a success? The answer to that question begins with another question, 'Who are the determiners of merger valuation methodology?'

Continuing shareholders of the acquiring firm are that 'who'. Those who own the buying firm command primacy when it comes to determining merger valuation criteria and methodologies, because they are ultimately responsible for providing the risk capital for the merger transaction. *It's their ball.* If those shareholders don't like the merger game or how the score is kept, they may decide to take their ball away (with the consequence of no transactions at all).

But how is the vital M&A interest of buying firms' owners to be interpreted? Company shareholders are diverse and dispersed. They rarely if ever speak with a unified voice. Rather than these considerations making the task of determining shareholders' vital M&A interests more difficult, they instead render that task simpler, as the one criterion common to all of those shareholders is returns: how much money their wealth position increases (or decreases) as a consequence of the merger. Precedent and experience suggest that shareholders will consistently choose the approach resulting in the superior financial returns to them – which means that the

TABLE 8.2 Merger success key 1: Getting the merger valuation criteria right

Key to Merger Success: 1	
Following the Right Merger Success Criteria Begins with designation of the merger valuation criteria-setter. From the four primary financial-qualitative methods, value gap (VG) and incremental value effect (IVE) for different reasons. Confirmation role *only* for multiples, arguably the most extensively *mis*-applied merger 'valuation' approach when relied upon as primary method.	
Implications	**Issues**
Quantitative vs qualitative merger valuation debate is moot: *criteria-setters establish the criteria, not valuation pundits, deal intermediaries or conflicted acquiring company management.* Incorporates recognition that 'meeting the prevailing market premium' (APP) may still result in a non-viable deal.	Comprising the best merger valuation *combination*, since no single merger criteria is complete. Separate merger valuation criteria for round-turn, intermediate round-turn acquirers? Methods which explicitly reflect synergies (VG, IVE) only as good as quality of pre- and post-close synergy diagnosis, implementation.

merger valuation methodology of greatest interest to that group is whatever measure or approach most clearly reveals the wealth effect to them from the merger.

No merger valuation methodology is without limitations, which is one of the reasons why what is described in Chapter 3 as today's emergent approach is composed not of one method but of two. In tomorrow's well-analyzed, carefully planned business combinations, value gap (VG) and incremental value effect (IVE) methodologies are conducted in parallel, separate analyses in judging the deal. VG is complemented by comparative analysis of the two acquisition partners on a standalone and combined comparative basis.

VG analysis reflects the no-nonsense question: 'are readily realizable synergies from this acquisition sufficient to cover the acquisition purchase premium (APP) paid for this deal?' Whether applied while bidding is still underway or after the close, the quality of the VG analysis is no better than the acquiring firm's NRSs.

IVE is a comparative discounted cash flow (DCF)-based analysis of two separate projections involving the acquirer and its target: combined (including purchase premia and assumed synergies) and separately as standalone entities (as if the merger never occurred). In this merger valuation analytical structure, important albeit supportive roles exist for multiples and for total shareholder returns (TSR).

Multiples are most credibly expressed in the form of analyzed share price over 10–20 sessions (numerator) divided by free cash flows (FCFs, denominator), multiples are correctly viewed as a form of historical measure, rather than as a true M&A methodology. Nonetheless, comparisons of transactions involving different companies and industries have long been used to provide supplementary insight into merger feasibility.[1]

TSR's limitations include a negative statistical bias, since successful acquisitions are rarely disposed of, except by transitional owners involved in buying and selling those portfolio acquisitions. For these types of short- and intermediate-term buyers TSR is sometimes the only merger valuation method used.

The valuation academicians' preferred method, event study (ES) analysis, stretches rational market (SSME) theory to breaking point: the supposition that a few months' post-announcement date share price movement foretells the future success of the deal is the analytical equivalent of picking hot stocks by examining tea leaves. At best, such share price movements reflect numerous influences, including pricing, lawsuits, competitive position, bad debts or market share trends. Isolating those contaminating influences on share price from influences solely attributable to the recent merger becomes an exercise in futility.

Supporters of 'soft' qualitative methods for measuring merger performance raise some secondary considerations of importance once required financial returns are first achieved, but *they* are not the owners of the acquiring business and their interpretations are subjective musings.

M&A success key 2: Optimal timing within the merger wave

While deft merger timing doesn't necessarily increase the prospects for acquisition success, *mis*timing may significantly reduce chances for merger success based on the VG-IVE two-method merger valuation approach.

Each business-merger cycle exhibits four distinct, identifiable phases, with different pitfalls and opportunities for each. Either a) misunderstand which phase of the wave is now in effect, and/or b) misinterpret that phase's signal, and chances of a failed deal increase significantly.

TABLE 8.3 Merger success key 2: Optimal timing in the four phase merger wave

Key to Merger Success: 2

Optimal Timing Within the Merger Wave

As the fourth post-1980 merger wave (2011–2019) continues, applying an understanding of the *patterns* and *critical characteristics* of the three waves is important to help:

- identify early phase opportunities for those acquirers not highly dependent on external acquisition financing;
- understand M&A whipsaw: by the time that the merger boom is widely acknowledged, (a) the wave's 'sweet spot' has already been underway for longer than a year and (b) the cycle's end is just over the horizon;
- comprehend and respond effectively to landmark events over the course of the new merger wave: the signature event (IPO), indications of approaching maturity, specific indications of imminent merger wave climax.
- avoid the value-destruction from mid-Phase IV onwards – *do the extreme risks of end-of-wave deal closings exceed the realistic returns?*

Early in the wave: this certainly does not yet feel like a merger boom yet. In phase I and into the initial weeks of phase II, general business and acquisition sentiment is negative, largely because financial markets are still spooked by the last severe recession. But presuming that the would-be buyer has excess cash reserves and/or access to some acquisition financing, this is often the best time in the merger wave to acquire. Supplies of quality targets are plentiful and APPs are modest. When the buyer proclaims that synergies exist to cover that premium, financial markets are inclined to believe such claims, since the amount of post-acquisition improvements required for the deal to be viable on a VG analysis basis is minimal.

The end of the merger wave is near (we just don't know how near). Phase III transitions into the wave's fourth, final phase. The merger boom has been roaring like a wildfire for multiple years by now. Anyone who has missed the merger market's major upward move has either been fired or soon will be. Merger financing is overly-plentiful and available at such low rates that some will miscalculate their merger cost of funds as being this marginal debt only. This basic analysis mistake adds to the number of deals that appear to be encountering difficulty.[2] Target companies rejected four years ago are now acquired at twice the asking price, even though synergies are unchanged. Braggarts boast that they can get out with merger profits before the bubble bursts. One or two manage to do so.[3]

M&A success key 3: Exploiting superior understanding of merger segmentation

The era of merger segmentation has arrived. Improving merger performance is no longer a matter of this week's vapid M&A concept from consultants or bankers trying to hype M&A volume (it never was). Today's and tomorrow's successful operating company acquirer knows where to look – and what to avoid – to improve their future M&A performance.

Primitive diagnosis of targets and deal types concentrated on either the structural nature of the business combination (vertical versus horizontal versus conglomerates), the target's initial reaction to a would-be acquirer's expression of interest (hostile versus friendly) or the form of payment made (all-cash versus all-stock versus combination). Factor in considerations such as the relative size of merger partners and relatedness of their business, and the beginnings of a considerably more advanced understanding of the difference between successful and failed deals emerges. Add in historical performance tendencies of the nine different key types of business combinations, and acquiring management is no longer flying the merger plane blindfold (see Figure 4.2 in Chapter 4).

Second generation 'merger segmentation' as described in Chapter 4 in this book refers to nine identifiable merger types, organized into four categories. Opportunity arises for considering the potential of that acquisition to revitalize the acquirer's business model along with the expected chances of success, rather than becoming myopically blinded by the siren song of unknown future promise. It's the beginning of the end of the visionary deal, the dead-on-arrival transaction gushed about by its champions as revolutionary in nature.

TABLE 8.4 Merger success key 3: Exploiting the new merger segmentation

Key to Merger Success: 3	
Exploiting Superior Understanding of Merger Segmentation Identification of those limited characteristics pertaining to the merger which are most important in terms of transaction success or failure. Adapting research insights to date (relatedness, size, number of bidders & bid cycles, others) to a structural framework for addressing different merger types (Table 4.2, Nine merger types framework, Chapter 4). Adaptation of Merger Segmentation Framework for adjustments directly related to deal success: timing in merger wave (Phase I, II, III or IV?), geography, APP% relative to bids for comparable targets & timing.	
Implications	**Issues**
Merger learning begins: instead of every deal being treated as unique (and thus the same mistakes are repeated with each new merger wave) patterns of success performance guide. Mundane is good (or at least, less likely to destroy value in the new combined company): true reality of visionary-transformational deals as value black holes for acquirers.	Matching the company's (external) investment return requirements with Table 4.2 model risk profiles: can we grow fast enough with just bolt-ons (2A) and line extension equivalents (2B)? Last man standing dilemma in *both* types of consolidation mergers: 3A Mature and 3B Emerging.

Saying no to certain kinds of deals is a matter of self-preservation. But without a merger segmentation framework that works, the acquirer is pursuing target companies without the support expertise needed to succeed.

M&A success key 4: Guiding acquisition strategy in accordance with absolute and relative limits on APPs

TABLE 8.5 Merger success key 4: Consideration of APP indicated maximums

Key to Merger Success: 4

Adhering to Absolute and Relative Limits on Acquisition Purchase Premiums (APP percentages, amounts)

The importance of overpayment as a factor in merger failure is better understood when acquisition bids are viewed in a *shareholder value context*:

There are ***no*** *'undervalued' publicly-traded target companies.* Rational Market Theory identifies the target's pre-announcement purchase price (Appendix A) as corresponding to the correct worth of that company.

Thus, all positive APP deals are value destroying, at least as of the closing date.It is what acquiring company management achieve *after* the close which determines whether or not this value deficit remains, along with indicated merger failure.

APP maximum: around 38%, largely because of extreme challenges in developing synergies corresponding to APPs above that level.

Relative APPs: Whether or not purchase premia in line with comparable transactions (by industry type, timing) provides only a secondary indicator of the reasonableness of the bid. In Buyers' Panic periods, most APPs are value-destroying.

Implications

Targeting, **pricing** and **synergy** are equally important to merger success: The Good Company, Bad Company is value-destroying.

Futility of 'We have not overpaid' self-proclamation or financial PR.

The price paid for the target is an integral element in the ultimate determination of the success – or failure – of that merger transaction. Those who misdiagnose bidding technique for a target as an important part of value creation in mergers (come now, anyone can overspend!) imagines that first the deal has to be secured, and then the synergy story devised to make the deal appear somewhat more palatable. This is backwards. The reality of most mergers fail (MMF, Chapter 5) affirms that bid-first myopia results in a) completion of some deals that shouldn't happen at *any* price, along with b) value-destroying purchase bases in the case of many completed transactions. (It isn't exactly rocket science: avoid deals that require purchase premiums that are several times the level of conservative estimates of synergies and stay away from ABN Amro/3Par-type bidding wars, and suddenly, merger performance improves.)

In such instances, the essential interests of the acquiring company's continuing shareholders are best served by doing nothing at all, even if the target company was and is highly successful as a standalone concern. The overbid APP means that credible synergies can never match the amount of the payment, rendering that transaction value destroying – regardless of any make-believe math fantasies foisted on the financial community by the overspending acquirer's financial public relations mouthpieces.

In response to the threat to the viability of the deal caused in large part by reckless overpayment, responsible (read: successful) acquirers ask the question: 'What is the amount over the target's present share price that can be paid without jeopardizing the transaction?' There is no singular, one-percentage-fits-all-circumstances answer to this APP ceiling question. Based on the VG method in Chapter 3, the acquirer can pay up to the amount of realizable synergies for the deal. In theory, a triple-digit percentage APP *might* be matched by expense- and revenue-related synergies, the two largest synergy categories as described in Chapter 7, but not when the sophistication of synergy diagnosis is limited to the story-telling stage, as in the late 1990s.

In an attempt to avoid some of the penalties of deal-killing overpayment, some practical APP ceilings begin to emerge, separate from the machinations of synergy description and measurement. Research studies by Azofra *et al* (2007) and Andrade *et al* (2001) suggest that APP percentages in excess of 37–38 per cent mean a failed transaction. Indirectly, this guideline for merger success is consistent with Merger success key 2, above, as few final or phase 4 deals occur at premiums of less than 40 per cent. The other ceiling – *relative APP* – is less precise but possibly more practical. The related question is: 'Is the APP percentage paid in line with other similar transactions by other acquirers?'

An equally important contribution of this step to modern M&A success is to destroy the Huffington-3Par fiction of the quality target company that is described by the acquirer (but almost no one else) as a worthwhile acquisition in spite of gross overpayment. A sure signal of merger value destruction is that the elements of the VG method (APP and S) are not even mentioned. The acquirer knows the result of that diagnosis already.

M&A success key 5: Bid pricing integrated with in-depth four-type PMI investigation

So long as bid pricing is treated as a separate activity from synergy identification and implementation, history is doomed to repeat itself as the majority of mergers will continue to fail in the future. But there is an antidote, composed of two parts: 1) synergy analysis during both the pre-bid and pre-close due diligence periods sufficient to act as a counterweight to merger chase mania; and 2) the board and management's conviction to apply both sides of the VG equation (APP and S) simultaneously.

Without a synergy counterweight to offset or at least slow the buy-side acquirer's proclivity towards ever-increasing bid prices, the only limitation to the soaring APPs is the availability of financing – and that limitation is

TABLE 8.6 Merger success key 5: Synergy integrated with target bid dynamics

Key to Merger Success: 5
Bid Pricing Integrated With In-Depth Four Synergy Type PMI Investigation The answer to the question *What is the maximum APP that may be justified in the bid?* has almost nothing to do with bid theatrics, but *everything* to do with the answer to a different but related question: *What is the present value of the realizable synergies, adjusted for offsets, synergy duration and/or feasibility adjustments, implementation delays, relating to expense (e-), revenue (r-), tax (t-) and other financial (f-) categories?* Challenges include: (a) useable synergy intelligence before the bid (and even before the announcement) despite perceived extreme information limitations; (b) advance limiting to those parts of the four synergy categories where the major improvements reside.

TABLE 8.6 *continued*

Implications	Issues
Beginning of the end for the 'gut-feel' value-destructive merger mistake. Change in relative importance of bid negotiation vs pre-bid synergy acumen in successful bid, correctly defined. Synergy expertise required in place or accessible *before the announcement* rather than *after the close.*	Pre-bid synergy intelligence: expertise vs PR (or worse, role in covering bid negotiating errors). Ensuring the analytical independence of the synergy team, veto role. Consistent method for resolving inevitable conflicts between bid and synergy parts of pre-bid group. Retreat when the synergies just aren't there (WBWA). Resources: Minimum number of bid-synergy errors.

sometimes an accelerant, instead. As the merger wave progresses, a flood of new financing emerges in phase III as bankers compete for what at the time appears to be high return financing with minimal downside risk. That's hardly protective investigation of the caliber mandated by the large merger transaction's status as the buying company's largest and most important investment expenditure.

In the absence of consistent and complete synergy insight relating to the deal overall and especially the target, APPs soar to unconscionable heights, causing repeats of the RKR Nabisco (1980s, merger wave 1) and ABN Amro (2000s, merger wave 3) fiascos: transactions that might have been successful at moderate premiums, but which were doomed to failure because of the inadequacies of the VG diagnosis then in place, combined with the Wild West reluctance to apply the diagnostics available at the time.

Towards a robust pre-close synergy diagnostic capability

Absent an applied understanding of the critical differences between each of the four synergy types (expense-, revenue-, tax-, other financial-, see Chapter 7), all synergies are subject to hopelessly optimistic guesses and overreliance on synergy stories that provide little insight into what to do differently. A framework that reflects the differences in synergy types is worthless without access to actual or surrogate information upon which knowledgeable synergy insights can be developed. Particularly in the two major synergy categories, the substance of specific e- (expense) and r- (revenue-) opportunities must either be known from fact or conservative estimates made on the basis of reliable indirect intelligence.

Synergy-informed bidding strategy

With no synergy-confirmed insight into the incremental value that might be generated from the proposed combination, the would-be acquirer is left with throwaway non-analytical fluff: notions of 'fair value' or 'intrinsic value' based on readily refuted comparative share prices. As with dot com bubbles past and present, no one stops to ask, but what if the comparative prices are tissue paper – plumped only by the mania of the speculative bubble?

For financial public relations purposes, every acquirer insists that their bid pricing reflects exacting assessment of realizable synergies, even when synergies are nothing more than the guess of a middle management flunky who backwards-justifies each increasing bid as 'not value destroying'. Some control: no analysis, no veto – and no job in the future if he or she comes up with a number that might contradict management's wishes.

Dealmakers and others dependent on deal completion for their fees can hardly be expected to act against their self-interest. Chief executives? Once the deal chase has been announced as started, perverse non-logic takes hold as in the macho merger world it is more permissible to destroy shareholder value in the acquiring company by overreaching on the deal than wimp out by walking away. The merger bid chase to value destruction requires minimal skill, except perhaps to know when to drop out (or the equivalent, when to set a final bid and then allowing the chase to proceed still further). Overspending, using other people's money? Not a skill set, never was. Not particularly bright animals can be trained to push the big, red 'spend even more' button whenever prices surge beyond a specified level.

The evolutionary transition from bidding to synergy-informed bidding depends on a) the quality of pre-close synergy analysis, and b) overcoming almost assured opposition from defenders of the previous, failed target bidding method. Without the board's firm resolve to place paramount importance on company merger performance in terms of the VG-IVE criteria, and to understand that independent intelligence-gathering is at the center of that analysis, the company's M&A effort is directionless, floating towards the next overpayment relative to achievable synergies, one more addition to the MMF list.

Developing quality synergy intelligence

Figure 8.1 considers the dilemma of developing credible synergy analysis despite limited availability of information. Synergy intelligence issues arise over four M&A periods: announcement, pre-bid acceptance, commencement of exclusivity period, and post-close.

1. Announcement date: initial expression of possible purchase interest

The prospective acquirer acknowledges possible purchase interest in the target firm, either deliberately (usually with initial indication of bid price) or less openly, as accumulated share position reaches the reporting threshold. Synergy guidelines at this time are extremely limited. Valuation development potential of companies in that sector, and legacy management's capabilities (or limitations) represent the primary synergy intelligence sources at the time.

Developing a defendable projection of bidders and bid cycles involved in the coming acquisition pursuit is mandatory at this time, rather than later in the bid-synergy progression. While not directly related to synergy development, this consideration is vital to the success of the overall synergy-informed bid progression.

As Andrade *et al* and others observe (see Table 3.6 in Chapter 3), the number of bidders and bid cycles appear to influence purchase premium levels, both individually and collectively. In order to avoid the adverse publicity and criticism from the board and financial markets about wasted costs and efforts that go with prolonged, futile bid chases, early diagnosis is necessary to ensure that the APP for the target is likely to be justified, based on expected NRS. Consider the different circumstances arising with acquisitions in a) cloud computing and b) metal fabricating businesses in the early years of the present merger wave.

a) Chasing merger mirages. The Dell versus Hewlett-Packard contest for 3Par ('won' by H-P) involved just one of the companies in the new must-have-can't-miss technology sector. In a familiar tactic from tech bubbles past, planted articles in pop-biz press gushed about firm's 'cloud strategies', with bloggers adding to the hyperbole. In such a carnival atmosphere, the chances of securing a quality target company without overpaying are remote. A stratospheric APP effectively means that NRSs are not even mentioned. There's no chance of the APP-NRS VG being narrowed to permit the deal to be described on a VG basis at least.[4]

b) Substantive, but unsexy. During the first phase in each new business-merger cycle – when half the world is proclaiming that the recession is still

FIGURE 8.1 Pre-bid synergy insight – the two major synergy categories, classified by forecast reliability

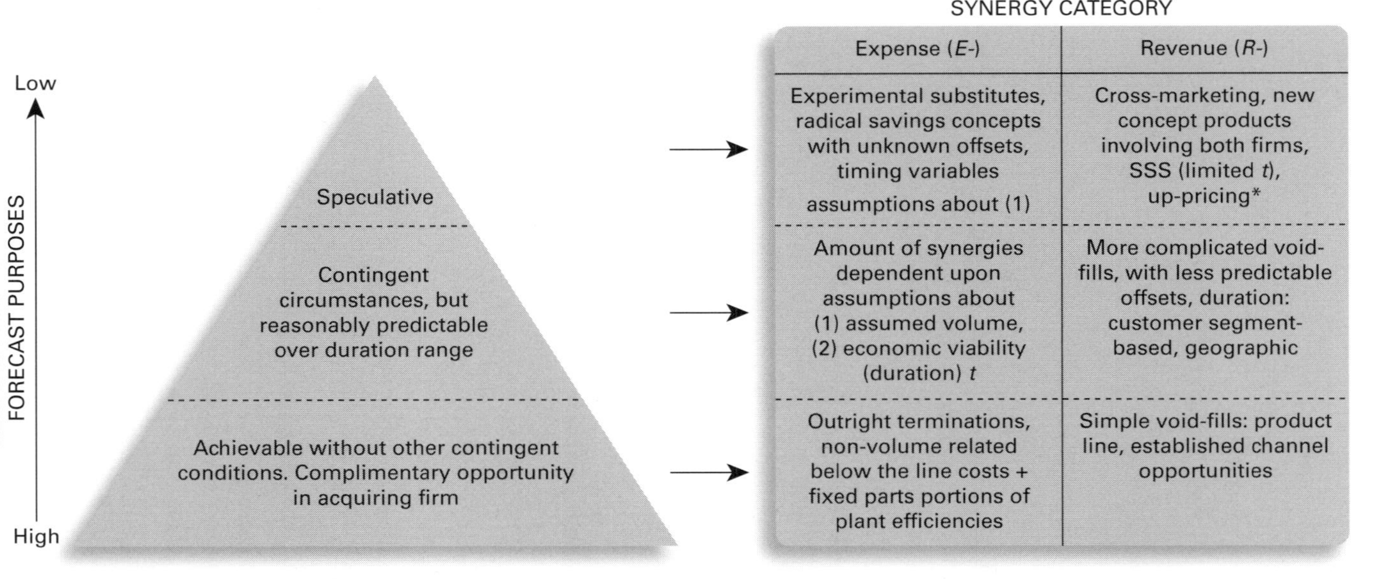

Note:
* Unless already underpriced on price–demand elasticity basis

in place – bargains in basic manufacturing arise (see Chapter 1). Premiums are minimal given the timing and the industry choice. The offsetting consideration is funds availability: with adverse economic conditions still presumed to exist, many financial institutions drop out on the basis that conditions are too risky. To proceed, the acquiree may have to rely on its own funds and/or shares to finance the deal.

2. Pre-bid acceptance period (active chase period)

The chase is underway. Other bidder(s) for the target have either expressed their interest formally or are waiting to see how many cycles are likely before pouncing at the last moment. The bid range changes dramatically, and management must be capable of justifying significantly increased bids.

Conventional practice is to imply – but not to specify – that existing synergies are thought to be sufficient to cover ever-rising bids. Management's primary defense mechanism dealing with rising bids is opaqueness. With no specific numbers offered as the bids rise, the unsupported implication is that an extra reserve of analyzed synergies is known. Some of the more investigatory-oriented analysts from institutional research (investors) may attempt to do the APP-NRS VG math to come to their own opinion that the deal is not value-destroying and thus warranted.

Widening awareness of MMF undermines reliance on synergy-light forms of justification for proceeding with the deal. 'Trust me' might work for some acquirers under two circumstances: a) most mergers are perceived as succeeding, and b) that specific acquirer has a well-established track record. Since a) is non-existent and b) applies only to a few top performers, the attitude of increasingly skeptical owners of the company and the boards of those firms today tends to be 'In God We Trust' while would-be acquirers require substantive justification. Slick public relations tactics designed to divert the eye no longer suffice.

3. Exclusivity period commences

The acquirer has taken the next step towards securing the object of its ardor, having offered a sufficiently high bid to exclude discussions with other suitors. The deal can still come undone, but one acquirer has the inside track.

But the dilemma from the two previous points in the process remains: a positive APP means value damage to the acquiring company until and unless offset by credible NRSs. Up to this point in time, attempts at amassing synergy intelligence have been limited by the level of formal information available for investigation.

4. Initial days following the close

Time to discover how great the discrepancy is between the acquiring company's bluff about not overpaying and the truth. In the case of a major merger, the acquirer's major institutional investors are already investigating that issue, particularly if those major investors are of an activist bent.[5] Regardless of the fables fed to pop biz press and in investor briefings, the persistence of MMF means that synergy gaps – differences between acquiring management's purported achievable synergies and true NRSs – should be presumed to exist.

Unless the acquiring company's top management is in complete denial, this is the point in time that the CEO insists on knowing the full extent of this synergy gap (the possibility that the CEO might be inclined to sabotage the investigation of the synergy gap for fear of being accused of entering into a value-destructive transaction) provides support for the argument that the synergy investigation reports directly to the board.

Informal sources of synergy intelligence

Our experience is that difference between the excellent synergy program capable of fully supporting *both* post- and pre-merger stages of the merger stages is the informal and indirect sources of intelligence. The common excuse of synergy-development teams that fail to do enough is that they weren't provided enough information from the target company. That's an inadequate excuse from a mediocre synergy team – a group insufficient to support the synergy-informed bidding process. A poor carpenter blames his or her tools.

Almost any junior analyst can come up with a diagnosis when all of the critical information is pre-screened for completeness and relevance. But such situations are extremely rare.[6] The seller cannot ever be expected to provide the level of information that buyer's analysts' require, as that would mean special insights into foibles and vulnerabilities that never appear on the balance sheet and exist only in the knowing glances and code words of the seller. As noted in the preceding chapter, even after the closing, such critical intelligence is sometimes difficult to extract.

So how to bridge the synergy knowledge gap with alternative sources? Start with the proprietary information that the knowledge bearers in the target company (corporate key contributors) know to be true. There are concerns that keep former financial officers and some forensically-oriented auditors awake at night and there are persistent but rarely acknowledged suspicions of suppliers, key accounts and regulators. The list of possible sources includes:

- *Past senior managers.* Briefer non-compete arrangements are becoming more commonplace, and the middle managers who actually know how things work at the target companies – rather than the executives who merely peruse the results – are often missed in the non-competes, as are temps.
- *Key suppliers.* Finding key suppliers to several competitors in the target company's sector represents a fast way to highlight possible cash flow and/or supply chain opportunities for future improvement. Care must be taken to apply indirect questioning techniques so as not to compromise the confidentiality of either target or pursuer.
- *Analysts.* As the ranks of investment analysts shrink – in part because banks' slow progress out of their subprime mess will continue well into the middle phases of the present boom – knowledgeable insight into some targets may be found walking the street.

Figure 8.1's triangle indicates the reliability of each of three tiers of forecast synergy data. The base of the triangle is comprised of e- and r-synergies that can be achieved without other contingent developments and conditions. The improvement opportunities correspond to complementary characteristics in the buying firm: the acquirer's IT department is world-class and under-capacity, suggesting a priority synergy opportunity in the form of the immediate and continuing costs associated with the target's parallel function. Simple revenue void fills pertaining to product lines or channel gaps at either the target company or the acquirer suggest a comparable high level of credibility and thus a higher percentage.

Moving upward in the triangle brings the middle tier of expense- and revenue-synergies. These opportunities are not sure things, but are accurately depicted as probable, resulting in a feasibility percentage only slightly lower than assigned to the base (above). The e-synergies corresponding to this tier vary depending on presumed efficiencies and the plant's remaining economic life. The level of volume efficiencies that can be counted upon as credible synergies depends on variables such as the remaining capacity and effectiveness of the continuing plant. The mid-tier revenue-synergies also involve void fills, but are less predictable.

The top of the triangle – the least predictable of the prospective synergies – represents outright bets. Chances of these prospective synergies actually being achieved are remote compared with the other two tiers. Experimental savings concepts and chancy new revenue concepts are included in this category.

M&A success key 6: Distinguishing real synergies from illusions

A synergy-directed APP process is only credible when the PMI capability is in place and perceived as fully complete, in terms of the four separate synergy categories: expense, revenue, financial, measurement.

TABLE 8.7 Merger success key 6: Real synergy elements distinguished from illusions

Key to Merger Success: 6

Synergy Elements: Real Distinguished From Vapor, Offsets Included

Business Combination Improvement Diagnosis: *synergy's* true identity, developed and implemented correctly.

The breadth of theoretically possible synergies does *not* indicate an unstructured approach. *Out*: experimental brainstorming. *In*: pursuing the most achievable net realizable synergies amongst the four established, well-diagnosed types.

Defendable range analysis, feasibility adjustments, timing factors, diagnosis of offsets encompasses both e's (expense, expenditure) and r (revenue).

Level of emphasis, resource, time allocation: 60+% to e-, 80+% e and r, combined.

Implications	Issues
Synergy as the *starting* point in the value-creating acquirer's M&A process, rather than a *post-close* afterthought.	While helpful as illustrations, stories about synergy miscues involving slightly similar combinations are no more effective in preventing M&A value destruction than Worst Deal lists.
Merger-related synergy investigation evolves to its next stage. Decisions based on credible future projections are nothing new in business.	Spotting of the single-functional distraction, in advance.
Especially as time is a critical factor in net realizable synergies (NRS), eradication of hollow process: *meetings per se are not synergies.*	Illusory management synergies.

E- and r-synergies are the major categories. Any synergy measurement or implementation approach that does not take into account the critical differences between each of the four categories, and/or which places over-reliance on vapor financial and management synergies is also suspect.

M&A success key 7: Avoidance of transactions involving 'wounded quail' acquirers, overreaching egos

TABLE 8.8 Merger success key 7: Avoiding the desperate acquirer's journey to value destruction

Key to Merger Success: 7
Avoidance of Transactions Involving Wounded-Quail Acquirers, Overreaching Egos
Desperate acquirers contribute to buyers' panics and may destabilize the M&A market overall because of: (a) acquisition decisions made on a non-economic basis; and (b) extreme overbidding – far beyond levels suggested either by realizable synergies or comparables.
Mergers are not a solution for underperformance or irreversible decline of legacy business; instead, the odds against merger success instead *add* to the acquiring firm's difficulties.
Absence of pricing leverage. Troubles are well-known to would be buyers, who take advantage: the well-shopped company able to temporarily disguise its true business issues (Conseco/Green Tree). The quality company sold at a company which renders a value-creating acquisition almost impossible (H-P/3Par, AOL/Huffington Press).
The high-ego acquisition means a deal made on the most indefensible of qualitative reasons (temporarily boosts struggling management's image), increases threat of Winner's Remorse caused by hubris (Roll, 1986).
Implications
Target prospecting: Stretch targets likely reappear over 2–5-year time periods.
APP benchmarking: Deletion from bid range indications, as non-representative.

Nothing condemns a deal to a fiery death faster than the intervention of a desperate acquirer, because that acquirer believes that he or she *must* consummate a deal and thus all six of the preceding keys to merger success are ignored.

There's the overly eager acquiring company CEO interested first in generating a personal image of management dynamism, who is only secondarily concerned with returns to continuing shareholders: the at-risk capital providers who ultimately support that hubris-driven chief executive's merger misadventures (Roll, 1986). Influenced by media acclaim which even today awaits almost all 'winners' (read: the over-bidders whose bids are accepted by sellers) except for those presiding over those few deals that are so fatally flawed that they are immediately dismissed as dead on arrival at the time of close (for example, PennCentral, AOL/TimeWarner), the distracted leader is poised to fail, in merger terms.

Mesmerized by his or her own perception of management aura, this distracted CEO doesn't only ignore signals of trouble in the target company but also misperceives his or her enthusiasm as evidence of the target's appeal. A similar dilemma – and consequence – arises with the savior acquisition: the business combination counted on to reverse the fortunes of the fast-fading mature company or, failing that, to buy the imploding firm a few quarters more life (AOL/Huffington Post).

In this instance, the desperate CEO may sincerely believe that the business combination is essential to protect the financial interests of the acquiring company's shareholders. Assuming that the target's business segment and model are complementary, such suppositions may appear to have some justification. It is the 'savior' aspect of the acquisition that is problematic. Especially if the company is mired in a chronically unprofitable segment, the possibility arises that the financial interests of the firm's shareholders may be better served by terminating the company in some manner, such as by sale to another firm or possibly even liquidation.

The only way to deal with such ballasts on merger performance is identification, followed by prevention. Company shareholders are typically dispersed and thus not always in a position to prevent value-destroying digressions by charismatic leaders, but boards of directors are better positioned to prevent merger underperformance resulting from this cause, and arguably have the obligation to help prevent such corporate self-destruction.

8.2 Some implementation considerations

Drucker's merger rules (1981)

1 Acquirer must contribute something to the acquired company.
2 A common core of unity is required.
3 Acquirer must respect the business of the acquired company.
4 Within a year or so, acquiring company must be able to provide top management to the acquiring company.
5 Within the first years of merger, managements in both companies should receive promotions across the entities.

(Weston *et al*, 1990: 640)

The opposite of the desperate acquirer who overreaches for low-probability deals (key 7) is the patient buyer who knows where and how to search – selectively. The reality that MMF means that for the aspiring buying firm, maximizing value through M&A may sometimes mean standing aside: *not doing a deal at all*. In a few instances, a resolve to put financial returns to the company's shareholders first may even persuade a few companies to cross over to the other side of the M&A transaction, becoming seller, rather than buyer-pursuer.

The patient, analytical acquirer acts

If overly eager acquirers (key 7) are M&A's south-pointing compasses, foretelling of tomorrow's acquisition disappointments, does that mean that the opposite – patient, careful acquirers – are well-positioned to excel? Possibly. The absence of the self-destructive acquiring chief executive is a start, enabling others in the organization – the chairman, the head of the acquisition performance review committee of the board, representatives of major investor groups, selected intermediaries – to better understand both the potential risks of the 'bet the company' acquisition and the hoped-for rewards possible from that wager.

If the high risk transformational-type transaction (category 4, Table 4.2 in Chapter 4) foisted on a frantic buyer by deal arrangers means trouble, where *should* the acquirer search for merger success? Table 8.9 identifies three possible opportunities, discussed below.

TABLE 8.9 Searching for promising targets

Type	Nature of Opportunity	Capture	Examples
Non-continuing units of 'shoot-first' acquirers	Change in direction and possibly management has brought in new openness to correcting unwise and/or unrelated acquisitions by departed executives.	Anticipating which of that acquirer's prior acquisitions probably excluded in next strategic review.	Non-banking operations of '00s genre 'universal banks', jettison targets of previous desperate acquirers.
Left on the shelf (LOTS) target	Seller missed its best offer, still wants to exit. Self-identified by PR-placement articles in financial media hinting at possible availability but also specifying an aggressive, above-market APP *requirement.*	Re-orienting seller away from unrealistically high (missed) bid offer: *That ship has sailed.*	Cablevision (early 2012), Post 1980 Wave 3 Phase IV (2005–2008) misjudgments by financial acquirers.
Near or actual last man standing (LMS)	Appealing to knowledgeable sellers that consolidation and contraction has advanced to the point that offer quality likely to decline continually in future.	Acting while existing participants still support smoke screen of the sector as 'not yet in decline'	Printers, remaining standalone quality small pharma, luxury brands?

Disposals: non-continuing units of the shoot-first (ask questions later) acquirer

The initial focus of this first approach is not specific targets – not directly, at least. Instead, the preliminary search is for the Icarus acquirer: the buyer who flew too close to the sun and later had to correct for his or her error by forced dispositions represents a promising potential source of new candidate acquisition target firms, but only for those who know where to look and can act quickly.

Consider some of the zombie financial holding companies brought low by their failed subprime derivative bets in the 2000s. In several instances, these are institutions with historical expertise in consumer and wholesale commercial banking, but also exhibiting a pattern of profit warnings whenever they wander away from their strengths. It is only a matter of time before some of those toxic subprime-related financings default, activating losses and jeopardizing that bank's fragile recovery. What better time to extend a mid-range offer for that financial holding company's non- or only slightly related units in insurance, credit cards or brokerage?

Comparable opportunities arise in technology manufacturing, consumer electronics and other consumer products. Falling behind in their fields, overly eager acquirers convinced themselves a few years earlier that they had no choice but to overpay to ensure that they snared their target, even if the purchase premium is two-plus times *greater* than NRS. It is not long before adverse VG consequences and high debt servicing costs take their toll, and divestments are imminent. One caveat: check that the specific target companies have not been plundered in order to prop up the struggling original acquirer.

Kaplan and Weisbach estimate total divestments that are also failed mergers at approximately 34 per cent (1992: 106). While the authors suggest that about 44 per cent of all acquisitions are divested, 'we classify only 34 per cent of the divested acquisitions as unsuccessful, that is, the reason for the divestiture appears to be performance-related'.

Left on the shelf targets and last man standing

Consolidation is a major theme in the present merger wave, comprising two separate major merger types in Table 4.2 (Chapter 4), categories 3a and 3b. Escalating investment requirements, shrinking product-service lifecycles and the tendencies of emergent internet-based sectors towards eventual duopolies combine to suggest that the 2011–19 merger megaboom will be composed of more than 60 per cent consolidation-type transactions as measured by the percentage of transactions over the period.

But there are always some valuable companies that have missed out on that industry's primary merger movement in the past and today face the risk of being orphaned. Particularly in mature industries where capacity has reached a plateau, the penalty for holding out for too high a price and/or responding venomously to *all* expressions of interest is that bidders move on to those who are more receptive.

At some point, management at the left on the shelf company realizes the consequences of their actions: others in the sector await a collapse, when they might pick up the assets of the firm at near-liquidation prices. At that point, an analyzed bid above liquidation levels sometimes results in a surprisingly receptive response.

Winning by standing aside

Achieving Success in Mergers and Acquisitions (along with near-equivalents) *has* to be the leading title of print and online infomercial brochures from fee-ravenous bankers and consultants eager to insert their snouts in the M&A fee trough. Implying secret knowledge but deliberately vague on the specifics, the easily persuaded might actually believe that merger success is there for the taking.

It isn't. The historical reality that MMF is cited throughout this book with an avalanche of supportive studies and references in preceding chapters. And while merger performance improvement is possible with the right frameworks and analytical tools (some of which are introduced in this book), responsible merger advisers avoid the bombast. Of all of the techniques and tools available to help increase the percentage of deals that are value-creating for shareholders of the acquiring firm, the number 1 improvement action is one which has only indirectly been referred to earlier in the book: *get out* –

> *Do not proceed any further with the acquisition chase.*
> *Abandon the target chase.*
> *Quit.*

By developing and revising VG *and* IVE analyses as soon as the pursuit of the target begins, management of the acquiring company should have no illusions about whether the deal is value-creating or value-destroying. Bluff and bluster designed for media sound bites have no effect at all on major investors in particular, who are probably applying their own forms of VG and IVE. Do you want to avoid failed mergers becoming a future target of agitated major investors? Start by viewing merger performance the same way that the owners of major blocks of the corporation do, already.

Crossing over to the other side?

Maybe M&A should be called M&D (mergers and *divestitures*), instead. Assuming that returns to the (acquiring) company's shareholders are paramount in the minds of management, and considering that the purchase premium represents a wealth transfer from the buying company's owners to the shareholders of the buying firm, the unthinkable becomes conceivable: cross over to the sell side.

The best value creator in M&A (M&D)? A compelling case can be made for some of the sellers in major deals, such as Arianna Huffington. Well run and at the cusp of profitability when AOL first indicated purchase interest, the message was clear to all would-be suitors: don't even bother contacting us unless your purchase premium is outrageous. So while shareholders wonder for months after the acquisition whether management's PR smokescreen (the deal is a success) or instead, the doubts expressed by some analysts (deal success is threatened) will turn out to be true. Ms Huffington's former shareholders just count their money.

Notes

1. Such a supportive role in merger valuation is consistent with Cornell's description of multiples' role in company valuation (1993: 146–63).
2. The erring acquirer who bases his or her acquisition decision on one capital cost component (typically low cost debt) disregards the elementary rule of investment: that the correct basis for evaluating cost of capital is on a company-wide basis, including the full breadth of both debt and equity sources.
3. For example, Mukherjee, S (2011) *Synergy Premium in Mergers and Acquisitions of Steel Companies: A look at the rationale behind the multi-million M&As of steel companies*, Marston Gate, England, Lambert Academic Publishing, 1–2; Goedhart *et al* (2010: 2–3); Bieshaar *et al* (2001: 68–9).
4. The dual diagnostic merger valuation approach, with both VG and IVE methodologies being applied, separately, emerges to permit accurate valuation of such situations. In theory at least, it is possible that the standalone versus combined IVE analysis could indicate a possible viable deal, despite the negative VG indication. A judgment of the deal as being value-creating (and thus, successful) using the IVE methodology depends on future projections of incremental cash flows from sales in new sectors.
5. Major investor groups such as pension funds, accustomed to retroactively monitoring the performance of the companies in which they hold positions, have become more activist on issues such as executive bonuses, presumably because of the importance of systematic overpayment to corporation performance in value terms. On that basis, it would not be a surprise for their scrutiny to next be directed to what is arguably an even greater source of value destruction: the large, high APP acquisition.
6. Danger sign: when such extreme openness does arise, the acquirer is right to suspect desperation by the seller. The underlying reason for such urgency for openness must be fully understood first, before proceeding further.

Epilogue

Any book that is research-oriented and also seeks to develop formidable answers to the vexing problem of historical merger underperformance tends to be years in the making. Work on *Masterminding the Deal* began at the end of 2010, when unexpected early-in-cycle deal volume and some on-off signals of a possible end to the recession appeared. That momentum continued into 2011 (see the confident statement from Evercore Partners' Altman in May 2011 at the beginning of this book's first chapter), but then merger momentum seemed to disappear for much of 2011.

Facebook pre- and post-IPO hangover? Fear of the effects of withdrawal of QE stimulus? The European sovereign debt crisis? For those who believe that the market reflects the delicate balance between fear and greed, there was certainly a great deal of the former as merger markets hit an air pocket in 2012.

Does that pause derail the resurgence of mergers for the balance of this decade? We think not. At this writing, as the autumn of 2012 gives way to winter, a day doesn't pass without two new deals being announced. Private equity firms no longer wonder if their earlier acquisition will have to be given back. The Facebook-Instagram deal does suggest the beginning of the second phase (of four) in the present business-merger cycle, and acquisition purchase premiums are consistent with what we have come to expect when the US and UK economies are both thought to have turned the corner, around late October 2012.

APPENDIX A
Acquisition purchase premium-related issues

RELATED CHAPTERS AND PARTS:

1.4 Merger wave issue I: (T)APP-synergy divergence

3.6 Value gap (VG): do synergies offset the price necessary to pay?

7.1 Value gap revisited: the integrated synergy-bid approach

Acquisition Purchase Premium (APP) is calculated based on the difference between the accepted purchase bid price for the acquiree versus that target's share price days prior to the first prospective acquirer's explicit expression of possible purchase interest.[1]

APP is often expressed as a percentage, to help assist in determining whether or not overpayment has occurred (Andrade *et al*, 2001; Azofra *et al*, 2007).[2] In a related application, the APP financial amount serves as the standard against which the success of the merger is assessed based on the VG merger valuation methodology described in Chapter 3.

The deal is viewed as probably value-creating if the present value of net realizable synergies (NRS, Chapters 3 and 7) associated with the proposed business combination match the APP amount.[3] Both the APP and NRS elements of VG-type method are frequently cited by the investigatory financial media, especially if there are suspicions that the acquirer has overpaid and thus completed a deal that is probably value-diminishing, from the perspective of the buying company's shareholders.

Two issues addressed in this Appendix are 1) possible adjustments for phase in merger cycle and, 2) timing practices, which may result in distortions to APP indications.

A1. TAPP and late phase merger bids

As customarily calculated, APPs for mergers closed during the last two phases (III and IV) of the merger wave. The recommended beginning date for calculating the earlier date in the APP analysis is 40–60 trading days prior to the first formal expression of possible purchase interest. Andrade *et al* (2001) contend that 20 days is sufficient, but that was before recent heightened concern about insider trading tips based on advance knowledge of acquirers' actions, occurring well before the close. In later phases of the economic expansion period/merger boom, increasing pre-announcement share prices may distort APP, as illustrated in Figure A.1.[4]

FIGURE A.1 The rising tide dilemma and TAPP

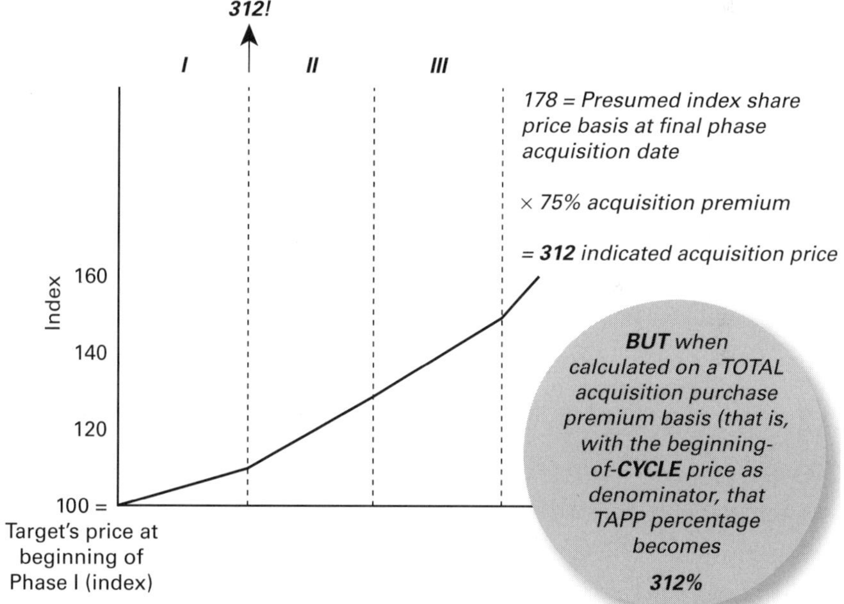

In Figure A.1, the apparent APP based on the target's share price 45–60 days before expression of interest indicates 75 per cent: a full but not outlandish APP percentage for latter phases of a merger bubble. But the 75 per cent APP only provides one part of the full overbid picture.[5] In Figure A.1, the general price index of *all* shares has risen from 100 at the beginning of phase

I to 178 by phase IV. Factor in a 75 per cent APP percentage for a deal in its final phase (a higher percentage than earlier in the wave) and the combined result is a significant increase in the total price paid: in that exhibit, from 100 to 312!

Part 5 in Chapter 1 explains why this rising tide dilemma contributes to the problem of late phase deal failures (Clark, 1991: 27–8). The possible offset to overbids – synergies – change little over the course of the merger price. Since both target company share price and APP percentage tend to increase over that same period, the consequence is an increasing disparity, with this gap becoming chronic sometime in phase IV: so significant that no reasonable estimate of achievable synergies can fully offset the purchase premium.

The 'T' in Figure A.1 stands for 'total'. Some adjustment to the base share price for APP analysis purposes is advisable to help prevent a situation such as shown in the figure in which the nominal APP percentage is 75 per cent but TAPP is more than three times greater at 312 per cent. The logical adjustment for 'T' is to set the price at the target's share price as the analyzed price as of beginning of the merger wave, regardless of when the transaction is closed. But at this writing there is no standardized method for setting this first TAPP date. Also, such clarification would almost assuredly be an anathema to buy-side merger advisers and dealmakers, as late phase deals would appear to be especially dangerous. But given the often-disappointing results of transactions closed in the waning moments of the merger wave, perhaps that isn't such a bad thing – particularly from the perspective of the acquiring company's shareholders.

A2. On departures from conventional APP calculation timing, resulting in possible distortions

A credible APP calculation begins with the correct measures for the ending and beginning time points for that calculation. As with A1, the more straightforward part of the APP calculation is the ending price. There is little debate about the target's correct analyzed share price as of the closing date of the deal. As with A1, the issue is with the beginning date.

Our recommended practice for the APP calculation differs based on whether or not multiple bidders are involved.[6] If the aspiring acquirer whose bid is accepted by the seller is either the sole bidder or the first of several bidders for the target, then the recommended beginning date is consistent with A1: 45–60 trading days prior to the first formal expression of possible purchase interest by the acquirer. If however the high bidder is neither the only bidder for the target nor the first to express interest in that target, then the appropriate APP first date appears to be 45–60 days prior to the *first* major bidder's expression of interest. This adjustment is necessary to prevent the scenario of a last minute bidder proclaiming to offer a modest bid at say 10 per cent over the prevailing price for the target at the time 45–60 days before it first expressed interest, whereas the chase for the target has been taking place for months before that time, and starting from a much lower bid-price level.

Imprecision about how and, more important, when the earliest date in the APP calculation is made sometimes manifests itself in the way that acquirers explain deals considered by the financial community at the time as 'very full' (possible overpayments). Consider *The Economist's* commentary about Lloyds Banking Group's description of its controversial acquisition of imploding UK bank holding company HBOS as described in LBG's 2008 annual report:[7]

> The bank told its shareholders that the decision to buy HBOS, widely thought to be disastrous, was the 'right decision' because the firm paid in shares £7.7 billion for a bank with a book value of £17.9 billion. As a gauge of the board's wisdom this was daft. It computed the bill based on Lloyd's share price on 15th January 2009, when the deal closed, by which time the shares had collapsed as investors discounted the consequences of the takeover... HBOS's book value was adjusted to... market price, of both its assets and liabilities. The acquisition's debts were trading below par, largely reflecting investors' worry that it might go bust. This, perversely, boosted the reported net asset value by about £12 billion. The bulk of the acquisition's supposed book value at that point, then, consisted of an accounting anomaly that reflected the risk of bankruptcy.

The Economist's point is well taken. APP is intended as an indicator of one element of management's merger performance, of particular importance to those in the financial community adopting VG-type perspectives on merger success. But if those dates are not consistently applied, then the purported indication of acquisition overbid may prove inaccurate and even misleading.

Notes

1. APP calculations typically presume an all-stock basis, even though most deals involve at least some cash as payment. Analysts at the acquiring firm apply an adjustment-to-cash assumption to the shares tendered, reflecting both the nature of the security tendered, the striking price and possible volatility of the value of the shares over time.
2. Diaz *et al* (2009) is another study on APP ceilings and the primary author frequently collaborates with Azofra. However, at 21 per cent, the indicated limit in Diaz's paper is significantly lower than the ceilings suggested by the other two studies (37–38 per cent) and thus is treated as an outlier here. Per Chapter 1, APP percentages invariably exceed the 21 per cent level early in phase II, even though that is early in the merger wave.
3. While it is theoretically possible for synergy amounts to exceed the APP amount, such instances are rare in actual PMI program implementation. If the seller even suspects that a major synergy source is being under-counted, rational action to maximize returns to *their* shareholders is either to insist in an upward revision in the sales price or to withdraw.
4. Calculating APP during phase I–II presents few if any such issues, as prices indices are still modest. Stated another way, the boom has not yet gathered momentum, and thus the base share price upon which the purchase premium is applied is still modest, at least in comparison to share prices at later phases in that business expansion/merger cycle.
5. Overbid (Encarta definition): 'bid more than the worth of something'. By semi-strong concepts of market efficiency, the share price of the target company already reflects the full worth of the company. On that basis, any and all bids over that level are value-diminishing – at least until and unless some synergies can be achieved that offset the amount of that overpayment.
6. As noted in Chapter 3, there is a correlation between both the number of bidders and the APP and also the number of bid cycles and APP (see Table 3.1).
7. *The Economist*, 'Lloyds' Results: Of mad dogs and English banks', Feb 25 2011.

APPENDIX B
Debunking the extreme acquisition leverage fallacy

RELATED CHAPTERS AND PARTS:

2.2 Significant increases to target company's debt levels do not significantly reduce the probability of the related deal's success

7.3 A key category-based net realizable synergy investigatory framework approach

Chapter 2, part 2 explores how the misapplication of a refinancing technique designed to deal with a temporary condition of underleverage in a few companies in the early 1980s, in later years result in the targets sometimes being significantly worse off because of the effects of the commercial and financial consequences of destabilizing debt.[1] Today, those acquirers misapplying such HLT techniques are primarily private equity firms. Traditional corporate shareholders exert negligible influence over day-to-day management of the firms in which they invest. Not so these latter-day HLT acquirers, who aim to divert the target's CF into fees under the 'Two' part of the private equity sector's controversial 'Two and 20' fee structure:

- The Two and 20 fee structure is a standard charging mechanism utilized by what are referred to in this book as transitional or temporary acquirers who are in the business of buying and then reselling firms, presumably after improving operations and/or financing in some manner. Private equity firms are probably the most visible companies in this category.
- One part of the fee (the '20') is performance based, awarded by the acquirer to itself based on that firm's formula for wealth created. Typically this is based on the differences between share prices of the

acquiree at the time of initial purchase and subsequent resale, usually a few years later. Phantom share appreciation assumptions are occasionally put into effect. Cash out time is typically the resold unit's new IPO.

- The 'Two' part of the fee structure is much smaller in percentage terms but is applied to a significant base, typically capital provided (total financing provided); exact terms vary from firm to firm.

To some observers, the controversy associated with this structure is that it may encourage loading up the recently acquired with debt that destabilizes the firm but generates fees to the private equity acquirer. Such acquirers typically require control in order to implement the scheme, as management would otherwise direct available CF into growth investments and liquidity reserves. Opinions vary: while the group has its share of supporters, others contend that too often the target's competitiveness is sacrificed for short-term fees.

Increases in the portion of debt relative to total capital (long-term debt plus equity) may be value-creating in the case of a chronically underleveraged situation. However, since the mid-1980s, such circumstances are so rare as to be almost non-existent in developed markets (not necessarily so in lesser developed areas). Instead, the opposite problem has arisen: company management becoming so enthralled with the apparent financial alchemy of hyper leverage that they sometimes rush into destabilized capital structures, while underestimating the financial and operational risks associated with their 'bet the company' gambles.

If the firm's capital structure is already at or approaching optimal, then adding further debt often makes things worse, although the damage caused by destabilizing the company's capital structure may not immediately be apparent. At first, it may be asserted by some self-interested proponents of the HLT technique that adding yet more debt to a company with an already near-optimal capital structure[2] decreases WACC, thereby increasing value assuming that all other things remain unchanged. But all other things *don't* remain unchanged. Bankruptcy risk increases significantly, in two forms – financial risk (risk of default on borrowings) and operating risk (risk of under-investment in areas critical to becoming or remaining commercially competitive). Correctly diagnosed, both cost of debt (WACD) and cost of equity (WACE) components soar, often causing overall WACC to increase – the exact opposite of the financier's contention.[3]

A deteriorating situation such as described above might temporarily be delayed, but those tactics do not work indefinitely. Assuming adequate disclosure, semi-strong market efficiency (SSME)[4] eventually prevails, and financial markets realize the true nature of the HLT shell game: that the acquired company is worse off than before, directly as a result of the short-term acquirer's destabilizing actions. That value has been destroyed was already suspected by the financial community because the company has been moved further away from its optimal capital structure, rather than closer to that ideal. Narrow financial acquirers with little applied knowledge of the business (besides being able to cite some industry buzz words) are hardly credible when it comes to analysis of operational investment requirements required for the company to remain competitive. The potential for conflict of interest by an acquirer concerned first about its fee formula is not lost on independent minds in the financial markets.

Table B.1 shows the advantages and disadvantages of imposing excessive debt on a target company that is not chronically underleveraged (scenario 1 in the table), plus three other alternatives that are somewhat less damaging to the ongoing value of the acquired target company.

TABLE B.1 Four scenarios: HLT resulting in extreme overleverage, plus three alternatives

Category	Description	Presumptions	Advantages	Disadvantages
1 Exploiting target's remaining marginal debt servicing capacity (CADS, TIE)	Increasing debt-to-capital (D/C) short-term ratio to the highest level possible while still covering debt servicing over near-term. As debt is significantly lower cost after tax than equity, it lowers nominal WACC, thereby increasing value all other things being equal	Significant levels of operational waste persist, and that excessive debt is best way to resolve that. Austerity budgets caused by unbalanced ST capital structure do not permanently harm company	Lowest marginal WACC rate possible in theory, but only if financial markets ignore or miscalculate increases in financial, operating risk	Subordinating firm's value-optimal capital structure to acquirer-financier's compensation scheme. Myopic orientation. Risk factors may mean *increase* in cost of capital. Outdated notion of using indirect financial influences to improve operating performance. May encourage manipulation of debt type and form (P+I). Possible to probable corporate value destruction

TABLE B1 *continued*

Category	Description	Presumptions	Advantages	Disadvantages
2 Approach 1, but with normalized debt including P+L, coverage contingency	Prevents some of the more egregious manipulations of debt servicing requirements possible in (1). Adequate contingency provisions help to prevent optimal-peak financing risk (debt coverage dependent on unrealistic CF performance)	Refer to (1) above	Maximizes short-term D relative to C, but with some safeguards against the worst abuses of (1)	Still a myopic capital structure driven more by the financier's objectives than what is best for the target. Prospect of higher rather than lower WACC persists. Opposition by those acquirers-financiers who resist effective caps to extreme over-leverage
3 Cap structure aligned with industry leaders' practice	Designed to correct the outlier capital structure	In order to remain competitive, company cannot afford a capital structure which is significantly out of sync with industry/segment leader	Pursuit of the optimal capital structure *in competitive terms* at the forefront of capital planning	Another spot (current) technique, with little if any attention to company's ongoing financing requirements. Effective presumption that leaders are at or approaching OCS. But if leaders are chronically over-geared, value destruction for all
4 Adjusted for CAP lifespan capital cost implications	Capital structure adapted to life stage changes in firm's competitiveness, CF generation, risks	Formulistic cap restructuring approaches that ignore life stage considerations are incomplete	Helps to avoid short-term capital planning	To champions of extreme leverage, reductions of D/C in latter life stages. Eliminates some mature and declining companies as HLT targets

Scenario 1: Maximum debt load

The HLT technique is applied to a company that is not chronically under-leveraged as a technique designed to increase debt and thus to increase fees under the 'Two' part of the 'Two and 20' scheme.

With paramount emphasis on increasing nominal servicing capacity – and thus the amount of extra debt which the company can withstand before collapsing – suspect assumptions may arise. Establishing debt servicing forecasts based on today's CF generation levels may be precarious, especially in the mature companies that are often the targets of the HLT technique. Depleting contingency reserves, or fully replacing debt with amortizing principal and interest (P+I) term with interest-only debt might distort coverage statistics.

Additional debt servicing capacity is imagined as coming from elimination of 'wasteful' company operational expenses and expenditures. Whether or not the acquirer now inserting itself into the day-to-day operations of the target is creating or destroying value by this boilerplate HLT attitude may not be known for several quarters. If the company has poor cost controls and the proposed cuts are irrelevant to the key sources of today's and tomorrow's value, then the financial acquirer's actions might enhance company worth. If however expense controls are already effective and critical investments are incorrectly evaluated as 'waste', then value will probably be destroyed.

Scenario 2: Adjusted HLT

This is not a separate alternative, but rather a slight adaptation of scenario 1 designed to mitigate some of the areas of greatest abuse, based on recent failures.

Debt capacity in this scenario is based on ongoing, average CF generation, rather than on peak CF generation years. Assumptions about additional servicing capacity from elimination of 'waste' are subject to skeptical review *before* being accepted: until and unless it can be shown that eliminating the expense item increases value including consideration of all offsets and side-effects, no action is taken. Interest-only debt is replaced by fully amortizing debt at full market rates for purposes of CADS-type coverage analysis.

The intrinsic problem of the past-its-prime HLT technique – that the capital structure of the target company is degraded – remains. The short-term fee generation objectives of the temporary owner of the company continue to prevail, to that acquirer's financial disadvantage if and when the deterioration in the value of the target company is realized by financial markets, affecting future re-sale price.

Scenario 3: Capital structure aligned with industry leaders

The key consideration in this alternative is market competitiveness rather than a temporary owner's fee extraction objectives as in scenarios 1 and 2.

The underlying hypothesis is that a company with a capital structure that is significantly out of synch with that of the industry/segment leader relegates itself to relative underperformance over the near and intermediate terms. Longer-term consequences may include economic non-viability and, eventually, bankruptcy.

The conception underlying this scenario is that a company deprived of adequate investment capital at competitive cost cannot hope to keep up with market leaders, and eventually decline and/or disappear. A simple D/C or D/E ratio is not designed to indicate the adequacy of the amount and timing of supportive financing; however, an extremely high D/C ratio suggests a company that is endangering its competitiveness because of insufficient funds earmarked for internal reinvestment.[5]

'Outlier' in the Table refers to companies with capital structures significantly out of step with leaders, based on D/C. A chronically underleveraged firm (as suggested by low debt relative to capital ratio) suppresses value by an excessive WACC rate and – assuming sufficient internal CF generation – insufficient borrowing to grow the company. Although at the other extreme in debt-to-capital terms, the chronically overleveraged exhibits the same disadvantages, but for different reasons: a high WACC arises because of the financial and operating risk factors caused by the introduction of destabilizing levels of extra debt, while cash necessary for investment is siphoned off to short-term transitional owners.

A key limitation of this approach is that the leader(s) may themselves exhibit value-diminishing capital structures: market share leadership does not ensure a value-optimizing capital structure. To some, that consideration may suggest the development of an idealized comparable instead. Also, this approach is limited to today's capital ratios only, whereas the competitive investment issue involves investment into the future periods.

FIGURE B.1 Towards capital structure reflecting present, future CAP lifespan positioning, dynamics

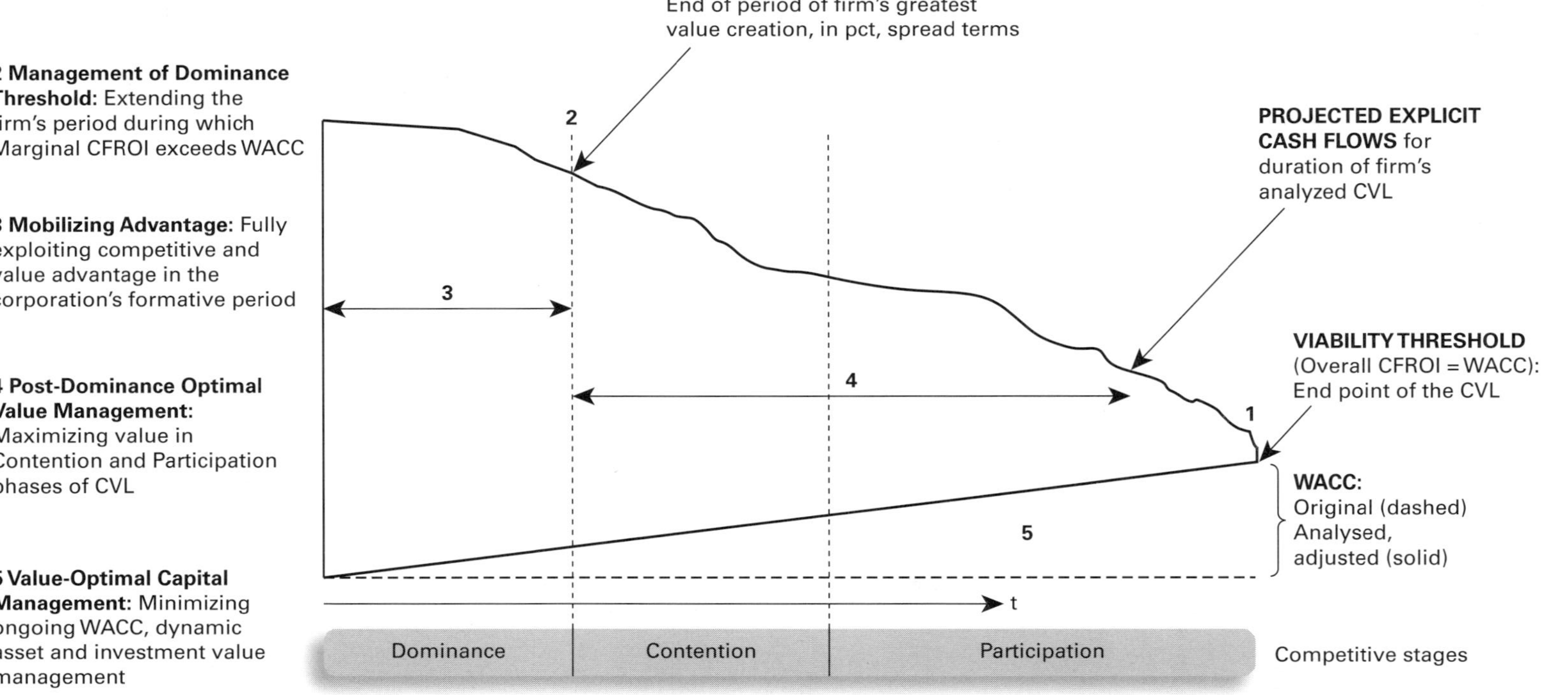

SOURCE: Clark (2010B) Figure 5.6.4, 192; based on June 6 2006 'Time is Value', presentation at Henley Centre for Value Improvement (HCVI) colloquium. This CVL5D structure represents an adaption of Competitive Advantage Period (CAP as described in Mauboussin and Johnson, 1997).

Scenario 4: Adjusted for CAP[6] lifespan capital cost implications

Disadvantages of scenarios 1, 2 and 3 include the fact that all three are myopic, in both financial and general management terms. The first and second scenarios risk destroying value of the target firm by diverting the target company's competitive lifeblood away from critical investments. Scenario 3 involves spot ratios, and presumes that the sector's market leaders are at – or at least approaching – OCS. Scenario 4 instead considers the appropriate capital structure in terms of where the company is today along its 'competitive value lifespan/five domain' (CVL/5D in Figure B.1).

At any point in time along that continuum, the company faces differing capital structure-relevant considerations. These include funding availability, borrower's capability to service debt, and customary debt structure. While a company in the second (contention) life stage period may well generate sufficient internal CF to cover extra borrowings corresponding with a very high (eg >75 per cent) debt-to-capital percentage, fading companies in the latter half of the participation phase often find that borrowers impose a much more conservative (lower D/C ratio) capital structure as decreasing CF begins to raise questions about economic viability.

The complete capital structure approach based on these principles include consideration of where the company is today along the CVL/5D continuum and also the rate of deterioration, in CFROI/WACC economic viability terms.

Notes

1. Although commonly thought to have originated in the early 1980s with the 1982 Wesray/Gibson Greeting Cards transaction, Miller (2005: 106) suggests earlier origins: 'Leveraged buyouts (LBOs)... were an established feature of the corporate landscape long before Franco Modigliani and I published our first joint paper on leverage and the cost of capital in 1958.'
2. The phrase 'chronically underleveraged' refers to a company exhibiting a level of debt in relationship to total capital (D/C) which is both suboptimal in the sense that value is destroyed by an excessively high WACC and which undermines company maximum value creation by hindering growth and/or competitiveness. A classic example is Eastman Kodak in the early 20th century, run by the penurious George Eastman, who insisted that his company (now defunct) have almost no borrowing. As a consequence, Kodak's growth and value were suppressed for decades and the firm was unable to withstand

an assault on its primary cash-generating business, consumer photo film, from Japan's Fuji Photo.

3 As noted in Chapter 2 part 2, different interpretations about optimal capital structure exist. The OCS interpretation applied in Chapter 7 part 6 in the examination of financial ('f-') synergies, is simply that combination of debt and equity which is analyzed as consistent with maximum shareholder value, expressed in terms of debt-to-equity portions, amount and, timing of those amounts, consistent with adequate debt servicing coverage as measured on a CADS (cash available for debt servicing) basis.

4 SSME is described in Campbell, J *et al* (1997) *The Econometrics of Financial Markets*, Princeton NJ, Princeton University Press, and also in Mills and Dahlhoff (Jul 2003) 'Competitive analysis period (CAP) analysis: looking at share price and firm value from a different perspective', Henley Discussion Paper Series, Henley-on-Thames, England, Henley Management College.

5 Examples include Palm in PDAs (dominant competitor Apple), Circuit City in consumer electronics merchandising (dominant competitor Best Buy), and Eastman Kodak in photographic film (dominant competitor Fuji Film). If the subject firm is thought to be segment/industry MS leader, the capital structure standard is provided by the fastest growing major rival(s).

6 Mauboussin and Johnson, 1997. 'CAP' refers to 'competitive advantage period': the period of time that a company's cash flow return on investment (CFROI) exceeds that firm's analyzed WACC.

BIBLIOGRAPHY

Andrade, G and Stafford, E (2004) 'Investigating the economic role of mergers', *Journal of Corporate Finance*, 10, 1–2

Andrade, G, Mitchell, M and Stafford, E (2001) 'New evidence and perspectives on mergers', *Journal of Economic Perspectives*, 15:2, 103–20

Andre, P (2004) 'Good acquisitions', *CA Magazine*, Mar, http://www.camagazine.com/archives/print edition/2004/march/regulars/camagazine15502aspx. Accessed July 25, 2011

Azofra, S, Diaz, B and Gutierrez, C (2007) 'Corporate takeovers in Europe: Do bidders overpay?' Seventh Global Conference on Business & Economics, Oct 13, 1–28

Baker, H K and Kiymaz, H (eds) (2011) *The Art of Capital Restructuring: Creating shareholder value through mergers and acquisitions*, Hoboken NJ, Wiley

Bazerman, M and Samuelson, W (Dec 1983) 'I won the auction but don't want the prize', *Journal of Conflict Resolution*, 27:4, 618–34

Betton, S, Ecko, B E and Thorburn, K S (2008) 'Corporate takeovers', ch 1, in (ed) B E Eckbo, *Handbook of Corporate Finance: Empirical corporate finance, Vol 2*, North Holland

Betzer, A *et al* (2009) 'Disentangling the link between stock and accounting performance in acquisitions', *Cardiff Business School Working Paper Series*, 2, May

Bieshaar, H *et al* (2001) 'Deals that create value', *McKinsey Quarterly*, 1

Bouwman, A *et al* (2003) 'Stock market valuation and mergers' *MIT Sloan Management Review*, Fall

Bradley, M A, Desai, A and Kim, E H (1998) 'Synergistic gains from corporate acquisitions and their divisions between the stockholders of target and acquiring firms', *Journal of Financial Economics*, 21, 3–40

Brochet, F and Weber, J (2012) LinkedIn Corporation', *Harvard Business School Case 9-112-006*, Boston, Harvard Business School Publishing

Brouthers, K, van Hastenburg, P and van den Ven, J (1998) 'If most mergers fail, why are they so popular?' *Long Range Planning*, 31:3, 347–53

Bruner, R (2004) 'Where M&A pays and where it strays: a survey of the research', *Journal of Applied Corporate Finance*, Fall 16:4, 63–78

Bruner, R (2002) 'Does M&A pay? A survey of evidence for the decision maker', *Journal of Applied Finance*, Spring-Summer, 48–68

Carroll, P and Mui, C (2009) *Billion Dollar Lessons: What you can learn from the most inexcusable business failures of the last 25 years*, ch 1, 'Illusions of synergy', New York, Portfolio, 15–36

Christofferson, S, McNish, R and Sias, D (2004) 'Where mergers go wrong', *McKinsey Quarterly*, 2, 93–9

Clark, P (1991) *Beyond the Deal: Optimizing merger and acquisition value*, New York, Harper Business

Clark, P (2010a) 'Exploration of some issues relating to variable weighed average cost of capital (WACC) over a firm's competitive value life span', April, *Value, The Magazine of the Institute of Value Management, UK*, 19:1, 22–6

Clark, P (2010b) *Time is Value*, Henley Business School Henley-on-Thames, Oxon, England

Clark, P (2009) 'Considerations in the development of alternative discounted cash flow (ADCF) valuation: a value management perspective', *Value: the magazine of the Institute of Value Management UK*, 18:1, 16–24

Clark, P (2001) *The Value Mandate: Maximizing shareholder value across the corporation*, New York, Amacom

Clark, P (2000) *Net Value: Valuing dot-com companies – uncovering the reality behind the hype*, New York, Amacom

Coley, S and Reinton, S (1988) 'The hunt for value', *McKinsey Quarterly*, Spring, 2, 29–34

Copeland, T and Dolgoff, A (2006) 'Expectations-based management', *Journal of Applied Corporate Finance*, Spring, 18:2, 82–97

Copeland, T, Koller, T and Murrin, J (1990, 1994, 2000) *Valuation: Measuring and managing the value of companies*, New York, Wiley

Cornell, B (1993) *Corporate Valuation: Tools for effective appraisal and decision making*, New York, McGraw-Hill

Cyriac, J *et al* (2012) 'Testing the limits of diversification', *McKinsey Quarterly*, Feb, 3

Damodaran, A (2005) 'The value of synergy', New York, Stern School of Business, 1–47 and in *Journal of Finance*, 60:2, 757–82

Damodaran, A (2012) *Investment Valuation: Tools and techniques for determining the value of any assets*, Hoboken NJ, Wiley

Diaz, S *et al* (2009) 'Are M&A premiums too high? Analysis of a quadratic relationship between premiums and returns', *Quarterly Journal of Finance and Accounting*, 48:3, 5–21

Dobbs, R *et al* (2010) The CEO's Guide to Corporate Finance, McKinsey & Co, 5

Eckbo, B E (2010) 'Introduction to corporate takeovers: Modern empirical developments', in *Corporate Takeovers Modern Empirical Developments: Takeover Activity*, North Holland

Epstein, M (2005) 'The determinants and evaluation of merger success', *Business Horizons*, 48, 37–46

Flanagan, D J and O'Shaughnessy, K C (2003) 'Core-related acquisitions, multiple bidders and tender offer premiums', *Journal of Business Research*, 56, 573

Fox, J (2009) *The Myth of the Rational Market: A history of risk reward and delusion on Wall Street*, New York, Harper Business

Fruhan, W (1998) *Note on Alternative Methods for Estimating Terminal Value*, Case 9-298-166, Boston, Harvard Business School Publishing

Geneen, H (1997) *The Synergy Myth and Other Ailments of Business Today*, New York, St Martin's Press

Goedhart, M, Koller, T and Wessels, D (2010) 'The five types of successful acquisitions', *McKinsey Quarterly*, July, 2–3

Gordon, M and Shapiro, E (1956) 'Capital equipment analysis: the required rate of profit', *Management Science*, 3:1, 102–10

Harford, J (2005) 'What drives merger waves?', University of Washington Business School 1–49; and *Journal of Financial Economics*, 77, 529–60

Hayward, M (2002) 'When do firms learn from their acquisition experience? Evidence from 1990–1995', *Strategic Management Journal*, 23:7, 21–39

Healy, P, Palepu, K and Ruback, R (1992) 'Does corporate performance improve after mergers?'*Journal of Financial Economics*, 31, 135–75

Henry, D (2002) 'Mergers: why most big deals don't pay off', *BusinessWeek*, http://www.businessweek.com/magazine/content/02_41/b3803001htm. Accessed May 1 2011

Hogarty, T (1970) 'The profitability of corporate mergers', *Journal of Business*, 317–27

Holt, C and Sherman, R (1984) 'The loser's curse', *American Economic Review*, 84:3, 642–52

Ingram, P *et al* (1992) 'Mergers and profitability: a managerial success story?', *Journal of Management Studies*, 29:2, 197

Kaplan, S N and Ruback, R S (1995) 'The valuation of cash flow forecasts: an empirical analysis', *Journal of Finance*, 50 (4), pp 1059–93, September

Kaplan, S and Weisbach, M (1992) 'The success of acquisitions: evidence from divestitures', *Journal of Finance*, Mar, 47:1, 107–38

Kauffman, D (1988) 'Factors affecting the magnitude of premiums paid to target-firm shareholders in corporate acquisitions', *Financial Review*, 23:4

KPMG (1999) 'Unlocking shareholder value: The keys to success', *Mergers & Acquisitions, A Global Research Report*, KPMG

Lehn, K and Zhao, M (2006) 'CEO turnover after acquisitions: are bad bidders fired?', *Journal of Finance*, 61:4, 1759–811

Leschinskii, D and Zollo, M (2004) 'Can firms learn to acquire? The impact of post-acquisition decisions and learning on long-term abnormal returns', *INSEAD*, 1–51

Lictenberg, F (1992) *Corporate Takeovers and Productivity*, Cambridge MA, MIT Press

Luehrman, T (2009) *Corporate Valuation and Market Multiples*, 9-206-039, Boston, Harvard Business School Publishing

Luehrman, T (1997) 'The pitfalls of using WACC', in 'Using APV: a better tool for valuing operations', *Harvard Business Review*, May-June, 9

Magnet, M (1984) Acquiring without smothering, *Fortune*, Nov 12, 22–8

Maksimovic, C *et al* (2008) 'Post-merger restructuring and the boundaries of the firm', Working Paper, University of Maryland

Malkiel, B G (1990) *A Random Walk Down Wall Street*, 103–4, New York, WW Norton & Co

Martynova, M and Renneboog, L (2008) 'A century of corporate takeovers: what have we learned and where do we stand?', *Journal of Banking & Finance*, 32, 2148–77

Martynova, M, Oosting, S and Renneboog, L (2006) *The Long-Term Operating Performance of European Mergers and Acquisitions*, ECGI Finance Working Paper No 137, Nov, 1–39

Mauboussin, M and Johnson, P (1997) 'Competitive advantage period: the neglected value driver', *Financial Management*, 26:2, 67–74

Miller, M H (2005) Leverage, *Journal of Applied Corporate Finance*, 17:1, 106–11

Mills, R (2005) 'Assessing growth estimates in IPO valuations – a case study', *Journal of Applied Corporate Finance*, 17:1, 73–8

Mills, R (1998) *The Dynamics of Shareholder Value: The principles and practices of strategic value analysis*, Glos Mars

Mitchell, M L and Mulherin, J H (1996) The impact of industry shocks on takeover and restructuring activity, *Journal of Financial Economics*, 41 (2), pp 193–229

Moeller, S and Schlingemann, F (2005) 'Global diversification and bidder gains: a comparison between cross-border and domestic acquisitions', *Journal of Banking & Finance*, 29:3, 533–64

Moeller, S, Schlingemann, F and Stulz, R (2003) 'Wealth destruction on a massive scale? A study of acquiring-firm returns in the recent merger wave', Cox School of Business, 1–38 (published 2005 in *The Journal of Finance*, 60:2, 757–82)

Morck, R A *et al* (1990) 'Do managerial objectives drive bad acquisitions?', *The Journal of Finance*, 45, 31–48

Mueller, D and Sirower, M (2003) 'The causes of mergers: tests based on the gains to acquiring firms' shareholders and the size of premia', *Managerial and Decision Economics*, 24, 373–91

Mukherjee, S (2011) *Synergy Premium in Mergers and Acquisitions of Steel Companies: A look at the rationale behind the multi-billion M&As of steel companies*, Marston Gate Eng, Lambert Academic Publishing

Norton, L (1998) 'Merger mayhem: why the latest corporate unions carry great risk', http://online.barrons.com/article/SB892852735409795000.html. Accessed May 14 2011

Parsa, H G *et al* (2005) 'Why restaurants fail', *Cornell Hotel and Restaurant Administration Quarterly*, 46:3 Aug, 304–22

Porrini, P (2006) 'Are investment bankers good for acquisition premiums?', *Journal of Business Research*, 59

Reinhart, C M and Rogoff, K (2009) *This Time is Different: Eight centuries of financial folly*, Princeton NJ, Princeton University Press

Rhodes-Kropf, M and Viswanathan, S (2004) 'Market valuation and merger waves', *Journal of Finance*, 59:6, 2685–718

Roll, R (1986) 'The hubris hypothesis of corporate takeovers', *Journal of Business*, 59:2, 197–216

Salmon, F (2009) 'Recipe for disaster: the formula that ruined Wall Street', *Wired*, 17 March

Scherer, F (1988) 'Corporate takeovers: the efficiency arguments', *Journal of Economic Perspectives*, 2:1, Winter, 69–82

Schwert, G W (2000) Hostile takeovers: in the eyes of the beholder?' *Journal of Finance*, Dec 55:6, 2599–640

Sirower, M (1997) *The Synergy Trap: How companies lose the acquisition game*, New York, Free Press

Smith, W R (1956) 'Product differentiation and marketing segmentation as alternative marketing strategies', *Journal of Marketing*, 21:1, 38

Stern, J (1974) 'Earnings per share don't count', *Financial Analysts Journal*, 30:4, 39–52

Sudarsanam, S (2002) 'Are acquisitions successful?' ch 4 in *Creating Value From Mergers & Acquisitions*, Harlow, England, FT Prentice-Hall

Tichy, G (2001) 'What do we know about success and failure of mergers?' *Journal of Industry, Competition and Trade*, 1:4, 347

Thomas, R and Gup, B (eds) (2009) *The Valuation Handbook: Valuation techniques from today's top practitioners*, Hoboken NJ, Wiley

Trautwein, F (1990) 'Merger motives and merger prescriptions', *Strategic Management Journal*, **11** (4), pp 283–95, May–June

Trimbath, S (2002) *Mergers and Efficiency: Changes across time*, Milken Institute, Boston, Kluwer Academic Publishers

Tuch, C and O'Sullivan, N (2007) 'The impact of acquisitions on firm performance: a review of the evidence', *The International Journal of Management Review*, 9:2, 141–70

Varaiya, N and Ferris, K (1987) 'Overpaying in corporate takeovers: The Winner's Curse', *Financial Analysts Journal*, May-June, 64–70

Vojtkova, B (2012) 'First day price fluctuations in Initial Public Offerings (IPO Pop)', *MSIN9001 Dissertation*, London, Management Science & Innovation Dept. (MS&I), University College London (UCL), unpublished

Walter, G and Barney, J (1990) 'Research Notes and communications management objectives in mergers and acquisitions', *Strategic Management Journal*, 11, 79–86

Weston, J F, Chung, K S and Hoag, S (1990) *Mergers, Restructuring and Corporate Control*, Englewood Cliffs NJ, Prentice Hall

Zollo, M and Meier, D (2008) 'What is M&A performance?' *Academy of Management Perspectives*, Aug, 55–77

FURTHER READING

Ang, J and Cheng, Y (2006) 'Direct evidence of market-driven acquisition theory', *Journal of Financial Research*, 29:2, 199–266

Becketti, S (1986) 'Corporate mergers and the business cycle', *Economic Review*, 13–26, May

Cassia, L and Vismara, S (2009) 'Valuation accuracy and infinity horizon forecast: empirical evidence from Europe', *Journal of International Financial Management and Accounting*, 20:2, 135–165

Damodaran, A (2002) *Investment Valuation: Tools and techniques for determining the value of any asset*, New York, Wiley

Dong, M *et al* (2006) 'Does investor misvaluation drive the takeover market?', *Journal of Finance*, 61:2, 725–62, April

Fama, E F and French, K R (2004) 'The capital asset pricing model: theory and evidence', *Journal of Economic Perspectives*, 18:3, 25–46

Fan, J and Lang, L (2000) 'The measurement of relatedness: an application to corporate diversification', *Journal of Business*, 73, 629–60

Franks, J and Mayer, C (1996) 'Hostile takeovers and the correction of management failure', *Journal of Financial Economics*, 40, 163–81

Ghosh, A (2002) 'Increasing market share as a rationale for corporate acquisitions', Working paper, Baruch College, May, as referenced in Bruner 2004

Ghosh, A (2001) 'Does operating performance really improve following corporate acquisition?', *Journal of Corporate Finance,* 7, 151–178

Golbe, D and White, L (1988) 'A time-series analysis of mergers and acquisitions in the US economy', in *Corporate takeovers: Causes and consequences*, Auerbach, A (ed), Chicago, University of Chicago Press/NBER

Gondhalekar, V *et al* (2004) 'The price of corporate acquisition: determinants of takeover premia', *Applied Economics Letters*, 11:12, 735–39, December

Gort, M (1969) 'An economic disturbance theory of mergers', *The Quarterly Journal of Economics*, 83:4, 624–42

Harding, D and Rovit, S (2004) 'What should you do when the deal goes off track?', *Mastering the Merger: Four critical decisions that make or break the deal*, Cambridge MA, Harvard Business School Press

Heron, R and Lie, E (2002) 'Operating performance and the method of payment in takeovers', *Journal of Financial and Quantitative Analysis*, 37, 137–56

Hirshleifer, D and Titman, S (1990) 'Share tendering strategies and the success of hostile takeover bids', *Journal of Political Economy*, 98:2, 295–324

Houston, J and Ryngaert, M (1994) 'The overall gains from large bank mergers', *Journal of Banking and Finance*, 18, 1155–76, December

Kumar, M (1997) *Growth, Acquisition and Investment: An analysis of the growth of industrial firms and their overseas activities,* Cambridge, Cambridge University Press

Lang, L and Stultz, R (1994) 'Tobin's Q, corporate diversification, and firm performance', *Journal of Political Economy*, 102, 1248–80, December

Levy M, Solomon, S and Ram, G (1996) 'Dynamical explanation for the emergence of power law in a stock market model', *International Journal of Modern Physics C*, 7:01, 65–72

Limmack, R, 'Shareholder wealth effects of diversification strategies: A review of recent literature', in C L Cooper and A Gregory (eds) (2003) *Advances in Mergers and Acquisitions Vol. 2*, Oxford, Elsevier Science, 207–29

Limmack, R and Rahman, R (2004) 'Corporate acquisitions and the operating performance of Malaysian companies', *Journal of Business Finance and Accounting*, 31, 359–400

Loughran, T and Vijh, A (1997) 'Do long-term shareholders benefit from corporate acquisitions?', *Journal of Finance*, 52:5, 1765–90, December

Lucas, R and Stokey, N (1987) 'Money and interest in a cash-in-advance economy', NBER Working Paper No. 1618, *Econometrica*, 55:3, 491–513

Madden, B (2010) *Wealth Creation: A systems mindset for building and investing in businesses for the long term*, Hoboken NJ, Wiley, 79–105

Mauboussin, M (2007) 'Death, taxes and reversion to mean', *Mauboussin on Strategy*, Legg Mason Capital Management, December

Melicher, R *et al* (1983) 'A time-series analysis of aggregate merger activity', *Review of Economics and Statistics*, 65, 423–30

Palepu, K (1986) 'Predicting takeover targets: a methodological and empirical analysis', *Journal of Accounting and Economics*, 8:1, 3–35, March

Pautler, P (2003) 'The effects of m and post-merger integration: a review of business consulting literature', Bureau of Economics, Federal Trade Commission, 1–41, January 21, Draft

Pautler, P (2001) 'Evidence on mergers and acquisitions', *Bureau of Economics*, Federal Trade Commission, 1–84, September 25

Perold, A (2004) 'The capital asset pricing model', *Journal of Economic Perspectives*, 18:3, 3–24

Rappaport, A (1986) *Creating Shareholder Value: A guide for managers and investors*, New York, Free Press

Rehm W *et al* (2012) 'Taking a longer-term look at M&A value creation', *McKinsey Quarterly*, 1–7, January

Rhodes Kropf, M and Viswanathan, S (2004) 'Market valuation and merger waves', *Journal of Finance*, 59:6, 2685–2718

Shelton, M and Dias, S (2002) 'Presentation to the Federal Trade Commission on issues in post-merger integration', McKinsey & Co, May 8, as referred to in Pautler (2003), 23

Shleifer, A and Vishny, R (2003) 'Stock market driven acquisitions', *Journal of Financial Economics*, 70, 295–311

Singh, H and Montgomery, C (1997) 'Corporate acquisition strategies and economic performance', *Strategic Management Journal*, 8, 377–86

Tvede, L (2006) *Business cycles: history, theory and investment reality*, 3rd ed, Hoboken NJ, Wiley

Zarnowitz, V (1999) 'Has the business cycle been abolished?', NBER Working Paper no. w6367, National Bureau of Economic Research, April

ACRONYMS AND GLOSSARY

Acronyms

APP	Acquisition Purchase Premium
C Capital	Long Term Debt + Equity
CADS	Cash Available for Debt Servicing
CAP	Competitive Advantage Period
CAPM	Capital Asset Pricing Model
CF	Cash Flow
CFFO	Cash Flow From Operations
CFROI	Cash Flow Return on Investment
CofD	Cost of Debt (alternatively CoD, WACD)
CofE	Cost of Equity (alternatively CoE, WACE)
CKC	Corporate Key Contributor
CVL	Corporate Value Lifespan
CVL/5D	Corporate Value Lifespan/5 Domain
D	Debt (generally refers to Long Term Debt, LTD)
DCF	Discounted Cash Flow
DCF2S	Two-stage Discounted Cash Flow Company Valuation Method
D/C	Debt-to-Capital Ratio
D/E	Debt-to-Equity Ratio
DEC	Digital Equipment Corporation
E	Equity
EBITDA	Earnings Before Interest, Taxes, Depreciation and Amortization
EPP	Explicit Projection Period (Stage 1 in DCF2S)
EPS	Earnings Per Share
ES	Event Studies
FCF	Free Cash Flow
g	Growth (Annualized FCF Growth Rate)
GCBP	Good Company Bad Price
GDP	Gross Domestic Product
HFC	Household Finance Corp
HLT	High Leverage Transaction
I	Investment (alternatively *i*)
IPO	Initial Public Offering

ITS	Invest to Save
IVE	Incremental Value Effect
KSF	Key Success Factors
LBO	Leveraged Buy Out
LMS	Last Man Standing
LOTS	Left on the Shelf
LTCM	Long Term Capital Management
LTD	Long Term Debt
M&A	Mergers & Acquisitions
MBO	Management Buy Out
MC	Market Capitalization
MICAP	Market Implied Competitive Advantage Period
MMF	Most Mergers Fail
MV	Merger Valuation
MVD	Market Value of Debt
MVE	Market Value of Equity
NOPAT	Net Operating Profit After Tax
NPV	Net Present Value
NRS	Net Realizable Synergies
OC	Opportunity Cost
OCS	Optimal Capital Structure
ODCAP	Operations Defined Competitive Advantage Period
PE	Price-to-Earnings Ratio (also P/E)
P/CF	Price-to-Cash Flow Ratio
P/FCF	Price-to-Free Cash Flow Ratio
P/R	Price-to-Revenue Ratio
PIK	Payment In Kind
PMI	Post-merger Integration
PV	Present Value (*see* NPV)
QE	Quantitative Easing
R	Return, or Residual (depending on context)
RBS	Royal Bank of Scotland
RMT	Reverse Morris Trust
ROA	Return on Assets
ROE	Return on Equity (reported earnings/equity)
RT	Round Turn
RV	Residual Value (*see* Terminal Value)
Ss	Synergies
SBU	Separate Business Unit
SIC	Standard Industrial Classification system
SN	Social Networking
SP	Share Price

SSME	Semi-Strong (concept of) Market Efficiency
t	Time (elapsed duration)
TAPP	Total Acquisition Purchase Premium
TRS	Total Returns to Shareholders
TSR	Total Shareholder Returns
TV	Terminal Value
TVP	Terminal Value Period (stage 2 in DCF2S)
VG	Value Gap
VM	Value Management
VOQ	Value Opportunity Quotient
VRQ	Value Risk Quotient
vWACC	Variable Weighed Average Cost of Capital
WACC	Weighed Average Cost of Capital
WACE	Weighed Average Cost of Equity
YCMWYCM	You Can't Manage What You Can't Measure

Glossary

Acquisition Purchase Premium (APP) Refers to the amount paid for a target firm in excess of that company's indicated market value (shares outstanding × share price = market capitalization) measured on the basis of the difference between the share price of the target at bid and a share price 40+ days prior to acquirer's initial expression of interest (*see* Appendix A).

Capital Asset Pricing Model (CAPM) A technique associated with deriving the cost of a business's equity from the risk free rate, the Beta β and the market risk premium. The formula for its calculation is:

$$\text{Cost of Equity} = \text{Risk Free Rate} + (\beta \times (\text{market risk premium})).$$

Capital Structure The composition of a company's sources of long-term funds, for example equity and debt.

Cash Flow (CF) The amount of cash flowing into or out of a business over a prescribed period of time. The formula for its calculation is: Net Operating Profit After Tax (NOPAT) + non-cash items (primarily depreciation and amortization).

Cash Flow Forecast The expression of the amount of cash expected to flow into or out of a business over a prescribed period of time (eg one elapsed year or longer) analyzed by shorter time periods (quarterly, monthly, weekly).

Combined Weighed Average Cost of Capital (Combined WACC) *See* Weighed Average Cost of Capital (WACC). This represents the projected combined cost of capital used for value analysis purposes in the combined scenario in the Incremental Value Effect (IVE) merger valuation methodology as described in Chapter 3 and Damodaran, 2005.

Continuing Value Formula (sometimes referred to as *Continuous* Value Formula) *See* Terminal Value (TV) (sometimes referred to as Residual Value)

Corporate Key Contributor An individual whose present and/or future role in the subject company is so closely associated with value creation that his or her departure means an assured reduction in worth as measured on a fundamental, DCF basis.

Cost of Capital The cost of long-term funds (debt, equity and mezzanine) to a company.

Cost of Debt The cost of loans to a business calculated after tax.

Cost of Equity The cost to a business of financing its share capital, typically calculated using a Capital Asset Pricing Model (CAPM)-based approach.

Discounted Cash Flow (DCF) A technique for calculating whether a sum receivable at some time in the future is worthwhile in terms of value today. It involves discounting, or scaling-down, future cash flows (CFs).

E-synergies 'E' stands here for 'expense' and on an expanded basis, both 'expense and expenditure'. This is one of the four principal categories of synergies described in Chapter 7.

Earnings Per Share (EPS) Earnings attributable to shareholders divided by the weighed average number of ordinary shares outstanding in issue (total shares authorized and issued minus treasury shares) during that period. The calculation and result are shown by way of a note in a company's annual report.

Event Studies (ES) Refers to a category of merger valuation (MV) methodological approach designed to make observations about the likely success or failure of a given merger transaction, comparing analyzed share prices of the acquiring firm before and after the time of initial expression of interest. Varying analysis time periods, primarily used in academic analysis of merger performance.

F-synergies 'F' stands for 'financial'. One of the four primary synergy categories described in Chapter 7.

Financial Risk The risk that results from a significant dependency upon capital funded by debt and which typically requires to be serviced by non-discretionary interest payments.

Free Cash Flow (FCF) Cash Flow (CF, above) minus period investment. www.Investopedia.com: 'A measure of financial performance calculated as operating cash flow minus capital expenditures... FCF is calculated as: EBIT(1 – Tax Rate) + Depreciation & Amortization – Change in Net Working Capital – Capital Expenditure. It can also be calculated by taking operating cash flow and subtracting capital expenditures.'

High Leverage Transaction (HLT) A transaction is which the debt-to-equity ratio of the acquired firm is significantly increased as part of an overall plan described by the acquirer as aimed at improving the affected company.

Incremental Value Effect (IVE) One of the merger valuation methodologies described in Chapter 3. Method involves a comparison of valuation of the acquirer and target on two alternative bases using Discounted Cash Flow (DCF) techniques: a) the two firms as standalones, b) the two firms combined, including estimated Acquisition Purchase Premiums (APP) in financial terms over time and Net Realizable Synergies (NRSs).

Leverage Expresses the relationship between some measure of present or prospective interest-bearing capital and some measure of equity capital or the total capital employed.

Market Capitalization (MC) Company share price × shares outstanding (shares authorized and issued minus treasury shares).

Merger Segmentation Categorization of target and transaction characteristics in combination, designed to distinguish between deals with higher probability of success from those with lower success chances.

Merger Valuation (MV) Assessment of acquisition transactions from the perspective of whether or not such acquisitions are thought to be value-increasing for shareholders of the acquiring firm and based on defendable calculation of the combined firm's present and projected Weighed Average Cost of Capital (WACC). For purposes of this book, whether or not the deal succeeds or fails.

Multiples A category of corporate performance ratios typically based on results to date (or extrapolations based on those results), in ratio form. Denominator: performance measure (earnings, CF, FCF, other)/share; numerator: analyzed share price. A popular but, on its own, limited method for estimating business worth.

Offsets As applied to synergies (S) analysis, refers to reductions in revenue and/or increases in expenses or expenditures necessary to achieve the candidate synergy. Measured on a DCF basis, this is one of the adjustments necessary to transform estimated synergies into achievable Net Realizable Synergies (NRSs).

Operating Risk As applied here to company future Weighed Average Cost of Capital (WACC), a marked increase in the risk of the company becoming economically non-competitive and thus no longer viable. This factor may increase a company's Weighed Average Cost of Equity (WACE) component in the Capital Asset WACC.

Opportunity Cost (OC) The company or business unit's next highest available return rate on investment of comparable type, size, risk, duration and timing.

Optimal Capital Structure (OCS) A theoretical ideal, in which the portions, timing and costs of the company's debt and equity structure coincide with achievement of maximum shareholder value on a continuing basis (Value Management, below), taking into account financial, operating and liquidity risks. Note: Sometimes misinterpreted as synonymous with a capital structure calling for the maximum percentage (of total capital) of debt that a company is imagined to be able to service, because of the much lower cost of debt after tax than equity. From www.investopedia.com: 'The best debt-to-equity ratio for a firm that maximizes its value. The optimal capital structure for a company is one which offers a balance between the ideal debt-to-equity range and minimizes the firm's cost of capital. In theory, debt financing generally offers the lowest cost of capital due to its tax deductibility. However, it is rarely the optimal structure since a company's risk generally increases as debt increases.'

PE Ratio One of the most significant indicators of corporate performance, it is widely quoted in the financial press. It is calculated by dividing the market price of a share by the earnings per share (or the total market value by the total profit attributable to shareholders), ie, PE Ratio = Market Price of a Share/Earnings Per Share (EPS).

Positive Value Gap *See* Value Gap. Since VG is typically calculated as Acquisition Purchase Premium paid minus Net Realizable Synergies, a positive Value Gap indicates a deal that is likely to be value-destroying for the acquiring firm.

R-Synergies 'R' stands here for 'revenue'. This is one of the four principal categories of synergies described in Chapter 7. Realistic calculations of revenue synergies reflect the CF effect of the incremental sales, adjusted for timing, feasibility and offset considerations.

Return on Equity The percentage rate of return provided to equity investors.

Shareholder Value Analysis A valuation approach that serves as a proxy for estimated Total Shareholder Returns, that considers in broad terms that the value of a business to shareholders may be determined by discounting its future Cash Flows using an appropriate Cost of Capital.

Terminal Value (TV) The second part of the Two-stage Discounted Cash Flow (DCF2S) company valuation methodology, in which company's projected future CFs are discounted at an analyzed future WACC rate, typically into perpetuity, utilizing the Continuing Value Formula (aka Gordon Formula). The analyzed present value of company future CFs over its Terminal Value Period (TVP). Terminal value can vary widely with changes in assumptions about the longevity of the company and other variables, most notably the growth rate to perpetuity. Sometimes referred to as continuing value, continuous value, residual value or horizon value.

Total Acquisition Purchase Premium (TAPP) This is an expanded version of the Acquisition Purchase Premium (APP) percentage concept, with TAPP representing the product of the publicly traded target company's pre-acquisition announcement share price × the APP necessary to secure control of that target. Typically expressed as an amount rather than as a percentage, TAPP provides a more complete perspective on merger success using the Value Gap method, as both the purchase premium and the appreciation of the share price over the merger cycle are taken into account (see Appendix A).

Value Gap (VG) One measure of acquisition success calculated on the basis of the difference between Acquisition Purchase Premium (APP) and comparable Net Realizable Synergies (NRSs) related to the acquisition. A positive VG suggests a value-destroying combination; a negative VG the opposite.

Weighed Average Cost of Capital (WACC) Refers to the weighed average cost of all sources of long-term capital utilized by the company at a given time. In its simplest form, WACC is calculated using cost of equity before tax and the cost of debt after tax, weighed according to the relative proportions of each in the firm's overall capital structure.

INDEX

NB page numbers in *italic* indicate figures or tables

3Par
  acquisition by Hewlett-Packard 53, 78, 97, 98, 104, 188, 282, 283, 286
  bid by Dell 286

Abelson, Alan 191
ABN Amro 18, 104, 146, 188, 282, 284
  bid by Barclays 28, 106, 146
Achieving Success in Mergers and Acquisitions 296
Akdogu, E *et al* 15, 155
Allen, Robert 78
Alpine Mutual Funds 117
Altman, Edward 164
Altman, Roger 7, 31, 299
Andrade, G and Stafford, E 11, 13
Andrade, G *et al* 96–97, 232, 282
Andre, P 31
AOL 199
  Huffington Press acquisition 27, 51, 53, 105, 187, 283, 293, 297–98
  TimeWarner acquisition 9, 18, 23, 53, 92, 95, 135, 144, 150, 159, 160, 234, 293
Apotheker, Leo 53, 78, 97–99
Apple 91, 99, 123
Armstrong, Tim 105
AT&T 21, 1, 106, 156
  acquisition by SBC Communications 163
  NCR Corporation acquisition 78, 91, 104, 144, 156, 188, 234, 253, 265
  Olivetti acquisition 156
Autonomy 53, 78, 97, 98, 105, 158
Azofra, S *et al* 96–97, 141, 144, 145, 188, 282

Bain & Co 44, 170
Baker, H K and Kiymaz, H 199
Bank of America
  Countrywide Financial acquisition 28, 175
  Merrill Lynch acquisition 28
Barclays
  ABN Amro bid 28, 106, 146
  Lehman Bros acquisition 28, 106
BCE, acquisition of 50
Bear Stearns 121
  acquisition by JPMorgan Chase 28
Best Buy 248
Betton, S *et al* 145
Betzer, A *et al* 171, 178
Bieshaar, H *et al* 147, 170
Big Blue 227
Blankfein, Lloyd 54
Bleak House 23, 29, 55
Blodget, Henry 210
BMC
  Harris Corporation acquisition 163
Bogan, V and Just, D 171
Bok, Scott 29
Boots plc 52
Bouwman, A *et al* 141, 273
British Airways 142
Brochet, F and Weber, J 123
Bronfman, Edgar 266
Brouthers, K *et al* 43, 69, 74, 173, 174, 176
Brown, Gordon 38
Bruner, R 43, 69, 79, 176
Bruner, R *et al* 107
BT 152
  Dialcom acquisition 163
Burt, S and Limmack, R 70, 71, 172

Capen, E *et al* 101
Carroll, P and Mui, C 44, 61–62, 94, 143, 170, 227
Case, Steve 53
cash available for debt servicing (CADS) 124
CBS 118
Chambers, John 51
Chand, Ranjeev 205, 206
Chandler, Harold 78
Chapman, T 173
Chase Manhattan Bank 175
Chassany, A 33
Chicago Tribune 35, 50, 238
Christofferson, S *et al* 55, 62, 78, 80, 219, 261
Chrysler 53, 92, 135, 144, 158, 258

Cinven
Spire Healthcare acquisition 35
Circuit City 151
Cisco Systems 51, 59, 260
Citicorp 143
Clark, P 13, *14*, 30, 48, 59, 87, 91, 157, 197, 218
Clickmango 205
Coca-Cola
Columbia Pictures acquisition 160
Coley, S and Reinton, S 89, *90*, 136–37, *137*, 140, 142, 170, 174, 178, 180, 185
Columbia Pictures 160
Comcast 51
Conseco
Green Tree acquisition 144, 175, 187, 188, 189, 265
Copeland, T and Dolgoff, A 11, 56, 74, 117
corporate governance 74
Countrywide Financial 28, 175
Cyriac, J *et al* 142

Daimler-Benz 106
Chrysler acquisition 53, 92, 135, 144, 158, 258
Damodaran, A 61, 77, 107, 141, 220, 222, 227, 235, 243, 246
Dell 21, 248
3Par bid 286
DeLong, G 180
Dialcom 163
Diamond, Robert 106
Diaz, B 145
Diaz, S *et al* 162
Diller, Barry 118
Dimon, Jamie 51–52
Disney
Pixar acquisition 144
Dobbs, R *et al* 101, 102, 103
Dorsey, Patrick 57–58, 119
Drucker, P 294

Eaton, Leslie 189
eBay 59, 123
PayPal acquisition 138, 158
Skype acquisition 53, 138, 160
Eckbo, B E 157
ecological sustainability 74
Elgers, P and Clark, J 237
EMI 35, 55, 94, 188, 234
Enron 150
Epstein, M 69, 175–76
Ericsson
Marconi acquisition 21, 152
Ernst & Young 30
'e-synergies' 103, 237, 238, 239, *240*, 241–42, 258, 292
non-volume-related 241–42
volume-related 242
event studies (ES) 67, 74, *75–76*, 77, 78–82
ease of use 80–81
origins 80
short-and long-term variants 79
shortcomings 81–82
vs incremental value effect (IVE) 108–11, *109*
Evercore Partners 7, 31, 299

Facebook 10, 31, 213
initial public offering 1, 28, 30, 192, 197, 202, 203, 208, 210, *210*, 211, *212*, 299
Instagram acquisition 1, 17, 24, 198–99, 201, 206, 207, 212, 299
possible acquisitions 204
Federal Express 52
Federated Department Stores
Neiman-Marcus acquisition 258
Flanagan, D J and O'Shaugnessy, K C 138
Fox, Bud 47
Fox, J 21, 81, 124, 226
Frick, K and Torres, A 173
'f-synergies' 237, 246–49

Gammeltoft, N and Vannucci, C 117
Gekko, Gordon 26, 45, 47
Geneen, H 151, 219
General Dynamics 163
General Electric 11
Gerstner, Lou 51, 159, 226–27
Ghosh, A 69
Gibson Greeting Cards 247
Gillette 156
Gimein, M 211
Glass-Steagall Act 27
Gleacher & Company 145–46, 159
Goedhart, M *et al* 150
Goldman Sachs 54, 196
good company bad price (GCBP) 105
Google 205, 260
Gordon, M and Shapiro, E 127
Gordon-Shapiro Formula 228
Greenhill & Co 29
Greenspan, A 27
Green Tree 144, 175, 187, 188, 189, 265
Gresham's Law 9, 200
Groupon 121, 122, 197, 204, 207

Harding, D and Rovit, S 150
Harford, J 20
Harris Corporation 163
Hayward, M 170, 185, *186*
HBOS 106
Healy, P *et al* 175, 176–79
Henry, D 143, 173, 175, 188
Heron, R and Lie, E 178
Hewlett-Packard 21, 106, 123, 199, 248
  3Par acquisition 53, 78, 97, 98, 104, 188, 282, 283, 286
  Autonomy acquisition 53, 78, 97, 98, 105, 158
  Palm acquisition 53, 55, 78, 91, 98, 99, 151, 153, 175
Hitt, M *et al* 171
Hoffman, Reid 198
Hogarty, T 71, 72
horizontal mergers 144–45
Houston, J and Ryngaert, M 145
hubris 37, 69
Huffington Press 27, 51, 53, 105, 187, 283, 293, 297–98
Huffington, Arianna 27, 51

Iannuzzi, Sal 206–07
IBM 51, 159, 227
  Lotus acquisition 96
incremental value effect (IVE) 67, 74, 75–76, 77, 92, 107–11, 277
  synergies 220
  vs event studies (ES) 108–11, *109*
Ingham, H *et al* 71, 174
Ingram, P *et al* 144–45
Instagram 1, 17, 24, 198–99, 201, 206, 207, 212, 299
'irrational exuberance' 27
ITT 219

Jackson, Reggie 192
Jensen, Michael 11, 24, 48
Johnson & Johnson
  Neutrogena acquisition 259
JP Morgan
  Chase Manhattan Bank acquisition 175
JPMorgan Chase 51–52, 196
  Bear Stearns acquisition 28

Kaplan, S and Weisbach, M 9, 91, 141, 296
Kaufman, D 96, *98*
Kellaway, L 54, 180
KPMG 173, 181, 228

Lehman Bros 28, 106
Lehn, K and Zhao, M 106
Levin, Gerald 9
Lewis, Michael 226
Lex (*Financial Times*) 45, 55, 118, 159
Li, David
  Copula 27–28
Lictenberg, F 116
LinkedIn 123, 192, 197, 198, 203
Lintner, J 85
LivingSocial 197, 204
Lloyds Banking Group 106
Lotus 96
Luehrman, T 56, 87, 88
Luo, T 172

'Mad Men' 252
Magnet, M 170, 174, 179
Maksimovic, C *et al* 155, 242
Malkiel, B G 115
'managed retreat' 19
Marconi 21, 152
market implied competitive advantage period (MICAP) 116, 118–19, 124, 127–28
Martynova, M and Renneboog, L 8
Martynova, M *et al* 178
Mathiason, N 51, 185
Mauboussin, M and Johnson, P 58, 84, 116, 118, 124, 127, 155
Maxwell Communications Company (MCC) 26
McKinsey & Co 44, 170
Melicher, R *et al* 199
merger fallacies
  inherent conflicts of interest 53–55
  multiples as a valuation methodology 56–60
  post-merger integration 60–62
  underleveraged target companies 45–50
  understanding of historical merger failure 43–45
  victim-acquiree characterization 50–53
'merger learning' 44, 280
merger research, dimensions of *138–39*
  geography 145–46
  horizontal vs vertical merger 144–45
  overpayment 146
  phase timing in merger wave 146–47
  relatedness 140–43
  relative size of partners 143–44
merger sources
  disposals 295–96
  last man standing 296
  left on the shelf targets 296

merger success keys *274–75*
absolute and relative limits on APPs *281*, 282–83
bid pricing and synergies *283–84*, 283–90, *287*
ego and hubris *292*, *293*
following merger success criteria 275–78, *276*
merger segmentation 279–81, *280*
real vs illusory synergies *291*, 291–92
timing within merger wave *278*, 278–79
merger types and success profiles *148–49*, *182*
adjustments to 160–63, *161*
bolt-ons 153–54, 181
bottom trawlers 151–53, *152*, 181
consolidation mature 155–56, 181
consolidation-emerging 157–58, 181
line extension equivalents 154–55, 181
lynchpin strategic 158–59
multiple core related complementary 156–57, 181
single core related complementary 158, 181
speculative strategic 159–60
merger valuation criteria-setting 70–72, 73
Merrill Lynch 28
Messier, Jean-Marie 51, 53, 160, 266
Metcalfe's Law 209
Microsoft
Skype acquisition 53
Mider, Z and Foley, B 54
Mills, R 92, 247
Milmo, Dan 50
Moeller, S, Schlingemann, F and Stulz, R 172
Monster.com 206
Morck, R *et al* 135
Morningstar Reports 57–58, 119
M-Score 164
'm-synergies' 234–35, 237
Mueller, D 172
Mueller, D and Sirower, M 68, 70, 78, 170, 175
'multi-companies' 10
multiples as a valuation methodology 56–60, 117, 277
to support other methodologies 118–28
MySpace *210*, 248
Myth of the Rational Market, The 226

NatWest
acquisition by Royal Bank of Scotland (RBS) 52, 145
Gleacher & Company acquisition 145–46, 159
NCR Corporation 78, 91, 104, 144, 156, 188, 234, 253, 265
Neiman-Marcus 258
net financial returns 77–78
Netscape 26, 28, 192, 197
Neutrogena 259
new product development (NPD) 11
Nomura 55
Norton, L 72, 173

Olivetti 156
OMGPop Inc 204
operational mergers 147
operations defined competitive advantage period (ODCAP) 124
opportunistic mergers 147

Palepu, K and Ruback, R 178
Palm 53, 55, 78, 91, 98, 99, 151, 153, 175
Pantene 153–54, 258
Papadakis, V and Thanos, I 78, 171
Parsa, H G *et al* 135
Paul, P 171
Pautler, P 134
PayPal 138, 158
PennCentral 135, 293
PepsiCo
Tropicana acquisition 153, 154
Perlroth, N 206
Peter Principle 51
Philippine Airlines 159
Phyrr, Peter 239
Pickens, T Boone 11, 24, 47, 48
Pixar 144
Pondbridge Limited 164
Porrini, P 96, 187
Porter, M 239
post-merger implementation team 261–68, *262*
external members 265–68
internal members 263–65
post-merger priorities 249–61, *250–51*, *256*
attack on competitors 259
defense against competitor action 250, 252
independent audit 260–61
invest-to-save 257–58
missed opportunities 258–59
move to post-merger bureaucracy 259–60
post-merger timeframe 253–54
reality check for synergies 252–53

return to normalcy 255, 257
visible quick wins 254–55
Pratley, N 211
Preqin 33
Private Eye 37
Procter & Gamble
Gillette acquisition 156
Pantene acquisition 153–54, 258
Shulton acquisition 156
Project for Excellence in Journalism 50
Provident 78, 94, 104, 143, 175, 188, 265

Quaker Oats 106
Snapple acquisition 78, 91, 104, 105–06, 175, 187
quantitative easing (QE) 30
CBS bid 118

Rahman, R and Limmack, R 178
Rappaport, A 116
RBS Fortis
ABN Amro acquisition 18, 104, 146, 188, 282, 284
Reinhart, C M and Rogoff, K 17, 205
Renren 56, 116, 122, 206, 210
Rhodes-Kropf, M and Viswananthan, S 146
RJR Nabisco 26, 284
Rogers, E *211*
Roll, R 37, 69, 135, 293
Roubini, Nouriel 10
Royal Bank of Scotland (RBS) 106
NatWest acquisition 52, 145
'r-synergies' 62, 103, 237, 238–39, 242–43, *244*, *245*, 258, 292
Rutberg and Co 205

Saito 105
Sakoui, A 171
Salmon, Felix 27–28
Samsung 91, 99
San Miguel
Philippine Airlines acquisition 159
SBC Communications
AT&T acquisition 163
Schrempp, Jurgen 53
Schwert, G 26
semi-strong market efficiency (SSME) 124, 225, 277, 307
Shacknofsky, Kevin 117
Shiller, R 27
Shulton 156
signature events *16*, 16–17
Sirower, M 61, 80, 91, 94, 96, 100, 104, 173, 227
Škoda 154
Skype 53, 138, 160
Smith, Wendell 135
Smithburg, William 78
Snapple 78, 91, 104, 105–06, 175, 187
social networking acquisition rationales *202*, *203*
APP built into share prices 206–07
bricks-to-SN, other clicks-to-SN 205
catch-up, emerging consolidation 204
expansion-defensive 203–04
new value paradigm 205–06
social networking valuation 207–13
'soft landing' 18
Sorkin, Andrew Ross 97, 121
Southwest 142
Spire Healthcare 35
Steger, U and Kummer, C 171
Stern, J 56, 57, 80, 92, 108
Sudarsanam, S 71, 72
Summify 204, 207
synergy categories
'e-synergies' 103, 237, 238, 239, *240*, 241–42, 258, 292
'f-synergies' 237, 246–49
'm-synergies' 234–35, 237
'r-synergies' 62, 103, 237, 238–39, 242–43, *244*, *245*, 258, 292
't-synergies' 237, 243, 246
synergy scope *224*
target-expansive 225
target-expansive plus missed opportunities 225–27
target-immediate 223, 225
Synergy Trap, The 100
Systemax Inc
Circuit City acquisition 151

Terra Firma
EMI acquisition 35, 55, 94, 188, 234
This Time is Different 17
Tichy, G 144
TimeWarner 9, 18, 23, 53, 92, 95, 135, 144, 150, 159, 160, 234, 293
TNT 52
total shareholder returns (TSR) 67, *75–76*, 77, 82–91, 112–13, 277
analytical limitations of 90–91
base TSR ratio 84–85
basic equations 82, *83*
shortcomings 82–83
variants 85–89, *86*
transformational mergers 150
transitional mergers 150
Trautwein, F 69

Travelers
    Citicorp acquisition 143
Trimbath, S 48, 143, 169
Tropicana 153, 154
‘t-synergies’ 237, 243, 246
Tuch, C and O’Sullivan, N 71, 82, 135
Twitter 31, 192, 203
    Summify acquisition 204, 207
Two and Twenty fee structure 49, 72

Unum
    Provident acquisition 78, 94, 104, 143, 175, 188, 265

value gap (VG) 34, 67, 74, 75–76, 77, 91–107, 277
    bidding groupthink 107
    calculation dynamics 92–94, *93*
    company overpayment 96–100
    good company bad price (GCBP) 105
    losing and professional reputation 105–06
    merger market dynamics 94–95, *95*
    synergies and net realizable synergies (NRSs) 99–101, 106–07, 202, 228–35
Varaiya, N and Ferris, K 58
vertical mergers 144–45
Vivendi Universal 53, 106, 150, 160, 175
Vodafone 127
Vojtkova, B 211
Volkswagen
    Škoda acquisition 154

Wachovia Bank 90
Ward, Robert 192
Wells Fargo 51
    Wachovia Bank acquisition 90
Weston, J F *et al* 294
Who Says Elephants Can’t Dance? 159
Williams Companies 150
Wired 28
Woolworths 152

Yook, K C 172

Zell, Sam
    Chicago Tribune acquisition 35, 50, 238
Zipf’s Law 210
Zollo, M and Meier, D 74
Z-Score 164
Zuckerberg, Mark 204
Zynga 207
    OMGPop Inc acquisition 204